AMERICAN CATHOLIC SOCIAL ETHICS

Other Books by Charles E. Curran

Christian Morality Today
A New Look at Christian Morality
Contemporary Problems in Moral Theology
Catholic Moral Theology in Dialogue
The Crisis in Priestly Ministry
Politics: Medicine and Christian Ethics:
    A Dialogue with Paul Ramsey
New Perspectives in Moral Theology
Ongoing Revision in Moral Theology
Themes in Fundamental Moral Theology
Issues in Sexual and Medical Ethics
Transition and Tradition in Moral Theology
Moral Theology: A Continuing Journey
Dissent in and for the Church (Charles E. Curran *et al.*)
The Responsibility of Dissent:
    The Church and Academic Freedom (John F. Hunt and
    Terrence R. Connelly with Charles E. Curran *et al.*)
Absolutes in Moral Theology? (editor)
Contraception: Authority and Dissent (editor)

AMERICAN CATHOLIC
SOCIAL ETHICS:
TWENTIETH-CENTURY APPROACHES

Charles E. Curran

UNIVERSITY OF NOTRE DAME PRESS
NOTRE DAME   LONDON

BX
1753
.C86
1982

Library of Congress Cataloging in Publication Data

Curran, Charles E.
  American Catholic social ethics.

  Includes index.
    1. Sociology, Christian (Catholic)—History
of doctrines—20th century. 2. Christian ethics—
History of doctrines—20th century. 3. Social eth-
ics—History—20th century. 4. Catholic Church
—United States—History—20th century. I. Title.
BX1753.C86   261.8′0973   82-4829
ISBN 0-268-00603-2   AACR2

Manufactured in the United States of America

To all those who have dedicated their lives and talents
in the service of theology
and in particular
on the occasion of his seventy-fifth birthday

WALTER J. SCHMITZ

former Dean of the School of Theology
of the Catholic University of America
whose loyal support and friendship I will always cherish

and

on the occasion of their seventieth birthdays

BERNARD HÄRING
JOSEPH FUCHS
PAUL RAMSEY

three important contributors to contemporary moral theology
who in significant ways have been
my teachers, colleagues, and friends

CONTENTS

ACKNOWLEDGMENTS

Many people have been of great help to me in researching and writing this volume. Richard Miller as my graduate assistant was especially helpful in preparing the manuscript. Patricia Whitlow assisted with the typing. Johann Klodzen, Sally Ann McReynolds, and Cindi Vian also helped. Once again I am grateful to John Ehmann, my editor at the University of Notre Dame Press. I continue to be indebted to the librarians at The Catholic University of America, especially Carolyn T. Lee, Bruce Miller, David Gilson, and Alan Flood. Daphne Burt has prepared the index.

From the beginning of this project Msgr. George G. Higgins has encouraged and assisted me with his advice and counsel. Msgr. John Tracy Ellis gave me the benefit of his extraordinary knowledge of the history of American Catholicism. Both of these colleagues, pathfinders in their respective fields of competency, kindly read the manuscript and offered criticisms and suggestions.

In my own academic field of moral theology I have come to appreciate deeply the colleagueship of my peers with their advice, criticism, and support. Recently I have been privileged to experience the same rapport with experts in American Catholic history who have been most generous and helpful in discussing my project. The references given in the text record my dependence on their published works. However, I have also benefited from the personal help of Jay Dolan, Philip Gleason, Patricia McNeal, David O'Brien, and Robert Trisco.

A number of institutions invited me to give lectures which served as an opportunity for developing some of the ideas presented in this volume: The Catholic University of America, Maryknoll School of Theology, St. Meinrad School of Theology, University of Notre Dame, University of Rochester, and Villanova University.

My students in seminars and courses on this subject matter at The Catholic University of America have helped me to develop my thought. I have especially profited from dialogue with those who have written doctoral dissertations in this area: John Stuart Sandberg, "The Eschatological Ethic of the Catholic Worker"; John W. Gouldrick, "John A. Ryan's Theory of the State"; and Joseph A. Serano, "The Social Mission of the Church in the Writings of Paul Hanly Furfey and John Courtney Murray: Analysis and Assessment."

Finally, I am exceedingly grateful to two of the subjects treated in this volume for their gracious response to my many requests: Paul Hanly Furfey and James W. Douglass. These two have contributed much not only to Catholic social ethics but also to the living out of the gospel call to peace and justice. I have criticized them and the other authors studied in these pages, but the reader will also recognize my great admiration and respect for all the figures treated herein. The main purpose of this book is to bring about a greater understanding and appreciation of what they did so that we might develop better approaches to Catholic social ethics in our day.

1. SETTING THE STAGE

This book will study American Catholic social ethics in the twentieth century. Historians have contributed much to our understanding of American Catholic social ethics, but unfortunately ethicists have not made similar analyses and studies.

A number of various reasons explains the lack of ethical studies as such. First, even in the training of Catholic priests in the United States American Catholic ethics was seldom considered. Catholic moral theology, as taught in seminaries and colleges before the Second Vatican Council, used textbooks either written in Europe or derived from European treatises. In the area of social ethics the manuals of moral theology make few if any references to the American scene. In contrast, American Protestant social ethics stresses its American background, and many studies have discussed the major figures of that tradition such as Walter Rauschenbusch or Reinhold Niebuhr.

Second, the role of the universal and authoritative Catholic teaching put primary emphasis, especially as the twentieth century progressed, on the official papal teaching as found in the encyclicals and addresses of the popes, so that little or no mention was made of a specifically American Catholic contribution. Especially after the 1931 encyclical of Pius XI entitled *Quadragesimo anno* the books and textbooks which did appear on social ethics tended to be commentaries on the official papal documents.[1] Thus, even when there did exist textbooks differing from the manuals of theology, they tended to give little or no importance to the American Catholic tradition itself. In 1959, for example, John F. Cronin published his *Social Principles and Economic Life*, which was designed as a textbook for seminaries, colleges, and universities, offering the readers a structured ex-

1

planation of Catholic social principles in the light of American economic life.[2] However, the book is merely a commentary on the official teachings on social ethics and makes almost no mention of Catholic social ethics in the United States. This 1959 book, together with its 1964 revision, leaves out an entire section of over one hundred pages discussing American Catholic social thought which Cronin had published in a somewhat similar work in 1950.[3]

Third, in general the American Catholic Church in the United States until recently has aptly been described as a brick-and-mortar church which has not been known for its academic achievements. One finds little intellectual contribution to the universal church or to the American scene by American Catholics until the last few decades.[4] However, there were some figures grappling with the question of the relationship between Catholic social ethics and American life in both its theoretical and practical ramifications who are deserving of an extended discussion and analysis. In addition, anyone attempting to do Catholic social ethics in the United States today should have some familiarity with the ways in which people in the past tried to come to grips with the same questions.

This study will focus on American Catholic social ethics as such and will not attempt to duplicate or repeat the many historical studies that have already been done.[5] "Social" indicates the area of concern. Social ethics is usually distinguished from private ethics, but in the Roman Catholic understanding especially in the first part of the twentieth century the social question or social problem generally refers to the economic order and the rights and duties of all those involved in that order.[6] In more contemporary times the social problem or question has broadened to consider other aspects, especially the political and the cultural. "Ethics" refers to a systematic, reflexive, and thematic discipline. Methodological questions loom large in any discussion of ethics or theological ethics as such, since it is a systematic discipline; substantive and content questions cannot be ignored. Even more importance is given to substantive questions in the light of the church-related aspects of Catholic social ethics. Catholic moral theology is intensely interested in asking how the church and individual Christians should act in the social realm. Catholic social ethics as a discipline has significant theoretical concerns but also entails a more acute interest in what is done in practice than some other types of ethics. "Catholic" and "American" specify the area

of social ethics to that which has developed in the American
Catholic context.

Such an understanding of American Catholic social ethics
focuses the structure of this study. The primary purpose is not
merely to report the stands that have been taken on specific
moral issues such as labor unions and government intervention,
but rather to study the Catholic social ethics developed by the
more significant figures in the American Catholic experience. The
following individuals and groups will be considered in chronological order: John A. Ryan, German-American Catholics, the
Catholic Worker and Paul Hanly Furfey, John Courtney Murray,
and the Catholic left in the 1960s and 70s. The choice of these
individuals or schools can be justified on the basis of the importance and/or distinctiveness of their contributions to American
Catholic social ethics.

No one is apt to challenge or question the inclusion of Ryan
and Murray, who are without a doubt the two most significant
Catholic theologians on the American scene in the first part of
the twentieth century.[7] The Catholic Worker movement has had
a significant impact on the lives of a few American Catholics and
on the consciences of many others and has presented a distinctive
radical alternative in social thought and action. Although *The
Catholic Worker* paper is neither scholarly nor systematic, Paul
Hanly Furfey has more systematically than anyone else developed the theory behind the Catholic Worker experience. German-
American Catholics were primarily derivative in their theory as
expressed in their journal *Central-Blatt and Social Justice,* but
their approach offered a significant alternative to others, even
though its impact was quite restricted by its own German character. The Catholic left in the 1960s and 70s was quite significant
and well publicized in the media, but the problem lies in trying
to find a systematic development of the position, since most of
the writing tends to be ad hoc and in essay form.

Perhaps the most glaring omission in our study concerns the
position opposed to the social involvement of the church or positions generally labeled conservative in these approaches. There
can be no doubt that such positions were very strong in practice,
but there was little or no sustained intellectual development of
the theories behind such positions. This omission points to the
very practical differences between a history of American Catholic social thought and action and a study of its social ethics. Any
history of Catholic social involvement and thought in the twen-

tieth century would have to devote many pages to such figures as
Father Charles Coughlin or Senator Joseph McCarthy, but these
people contributed little or nothing to American Catholic social
ethics as such.[8] Similarly, some important social movements in
the American Catholic Church such as Catholic Charities or the
Catholic Rural Life Conference will not be discussed. The
"American-Catholic" aspect of the study also eliminates the contributions of European Catholics who lived in this country for a
period of time and published here, such as Jacques Maritain,
Heinrich Rommen, and Yves Simon.

Although social ethics is deeply interested in what is actually being done in the life of the church, the discipline as such
does not enter into questions about what was actually occurring
in the American Catholic community in terms of social action and
involvement. Despite the efforts of the authors mentioned here
and many other publicists and activists, the Catholic Church on
the grass roots level has not been significantly known for its social involvement. Very often the pulpit and the parish mirrored
little or none of the discussion to be analyzed here. There have
been individuals and small groups of American Catholics working for social justice, but especially in the first part of the twentieth century there was comparatively little involvement of Catholics in social action and even a glaring lack of knowledge about
the social teaching of Catholicism. For example, John Brophy
(1883–1963), a Catholic and one of the founders of the CIO, commented in his autobiography, "Had I known of the papal encyclicals I could have been saved much distress of mind. . . . I never
read *Rerum Novarum* until a generation after it was issued."[9]
Much better known is the remark of Al Smith that he did not
even know what an encyclical was until the question was brought
up to him in the 1928 presidential political campaign.

To understand better American Catholic social ethics in the
twentieth century, the roots and background must be explored.
Three aspects will now be considered—the American Catholic
context, Catholic social ethics in general, and American Catholic
social ethics in the nineteenth century.

I. The American Catholic Context

What is the relationship between being Catholic and being
American? Are they compatible or opposed? Can one be both a

good Catholic and a good American at one and the same time?
No other single question has been of such practical significance
for the life of the Catholic Church in the United States. No other
problematic has been as influential in shaping American Catholic
social ethics. In the last paragraph of his 1956 *American Catholicism* John Tracy Ellis, the dean of American Catholic historians, pleads for the acceptance of Catholicism on the American
scene and points out that history reveals among American Catholics "the maximum of loyalty and service to every fundamental
ideal and principle upon which the Republic was founded and has
endured."[10]

One can readily appreciate the possible incompatibility between Catholicism and the American ethos especially as seen in
the nineteenth century. Roman Catholicism was primarily an
authoritarian and conservative institution which had traditionally been opposed to many modern political developments and to
the modern freedoms. On the other hand, the United States insisted on the importance of freedom and gloried in being a part
of the new world. The American democratic system proposed
separation of church and state and espoused religious liberty,
whereas Roman Catholicism called for union of church and state
and refused to accept religious freedom. However, by the end of
the nineteenth century the main-line approach in American Catholicism under the leadership of Cardinal James Gibbons of
Baltimore, with the crusading help of Archbishop John Ireland
of St. Paul, Minnesota, Bishop John Lancaster Spalding of
Peoria, and Bishop John J. Keane of Richmond, adopted a position often described as American Catholic liberalism. This position saw no basic incompatibility between being Catholic and
being American, urging strong Catholic participation in American life and espousing cooperation with non-Catholics in areas of
political, social, and economic life.[11]

The ultimate emergence of the mainstream position of
American Catholic liberalism can be traced to an interplay of
various factors—the ethical methodology in Catholic self-understanding (to be considered next), the self-interest of the American Catholic Church to protect itself and to insure its growth,
and the intermeshing of a variety of different historical circumstances. This position finally triumphed in response to the attitudes of non-Catholic Americans, of Rome, and of some American Catholics themselves. The majority of Americans wondered
if the immigrant Catholics would be truly Americans, and suspi-

cion of Catholics and even prejudice against them often surfaced. At the same time the Roman authorities were worried that American Catholics would too readily absorb the Protestant ethos existing in the new country. American Catholics struggled with the existential problem of being both loyal Americans and loyal Catholics.

The question first surfaced pastorally in terms of the attitude to be taken regarding the new Catholic immigrants. Should the immigrants become Americanized and enter fully into American life? Those who accepted the thesis of no basic incompatibility urged rapid Americanization. On the other hand, opponents of Americanization argued that if the immigrants lost their language, their customs, and their traditions, they would also very quickly lose their faith. The United States was basically a Protestant country, and Catholics had to retain their own identity or else suffer the loss of faith or absorption into the non-Catholic environment of the new world.

Archbishop Hughes of New York (+ 1864) strongly urged the Americanization of immigrants and defended a basic compatibility between the American ethos and Catholicism. He pointed to the progress and growth of the immigrant Catholic Church in the United States as a sign of such basic compatibility refuting the charge that the Catholic Church cannot thrive in a free country where there is no special protection of the law. At the same time Hughes pointed out the loyalty of Catholics to America and its ideals as illustrated in their willingness to fight in war to defend the American cause not only against Great Britain but even against Catholics in Mexico. Hughes frankly acknowledged that many immigrants had lost their faith and had fallen into indifference or even infidelity. But the archbishop of New York quickly refuted the calumny that the leakage came about because Catholics had examined their religion and had found it wanting. Physical hardships, poverty, and lack of pastoral care can explain the losses.[12] Hughes also maintained there was no real need for social reform in the United States because all was well and blessed in our country.[13]

However, throughout the nineteenth century and even later there was opposition to the Americanization of the immigrants especially among some German-American Catholics. Since the Germans, unlike the Irish, spoke a foreign language, it is readily understandable that they would be more apt to hold on to their language and their traditions. In 1891 Peter Cahensly, a German merchant, presented a memorial to the pope which claimed that 10 million Catholic immigrants had lost their faith in America and urged the pope to appoint bishops who would work to preserve the language, the customs, and the faith of the various immigrant groups.[14] Although differences between the German Catholics and the Irish Catholics remained strong, they all belonged to the same church. With decreasing immigration after 1890 and the anti-German feeling aroused by the First World War, the German Catholics clung less and less to their own German language, customs, and traditions.

Pressure from other Americans also encouraged American Catholic liberalism. Catholics, as an immigrant minority owing allegiance to a foreign ruler in Rome, could easily be the object of derision, prejudice, and persecution. The position of Catholics became even more vulnerable as immigration grew. In the decade of the 1820s 54,000 Catholics entered the United States; in the 1840s 700,000 Catholic immigrants came to those shores. Between 1850 and 1900 nearly 5 million Catholics came to America from their native lands.[15]

The nineteenth century saw three waves of anti-Catholic feeling swell up in the United States.[16] The nativist prejudices against all foreigners and especially Catholics began as early as 1830. There were many complex factors entering into this, including the economic aspects. Anti-Catholic feeling was present in the large urban centers of the east where many of the new immigrants settled. Violence also erupted in this context. In 1837 at the third provincial council of Baltimore the bishops of the United States painfully acknowledged the misrepresentation and persecution of Catholics. The bishops' defense against the attacks was to separate the spiritual life of Catholics from their civil life and to point out the compatibility between being Catholic and being American. The outburst of persecution made Catholics even more self-conscious and also occasioned the growth of distinctively Catholic newspapers and schools. Catholic participation in the war against Mexico in 1846 eventually helped to dampen the strength of the nativist movement.

In the 1850s the Know-Nothing party came into existence and exerted a great influence against Catholics and foreigners. But this wave of bias and persecution ran its course, again with help from the crisis of war—this time, the Civil War. In 1887 a third wave of anti-Catholic prejudice appeared in the form of the American Protective Association. Again in the face of opposition and bigotry the natural response on the part of Catholics was to stress their American loyalties. Social opposition tended to bring Catholics closer together and to make their leaders ever-more conscious of avoiding antagonisms by showing the compatibility between being Catholic and being American.

In a more theoretical vein Issac Hecker (1819–1888) and Orestes Brownson (1803-1876), both converts to Catholicism, espoused a basic compatibility between Catholicism and Americanism.[17] Brownson, the leading Catholic intellectual in the nineteenth century (in a context in which the Catholic intellectual life could not easily flourish and develop to any great degree), believed that American democracy was totally compatible with Catholic self-understanding. He envisioned that many progressive Protestants would embrace Catholicism because they could be convinced that Catholicism is perfectly at home in the American ethos. Even if Catholics became a majority in the United States, principle and not expediency would demand that religious freedom still exist.[18] Hecker founded the Paulist Fathers and had a vision of America ripe for Catholicism. The Paulists believed that the Catholic faith was uniquely geared to the American spirit, since it was reasonable, accepted the goodness of the human, encouraged the importance of the active virtues, and guaranteed the basic liberties of democratic society. Catholics would have to shed some of their authoritarianism which had been occasioned by responses to the Protestant Reformation, but the perennial Catholic humanism is most appealing to the American spirit.[19]

Of the hierarchy Archbishop Ireland, Bishop Keane, and, in a somewhat more critical way, Bishop Spalding were in the forefront of American Catholic liberalism. Ireland and Hecker developed followings in Europe, especially in France. Their liberal position aroused some conservative opposition not only in the United States but also in France. Generally speaking, Archbishop Michael A. Corrigan of New York and Bishop Bernard J. McQuaid of Rochester led the conservative forces against the liberalism of Ireland and Keane. Cardinal Gibbons as leader of the American hierarchy generally sided with the progressives. These controversies involved a number of different issues, but even the conservative bishops did not want to be looked upon as un-American, even though they strenuously opposed aspects of the liberalism proposed by Ireland and his followers.[20] Some brief historical episodes will illustrate the development of American

Catholic liberalism in the historical context of the last decades of the nineteenth century.

Perhaps the most significant event was the support of Cardinal Gibbons and the majority of the American Catholic hierarchy for the Knights of Labor.[21] The Knights of Labor, founded in 1869 and coming under the leadership of Catholic Terrence Powderly, grew quickly because of success against some railroads controlled by Jay Gould. In 1886 Rome reaffirmed the earlier condemnation of the Knights of Labor in the ecclesiastical province of Quebec under Archbishop Elzéar-Alexandre Taschereau. The significant issues revolved around the fact that the Knights of Labor was an organization which included all workers of whatever religion or even of no religion and that Catholic members would be exposed to great dangers to their faith. This problem of Catholics cooperating with non-Catholics for social justice would continue to be a problem in the universal church and even in the American church, as illustrated in the debate over intercredal cooperation. In addition, because of the oath taken by all members, the knights seemed to be a secret society which fell under Roman condemnation.

Most, but not all, American bishops were opposed to the condemnation. Archbishop Corrigan was hostile and unfriendly to the organization. Corrigan did not openly call for condemnation at this time, but apparently he used his Roman influence to undermine the knights. Since the American archbishops' meeting in October 1886 could not unanimously agree on a position regarding the knights (only two archbishops favored condemnation), the matter was referred to Rome and the Congregation for the Propagation of the Faith, which directed church affairs in the United States. Gibbons himself was in Rome in early 1887 to receive officially the red hat of the cardinalate and on that occasion prepared, with the help of Ireland, Keane and Denis O'Connell, a memorial for the Propagation of the Faith urging that the Knights of Labor not be condemned.

The reasons proposed in Gibbons' memorial well illustrate the issues involved: the knights do not fall under the category of secret societies condemned by the Holy See. Grave social evils exist, and even the Congress and president of the United States have acknowledged this. Note how Gibbons delicately handled the matter by recognizing there was a problem in the United States and quickly adding that the highest authorities acknowledged the existence of such evils. Workers have a right to join together in

associations and defend their rights. Yes, Catholics would participate with Protestants and even nonbelievers in these trade
unions, but Catholic confraternities are not possible. In addition
there seems to be no danger to the strong faith of American
Catholics. A condemnation would have very negative effects for
the church, since working people would be alienated from the
church, which would appear opposed to their efforts for social
reform. Many might even leave the church and thereby affect the
temporal well-being and collections of the church. Even the political powers of the United States who have supported workers
would be rendered hostile to the church. "The accusation of being
un-American, that is to say, alien to our national spirit, is the
most powerful weapon which the enemies of the church can use
against her." Finally, Gibbons points out that condemnation
would be impractical because, according to many reports, the
organization is not going to last very long.[22]

The memorial is obviously the work of a shrewd and practical administrator mixing together arguments based on gospel
principles and pragmatic considerations involving both the spiritual and temporal self-interest of the church. As a result of Gibbons' efforts Rome did not condemn the knights. This incident
is often cited by American Catholics as the basis for the church's
support of and rapport with working persons in the United
States—a position that was always a legitimate source of pride
for American Catholics especially in contrast to the European
scene where the Catholic Church had lost the working person.[23]
For our purposes this incident shows official church approval for
the fact that Catholics can participate and cooperate with all
other Americans in working to defend their rights and for the
cause of social justice.

A second significant incident involved Father Edward Mc-
Glynn, a well-known and apparently zealous priest of the Archdiocese of New York who publicly supported Henry George in his
independent candidacy for mayor of New York City in 1886.[24]
In his 1880 book *Progress and Poverty* George espoused the single-tax theory. Increase in land value was in no way due to the
landowner but to the community which in various ways had contributed to making the land more valuable. This increased value
in land should be confiscated for public purposes and thus provide the government with funds while at the same time holding
down rents for people and eliminating poverty.[25] McGlynn was
suspended by Archbishop Corrigan and later excommunicated

(July 3, 1887). Also Corrigan with the help of Bishop McQuaid tried to have Rome put George's book on the Index.

The American Catholic liberals were opposed to Corrigan on both issues. The excommunication of McGlynn provided ammunition for those who claimed there was no freedom in the Catholic Church even on civil and political questions. Likewise, Corrigan's proposed condemnation of George's book could also readily give the impression that the church was always against the poor and sided with the rich and the status quo. Gibbons and liberal American bishops tried to prevent Rome's placing Henry George's book on the Index. The final result could be called an illustration of diplomacy at its best. In 1889 the Holy Office decided George's positions were deserving of condemnation but refrained from officially and publicly promulgating a decree of condemnation. Through the intervention of the liberals and with the help of the apostolic delegate to the United States, Archbishop Francesco Satolli, McGlynn was reconciled in 1892 after four professors at The Catholic University of America found nothing opposed to Catholic doctrine in McGlynn's defense of Henry George.

National Catholic congresses were held at Baltimore in 1889 and at Chicago in 1893 to celebrate the growth of Catholicism in the United States. Great care was taken in preparing for these meetings so that they would give no cause for suspicion, opposition, or prejudice on the part of other Americans who were not Catholic. There were some areas of friction, especially the school question and support for the temporal power of the pope after the occupation of Rome in 1870 by the Kingdom of Italy, but a committee of bishops was set up to screen the papers proposed by lay people at the Baltimore congress lest they overstress Catholic grievances and awaken latent hostility among non-Catholic Americans. Any differences between Catholicism and Americanism were toned down. At the Chicago congress of 1893, which incidentally discussed at some length the social problem in the light of the 1891 encyclical *Rerum novarum*, Archbishop Satolli delivered his famous speech in which he urged his hearers to go forward with the book of Christian truth in one hand and the Constitution of the United States in the other. One conservative Catholic, Condé B. Pallen, commented publicly that it would be better for Catholics to march forward with the Bible in both hands.[26]

By the end of the century it was evident that the Catholic Church was flourishing in the United States, but American Cath-

olic liberals had to yield some ground, for in 1899 Pope Leo XIII
condemned Americanism in his letter *Testem benevolentiae* sent
to Cardinal Gibbons.[27] The events leading up to this condemnation included continuing controversies between liberal and conservative bishops. In 1893, for example, Bishop Keane participated in and read a paper at the World's Parliament of Religions
held in Chicago. Both his presence at the meeting, thus acknowledging the equality of other sects and denominations, and the
content of his address on "The Ultimate Religion" were criticized.
Civiltà Cattolica, a semiofficial, Jesuit, Roman publication, wrote
an editorial accusing some American prelates of neo-Pelagianism.
Archbishop Ireland, on the occasion of Cardinal Gibbons' silver
jubilee as a bishop, optimistically proclaimed the goodness of
the times. He called upon the church to accept the age and join
with it through the acceptance of democracy as the best form of
civil government even for the good of the Catholic Church, which
is above all the church of the people. In 1894 conservative and
liberal bishops in the United States clashed over the application
of the Holy Office's decree on June 20, 1894, against Catholic
membership in secret societies, specifically the Odd Fellows, the
Sons of Temperance, and the Knights of Pythias. Meanwhile
liberals in France were appealing to the church there to accept
many of the ideas of the youthful and vigorous American Church,
especially as practiced by Hecker and Ireland, who often spoke to
enraptured audiences in France. Controversy about Americanism
thus spread to Europe.

Finally, in 1899 Leo XIII issued his condemnation of the
ideas connected with Americanism: the need to modify doctrine
in accord with the times in order to attract converts; a downplaying of external guidance, of the supernatural, of religious
vows, and of the so-called passive virtues; discussions with heretics. Conservatives in the United States and abroad saw the letter as a great victory. Liberals in the United States claimed these
condemned teachings were never proclaimed or held in their
country but were based on poor understandings current in Europe, especially France, due to some inaccurate translations of
American works. Gibbons wrote to Pope Leo XIII: "This doctrine, which I deliberately call extravagant and absurd, this
Americanism as it is called, has nothing in common with the
views, aspirations, doctrine and conduct of Americans."[28]

At the beginning of the twentieth century the Catholic
Church in the United States was growing and flourishing. The

mainstream of the church under the leadership of Cardinal Gibbons saw no basic incompatibility between being Catholic and being American. Even the leaders of the conservative wing of the Catholic bishops, Corrigan and McQuaid, were as nationalistic as the liberals.[29] However, certain suspicions of both other Americans and of Rome continued to exist during the twentieth century.

The problem of unity and plurality in the United States for the first six decades of the present century often focused on the question of religious differences rather than the question of racial, ethnic, or sexual differences, which have come to the fore in the last few decades. In the twentieth century there were still many areas of possible friction between Catholics and other Americans.[30] Even after Catholics entered the mainstream of economic life following the Second World War and were no longer immigrants, the tensions continued. Witness the debates over aid to Catholic schools, the sending of an ambassador to the Vatican, and the Blanshard thesis about the fear of Catholic power.[31] In a sense the 1960s marked the culminating point in the long history of the struggle for American Catholics to prove they could be both good Americans and good Catholics at the same time. On a practical level the election of John F. Kennedy as president proved that Catholics were now an integral part of the American scene. John Courtney Murray made his contribution in the theoretical realm. The Romans had always been suspicious of the American system of separation of church and state and religious liberty, at best tolerating the American approach. Murray through his writings and the ultimate acceptance of his position (also proposed by many others) by the Second Vatican Council was able to prove that the church can and should fully endorse the American approach to religious liberty and the separation of church and state. At the same time Murray also gave a response to other Americans who feared that Catholics could never accept the basic American political principles with their heavy emphasis on the rights and freedoms of the person. Murray maintained that the basic American doctrine, as contained in the Declaration of Independence, found its ultimate grounding in the natural law theory proposed by Catholics. Catholics could be both truly Catholic and truly American at one and the same time. No sooner had the long struggle of American Catholic liberalism been capped by practical and theoretical success than some American Catholics insisted that being Catholic meant they had to oppose much of their contemporary American society. But we are getting ahead of our story. The main point is that a proper understanding of American Catholicism in general and American Catholic social ethics in the twentieth century can only be fully appreciated in the light of this basic question of the relationship between being Catholic and being American.

II. Catholic Social Ethics

To understand American Catholic social ethics, it is necessary not only to know the setting in which it evolved but also to be familiar with the general characteristics of Catholic social ethics as such. Catholic social ethics has a long tradition, for the church fostered systematic reflection in all areas. Questions of the meaning and structure of political, cultural, and economic life have been addressed almost from the beginning of Christianity. The two most significant aspects of Catholic social ethics in the twentieth century are the existence of a body of authoritative church teaching found especially in the papal encyclicals and the natural-law methodology which served as the basis for Catholic social ethics. First, a brief description of the authoritative church teaching.

In the second half of the nineteenth century some Catholic leaders in Europe began to address the social question—that is, the problems of the economic system and the plight of the workers in the new industrial era.[32] Even at this time there was a diversity of opinion among Catholic approaches. The school of Angers, following the inspiration of Charles Périn and Frédéric Le Play, believed the solution to the social problem lay in the application of the principle of Christian charity and not in state intervention or the reform of institutions. On the other hand the Catholic social school of Liège favored state intervention in terms of social legislation and insurance. Karl von Vogelsang and Albert M. Weiss, O.P., in the German-speaking countries condemned the existing capitalist system and called for its replacement with a new corporative system based on medieval guilds. The Fribourg Union under Bishop (later Cardinal) Gaspard Mermillod endorsed many of the corporatist views. The *Circolo dei studi sociali ed economiche* in Rome, which was set up under the auspices of the Congregation for the Propagation of the Faith, generally accepted a less radical position which could be characterized as a realistic and reforming approach. Perhaps the most significant individual figure, and recognized as such by Pope Leo XIII, was Bishop Wilhelm Emmanuel von Ketteler of Mainz. Von Ketteler originally espoused a corporatist view calling for a radical change in society, but as time went on he became a strong advocate of reforming social legislation as a means of alleviating the more serious and immediate problems of the worker. Also in England under Cardinal Henry Edward Manning there was a great stress on the social mission of the church in defending the rights of the workers. The role of the young American church in supporting the Knights of Labor formed a part of this general picture.

In this context Pope Leo XIII issued in 1891 his encyclical *Rerum novarum*. The encyclical recognizes the misery and poverty suffered by the workers but condemns the socialist solution which denies the natural right of private property. The solution to the problem of the misery of the worker is to enable each person to procure the necessary private property to provide for one's needs and dignity. Leo also calls for the intervention of the state to alleviate the problems. Whenever the general interest or any particular class suffers or is threatened with a harm which can in no other way be met or prevented, the public authority must step in to deal with it. However, there are limits to state intervention—the principle being that the law must not undertake more or proceed further than is required for the remedy of the evil or the removal of mischief. Leo also recognizes the obligation of employers to pay a living wage and the rights of workers to organize. However, commentaries later questioned if Leo was referring to unions composed exclusively of Catholic workers or to secular unions involving all. In general the encyclical condemns both the existing laissez-faire spirit and the opposite extreme of socialism, all the while recognizing the problem of the workers and trying to bring about the social reform of institutions.[33]

The encyclical of Pope Leo XIII began a long line of official, authoritative church teachings on social issues. The most important of these documents are: Pius XI, *Quadragesimo anno* (1931); various addresses and allocutions of Pope Pius XII; John XXIII, *Mater et magistra* (1961) and *Pacem in terris* (1963); The Pastoral Constitution of the Church in the Modern World of the Second Vatican Council; Paul VI, *Populorum progressio* (1967) and *Octogesima adveniens* (1971); the document of the World Synod of Bishops, *Justice in the World* (1971); John Paul II, *Redemptor hominis* (1979) and *Laborem exercens* (1981).

Catholic social teaching was based on these authoritative documents, and much of Catholic social teaching, especially after *Quadragesimo anno* in 1931, consisted in commentaries and explanations of these official teachings. Generally speaking, the documents before 1960 condemned the extremes of both laissez-faire capitalism and socialism while recognizing the natural-law rights of the individual, the basic rights of the family, and the subsidiary role of the state to intervene and protect these rights as well as work for the common good of the society.

As was frequently pointed out, the popes gave the general principles of social ethics, but there was room for differing applications. In addition, the papal teaching itself allowed for different interpretations on many significant points. Those in favor of state intervention could point to Leo's endorsement, but opponents of state intervention could point out in the same paragraph the careful limits placed on such a role by the pope. Reformers could find many things in the encyclicals to support their position, but proponents of more radical changes, especially those calling for a corporate society, could also find backing. In later encyclicals there is a greater tension between short-term reforms and long-term, more radical changes. There can be no doubt that Leo XIII recognized the need for institutional change and reform throughout his encyclical, but advocates of personal change of heart as the absolute cornerstone and basis of social reform could point to the concluding exhortations that the happy results longed for by all must chiefly be brought about by the outpouring of charity which is the surest antidote against worldly pride and immoderate love of self. All American social ethicists in the twentieth century appealed to the official papal teaching, but there was still room for many different positions. The question of the possibility of dissent from such teachings did not arise until the 1960s.

The second significant characteristic of Catholic social ethics is the natural-law methodology employed. Even a cursory reading of *Rerum novarum* and the later documents until 1963 indicates heavy emphasis on natural law and human reason. Anyone familiar with Catholic theology should recognize that the popes are merely continuing in the traditional Catholic approach. In

1879 Leo XIII had made Thomas Aquinas the patron of Catholic theology and philosophy and called for a restoration of Thomism.[34]

To appreciate and evaluate the natural-law tradition one must distinguish at least two aspects of natural law—the theological and the philosophical.[35] From the theological perspective natural law responds to the question: Where does the Christian find ethical wisdom and knowledge? Only in the scriptures, in revelation, and in Jesus Christ? The natural-law view maintains that human reason examining human nature can arrive at true ethical wisdom and knowledge. The Catholic teaching has always accepted these two sources of ethical wisdom and knowledge—faith and reason; revelation and natural law. In practice, social ethics was based almost exclusively on natural law. The ultimate grounding of such an understanding rests on the goodness of creation. Redemption and the supernatural do not destroy but build on creation and the natural.

The acceptance of human reason and the natural, as distinct from the supernatural, grace, and faith, implies that on the level of political, cultural, social, and economic questions Catholics share much wisdom and knowledge with all other human beings. The supernatural level and the realms of faith and the church are the areas in which Catholics are distinctive. The natural-law approach does not call upon the distinctively Christian aspects of scripture, revelation, or grace to explain the morality of the "natural" life of human beings in political society. John Ryan and John Courtney Murray, the main proponents of reconciling Catholicism and the American ethos in the twentieth century, employed such a methodology to further their purpose. As will be seen, they were not uncritical observers of the American scene, but they saw no theoretical obstacles to full Catholic participation in American life and called for collaboration between Catholics and other Americans in working for social reform. American Catholic liberalism found firm theoretical grounding in a natural-law approach.

However, history reminds us that Roman Catholicism has very often been quite opposed to much of the world in which it was living and has insisted on real incompatibilities with different forms of contemporary thought and life. There are a number of factors contributing to this reality. Recall that the theological understanding of natural law proposed above does not entail an uncritical acceptance of what others are doing but rather proposes sources of ethical wisdom and knowledge that are available to all and not distinctively Catholic or Christian. Thus, for example, on the basis of reason Catholic thought condemned communism and socialism as opposed to the proper understanding of the human person with inalienable rights. In addition, there are two other reasons that explain why the Catholic Church in the course of history has seen itself in opposition to the current culture.

The first factor is the authoritative teaching of the church. Although the Catholic Church based its social teaching on natural law, the church, and more specifically its hierarchical magisterium, assumed an important role as the official interpreter of natural law. As a result, official Catholic teaching on a particular question, such as opposition to socialism, was readily known and contrasted with other approaches which also claimed to be based on human reason.

A second factor partially explaining the fact that the Catholic Church in the course of history has often found itself at odds with the contemporary political and cultural milieu is its tendency to identify with a previously existing worldview and culture. Roman Catholicism opposed the separation of church and state and religious liberty on the grounds of natural law, but its understanding of natural law was very much influenced by the historical circumstances of union of church and state in the Constantinian era and in subsequent historical periods. Both of these factors were also operative on the American scene as illustrated in the dispute about religious liberty. Roman Catholicism learned to use the best of Aristotelian thought for understanding faith but then failed to accept other, more contemporary ways of trying to express the faith in modern times. This explains the call of many in the last few decades for a de-Hellenization of theology and even of dogma.

At the Second Vatican Council in the early 1960s dissatisfaction with some aspects of the theological understanding of natural law resulted in some significant changes in methodology. The theological grounding of natural law in creation and incarnation was good, but unfortunately such an understanding never integrated the other Christian realities of sin and grace. Too often the older approach viewed the world as a two-tiered reality with the supernatural order built on the natural, but the supernatural did not really affect the natural. In practice there existed too great a dichotomy between faith and daily life. The gospel, grace, and eschatology should also affect our daily life and the political and social structures of our world. Catholic social ethics must overcome the false dichotomy between the natural and supernatural and integrate all the Christian realities into our understanding of the world in which we live. Compare the methodology of the Pastoral Constitution on the Church in the Modern World with the 1963 encyclical *Pacem in terris* of Pope John XXIII. *Pacem in terris* grounds the reality of peace not in the gift of Jesus to his disciples but rather in the order which the Creator has put into the world and which human reason can discern.[36] The Catholic peace movement in the 1960s in the United States employed a more integrated Christian methodology in its critique of American society.

The theological aspect of natural law is only one part of the entire natural-law question. Another very significant aspect is the philosophical. Granted that human reason on the basis of human nature can arrive at ethical wisdom and knowledge, how are human reason and human nature to be understood? Here, too, significant changes have transpired in Catholic thinking since the time of the Second Vatican Council. Until that time Catholic social ethics was based on the perennial philosophy as found in the manuals of scholastic philosophy and theology. There was one monolithic philosophical system proposed in Roman Catholicism. However, in the last few decades in place of such a monolithic philosophical understanding there now exists a growing pluralism of methodologies and philosophies in Catholic thought. Witness, for example, the dialogue between Catholic social ethics and Marxism in many parts of the world.[37]

Until recently classicism properly described Catholic natural-law theory. Classicism stresses the eternal, the immutable, and the unchanging and strives for certain knowledge of things in their causes. The natural law in this approach is the eternal plan of God for the world which can be applied in all different times and circumstances. The contemporary shift to historical mindedness, on the other hand, emphasizes the contingent, the historical, and the individual with a greater appreciation of historical and cultural pluralism. The classicist approach employs a very deductive methodology, whereas contemporary historical mindedness uses a more inductive methodology. Historical mindedness is perhaps best seen in the letter *Octogesima adveniens* of Paul VI. The pope declares it is neither his intention nor purpose to utter a unified message which has universal validity for all peoples today in matters of social justice. The individual Christian communities themselves must come up with such solutions (par. 4).

A third change in contemporary Catholic understanding of human reason and of human nature gives much more importance to the subject and to the role of human subjectivity. An older approach before the Second Vatican Council saw the natural law as an objective ordering to which the individual had to conform oneself. Over the years, however, more importance has been assigned to the subject and to the freedom of the subject.[38] In *Octogesima adveniens* Paul VI uses as the cornerstone of his approach two aspirations of contemporary human beings—the aspirations to equality and to participation. The citizens are to participate actively in forming the institutions under which they live (par. 22). Gone is the image of an eternal plan, expressed in an ideal order of an historic age, to which all people should conform.

To appreciate and evaluate American Catholic social ethics as such, it is necessary to understand the two most significant characteristics of Catholic social ethics—the existence of an authoritative body of teaching and a natural-law methodology. In both cases there has been significant development especially in the last few years, but for the first sixty years of this century the understandings of both these realities remained fundamentally unchanged.

III. American Social Thought in the Nineteenth Century

Our study is primarily interested in American Catholic social ethics as a systematic discipline as it developed in the twentieth century. As might be expected, social ethics as a systematic reflexive discipline did not exist in the nineteenth century, but there have been studies about the social attitudes and thoughts of American Catholics at that time which serve as helpful background for understanding some of the positions and methodologies of American Catholic social ethics in the twentieth century.

Catholicism in the American setting began in the Maryland colony and was only an insignificant factor elsewhere in the colonies. Before the waves of immigration in the nineteenth century Catholics were not only a small minority in a Protestant

country, but even after American independence from England
they still faced institutional restrictions on their political activity
in several states. The early Catholics in Maryland were conservative and went along with the land tenure of the time, including
the plantation system with its acceptance of slavery. Some few
Catholics were influential in the war of independence and in the
framing of the Constitution, but their chief concerns were those
of their conservative compatriots—strong central government,
financial stability, and the rule of the property classes. In this
very early period the Catholic Church was quite aware of its spiritual mission, but there was practically no consciousness of the
social mission of the church. C. Joseph Nuesse concludes his study
of the social thought of American Catholics from 1634 to 1829
with the observation that American Catholics maintained a social
attitude best described as conformist.[39]

The general American Catholic attitude to slavery before the
Civil War bears out the conformist description. American Catholics accepted the system of slavery, and many, including Bishop
John Carroll and a number of religious communities, owned
slaves. Catholics relied on a theological tradition which condemned slave trading but not slavery in itself. Slavery could be
permitted to continue for the good of society if it was necessary.
Catholics as a whole strongly opposed the abolitionist position
for a number of reasons. As Democrats (and most Catholics
were), their party was opposed to the abolitionists, but also
Catholics tended to look upon the abolitionists as enemies of religion, public order, and even of the Union itself. During the Civil
War it is fair to say as a generalization that Catholics in the
north supported the Union, while Catholics in the south gave
their allegiance to the Confederacy.[40]

As the immigration in the nineteenth century increased,
Catholic social thought even after the Civil War could still be
called conservative, cautious, and individually oriented. There
was no talk about changing structures. Abell refers to the period
from 1865 to 1885 as the charity phase.[41] Steps were made to
Americanize the immigrants and have them fit into the American
mainstream. The president of the St. Vincent de Paul Society in
1865 assured the international organization in Paris that the
American Catholic poor were poor only temporarily. Where there
is health, temperance, and industry, there can be no poverty in
the United States. Schools, orphanages, and homes for working
women and even reformatories, which soon came under public

auspices, were important forms of the social apostolate.[42] In February 1872 the Catholic Total Abstinence Union of America was founded. There was no doubt that intemperance was a problem in the cities, and Catholics were often associated with the problem. Temperance societies were formed to warn people of the danger of drinking and to overcome one of the great problems of the day. A very significant motivating factor in the Catholic temperance movement was the recognition that other Americans frequently connected the drinking problem principally with Catholics. Strong opposition to the demon of drink was another way to prove that Catholics were just as good as other Americans and were united with them in fighting problems of morality. No one could point a finger at Catholics to prove that they were primarily the cause of the problems and were doing nothing about them.[43]

As time went on, however, the problem of poverty in the cities where most of the immigrants lived could not be denied, especially in the light of an economic depression in the 1870s. Two attempts to solve the problem at that time did not really accomplish very much. Benevolent societies had sprung up among the immigrants. Again, part of the motivation was self-protection —to keep Catholics from joining secret and dangerous societies such as the Masons. These societies tried to provide sickness and death benefits for their members. In the 1870s proposals for Western colonization became popular, but the movement never became truly effective. The idea was for Catholics to leave the poverty and misery of the cities in the east to settle in the newly created, small, Catholic communities on the vast lands in the west. The idea was proposed especially by western bishops such as Ireland in St. Paul and Spalding in Peoria, but the eastern clergy, bishops, and wealthly Catholics never wholeheartedly supported such schemes.[44]

A number of reasons contributed to the fact that before 1875 little or nothing was said about social change and reform. Catholic leaders had always been suspicious of social change because of the radical elements calling for such change. Many Catholics had looked upon the social and political changes in Europe as being inimical to the church. The danger of socialism was a constant threat. The fear of violence connected with calls for social change also had made the leaders of the American church very wary of change itself. There too remained the problems of secret societies and the question of Catholics joining in associations or trade unions with Protestants, nonbelievers, and even radicals. For all these reasons there was not much support before 1875 even for trade labor unions among Catholics; in fact there was a distrust of unions on the part of most Catholic leaders.[45] A good example was Catholic reaction to the Molly Maguires and the violence connected with this Irish group in the mines of eastern Pennsylvania. When many influential Americans condemned the violence of the Molly Maguires, many Catholics, wanting to prove they were no less American, went along with the condemnation. However, some Catholic voices pointed out there were serious grievances behind the action of the Molly Maguires, even though their violence was not to be condoned.[46]

In the last quarter of the nineteenth century the Catholic leadership recognized the need to support labor unions and even began to call for government intervention to prevent abuses in industry. The support of the Knights of Labor indicated the new position taken by the American Catholic bishops toward labor and social reform. In his autobiography Monsignor John A. Ryan, the dominant force for social reform in American Catholicism in the first half of the twentieth century, lauded the social vision and quest for social justice given by Gibbons, Ireland, and Spalding.[47]

Perhaps in Catholic circles a certain form of triumphalism has uncritically attributed too much to these hierarchical leaders. Both Gibbons and Ireland upheld the right of labor to organize, but they were very cautious. The boycott was condemned; strikes could be justified in theory, but in practice they were dubious. Recall that Gibbons' memorial on behalf of the Knights of Labor was not a ringing support of the rights of the worker but rather a very shrewd and pragmatic mingling of many different arguments in defense of Catholic participation in the knights. Ireland was personally quite friendly with leaders of big business and rather reluctant about state intervention. Ireland especially had an almost naive faith in all aspects of the American system including its economic institutions. Spalding was more intellectual in general and less public than the other two prelates. While definitely aligned with the liberal progressive camp, he was not as uncritical of the American way of life in general. In social matters he came to see that state intervention was necessary to protect the rights of the poor and the workers. Thus the theoretical positions of the leaders of the progressive wing of the American hierarchy were still somewhat cautious.[48] However, their deeds, especially in support of the Knights of Labor, spoke louder than their words.

By the end of the century the Catholic Church was somewhat identified with moderate social reform, although there would still be Catholics who opposed such a stance. The first two decades of the twentieth century culminated in official support by the American Catholic bishops for social justice and reform as embodied in a statement issued in 1919 by a committee of bishops of the National Catholic War Council. There were many elements leading up to this document, popularly known as the Bishops' Program of Social Reconstruction. The fear of socialism remained very strong, but many liberal Catholics stressed that social reform was necessary to counteract the effects of socialism. Father Peter Dietz tried to make Catholic unionists more familiar with the teaching of the church.[49] The Central-Verein, the central organization of all German-American Catholic groups, actively took up the social problem.[50] The National Conference of Catholic Charities was organized in 1910.[51] There were also a number of different developments occurring on the grass-roots level at this time.[52] The American bishops set up the National Catholic War Council in November 1917 to coordinate Catholic activities in support of the war effort. Here again Catholics were merely doing what Protestants and others had already done and thereby showing support for their country at war. This body ultimately became the National Catholic Welfare Conference, a national organization of the Catholic bishops for the realization of common Catholic objectives.[53]

The Bishops' Program does not formulate a comprehensive scheme of reconstruction but, recognizing that there probably will not be fundamental or revolutionary changes on the American scene, proposes reform and changes in the existing system. Short-term reforms include the following: continuation of United States Employment Service to deal with unemployment after the war; continuation of the National War Labor Board with its emphasis on a living wage and labor's right to organize; sustaining the present wage scale; developing housing for the working classes; reduction of the cost of living; government checks on monopolies and perhaps even governmental competition for monopolies; enactment of a legal minimum wage; provision by the state for insurance against illness, unemployment, old age, and other disabilities; labor participation in industrial management; vocational training; state laws against child labor. There are three major defects in the existing system—inefficiency and waste in the production and distribution of commodities; insufficient monies for the majority of workers; increasingly and unnecessarily large monies for a small minority of privileged capitalists. To fully remedy these defects the majority of people must not only be wage earners but must become owners at least in part of the instruments of production. This long-term goal can be reached through cooperatives and copartnership.[54]

The content of such a program was condemned by some as socialistic. There is no doubt that the program is progressive and in the reforming tradition. Only with the New Deal were many of its provisions finally put into effect. The methodology behind the statement is based primarily on human reason. There is no citation from scripture in the document itself. The only reference to papal teaching is in the last paragraph. (Compare such an approach with more recent statements by American bishops which tend to emphasize much more heavily the official papal teaching.) The solutions are in terms of structural reform, although the final paragraph exhorts all to a reform of the Christian life and institutions as being necessary for true social change.

This official statement of a committee of American bishops presented a progressive, reforming approach to American economic life and served as a platform for the mainstream of American Catholic social thought in the twentieth century. The real author of the statement was John A. Ryan, who in the first half of the century became the central figure in the reforming social approach of American Catholicism.[55] The stage is now set for our consideration of American Catholic ethics in the twentieth century.

2. JOHN A. RYAN

John A. Ryan was not only the best known Roman Catholic social ethicist in the United States in the first half of the twentieth century, but he was also the foremost "official" Catholic spokesperson for progressive social reform. Ryan's significance was enhanced by the two positions he held—professor of moral theology at The Catholic University of America in Washington, D.C. (1915-1939) and director of the Social Action Department of the National Catholic Welfare Council (N.C.W.C.), the national organization of the American Catholic bishops, (1920-1945). Ryan was also highly regarded outside the Catholic Church because of his many associations with non-Catholics in the work of social reform during those years.[1]

John Augustine Ryan was born in 1869, the first of eleven children, to Irish immigrant parents on a farm in Vermillion, Minnesota, near St. Paul. Ryan's formative years included an exposure to reforming and populist ideas as found in *The Irish World*, a monthly paper edited by Patrick Ford, in meetings of the National Farmers' Alliance, and in contact with and admiration for Ignatius Donnelly, whom Ryan later referred to as a statesman, politician, agitator, social reformer, and author.[2] He eventually studied for the priesthood and was ordained a priest of the Archdiocese of St. Paul on June 4, 1898. In addition to his philosophical and theological studies he showed an interest in social questions, spent one summer studying economics, and was influenced by the writings of the leaders of the progressive wing of the American Catholic Church—Cardinal Gibbons; Archbishop Ireland, his own ecclesiastical superior; and Bishop Spalding of Peoria. Interestingly, Ryan apparently read *Rerum novarum* for the first time only in 1894, even though he was a junior in a Catholic college seminary when the encyclical first appeared in 1891.[3]

Archbishop Ireland sent his new priest to study moral theology at The Catholic University of America to prepare for teaching at the St. Paul Seminary. At Catholic University Ryan, who was already interested in social reform and economics, was strongly influenced by his teachers William Kerby in sociology and the Belgian Thomas Bouquillon, who both insisted on the importance of the data of the sciences, especially sociology and economics, for appraising properly the moral aspect of social problems. His licentiate dissertation on "Some Ethical Aspects of Speculation" was finished in 1900, while his doctoral dissertation, "A Living Wage," was eventually published in 1906 with some prodding of the publisher by Richard Ely, a Protestant economist associated with the Social Gospel Movement and teaching at the University of Wisconsin, to whom the book is dedicated and who wrote the introduction. The book received plaudits in both secular and religious reviews and established Ryan as a progressive social reformer. Ryan had returned to St. Paul Seminary to teach before completing his doctorate and stayed there until he returned to Catholic University as a professor in 1915. Ryan remained in Washington the rest of his life.

As a scholar Ryan's most significant published works are *A Living Wage* (1906) and *Distributive Justice* (1916, revised editions in 1927 and 1942). In 1914 his debate with Morris Hillquit in *Everybody's Magazine* was published under the title *Socialism: Promise or Menace?* His serious and systematic scholarly publication did not continue apace after he came to Catholic University, but he continued to write lucid commentaries on the problems of the day and more popular explanations of Catholic social thought. His later books were either lectures given at other universities (*Social Reconstruction* in 1920, *A Better Economic Order* in 1935); compilations of previously published articles (*The Church and Socialism and Other Essays* in 1919, *Declining Liberty and Other Papers* in 1927, *Questions of the Day* in 1931, *Seven Troubled Years, 1930–1936* in 1937); or textbooks (*The Church and Labor* with Joseph Husslein in 1920, *The State and the Church* with Moorhouse F. X. Millar in 1922 and later revised as *Catholic Principles of Politics* with Francis J. Boland in 1940, *The Catholic Church and the Citizen* in 1928). His 1941 autobiography, *Social Doctrine in Action: A Personal History*, chronicled his career in a rather formal, impersonal, and documentary manner. In 1944 he published *The Norm of Morality* through the N.C.W.C. because he could not find a commercial

pamphlets on various subjects. Many articles of a scholarly nature and of a more popular type, often in the form of commentaries on the problems of the day, appeared in numerous journals
and periodicals.[4]

Ryan taught not only in the School of Theology of The Catholic University of America but also at Trinity College and at the
National Catholic School of Social Service. In addition he was
the director of the Social Action Department of the N.C.W.C., but
by his own admission the running of the department was often in
the hands of his associate and colleague, Father Raymond A.
McGowan.

As a social reformer Ryan frequently worked with progressive non-Catholic Americans for the cause of social justice. He
wholeheartedly accepted in practice the American political system and thought that the economic and social system could be
changed in accord with Catholic principles by extending democratic ideals to the industrial order. Ryan as a Catholic priest
wanted to prove to all that the Catholic Church was the friend of
the worker, of the poor, and of social reform. For Ryan there
was no incompatibility between being Catholic and being a progressive. His progressive friends were somewhat amazed but always happy to have him associated with their causes. He worked
for and helped to write minimum wage laws in a number of
states. Even before the First World War he was associated with
many progressive groups and causes—the National Child Labor
Committee, the National Consumers League, the National Conference of Charities and Corrections. His biographer Francis
Broderick remarks that in the decade of the 1920s Ryan joined
dozens of committees, councils, boards, and associations. Ryan
was the first Roman Catholic priest to be a member of the national board of the American Civil Liberties Union. His association with progressive movements aligned him early with many
of the supporters of the New Deal. In general, progressives were
glad to have him in their company, even though they could not
accept all his doctrinal and moral positions.

Ryan was saddened by two events in the 1920s. Many liberals failed to support the rights of the Catholic Church in
Mexico. Also the defeat of Al Smith in 1928 engendered much
anti-Catholic animus, and Ryan himself was involved in the controversy because of his teaching on church and state. He publicly
disagreed with Herbert Hoover and supported Franklin D.
Roosevelt even to the point of making a campaign speech for

Roosevelt in 1936 under the auspices of the National Democratic Committee. On that occasion, Father Charles E. Coughlin, the Detroit radio priest who had a large following and had by then broken with Roosevelt, dubbed Ryan "the Right Reverend New Dealer." Ryan proudly notes that, in giving the benediction at Roosevelt's inauguration in 1937, he was the first Catholic priest who had ever participated in such a ceremony. The tributes to Ryan, on the occasion of a banquet celebrating his seventieth birthday in 1939, came from many prominent politicians and leaders in American life including the president, justices of the Supreme Court, senators and congressmen, and cabinet members. Granted the inflated rhetoric on such occasions, these tributes nevertheless testify to Ryan's work for social reform.[5]

Within the Catholic Church Ryan was the foremost leader in the fight for social justice not only because of his writings, activities, and speeches but also because of his association with many groups such as the National Conference of Catholic Charities, the National Catholic School of Social Service, and the Catholic Association for International Peace as well as with the N.C.W.C. and The Catholic University. Ryan has been described by his biographer as a papalist.[6] There can be no doubt that John Ryan faithfully expounded papal teaching on social justice and in all areas, stressed his opposition to birth control, and even changed his teaching, which originally allowed for sterilization of the mentally ill, after the papal encyclical *Casti connubii* of 1930. However, all Catholic authors of this period could be called "papalists."

Our reformer's progressive stands on social issues did cause some tensions within the church. Conservatives in the church often accused him of socialism. Early in his career Ryan wondered if his views were acceptable in Rome, but he was reassured by an influential Roman cleric.[7] Ryan's appointment as a domestic prelate, or monsignor, in 1933 was looked upon as a vindication of the orthodoxy of his opinions and of his standing in the Roman Catholic Church.[8] Cardinal William O'Connell of Boston was upset with Ryan's position on a child labor law amendment and even tried to have him removed from his teaching post.[9] Archbishop Michael J. Curley of Baltimore, who in his capacity as chancellor of Catholic University defended Ryan against O'Connell, became unhappy with Ryan's support of Roosevelt and the New Deal but eventually was reconciled with Ryan.[10] Ryan, the shrewd politician, was publicly effusive in his praise for the academic freedom he experienced at Catholic University.[11] Ryan's support of the New Deal in the 1930s brought him into opposition with some other Catholics as represented by such journals as *America, Catholic World* and its editor Father James M. Gillis, and *The Tablet* of Brooklyn under Patrick Scanlan, all of whom feared that Ryan was giving too much importance to the role of the state.[12]

Ryan died on September 16, 1945, and again received the plaudits of leaders of the church and of the state. As previously mentioned, he had been the foremost Catholic theoretician and practitioner in the field of social reform in the first half of the twentieth century.

I. General Ethical Principles

The very first sentence of John Ryan's unpublished licentiate dissertation, written in 1900, proclaims his lifelong interest in applying ethical principles to contemporary economic life. "Every free economic action has ethical relations, and is subject to ethical laws."[13] By 1933 he noted with obvious satisfaction that even the dominant business opinion in the United States now admitted that economics is subject to ethics.[14]

What kind of ethics and ethical principles does Ryan apply to economic life? Although Ryan explained his methodology in the context of his discussions of particular questions, his full-scale treatment of ethical methodology was only published in 1944, the year before his death. He points out that while Catholic moral theology acknowledges the importance of divine revelation, most of the specific applications and rules of Catholic morality, as illustrated in the papal encyclicals, are derived from the law which is inherent in rational human nature. Even without revelation this law would have provided human beings with sufficiently adequate ethical guidance. God has raised us to a supernatural order, but this does not destroy the natural order.[15] Ryan's own corpus of books and articles well illustrates such a natural-law approach.

On the philosophical level the Catholic University professor follows the standard textbook views of natural law in its relationship to eternal law. The primary principles of the natural law are known intuitively, based on the inclination of human

nature itself—do good and avoid evil as well as the principles of
self-preservation, care of offspring, and social intercourse. The
other principles are deductively derived from these primary principles.[16] The ultimate norm of morality is the divine reason or
essence, but this is mediated through human nature and human
reason. The proximate norm of morality, to use the traditional
term also employed by Ryan, is rational nature in its constitution and essential relations.[17]

The constitution of rational human nature shows that the
human person is an end in itself and can never be used as an instrument or as a means for any other end. The human person has
inherent worth, sacredness, and dignity. The human person acts
through different faculties which are hierarchically ordered. The
rational part of human nature orders and directs all the lower
faculties so that they serve the higher human end. Eating and
drinking, for example, are to be moderated by human reason to
serve the good of the total person.[18]

There are three essential relations of human beings—to a
higher being, to lower beings, and to equals. The relationship to
God serves as the basis for the primary obligation of knowing
and loving God, from which flow all our other obligations to God.
Human beings' relationship to lower creatures is one of domination. Although Ryan dismisses the sentimentalists of the early
1940s who want to attribute rights to animals, he shows a concern for what is now called the ecological question. The present
generation must allow for reasonable provision of natural resources for those who come after us. Fellow human beings are
to be treated as ends in themselves, since they are equals who
have the same nature, intrinsic worth, basic needs, and fundamental rights as we do. Our obligations to fellow human beings
should be understood in light of the virtues of charity and justice. These two virtues often overlap in their material obligations,
but they have a formally different perspective. Charity arises
from the bond which unites people together, whereas justice considers human persons as mutually independent and as possessing
individual rights.[19]

What about the argument that human nature is an inadequate norm, since developing and evolving human nature cannot
constitute an enduring objective basis for morality? Ryan responds that if human beings are changed into angels or gorillas,
then a new set of rules will apply, but in the meantime, rational

nature serves as an adequate norm of morality. However, the applications of natural law require that one take account of varying circumstances and developing human existence.[20]

The above explanation shows that Ryan adopted a traditional Catholic natural-law approach to ethics. Unfortunately, Ryan in his own explanations of theory failed to mention or to integrate his own distinctive contribution—a more inductive approach. Ryan's early teachers, especially William Kerby in sociology and Thomas Bouquillon in moral theology, stressed the importance of empirical data in social problems.[21] Ryan himself often criticized the vague and a priori approach of Catholic moral theology in the area of economics. In social ethics the ultimate criterion for Ryan was what serves human welfare, but this was determined by what actually happens.[22] On the basis of what proved to be best for human welfare, Ryan accepted private property and rejected socialism, but with the recognition that if a better system comes along, there is an obligation to embrace it.[23] Ryan even proposed a basic principle of expediency that good morality and good economics are identical. Yet he never integrated his own inductive emphasis into his more formal discussions of theory.

The most fundamental content question in ethics is the meaning of the human person. Ryan, throughout his long life, constantly refers to this question, but his chapter considering the natural rights of persons in his 1940 *Catholic Principles of Politics* repeats with only an occasional verbal change the chapter from his published dissertation "The Basis and Justification of Rights."[24]

The rights of the individual are grounded in the dignity of the human individual. A right may be defined as an inviolable moral claim to some personal good. A more detailed definition understands a right as the moral and inviolable power of having, doing, or demanding something desirable. Natural rights are inherent in a person, are derived from human nature itself and cannot be annulled or destroyed by any other person or by the state. Legal rights, for example, the right to vote, are conferred by the state for a civil purpose. The justification and purpose of natural rights is the welfare of the person. Every person has the obligation of self-perfection or development of one's personality, which has its ultimate source in God and its proximate source in human nature. Natural rights are the moral means by which the human person is enabled to reach this obligatory end.

There are three basic levels of natural rights. The first type has as its object that which is intrinsically good—good for its own sake or an end in itself, namely, the right to life itself. The second class of rights has as its object those things which are directly and per se morally necessary for the individual to achieve one's end. Among natural rights of the second class the most important are the right to marry, to enjoy personal freedom, and to own consumptive goods such as food and clothing. Also included in this category would be the right to reasonable freedom and reputation. A third class of rights includes those things that are means to human welfare but which are not directly necessary for any individual. Such realities are indirectly necessary for the individual because they are necessary as social institutions. The right to private property belongs under this third category.[25]

There are two important characteristics of human rights—once it is acknowledged that these rights are necessary for the individual. First, these natural rights are absolute, not in the sense that they are subject to no limitations, but in the sense that their validity does not depend upon any other person or institution. They are absolute in existence but not in extent as illustrated by the fact that our right to liberty has within itself certain reasonable limits. The second characteristic of human rights accents a basic equality of rights among all human beings. All people are equal with regard to natural rights because all are of equal intrinsic worth. However, in the concrete there are inequalities because of differences among human beings. All are equal with regard to the existence of these natural rights, but their extension or content differs because of the demands of proportional justice. Some people might possess rights in excess of the minimum (based on greater needs, efforts, or capacities), but in every case natural rights refer to a certain minimum which is necessary for all.[26]

Ryan situates his theory on natural rights between two extreme positions—one claims that all human rights are derived from society and are merely conferred by society on the individual, and the other extreme insists on the antisocial character of individual rights, exalting the individual at the expense of other individuals and of society itself. The first position exaggerates the extent to which society is an organism. This theory of social utility and of social welfare subordinates the individual to society and thereby denies the basic intrinsic dignity and worth of all human beings. Hegel's philosophy adopts the same basic approach, although it is formulated somewhat differently. However, society is not an organism in the sense that it is an end in itself. The members of society possess intrinsic worth and sacredness. Society does have rights that individuals do not have, such as the right to make war, but every right that society possesses is ultimately for the good of individuals and not for the good of society.

At the opposite extreme is an individualistic, antisocial, and semianarchical concept of natural rights proposed by the political philosophers in France in the last half of the eighteenth century. They speak of natural rights, but nature refers, not to what is permanent and essential in human nature, but to the state of nature which is primitive and unconventional. The state is a later encroachment on this primitive human freedom. These theorists falsely exaggerate the freedom of the individual and claim that the individual has the right to do anything that does not interfere with the equal liberty of others. Our author, with a greater appreciation of the social nature of human persons, proposes as the true formula that the individual has the right to all things essential to the reasonable development of one's personality consistent with the rights of others and the complete observance of the moral law.[27]

Logically, the discussion now turns to the state and its origin, purpose, and function. In 1921 Ryan published some brief articles in *America* on the origin of the state and in the same year wrote three articles in *The Catholic World* which were later revised for *Catholic Principles of Politics*.[28] A total view of his understanding of the state can only emerge from a study of all his writings, but *Catholic Principles of Politics* presents his most sustained and systematic discussion of the state.

Father Ryan accepts the traditional Catholic position that the state is a natural society, since human beings are by nature social and cannot adequately develop their faculties or live reasonable lives without the state. Interestingly, this Catholic social ethicist nowhere refers to some Augustinian theories and the Lutheran notion, which see the state as based on sin with the primary purpose of keeping sinful human beings from destroying one another. The end of the state for Ryan is the promotion of the common good or the public welfare. Later Ryan understands the end of the state as the promotion of social justice, a term which he began to use after Pius XI employed it so frequently in *Quadragesimo anno*.[29]

Ryan from the very beginning accepts what in Catholic theology is now often called the principle of subsidiarity, even though he does not use the term. The state must respect the rights not only of individuals but also of the family and of voluntary associations. The end of the state is to promote the common good only to the extent that this object cannot be attained by the family or by voluntary associations. The common good refers to the external goods of soul and body comprising the spiritual, intellectual, moral, physical, and economic orders. The "common" aspect refers to the state's obligation to provide common opportunity for individuals and groups to attain these goods. There exists a danger of understanding common in too rigid a way, which forgets that the state is obliged to promote the welfare of its citizens as a whole, as members of families and as members of social classes. From his earliest writings on the subject Ryan supports his position with two quotations from *Rerum novarum* which he constantly repeats in his writings. "Whenever the general interest, or any particular class, suffers or is threatened with injury which can in no other way be met or prevented, it is necessary for the State to intervene." Likewise, "The richer classes have many ways of shielding themselves and stand less in need of help from the State; whereas those who are badly off have no resources of their own to fall back upon, and must chiefly depend upon the assistance of the State." Ryan relies heavily upon these passages to justify his emphasis on the role of the state in bringing about human welfare in the economic order.[30] His opponents claim that he forgets to mention the warning of Leo XIII in *Rerum novarum* (par. 36) "that the law must not undertake more, nor proceed further, than is required for the remedy of the evil or the removal of the mischief."[31]

The primary function of the state in Ryan's "welfare theory" of the state (to use his terms) is to safeguard all natural rights including the right to life, liberty, property, livelihood, good name, and spiritual and moral security. The secondary functions, recognizing the principle of subsidiarity, include the following aspects: public works; public education; public charity; public health, safety, morals, and religion; and industrial regulation. This view of the state occupies a middle position between individualistic theories and totalitarian theories of the state.[32]

The individualistic theory rests on an exaggerated individualistic freedom and conceives the role of government as primarily restrictive and coercive. This laissez-faire theory maintains that the best government is the least government. Philosophically, the theory was proposed by the eighteenth-century thinkers alluded to above and by Adam Smith. Politically, reaction to authoritarian and overly restrictive regimes paved the way for this overemphasis on individualistic freedom. Economically, the capitalist classes embraced the theory so that there would be no state interference in their quest for profit.[33]

In theory and in practice Ryan worked against this theory of the state and its functions throughout his long life. From the very beginning he appealed to the state to protect the rights of workers against the abusive power of capitalists.[34] In the 1920s and 1930s he constantly denounced the Supreme Court decisions which read an individualistic notion of freedom into the fifth and fourteenth amendments to declare unconstitutional the laws proposing eight-hour work days, minimum wages, and other provisions for the protection of labor.[35] After the Depression occurred in 1929, he intensified his criticism of the Court, which refused to accept much of the legislation proposed by the Roosevelt administration. His solution for the economic problems of the Depression called for heavy government involvement and even deficit spending.[36] Ryan was criticized by some Catholics for relying too heavily on the state.

When discussing erroneous views of the state in 1921, Ryan describes the opposite extreme as a socialistic theory of the state which calls for undue intrusion of the state in economic matters, in education, and in family life.[37] His 1940 book *Catholic Principles of Politics* adds a section on totalitarianism and treats fascism, nazism, and communism, all of which had often been discussed by Ryan in the intervening years.[38]

In the light of his understanding of the human person, human rights, and the state, one can understand better the approach which Ryan took to particular questions of social ethics. The first and longer section will discuss his economic ethics, the field in which he made his greatest contribution. The relevant aspects of his political ethics will be considered in a following section.

II. Economic Ethics[39]

Economic ethics discusses the proper distribution of the goods of this world. Ryan the economist knew full well the problems that existed. In his doctoral dissertation he pointed out that

60 percent of adult American males were not receiving a living wage, although the national income at that time could have been so divided as to provide all male workers with a living wage.[40] In his 1913 debate with Morris Hillquit, Father Ryan identified three great defects of the existing American economic system: insufficient remuneration for the majority of wage earners; excessive incomes for a small minority of capitalists, and the narrow distribution of capital ownership.[41] As time went on, our economist-theologian saw no improvement in the distribution of economic productivity in the United States. In 1929 one-tenth of 1 percent of American families received as large a share of the national income as the poorest 42 percent of families in the nation. The disproportionate growth of the incomes of the rich and the poor was particularly striking between 1900 and 1929.[42]

The cornerstone of Ryan's economic ethics is his understanding that the goods of creation exist to serve the basic needs of all, although he never really discusses this fundamental concept at great length. Three generic proofs are briefly proposed in *A Living Wage*. First, the practice of people throughout history proves it, as illustrated by the theory of primitive communism regarding land ownership, by the fact that scarcely any community regarded as thieves those of its members who seized their neighbors' goods as a last resort against starvation, and by the efforts of church and state to provide for poor people. Second, Christian conviction shows that every human being has a strict right to as much of the wealth of the community as is necessary to maintain life. Such was the teaching of the fathers of the church and of the older theologians, especially Thomas Aquinas. Third, human reason proves the point. All persons are of equal dignity and of equal intrinsic importance. All have a right to subsist upon the bounty of the earth.[43] Ryan's theory of human rights, together with his understanding of the purpose of the goods of creation, forms the basis for the human being's right to a decent livelihood.[44]

His systematic and comprehensive study of the distribution of the products of industry is entitled *Distributive Justice*, which serves as the criterion of just distribution. Here again Ryan never even treats the theory of justice and the relationship of distributive justice to other forms of justice. Only in chapter 16 does he discuss the canons of distributive justice or the rules that should be applied to the distribution of the products of industry. Ryan mentions five canons, all of which have some significance, but none of which is adequate and complete if applied only by itself—equality, needs, effort and sacrifice, productivity, and scarcity. Our author adopts the canon of human welfare, which includes and summarizes all that is "ethically and socially feasible" (note his word—feasible) in the other five canons. "It takes account of equality, inasmuch as it regards all men as persons, as subjects of rights; and of needs inasmuch as it awards to all the necessary participants in the industrial system at least that amount of remuneration which will meet the elementary demands of decent living and self-development. It is governed by efforts and sacrifices, at least in so far as they are reflected in productivity and scarcity; and by productivity and scarcity to whatever extent is necessary in order to produce the maximum net results."[45] As is evident from all his writings, the canon of needs and the right of the person to the minimum of goods necessary to satisfy these fundamental needs is superior to any other claim.[46]

In his 1931 encyclical Pope Pius XI used the term "social justice." Ryan analyzes his uses of the term and sees in it a general concept of justice involving both a distributive and a contributive aspect, which includes both legal and distributive justice and sometimes also commutative justice. Social justice is equivalent to the common good. After quoting from Pius XI that the distribution of created goods must be brought into conformity with the demands of the common good and social justice, Ryan concludes, "The sum of the matter is that the concept of social justice, adequately considered and comprehensively applied, would do more to bring about a reign of industrial peace and industrial justice than any other theory or formula that has ever obtained lodgment in the minds of men."[47] Perhaps Ryan would have made social justice his criterion of distribution if he were writing his major work after 1931, but he did not and would not change the canons of distribution with needs as the most fundamental and primary.[48]

Principle of expediency

The most creative and unique contribution of John Ryan to the justice of distribution concerns the principle of expediency. Writing in 1932, he proposes a definite and fundamental task for Catholic Action—to bring about the identification of morality and expediency in our industrial system, by persuading all classes that prosperity cannot be maintained unless the receivers of wages and salaries obtain a considerable increase in remuneration and purchasing power.[49] Especially in the Depression years Ryan appeals to this identification of morality and expediency, but from the very beginning it has been bubbling near the surface of his thought and occasionally breaking through. The development of his thinking on expediency is fascinating.

Since John Ryan is an ethicist interested in particular questions, an economist, and a reformer, he has to discuss the feasibility of a living wage. Ryan responds to the two arguments proposed against its feasibility. To the argument that the national product is not adequate to supply all with a living wage, Ryan answers that our natural resources are capable of sustaining a living wage for all, and there will even be an increase in our total resources from the living wage paid to all. To the argument that the machinery of distribution cannot be modified to bring about such a result, our author points to the reforming approaches he has suggested.[50] In the economic sphere the danger of overproduction would be diminished because there would be greater demand and consumption by the working classes.[51]

In the 1913 debate with Hillquit, Ryan explicitly formulates the principle of expediency. The ethical character of socialist proposals can only be evaluated by examining their bearing on human welfare. "In the matter of social institutions, moral values and genuine expediency are in the long run identical."[52] In the ensuing debate Ryan attacks socialism because of its expediency and because its theory that social welfare is the determinant of morality would be fatal to the rights and welfare of the individual. Hillquit responds with his trump card, that is, he uses Ryan's earlier remarks, just quoted, against him.[53] In his final summation our author clarifies his position. His previous statement on expediency was limited to social institutions and systems and did not apply to human actions. But it would have been better to write economic institutions, for this is what he had in mind. The Catholic priest clearly wants to separate himself from those who make social expediency the test of morality. For Ryan morality is the test of social expediency. The moral law and the rights of individuals are not mere conventions.[54]

This debate with Hillquit may have chastened his enthusiasm for the principle of expediency, for it does not appear in his major 1916 work on *Distributive Justice*. Again there are arguments for the feasibility of his position on a living wage. The living wage rests on the right of the worker and in no way comes from the state, but in one paragraph Ryan adduces an argument for the living wage on the basis of the good consequences this would have for society and social welfare.[55] He later shows that the enactment of minimum-wage laws is politically and economically expedient, but he does not make or develop the claim that good morality and expediency are identical.[56]

In 1926 Ryan remarks that the living-wage doctrine is now generally recognized to be in harmony with the best interests of industry and of the whole community. Our natural resources and productive equipment are capable of turning out more goods than people are able to consume. The solution is to increase consumption by increasing the purchasing power of the workers through a living wage. Our economist is here referring to the underconsumption theory which he had originally learned from John A. Hobson, although he does not explicitly refer to Hobson or the theory as such.[57] In *A Living Wage* Ryan incorporates an extended three-page quotation from Hobson on this theory.[58] However, there are only passing references to it in his other writings before the Depression.[59]

The crisis of the Depression and Ryan's proposed solutions in the light of the underconsumption theory occasion his insistence on the principle of expediency. According to Ryan there have been fifteen depressions in American industrial history, but the Depression of 1929 is the most severe. Ryan explains the cause of the Depression in the light of the underconsumption theory. Excess of productive capacity relative to profitable demand is the main cause of the Depression, but this situation exists because the masses of the people do not have the money to buy the goods of production. The basic problem is not overproduction but underconsumption.[60]

Ryan's proposals for overcoming the Depression are three: minimum wage laws, a thirty-hour work week, and federal expenditures for public works. The basis for these measures is the underconsumption theory.[61] In discussing unemployment in the Depression Ryan asserts that the teaching of Pope Leo XIII on a living wage and the rights of the workers is the most direct, prompt, and efficacious means of insuring the prosperity of industry.[62] This explains the identification of morality and expediency in our economic system—Ryan's principle of expediency.

At first glance one would not expect a Roman Catholic ethicist to propose even a nuanced theory of expediency. However, there are many factors entering into Ryan's acceptance of such a theory. As a Catholic natural-law ethician, Ryan recognizes that morality is based on the human and is in no way a restriction of the truly human. In his inductive approach the morality of all economic institutions and systems is determined by whether or not in practice they contribute to human welfare. His economic theory of underconsumption fits perfectly with his insistence on the moral need for a living wage. As a reformer, there is more chance to have his morality accepted if he can prove it would also be economically beneficial. However, such a theory of expediency raises significant theoretical and practical questions.

Having established the theoretical basis for a just distribution of the products of industry, our consideration now focuses on the content of Ryan's proposals. First, the rights and duties of the four classes contributing to the economic product will be discussed. Then our ethician's more systematic development of economic ethics will be treated under the rubric of economic democracy. Third, Ryan's approach will be contrasted with opposite extremes of capitalism and socialism which he was striving to avoid. Fourth, Ryan's understanding of the social mission of the church will be explored.

Distribution among the participating groups

There are four groups that share in the work of production and have some right to a return. Wages constitute the return to the worker; rent belongs to the landowners; profits belong to the business person; interest goes to the capitalists. Ryan considers these four groups and their right to recompense especially in his 1916 *Distributive Justice*, although the question of wages was the subject of his earlier doctoral dissertation.

Laborers and wages

John Ryan discusses and rejects three erroneous theories of wage justice. First, the prevailing-wage theory is rejected because it does not even make an appeal to any kind of justice but merely accepts the existing rate. Ethics does not even enter into the consideration.

Second, a number of theories fall under the general category of exchange-equivalence theories, which appeal to a principle of justice calling for equality in the wage contract between what is given and what is received. One version of this theory, called the rule of equal gain, maintains that the contract could bring to employer and employee equal amounts of net advantages or satisfactions. Such a theory is both impractical and unjust because it ignores the moral claims of needs, efforts, and sacrifices as regards the worker. Likewise, the theory of free contract is wrong because of its individualism and its failure to take account of the fundamental moral claim of needs. Another exchange-equivalence theory is based on the concept of objective value as found in the medieval concept of the just price, which is still proposed by some modern Catholic writers. Such theories fail because they try to compare two entities which are ultimately incommensurate—there exists no third term or standard or objective fact to determine whether a certain amount of wages represents the equivalent of a given amount of labor. Implicit in Ryan's condemnation of all these exchange-equivalence theories is their appeal to commutative justice and not to distributive justice.

Productivity theories constitute a third type of erroneous theories of wage justice. The radical version maintains labor's right to the whole product based either on a theory of value or on the fact that laborers, together with a few managers of industry, are the only ones who expend energy in the productive process. Such a theory cannot be theoretically proven and would lead to much greater evils and injustices than the ones it proposes to abolish. A modified productive theory proposes that the worker receive that portion of the product which comes from one's productive efficacy in relation to all the other productive contributions. Theoretically, such approaches erroneously make productivity the only canon of distribution; in practice these approaches are inapplicable.[63]

Ryan criticizes all these inadequate theories and constructs his own approach in the light of his understanding of human rights, of the universal destiny of the goods of creation to serve the needs of all, and of the canons of distributive justice. He develops a three-step argument to prove that the minimum of justice (not the fullness of justice) calls for a living wage for all workers. (1) God created the earth for the sustenance of all his children; therefore, all are equal in their inherent claims upon the bounty of nature. (2) The inherent right of access to the earth is conditioned upon and becomes actually valid through the expenditure of useful labor. (3) As a corollary, it follows that those who are in control of the opportunities of the earth are obliged to permit reasonable access to these opportunities by those who are willing to work. As a minimum, every worker has the right to a decent livelihood from one's labor because in the present economy this is the only way in which the worker can share in the goods of creation. A decent livelihood includes that quantity of goods and opportunities which is indispensible to live in the manner worthy of a human being and includes such elements as food, clothing, shelter, a healthy and moral environment, provision for the future, security against sickness and accidents, opportunities for recreation, education, and religion. This belongs to the average worker, even the woman worker.

Ryan maintains against some Catholic theoreticians that a living wage in justice must be a family living wage. The laborer has the basic human right to develop one's personality and basic human faculties. Without explicitly identifying his sources in the traditional Catholic understanding of natural law, our author argues that self-preservation is undoubtedly the first law of nature, but self-propagation is the second law of nature or at least the expression of one of the primary and strongest human instincts. A family living wage is the only way in which the worker can exercise his right to have and care for a family, which is an essential condition of normal life.[64]

Ryan the economist spells out the concrete demands of a family living wage which should be sufficient for an average-size family of four or five children. In 1906, in detailing a budget for such a family, Ryan concludes that anything less than $600 per year is not a living wage in any American city, and more is needed in the largest cities.[65] In 1916 the figure is raised to $750 in the light of escalating prices.[66] A living family wage meets the minimum standard of justice. Ryan goes on to discuss the question of complete wage justice, but he recognizes that the immediate practical problem is to insure the minimum family living wage and a decent livelihood for all.[67]

Ryan contends that a living family wage should go to male workers but not to female workers, since the support of the family falls properly and primarily on the husband and the father and not upon the wife and mother whose role is in the home.[68] Despite his position on the role of the woman in society Ryan still might have been able to argue for a living family wage for women on more pragmatic grounds. According to Ryan women

living at home deserve the same pay as women supporting themselves because otherwise employers would be tempted to hire
women living at home at lesser pay and take jobs away from
women living outside the home.[69] In addition to using in-princi-
pled reasons Ryan argues that nonmarried men should be paid
a living wage lest they take jobs away from married men because they could be paid less.[70] He might have made the same
type of argument for giving women a living family wage, but his
traditional view of the role of women is probably too strong to
entertain any practical reasons that would put women and men
on the same footing in industrial society.

Landowners and rent

A second class of agents contributing to the industrial product are landowners. In *Distributive Justice* Ryan discusses the
whole question of private property in the context of the ownership of land. His discussion involves three points: the right to
own land or private property, the right to rent from land, and
the limits on the right to private property and to rent. Our discussion will first consider Ryan's attitude toward private property as found throughout his writings.[71]

As one might suspect, Ryan's teaching on private property
tries to find a middle ground between the individualistic and
socialistic approaches. His teaching logically follows from his
understanding of human dignity and human rights, the primary
purpose of the goods of creation, the canons of distributive justice, and his own more inductive natural-law methodology. Generally speaking, Ryan defends the institution of private property
(which in his major works is considered only in the form of land
ownership) against the socialist position and stresses the limitations of the right to private property against the capitalists.

As already pointed out, Ryan defends the institution of private property as a natural right of the third kind—private ownership of productive goods or land ownership is only indirectly
necessary for the good of the individual because it is necessary
as a social institution. This defense of private property is based
on empirical and consequentialist grounds and not on the intrinsic human nature of the individual. If and when a better system is discovered, the state has a moral obligation to put it into
practice.[72]

The two approaches of socialism and the single-tax theory would ultimately not be as beneficial for human welfare and, consequently, should be rejected. The following aspects of socialism make it inferior to the system of private ownership in securing the welfare of society and indirectly the welfare of the individual: socialism lessens or takes away the incentive of the workers; it could not adjust wages satisfactorily; its organization would be highly inefficient whether in a centralized or subsidiary form; workers and all would be deprived of some freedom.[73] Many of Ryan's arguments against the practicality of socialism are rooted in a realistic view of human beings. He frequently criticizes socialism as being utopian and idealistic.[74] However, theoretically Ryan cannot readily ground his defense of realism because he fails to give enough importance in theory to the reality of sin. His recognition that the natural is quite different from the supernatural gives some but not enough basis from a theological perspective for his realistic view of human beings and his practical rejection of socialism as being unable to serve human and social welfare.

Ryan in his earlier writings also shows the impracticality of the single-tax theory proposed by Henry George. If rent were confiscated or totally taxed by the state, the following deleterious consequences would occur: the land would deteriorate and lose its productiveness; bureaucratic and administrative machinery to carry out such a tax would involve error, favoritism, and complexities; tenure would be unstable, because owing to misfortunes the individual in a particular year might not be able to pay the tax.[75] Ryan accepts the institution of private property because it best achieves the basic rights of human beings and the common destiny of the goods of creation to serve the needs of all.

However, Ryan's controlling notions of the basic rights of all human beings, including the right to livelihood, and of the common destiny of the goods of creation to serve the needs of all, also call for limitations on the right of private property. The individual right of ownership is always subordinate to the common right of use. Private property can never be an unlimited right, especially in the light of the fundamental right of all to a basic livelihood from the common destiny of the goods of creation.[76]

Ryan appeals to history, the teaching of the fathers, the teaching of the Scholastic theologians, especially Aquinas, and the teaching of the popes to back up his position on private property. However, in the process Ryan might too quickly pass over some of the different nuances in his own approach. There are significant differences between Ryan and Pope Leo XIII. Leo's argument for private property in *Rerum novarum* rests primarily on human nature and the rights of the individual person. Ryan is aware of his differences with Leo, for in his notebooks he expresses some disagreements with Leo, characterizing as of merely sentimental value Leo's argument for private property as an extension of the individual's personality.[77] However, our author apparently in his published works never explicitly calls attention to his differences with Pope Leo XIII.

Ryan has been criticized by some in the Catholic tradition precisely because he did not base the right to private property on individual human nature as such and thereby made the right conditional and based upon changing social realities rather than unchangeable human nature.[78] There can be no doubt that Ryan's methodology, his basis for defending private property, and his insistence on the limitations of the institution of private property differ somewhat from other views in the Catholic tradition, although they seem to be quite in harmony with the teaching of the fathers of the church and even with Thomas Aquinas. In short, Ryan relativizes the right of private property more than Leo XIII and some manualists in the Catholic tradition. The practical effects of this theory will be seen in his concrete discussions of the economic order.

Ryan defends the right of land ownership but also recognizes important limitations in the light of the common destiny of the goods of creation to serve the basic needs of all. As a reformer, he points out defects in the present system of land tenure in terms of monopoly, excessive gains, and exclusion of many from the land. His proposed reforms are numerous. Exceptionally valuable lands, such as those containing timber, minerals, oil, coal, gas, and water power, which are under public ownership should remain there. Deserving and efficient persons should be helped through loans to obtain possession of some land. Municipalities should sell no more land but only lease land and try to buy back some land. There should be much higher taxes on profits from land. To take all the future increase in land value would even be morally lawful if justice were done to the owners. A supertax on exceptionally large or valuable land holdings would also be beneficial.[79]

Capital and interest

A third factor in production is capital, which refers to all means of production except land. Interest is the return from capital as distinguished from rent, which is the return from land. However, the right to rent is based on the same principles as the right to interest.[80] Ryan first systematically discusses the Catholic teaching on interest or usury, as it was called in the Middle Ages, in a series of eleven articles published in the *Catholic Fortnightly Review* in 1909 and later published in pamphlet form.[81] The older Catholic teaching condemned interest taking or usury because one only had a right to strict equality—the return of what was given. Since the end of the seventeenth century other extrinsic titles were proposed such as the gain that one could make by investing the money in land or productive enterprises rather than loaning it to another (*lucrum cessans*). Today most Catholic authors justify the taking of interest on a loan on the basis that money itself is now considered to be virtually productive.

However, Ryan cannot accept this approach of many contemporary Catholic scholars. There is no intrinsic right to interest based on the right of the individual who puts up the capital. Neither productivity nor service establishes a title or right to interest. Not a single conclusive argument can prove the right to interest based on either of these titles. The title of sacrifice undergone by the one who lends the money justifies interest in some cases, but in most cases the lender is already rich and is therefore not sacrificing anything because the rich person has no immediate needs.[82]

Ryan ultimately justifies interest taking only on social and presumptive grounds. In a consequentialist and empirical argument he reasons that the state is justified in permitting interest because the suppression of interest would not be in the best interest of the community. What about the right of the individual to take interest? Our author ultimately justifies interest only on the titles of presumption, analogy, and possession in the light of the doubt about being able to prove conclusively the existence of intrinsic titles to interest. Its immorality cannot be proven, and meanwhile the right to take interest is in possession. The title to interest, however, must always cede to the stronger title of the laborer to a living wage.[83]

Ryan as an ethicist and economist is also interested in the
rate of interest. In the 1930s he recognizes as excessive more than
2 percent interest on loans, including mortgages and bonds. Somewhat larger returns are justified on stocks because of the risk
factor.[84] In the midst of the Depression, on the basis of his underconsumption theory, he urges businessmen and capitalists to
forego any return on capital as such, and in that way they will
ultimately help the economy and themselves by pulling the country out of the Depression.[85]

Serious questions can be raised about Ryan's treatment of
interest. In the light of his approach elsewhere stressing the social aspect, could not a stronger case be made for interest on
capital in the light of the good of society? Should interest on
loans and interest on capital really be treated together? Is the
meaning of capital the same today as in the preindustrial Middle
Ages? Possible inconsistencies also arise. According to Ryan rent
and return from capital are governed by the same principles, but
on the very first page of *Distributive Justice* he seems to give an
intrinsic title to rent by referring to it as a right included in the
institution of private ownership.[86] Another significant problem
concerns Ryan's treating interest on loans and interest on investments as the same reality. In the industrial age of the twentieth
century many economists and others often separate and distinguish the two. In fact, in 1936 our author agrees with John Maynard Keynes in making such a distinction.[87] If Ryan were writing
his major theoretical works after this time, would he have proposed a difference between the return on loans and the return on
investments? In the light of some of these problems one can
question the accuracy and helpfulness of his fourfold division of
the factors of productivity in the modern economic world into
landowners, capitalists, businessmen, and laborers.

Businessmen and profits

The fourth factor of production is the function of the businessman, to which corresponds the remuneration of profits.
Profits constitute the reward of the businessman for labor and
the direction of the enterprise and are distinguished from rent
and interest. Ryan's terminology thus differs from the generally
accepted notion that profits are what remain in a corporation
after all the other expenses are paid. Such an understanding
again argues against Ryan's fourfold division of the factors of

industrial productivity as adequately portraying modern economic life. Here he seems to be referring to the small businessman and not to the modern American corporation.

Profits, as the reward of the businessman for his efforts, are essentially just. The moral problem is one of degree and basically involves two questions—the right of the businessman to obtain indefinitely large profits and a right to a minimum of profits. As a general rule, businessmen who face conditions of active competition have a right to all the profits they can obtain so long as they use fair business methods. However, equity or fairness, which is less strong than justice and does not constitute a strict rule as such, calls for the businessman to share these exceptionally large profits with the wage earners and consumers. Ryan admits that in large corporations where management is done by salaried executive officers the revenues comparable to profits are the surplus gains that remain after all other obligations are met. The stockholders have a better claim to these surplus gains than anyone else, but they are held in equity to share the surplus with laborers and consumers. However, these principles suppose the conditions of competition and the absence of fraud. Questions of monopoly, the legal limitations of fortunes, and distribution of surplus wealth are discussed at great length.

Does the businessman have a right to a minimum profit? The basic principle is that all workers of average ability who contribute a reasonable amount of labor to the productive process have a right to a decent livelihood on two conditions—that such labor is the only means of sustenance and that their labor is economically indispensible to those who utilize it or its product. These conditions are usually present in the case of a worker but not of a businessman, who can readily become an employee. Otherwise, all inefficient and unnecessary businessmen would be kept in operation.[88]

Economic democracy

Everything that has been discussed thus far sets the stage for a consideration of Ryan's program of social reform. Ryan is neither an advocate of the status quo nor a radical. The existing structures can and should be reformed to bring about greater justice. In his earlier discussions with Hillquit, Ryan defends social reform as able to meet the problems and rejects more radical approaches.[89] In commenting on the Bishops' Program of Re-

construction Ryan acknowledges that the word reconstruction
is poorly chosen because the program calls for a considerable
amount of reform, readjustment, and improvement but no change
so great so as to justify the word reconstruction.[90] Such a reforming approach fits in well with Ryan's realistic personality,
his interest in economics, his inductive methodology, and his attempt to alleviate the problems faced by the worker as quickly
as possible. To Ryan's great credit as a reformer, he never
stopped seeking more reforms in the existing situation so that
his program of social reform continued to develop over the years.

Ryan's program of continuing economic reform might best
be called economic democracy—a term often used by Ryan but
not consistently employed to designate his developing program.
In 1909 Ryan defines economic democracy as the movement toward a more general and more equitable distribution of economic
power, goods, and opportunities.[91] On different occasions he employs this term to describe the changes that should be brought
about.[92] Ryan did not create this term, for it was used by many
others. Perhaps he was heavily influenced by the book *Industrial
Democracy* written by Sidney and Beatrice Webb in 1897, which
he frequently cites in his writings.

The term economic democracy fits in well with Ryan's role
as an American Catholic reformer. His ethics, with its basis in
the dignity of the person and the universal destiny of the goods
of creation, calls for all to share and participate in the products
of industry. The term has obvious appeal in the American ethos.
Ryan's economic reform is based on the principles of a democracy
which is both political and economic. To criticize and call for a
change in the existing American economic institutions is not un-
American but rather is calling for the American concept of
democracy to be applied also in the economic order.[93] As a proponent of economic democracy, Ryan uses a definite American
base in attacking the individualistic notion of freedom so often
upheld by the Supreme Court into the 1930s.[94]

Three developing stages can be pointed out in Ryan's program of economic democracy: social reform by legislation, a new
status for workers which began in 1913, and industry-wide councils which Ryan advocated after the encyclical *Quadragesimo
anno* in 1931. However, the succeeding developments did not do
away with the preceding stages but merely added aspects to
them. Undoubtedly a problem exists in determining the exact

relationship among all these proposals, but for Ryan the reformer they all worked toward the same goal of economic reform.

Social reform by legislation—first stage

In 1909 Ryan wrote an important two-part article for *The Catholic World* entitled "A Program of Social Reform by Legislation," which synthesizes his approach and remains the basic direction of his thought throughout his life despite a few changes. The state must intervene to protect the poor working people and to limit the power of the economically favored industrialist and the wealth of the few.[95] First, the intervention of the state to protect the rights of the workers will be considered.

First and most fundamental Ryan advocates a minimum wage law. As previously mentioned, Ryan wrote his doctoral dissertation on this subject, framed proposed laws for state legislatures, and worked in several states for the enactment of these laws. When the Supreme Court declared such laws unconstitutional because they violated the freedom of the employer to make a contract without such restrictions, Ryan severely criticized the Court and its individualistic concept of freedom. In fact, he had a running battle with the Court because of its refusal to accept as constitutional legislation which was passed to protect the worker. In the 1920s he proposed an amendment to the Constitution to allow Congress and the several states to pass laws on all aspects of protective social legislation for workers.[96] In 1936 he strongly supported the proposal of the Democratic platform calling for a constitutional amendment if this is necessary to enable the state and federal government to enact legal standards of industrial and social justice.[97] Ryan even defended Roosevelt's attempt to pack the Supreme Court and thereby do away with its conservative majority.[98]

Second, Ryan's 1909 program favors legislation limiting the work day to eight hours. In the Depression years, especially on the basis of his underconsumption theory, the Catholic University professor would call for a thirty-hour work week with the same pay as a means of overcoming the massive unemployment and of raising consumption to counteract the effects of the Depression.[99]

Third, Ryan supports selective labor laws to protect women and children. Later Ryan would advocate an amendment to the

Constitution to prevent child labor, even though he ran into much opposition on this score from other Catholics and particularly from Cardinal O'Connell, archbishop of Boston, who saw such a proposal as an undue intrusion of the state into questions of the family.[100] Ryan attacked the National Woman's party for its platform of abolishing protective labor legislation for women and of proposing an equal rights amendment. He saw their position as weakening the struggle for social justice and also as based on a false notion of equality and freedom. For Ryan labor legislation protecting women and children is the first step toward protection for all workers. Women are men's equal as persons, but outside this essential equality there are many biological and physical inequalities. Social justice which is proportional calls for laws adopted to the needs and capacities of different classes.[101]

Fourth, legislation is necessary to protect the rights of workers in industrial disputes and to make legal boycotts and other means used by labor to defend its interests. Through the years Ryan strenuously opposes the use of court injunctions as an arbitrary and oppressive way of preventing labor from using tactics such as strikes and boycotts which are not illegal.[102] His 1909 article advocates compulsory arbitration of labor disputes, but in 1922 he would reject such an approach.[103]

Fifth, the 1909 article calls for relief for the unemployed, who then constituted between 8 and 15 percent of the adult population, through such means as employment and state subsidies for private agencies to help in the care of the unemployed. During the Depression, Ryan would insist on the obligation of the state, when other resources were inadequate, to provide material relief and jobs for the poor, especially through public works.[104] In Ryan's view such pump priming would bring about more jobs, and the jobholders would then spend more money, thus creating jobs for others.[105] In Ryan's analysis strong government intervention is the only means capable of pulling the country out of its problems, but such efforts will be truly successful to the extent that other reforms of distribution are accepted. Priming the pump will not of itself solve the basic problem.[106]

Sixth, there must be security and provision against accident, illness, and old age with different groups contributing to the cost of such insurance.

Seventh, government should also work to insure adequate housing for workers, but here again the state is not expected to do everything.

The second part of Ryan's program for social reform through legislation tries to overcome the abuses in land ownership and excessive incomes of a minority of capitalists. Our author's program calls for public ownership of public utilities, mines, and forests. In a 1936 article Ryan distinguishes four different classes of businesses: (1) those that should be owned and operated by the government either federal, state, or municipal, such as public utilities, which are natural monopolies; (2) those that might be operated by a public corporation like TVA whether or not they are governmentally owned, such as coal mining and oil drilling; (3) those that should be subject to public control without public ownership or operation, such as those producing or marketing certain agricultural products; (4) the majority of industries which would be left to private ownership and operation even though subject to some degree of government control.[107]

A second aspect of Ryan's 1909 program deals with adequate control of monopolies. Ryan the realist is aware that history shows that human beings cannot be trusted to use such great power justly. Again one must note that Ryan proposes little or no theological grounding for the realism which often comes through in his writings. In the last revision of *Distributive Justice* the following suggestions are made for controlling monopolies: competition by publicly owned firms; prevention of price fixing and other unfair means of competition; strict enforcement of laws against illegal practices by monopolies.[108]

A third area of concern is taxes. In keeping with his concept of distributive justice and its proportional rather than arithmetic equality, Ryan calls for a progressive tax on income and inheritance. A considerable portion of the future increase in land values should also be taxed. Here, again, one sees Ryan's reaction to Henry George's proposal. Later Ryan would recognize that this proposal was not too realistic because land values had not continued to increase.[109]

Finally our reformer calls for the prohibition of pure speculation on the stock exchanges. In his licentiate dissertation he concluded that the institution of unproductive speculation, as it existed at that time, was of questionable morality.[110] In an earlier article based on the licentiate dissertation the young Ryan concluded that speculation as an institution is economically of doubtful utility, socially productive of great evils, morally vitiated by a great amount of dishonesty.[111] Ryan would later be heartened to see that the Securities and Exchange Act of 1933 accepted similar principles and conclusions.[112]

A new status for workers—second stage

Reform by legislation aimed at a better distribution of material goods, but Ryan soon realized there had to be a change in the role and status of the worker. Generally this new status can be described as cooperation and coparticipation in the industrial order. Our author implicitly and explicitly furnishes many reasons for this new status for workers. First, cooperative societies whether of producers or of consumers will help in bringing about a more equal share in the material goods of production and thus serve as a partial solvent to the evils of capitalism.[113] Since the economic and the material are not the only aspects of human nature, full human dignity calls for a greater participation of the worker in the whole enterprise. Traditional Catholic theology has called for people working together and cooperating for the common good rather than opposing one another in class struggle. Likewise, Catholic theology does not want to leave all to the role of the state.[114]

Ryan also supports this new status for workers by calling it the American way. In the American industrial situation in the 1920s the vast majority of men begin their adult life as workers who must be resigned to dependence on wages and salaries for the rest of their days, while functions of ownership and direction are limited to a few. The present system is autocracy or feudalism at best and opposed to the democratic genius of America. Ryan the reforming realist also carries a big stick—if these modifications are not made, the socialist alternative will be more attractive to many Americans.[115]

In his 1913 debate with Hillquit, Ryan insists that until the majority of workers become owners, at least in part, of the tools with which they work, the system of private capital will, in the words of Hilaire Belloc, remain essentially unstable.[116] In a 1913 pamphlet the Catholic reformer maintains that cooperation is an essential element in social reform, even though not many others emphasize it. Cooperation involves much more than merely material benefits.[117] At this time of development Ryan discusses the various types of cooperative enterprises: cooperative credit societies, cooperative agricultural societies, cooperative mercantile societies, cooperation in production. Since cooperative associations for production involve greater complexity and the need of specialized business ability, they have been less successful in the past, and their extension in the future will be slow. Some business enterprises are better suited to cooperation than others.[118] It is highly desirable that the majority, if not all, of the workers possess some capital, preferably in the productive and distributive concerns in which they are interested.[119]

In *Social Reconstruction* in 1920 Ryan devotes one chapter to labor sharing in management and profits and a following chapter to copartnership, by which he means ownership of the stock in the corporation, and cooperation.[120] However, near the end of the second chapter he comes to the formula which would remain constant with him throughout the rest of his life—a threefold sharing in management, in profits, and in ownership.[121] Ryan also cites with obvious delight the passage in which Pius XI in *Quadragesimo anno* calls for the same threefold sharing of the worker.[122]

Sharing in management does not mean involvement in all the business decisions but in those which directly affect the worker, such as shop conditions, shop discipline, installment of new machinery, improvement of the industrial process and organization. Sharing in profits calls for a change in the existing American practice which gives the profits to the owners of capital or stockholders. The existing practice is contrary to human welfare because it rewards idle ownership at the expense of labor. One can see here a practical application of Ryan's understanding of capital and his unwillingness to give an intrinsic title to interest from capital. After fair wages, a reasonable rate of interest, adequate compensation of management, and all other expenses of production have been paid, the wage earners should share the surplus not with the owners of capital but with the managers of the business. Sharing in ownership in our society should take the form of associated and partial ownership, for only a small minority of workers can expect to become individual owners. In these ways workers can purchase stock and perhaps even acquire some real control over the company, although ownership of stock does not always insure real control. In the midst of the Depression Ryan the realist recognizes that the most desirable and democratic arrangement would be productive cooperation in which the same persons would be capitalists, workers, and businessmen, but such a reorganization of industry cannot be hoped for at the present time. However, the cooperative movement remains the most effective means of improving the economic and social conditions of the farmer. In this second stage of his reform program Ryan calls for a new status for the workers but also continues to stress the need for economic sufficiency and security for workers.[123]

Occupational group system—third stage

In 1931 Pope Pius XI issued his encyclical *Quadragesimo anno* calling for a reconstruction of the social order. Not only the status of the worker but the whole order should be reconstructed in accord with what Ryan calls the occupational-group system and industrial self-government. His own development of the occupational-group system almost always occurs as a commentary on the papal encyclical. This system was seen by many as based on the guild system or at least on the organic principles behind the guild system.

The dangers of the existing economic order are individualism and class conflict, but collectivism should not be the solution. The papal plan calls for a graded hierarchical order, a system of subsidiary organizations between the state and the individual. The occupational group would bring people together not according to the position they occupy in the industrial order (labor or capital) but according to the diverse functions they occupy in society. These organizations would comprise both capitalists and workers in a particular industry such as railroading or steel. The occupational group of all people in this industry would be empowered by law to fix all wages, interest, dividends, and prices and to determine working conditions, to adjust industrial disputes, and to carry on economic plans. All the local groups would be federated under a national group for the whole industry. Likewise, there might be a federation of all the occupational groups in the nation. The state would bring these occupational groups into existence, and in accord with the principle of subsidiarity the state would perform those functions which the smaller groups could not do—direction, overseeing, stimulating, and restraining. According to Ryan the trade associations set up by the National Recovery Administration correspond to the papal plan, but unfortunately these trade associations do not include adequate representation of labor. Ryan the meliorist is always looking for ways in which these structures could develop from existing structures.[124]

There has been some discussion about Ryan's real attitude toward the occupational-groups system. Gearty sees it as the logical consequence and historical culmination of his thinking.[125] On the other hand, Karl Cerny maintains that Ryan never really accepted all the ramifications of the pope's plan. Ryan espoused the occupational-group system as a long-term goal that could be reached by intermediate steps from existing structures, but in his judgment this long-term goal did not call into question aspects of his reforming approach such as the heavy emphasis on state intervention.[126] David O'Brien claims that Ryan never integrated the occupational-group system into his thought.[127] As we shall see below, the judgment of Cerny and O'Brien seems correct.

Ryan accepts the occupational-group system only after the encyclical of Pius XI—obviously because of the authority of the papal teaching. Many Catholics in Europe and in the United States had been proposing such a solidarist or corporative approach for many years, but Ryan never adopted such an approach before 1931. In the United States the *Central-Blatt and Social Justice* espoused corporatism since the beginning of the twentieth century, as will be discussed in the next chapter. Many Catholics both before and after the encyclical saw the guild system as either the blueprint or at least the inspiration for the pope's approach. Ryan had earlier dismissed the guild system as utterly impractical. The principle underlying the guild system was what is important, but in Ryan's interpretation this turned out to be the recognition that the different economic classes must receive the measure of protection, encouragement, and privilege that is required to secure their rights and welfare.[128] He also mentioned that probably the only feasible association based on the older guild system is the periodic conference between employers and employees concerning wages and conditions of employment.[129] However, he would later refer to the papal plan for reconstruction as "the adoption and adaptation of the guild system."[130]

Despite verbally accepting the papal plan, Ryan never changes any other aspects of his program, especially the primary emphasis on state intervention. Even within the Social Action Department of the National Catholic Welfare Conference, his long-time associate Msgr. Raymond McGowan gives greater importance to the occupational-group system than does Ryan.[131] Ryan also downplays this approach at times by stressing the long-term aspect of the papal proposal. Ryan the reformer is primarily interested in improving the situation here and now, especially in the light of the terrible problems created by the Depression. In *A Better Economic Order*, the last somewhat systematic presentation of his economic reform program, Ryan devotes the last chapter to the new economic order as spelled out by Pope Pius XI, but he concludes the chapter by reminding his readers that in the meantime before this plan can be realized, there are certain definite and important industrial actions and functions that should be performed by the state. Ryan then summarizes the role of the state in overcoming the problems of the Depression.[132]

Having seen the developing stages in Ryan's economic democracy, now the various roles and functions in this order will be briefly summarized and analyzed—the individual, private associations, and the state.

First, the individual. Although Ryan stresses the need for structural reform through distributive justice and economic democracy, he briefly considers the role of the individual especially in terms of the obligation to give one's superfluous goods to the poor. Ryan accepts a hierarchical view of human nature in which the lower parts serve the higher. When the basic demands of food, clothing, shelter, health, and moderate comfort have been supplied, additional sense satisfactions contribute little or nothing to true human development, which is primarily qualitative and in accord with the higher aspects of human nature. The danger of materialism and sense satisfactions constantly threaten true human development. Ryan accepts the traditional thesis of the obligation to give away superfluous goods which are not required for the necessities of life or for the comforts in keeping with one's state in life. When the needs of an individual or community are grave, possessors of superfluous goods are required to contribute all that is necessary to relieve these grave needs. The inordinate attachment to wealth is one of the difficulties in the way of a better distribution of the goods of creation.[133] Ryan the practical reformer and economist on different occasions spells out the upper limits of family expenditures which are compatible with true human welfare and Christian living.[134]

Although in discussing the role of the individual in social reform Ryan emphasizes the dangers of materialism and the role of the rich, he also makes passing references to the individual laborer who would better one's condition by more energy, honesty, and thrift. Anyone teaching in a school of social work and associated with and editing the *Catholic Charities Review* realizes that some problems are caused by individuals themselves. Individual social work agencies are charged by Ryan with reforming those individuals whose character has caused their plight. Social agencies, especially those affiliated with the Catholic Church, should deal with the moral problems involved, but they should employ the scientific methods of organized charity such as investigation, specific treatment, attention to real causes, record keeping, and mutual cooperation among agencies. Ryan, together with his former teacher and colleague William Kerby, is a strong advocate of scientific charity.[135]

From his earliest writings Ryan recognizes the need for what he calls private associations between the individual and the state to work together for full social reform. In his earlier writings cooperative movements of all kinds are included under this category of voluntary associations. After 1931 the occupational-group system, even if somehow brought into existence by the state, fits under this category. These have already been discussed. Also mutual insurance societies, which protect their members against sickness, accident, and unemployment, are mentioned in his earlier writings.[136] Although employer associations are also mentioned, the labor union is the most significant private association which still needs to be considered.

Ryan published an article on labor unions even before the final publication of his doctoral dissertation.[137] Workers have a right to organize to achieve what is just provided they also use just means. Since powerful employers are not usually interested in the rights of workers and consumers are not interested, the workers must unite to achieve their rights.

Our ethicist-economist considers the means employed by labor unions to achieve their goals. Collective bargaining is obviously legitimate if the demands are just. The strike, as the most powerful instrument the union has, even though involving very significant effects, can be justified in accord with the principles laid down by the theologians and by common sense: (1) What is sought by the strike is just. (2) All peaceful and less harmful means have been exhausted. (3) The good to be attained should outweigh the evil that will occur. The boycott or refusal to do business with a particular firm is justified if the cause is just and the boycott is directed only against those who are acting unjustly. The secondary boycott, which is directed against innocent second parties, in all but extreme cases is against Christian charity. The closed shop, which calls for all workers to belong to the union, is not opposed to justice, since no one's rights are violated; nor is the closed shop often opposed to charity, for there are many reasons which can justify it. However, the employer has a right to oppose the closed shop provided such actions do not tend to impose unjust conditions on the workers.[138]

In the 1920s Ryan attacks as a fraud the open-shop concept proposed by some employers, which, on the basis of an individualistic notion of freedom falsely labeled as American, denies the very right of collective bargaining. Our author at this time continues to write against those Court injunctions which prevent the workers from doing what is lawful.[139] In his earliest writings Ryan favored compulsory arbitration of labor disputes, but in the 1920s he abandons such a position as being neither feasible nor desirable.[140]

Ryan the realist recognizes the danger of abuses in labor unions such as breaking contracts, making excessive demands, unnecessary strikes, disregard of public welfare, and restriction of output, but he hastens to add that more often employers are guilty of abuses.[141] Labor must continue to stand up for its rights, but labor, consumer, and capitalists must work together for the human welfare of all, including labor.[142]

Father Ryan praises labor unions as having done more for the betterment of the working population than all other agencies combined with the exception of religion.[143] However, he recognizes and regrets the fact that only a comparatively small number of workers belonged to unions. As a result, the state must intervene to bring about justice for the worker. However, organization and legislation should be seen as complementary in theory and in practice.[144] Ryan also points out another defect in labor unions in the United States until the mid-1930s—unions exist primarily among the highly skilled craft workers and not among the unskilled and lower-paid workers.[145] Such unskilled workers obviously need the protection which only the state could provide. Ryan strongly defends the new CIO in the 1930s precisely because this union tries to organize the assembly-line and unskilled workers.[146]

The state

The study of Ryan's thought shows the very important role he gives to the state both in theory and in practical proposals for social reform. Even after advocating occupational groups in the

1930s, during the Depression Ryan calls for massive involvement of the state to overcome the economic crisis. His only criticism of Roosevelt points out that the president did not go far enough. However, our reformer never forgets at least in theory the principle of subsidiarity—individuals, private associations, and intermediate groups should do all they can, and the state takes over when the lesser groups cannot accomplish what is needed.[147]

Fellow Catholics often disagreed with the heavy emphasis Ryan put on the state. In citing Leo XIII on the role of the state Ryan often forgot to include the limitations which Leo mentioned in the same paragraph about state intervention. The German-American Catholics consistently feared that Ryan gave too great a role to the state.[148] In the midst of the Depression Ryan's strong support of the New Deal (recall that long before the New Deal Ryan had proposed most of these measures) put him in disagreement with many of his former supporters such as *America*, the Jesuit weekly, or *The Catholic World* and its editor Father Gillis.[149] Such a reliance on the state led to the charge that Ryan had no real plan of reform but only a piecemeal and pragmatic approach that failed to see the long-range consequences of his call for state intervention. However, from Ryan's viewpoint as a meliorist the first steps were necessary now, and further steps could build on these. One could almost hear the practical reformer saying that the better should never become the enemy of the good.

Capitalism and socialism

Ryan develops his economic democracy as a middle position between capitalism and socialism based on a theory which recognizes the dignity and rights of the individual person, the social aspect of human nature, and the fact that the goods of creation exist to serve the needs of all. Our reformer struggles against the capitalistic system but at the same time often has to defend himself against the charge of favoring socialism.

John Ryan is not opposed to capitalism understood in an abstract and broad sense as the private ownership and operation of the means of production. Capitalism in this broad understanding could apply to the guild system and practically every other system which has ever existed.[150] From his earliest writings it is very evident that Ryan is not opposed to the institution of private property as such nor to some profit and the motivation based on profit. He could quote with conviction the teaching of Pope Pius

XI in *Quadragesimo anno* that capitalism is not of itself vicious and is capable of reform.[151]

However, Ryan never accepts what he terms historical and contemporary capitalism such as existed in the United States even in the 1930s. Historical capitalism is characterized by five elements—indefinitely high profits and interest, indefinitely low wages, unlimited wealth, and unlimited economic power.[152] There are three fundamental principles on which historical capitalism is built. The political principle espouses nonintervention in the economic order, which is often described as a laissez-faire approach. The economic principle maintains that unlimited production automatically provides unlimited markets and constant employment for all labor. The ethical principle espouses an extreme and individualistic concept of natural rights which presupposes the natural goodness of people and the substantial equality of all.[153] The errors in such principles are evident in the light of what Ryan holds and teaches.

Ryan makes a special effort to show that the Catholic Church does not support capitalism and the status quo in the United States. His life and work refute the charges that the Catholic Church is the unquestioning upholder or the tool of capitalism. In an apologetic manner he points out that it was the religious and social disturbances of the sixteenth century (read Protestant Reformation) that blocked the widespread distribution and diffusion of productive property.[154] Ryan mentions with approval the thesis of Weber and Troeltsch that the spirit of capitalism was considerably determined and promoted by the fundamental tenets of Calvinism and Puritanism with their emphasis on individualism, the calling, and success as a sign of God's blessing.[155] However, in 1936 our reformer cites Fanfani's thesis that unfortunately the spirit of capitalism as the unlimited quest for the pursuit of wealth existed before the Protestant Reformation and must be seen as a true weakening of the Catholic faith.[156]

Ryan's discussion of and opposition to socialism takes place on four different levels—religion, philosophy, morality, and the economic order. In this nuanced approach Ryan anticipates what later popes would do. Socialism as a movement is unfriendly and even hostile to religion according to its own proponents. Socialist philosophy is incompatible with religious convictions, since there is no room for belief in the spirit and the supernatural.[157]

The Catholic economist-ethician rejects the philosophy of socialism primarily because of its cornerstone theory of social evolution, which is based on the doctrine of historical materialism or economic determinism. There exists an inconsistency in socialism's passing any moral judgments in the light of its philosophical theory which rejects human freedom. Socialism pretends to be scientific, but in the last analysis it rests on a faith in this theory of evolution.[158] What is even more significant is that historical reality contradicts this faith. According to Marx the forces of economic evolution were surely bringing about a narrow concentration of wealth and capital, the elimination of the middle classes, and the ever deeper impoverishment of the wage earners. Actually the opposite has occurred.[159]

From the viewpoint of morality the basic incompatibility between determinism and morality is evident. More specifically, Ryan criticizes four aspects of socialist ethics—its general principle and its specific teachings concerning the individual, the family, and the state. According to the general principle of socialist ethics rules of morality are neither ethical nor immutable, since they are not based on either God's law or human nature. Human beings are morally free to set up their own code of conduct, and moral laws merely reflect how people act in a given set of circumstances. Ethics does not even deal with purely self-regarding actions of the individual. In addition, socialism attacks the family and the indissolubility of marriage. Socialism in its understanding of the state subordinates the individual to the state and justifies whatever is done to promote the coming to power of the socialist state.[160]

On the level of the socialist scheme of industry Ryan disagrees with the underlying socialist theory of value, which makes labor the sole explanation, creator, and determinant of value. The ultimate test of any scheme of industry is whether or not it achieves human welfare and not some metaphysical and a priori criterion. Socialism fails to provide for human welfare for three reasons—inefficient industrial leadership and management, inefficiency of labor, and a curtailment of human liberty. Boards of directors, especially if elected by the workers, would be so beholden to the workers that they would not be efficient. There would be no incentives for directors. Bureaucracy and the curse of bigness would characterize the industrial order and lead ultimately to despotic control. Labor law would be inefficient since it would follow the path of least resistance. Liberty would suffer in different ways. The tremendous social power concentrated in the state would reduce individual liberty. Freedom of expression in education and in newspapers would be hampered. Since the state would be the only buyer of labor and seller of goods, contractual liberty would be lessened.[161]

Many of Ryan's problems with the socialist scheme of industry are logically grounded in a realistic anthropology. Socialists try to explain away the evil consequences mentioned above by appealing to the achievements of government enterprises and of cooperatives as well as to the altruism of citizens in a socialistic regime, but Ryan refutes such arguments. The ability of the state to run some enterprises well, especially those which are of a more homogenous grouping (e.g., public utilities), does not prove that the direction of all industry by the state would be successful. Cooperatives in production have not been as successful as cooperatives in distribution, even though in productive cooperatives the workers themselves have direct ownership and management of the company, which would not be true in socialism. Appeals to altruism and honor are also unrealistic, for only a small minority of human beings have ever consistently acted on the basis of these virtues. The socialist argument presupposes that the natures and attitudes of average people can by some mysterious process be completely revolutionized.[162] Note again the lack of theoretical grounding for Ryan's more realistic anthropology.

As time went on, Ryan distinguishes between communism, orthodox socialism, and mitigated socialism. Orthodox socialism fits the description of what he was attacking earlier. Communism before the First World War is distinguished from socialism by insisting on common ownership of consumer goods as well as the goods of production. In the 1930s communism is distinguished from socialism by its insistence on using violence to achieve its goal and by the role of the Communist party.[163] The Socialist party in the United States represents mitigated socialism, for the party gives little or no importance to the philosophical basis of socialism and modifies many approaches to the industrial order. Ryan finds only two questionable planks in the 1932 Socialist party platform, and these could be totally compatible with Catholic teaching depending on what is meant by the "principal" industries to be owned socially and the "basic industries" to be socialized. In the light of Pope Pius XI's criticism and condemnation of even mitigated socialism for Catholics, Ryan advises Catholics to seek their goals of social reform elsewhere. However, he finishes his discussion in 1932 with the dilemma that neither of the two existing political parties is likely to undertake this vital task of social reform.[164] In 1935 Ryan appears to be a bit more critical in referring to American socialists as benevolent Tories who deprive the masses of freedom in order to enhance what is considered to be their welfare. Obviously Ryan agrees with many of the practical proposals put forward by the mitigated socialists in the economic order.[165]

Social mission of the church

Ryan steadfastly tries to foster the social mission of the church and to make Catholics more conscious of it. To convince Catholics he cites Pope Leo XIII. The social question is not merely an economic matter but a moral and religious question that cannot practically be solved without the church.[166] Ryan's justification of the social mission of the church reflects his understanding of the relationship between the natural and the supernatural, between this world and the next world. The primary object of the church is to save individual souls and to prepare them for the supernatural life with God which begins in earthly existence but is completed in eternity. Compared with immortal life and this otherworldly vision, all temporal goods such as wealth, education, liberty, and fame are utterly insignificant. The soul lives righteously and comes to its eternal reward through right conduct; therefore the church must teach and enforce the principle of right conduct. All free human actions whether in the field of economy or in any other endeavor come under the moral law, and it is the duty of the church to teach the moral law and help people save their souls by right conduct. The church's function is both as teacher and as doer—in word and in deed. Ryan points to the history of the Catholic Church to show that this social mission has always been present.[167]

There is a teaching role of the church in social and economic questions. In general all should recognize that the church inculcates the virtues of charity and justice in all areas of human existence. However, the advocacy of definite methods of political organization, of agriculture, and of finance lies outside the powers of the church. Ryan distinguishes three ways in which the authoritative teaching of the popes and bishops should function. First, the pope and bishops lay down the moral principles, as distinguished from methods, which govern industrial relations, such as the right of the worker to a living wage, the obligation of the worker to give an honest day's work, and the obligation of the state to intervene to remedy serious abuses when no other means are available. Second, the church can declare certain methods lawful or not as in the condemnation of socialism. Third, the church might even go further and advocate certain methods as Leo XIII did in supporting associations of laborers or as the American bishops did in their program of social reconstruction. The third approach does not have as much official force as the other two because it involves questions of practical expediency. In this way Ryan responds to a perennial question for Christian social ethics on how specific should church teaching be. In addition to its teaching, the church can supply much motivation for social reform among its people.[168]

Church action is also required. Ryan throughout his writings recognizes the need for Catholic laity to become involved in the different aspects of social reform either in terms of working for certain policies or in participating in particular organizations such as labor unions. However, in discussing the role of the church he especially stresses the role of priests as giving leadership in areas of social work and action. One can see here the effects of his hierarchical ecclesiology as well as his desire for results in achieving reform. The priests, depending on local conditions, should become involved in assisting and directing cooperative associations of all sorts, settlement houses, and consumer leagues, and not only orphan asylums and schools. From the very beginning Ryan insists on the need for seminaries to train priests in social thought and action and to offer courses in sociology and economics.[169]

Ryan the practical reformer cleverly supports his advocacy of the social mission of the church with an appeal to enlightened self-interest and to the pride of the American church. If the Catholic Church does not endorse social reform, many Catholics will be drawn away from their faith because of the appeal of socialism and other anti-Catholic organizations. We do not want working people to become estranged from the church in the United States as they are in some European countries.[170]

Although Ryan's main concern is to convince Catholics of the social mission and role of the church, in his earlier writings he distinguishes his understanding of the social mission from the exaggerated view of some proponents of the Social Gospel in American Protestantism. Ryan and Walter Rauschenbusch were contemporaries, but the Catholic priest makes little or no mention of the Protestant reformer in most of his writings except on this issue of the social mission of the church. A comparison of the theological and ethical methodologies of the two shows the differences between a liberal Protestant and a Catholic natural-law theoretician. Ryan stresses reason and natural law and engages in a comparatively detailed analysis of specific problems, whereas Rauschenbusch bases his approach on faith and the scriptures and tends to have a broader and more sweeping approach to social questions. Ryan probably too harshly and too quickly dismisses Rauschenbusch as a theological liberal who too willingly sacrifices dogma in his concern for social reform.[171] Ryan maintains in 1909 that among the Protestant churches which display any great vitality there is a tendency to identify religion with humanitarianism. The mission of the church is not to realize the kingdom of God on earth but to save individual souls and render them fit for the kingdom of God in heaven.[172]

There is no doubt in the little that he does say and the much that is left unsaid that Ryan in no way wants his position to be confused with a Protestant theological approach. Ryan is progressively American but also staunchly Catholic. Social ethics was not ecumenical in those days. Ryan vigorously defends an otherworldly view of the role of the church and thus avoids what he calls an exaggerated understanding of the social mission of the church. However, Ryan's own position is open to the serious charge of too great a distinction between the natural and the supernatural and between this world and the next. Many Christians, operating on these same presuppositions, have actually denied any social mission of the church. Ryan's own justification of the social mission is weak; yet his life and work as indicated in the title of his autobiography, *Social Doctrine in Action,* gave a living witness to the social mission of the church.

III. Political Ethics

Although for John A. Ryan social ethics is primarily economic ethics, he also touches on political ethics. Together with Moorhouse F. X. Millar, Ryan published *The State and the Church* in 1922, with subsequent reprintings in 1924, 1930, and 1936, a book of essays by different authors which often served as a textbook in Catholic colleges. Ryan himself wrote seven of the eighteen chapters. In 1940 Ryan and Francis Boland edited

Catholic Principles of Politics with the express purpose of re-
vising the earlier volume and making it more apt as a college
text. In 1928 Ryan wrote *The Catholic Church and the Citizen*,
a ninety-four page survey, again geared to a college audience or
to the general educated reader. The Catholic University professor
also wrote many essays that touched on topics of political ethics,
but in general Ryan's background in, and contribution to, political ethics was comparatively unoriginal and lacked the creativity
and depth of his approach in economic ethics. His greatest contribution involved a creative application of the Catholic tradition
to show its acceptance of the American political experience.
Ironically, Ryan is most often remembered today, especially in
non-Catholic circles, for his opposition to the American concept
of the separation of church and state.

On the issue of the relationship between church and state
Ryan assumes he was true both to the Catholic tradition and to
the American experience. But his was an uneasy solution which
was not accepted by most non-Catholic Americans. The Catholic
University theologian accepts the traditional teaching that the
church and the state are two independent societies dealing with
the spiritual and the temporal welfare of human beings. However, hierarchical ordering requires that the temporal serve the
spiritual. The state, as seen in the discussion of economic questions, must promote human welfare in all its aspects. Religion is
a very important aspect of public welfare. In addition, the emphasis on objective truth concludes that error as such has no
rights. As a result, civil authority must promote religion, and
more specifically the one true religion of the Catholic Church.

The thesis or ideal situation calls for the union of church
and state, and the state as such should profess the Catholic faith,
not allowing for the external profession of other faiths. However, this applies only to the completely Catholic state, and there
is good reason to doubt the existence of any such completely
Catholic state existing in the world—even in Spain. In a religiously pluralistic state, obviously meaning the United States
and probably all the states existing at the time, political toleration of all religions and basic religious freedom can be accepted
in practice because of the rational expediency which sees greater
harm in trying to proscribe activities of other religious groups
and because of one's loyalty to the constitution of existing
states.[173]

Ryan, however, went on to add a paragraph that ultimately had far more repercussions than he ever imagined when he wrote it. "But constitutions can be changed, and non-Catholic sects may decline to such a point that the political proscription of them may become feasible and expedient."[174] Our author assures his readers that practically speaking such a possibility is so remote and impractical that the prudent person will not be disturbed by the thought of it. However, to be fair and sincere, Ryan cannot yield on the principles of eternal and unchangeable truth. Our author pointed out earlier in the same discussion that there is some public profession of religion in the United States (a proclamation of Thanksgiving Day, military chaplains, church tax exemption, etc.), and there is no specious neutrality or opposition to religion as exists in some countries. Ryan apparently felt that he handled the situation quite well and in a manner that would be perfectly acceptable to Catholics and to Americans.[175]

His position apparently attracted no great attention until the preparations for the presidential campaign of Alfred E. Smith in 1928. In March 1927 Albert C. Dieffenbach, the editor of the *Unitarian Christian Register*, pointed out the problem of the Catholic view on church and state and quoted the positions proposed by Ryan that constitutions can be changed and that non-Catholic sects can be politically proscribed if they should decline. This article began a long series of letters and responses and put Ryan and his book in the center of the issue. Ryan basically defended his position and occasionally was happy to find some Protestant support for what he thought was his common-sense approach.[176] In his 1928 book on the *Catholic Church and the Citizen* Ryan repeats the same basic position and recounts some of the public discussion, all the time trying to dispel Protestant fears. Neither the pope nor any American bishop has ever called for a change in the present church-state relationship in the United States, and they would oppose any suggestion of union between the two powers.[177] Ryan, the political and social liberal, was bitter about the defeat of Smith in 1928, which he attributed to the religious factor.[178] In his autobiography Ryan devotes less than two pages to this rather significant controversy, and one page is a long quotation from his article written after the election.[179] However, long after the election itself and even after Ryan's death his handling of this issue

caused concern to many fair-minded, non-Catholic Americans and
not just to people who might be accused of anti-Catholic polemics
such as Paul Blanshard.[180]

Historical controversy and the resulting tendency on the
part of many to remember Ryan as a symbol of opposition between Americanism and Catholicism, when in reality he always
strove to show the compatibility between the two, call for a
somewhat more extended understanding of Ryan's political ethic.
The basic outline of his theory of the state has already emerged
in the discussion of economic ethics. The state is a natural society striving for human welfare or for the common good, which
is both distributive and collective. This theory, building on
Ryan's anthropology, tries to avoid the two extremes of collectivism and individualism. Ryan insists on natural-law rights
of individual persons which are prior to the state, but yet he sees
the state as a natural society which is in no way opposed to the
true good of the individual, for the person is by nature social.
Always recognizing the principle of subsidiarity, Ryan, however, calls upon the state to intervene to protect the weaker and
distressed classes.

Dr. Ryan at times proposes two different explanations for
the theoretical understanding of the way in which the government obtains its power. He first proposes a type of designation
theory whereby the ruler's right to govern comes ultimately not
from the consent of the people but from the ability to promote
the public welfare.[181] However, in 1928 in the midst of the election campaign Ryan espouses the translation theory, proposed
by Catholics such as Bellarmine, according to which the ruler
receives power from the consent of the people. Our American
Catholic liberal emphasizes the harmony between this traditional
Catholic position and that of the Declaration of Independence.[182]
Our author also considered other aspects of the question of a
legitimate government.[183]

A number of different forms of government—monarchy,
autocracy, or democracy—can be compatible with the basic purpose of the state according to Catholic teaching, but there is no
doubt that Ryan's personal preference is for democracy.[184] One
of the primary reasons in favor of American democracy is its
protection and guarantee of certain basic natural-law rights of
the individual. Happily for the United States, the doctrine of
natural rights is strikingly recognized in the Declaration of Independence itself—"We hold these truths to be self-evident that

all men are created equal, that they are endowed by their Creator
with certain inalienable rights, that among these are life, liberty
and the pursuit of happiness." Liberty, according to Ryan, is a
very comprehensive term including freedom of movement and
immunity from political oppression, freedom of education, religion, speech, and writing.[185] Ryan gives other advantages deriving from a democratic form of government and defends democracy against attacks by other Catholics. Democracy is in
keeping with the dignity of the individual person, for it stresses
the capacity of the individual to think. Democracy allows all individuals a voice in the government and thereby strengthens
their commitment to the nation. If leaders are elected by the
people, they will be more aware of their constituents' problems
and interests and will act more efficaciously on behalf of the
people.[186]

In his article refuting a Catholic attack on democracy Ryan
closes with a quotation from Thomas Aquinas calling for rulers
chosen by merit and elected by all. In Ryan's judgment the formula proposed by Aquinas for the best system of government
does not differ essentially from that which is actualized in our
American federal and state systems.[187] In *Catholic Principles of
Politics* our editor places as the concluding chapter the famous
address by Archbishop Ireland on Catholicism and Americanism.
Ireland here makes his profession of faith—his religious faith,
Catholicism; his civil and political faith, Americanism. The address closes with the words of Archbishop Satolli calling for
Catholics to go forward with the gospel of Christ in one hand and
the Constitution of the United States in the other.[188] So committed is Ryan to democracy that he appeals to economic democracy to support his program of social reform. Even when criticizing American political institutions, Ryan almost invariably
does it in the light of the needs of true democracy. Ryan thus
wholeheartedly accepts the democratic form of government as
found in the United States and sees no incompatibility between
that and his Roman Catholicism.

Perhaps the most obvious possible source of friction between Catholic self-understanding and American democratic
theory concerns the notion of freedom. The Roman Catholic
Church has traditionally stood for doctrinal orthodoxy proposed
by a God-given teaching function in the church as distinguished
from Protestant ecclesiology with its emphasis often on the freedom of the believer. The United States embraces the fundamen-

tal importance of freedom, whereas the Catholic Church both historically and theoretically stands opposed to some aspects of freedom. Catholic teaching and actions in the nineteenth century thoroughly opposed the modern liberties which called for freedom in political, intellectual, and economic life.[189] The Catholic teaching strongly upholds an objective social order and objective truth. The primary obligation of the individual is to follow the God-given natural order and the truth. Human beings have no right to go against the objective moral order and objective truth. To any objection about the rights of conscience, the rejoinder is simple—error has no rights. Catholic theology strongly opposes the concept of freedom as the right of the individual to do whatever one pleases. There appear to be great differences between the American ethos and the Catholic understanding, but John A. Ryan, to the happy surprise of many liberal non-Catholics, was able to overcome the apparent differences between the American and the Catholic understanding of freedom.

Ryan takes pride in his defense of civil rights and liberties; the tenth chapter of his autobiography is entitled "In Defense of Civil Rights and Liberties."[190] During the First World War Ryan defended government restrictions on free speech. The legal right of freedom of speech protected by the Constitution is not an unlimited right and can be limited by other constitutional provisions. Congress can restrict the freedom of speech to the extent necessary to prosecute the war.[191] However, after the war Ryan became an active member of the Joint Amnesty Committee which worked to obtain the release of so-called political prisoners who had been convicted in 1917 and 1918 of violating the wartime law proscribing actions or utterences tending to interfere with a successful conduct of the war. Ryan had not changed his mind about the earlier laws, but he maintained that two or three years punishment was sufficient for what had been done. In addition, in the hysteria of the time some may even have been imprisoned who committed no crime.[192]

Ryan defended the rights of five socialists who had been elected to the state assembly of New York in 1920 but then were expelled by the assembly itself. Ryan upheld the rights of aliens and foreigners whose freedom had been unduly restricted by the law. He strongly disagreed with the Supreme Court's decision maintaining that Benjamin Gitlow had not been deprived of his constitutional liberty of speech when he was imprisoned for advocating mass industrial revolt and revolutionary action that would lead to a politarian dictatorship. Ryan argued that since Gitlow did not advocate definitive and immediate execution of these methods, his writings and speech constituted no clear and present danger to the state.[193] In general Ryan referred to the time in the early 1920s as an era of hysteria unduly eroding the civil rights of people.[194]

In his article "Declining Liberty in America" the following areas are mentioned. Civil liberty is threatened by interference on the national, state, and local levels. Economic freedom is endangered by the Court's interpretation of the due-process clause based on an individualistic notion of freedom supporting the false freedom of contract, by injunctions in labor disputes which prevent workers from doing what is lawful, and by monopolistic practices. Ryan again brings political and economic freedom together but makes sure that economic freedom is understood in terms of freedom of economic opportunity for all, a truly democratic notion, and not just an individualistic freedom of contract. Finally, even political liberty has declined in the United States through indirect processes and influences such as propaganda.[195] In the 1940s the ever vigilant Ryan publicly fought two other attempts to restrict liberty: the Dempsey Bill which called for the deportation of aliens who believed in or advocated changes in the American form of government, and a bill passed by the House of Representatives which called for the immediate deportation of Harry Bridges, a west coast labor leader.[196]

All agreed Ryan was a staunch defender of civil liberties and freedoms. His position is perhaps best symbolized by his membership on the national committee of the American Civil Liberties Union, whose main object is to defend the rights and freedom especially of relatively weak people, such as "radicals," "foreigners," "socialists," and "communists." Ryan recognized that many Catholics could not understand his belonging to such an organization, although in his judgment the A.C.L.U., despite not a few mistakes, had been one of the most effective champions in America of civil and social justice. In 1935 Dr. Ryan resigned from the A.C.L.U. and its national committee when the organization took up issues of academic freedom. Such issues went beyond civil liberties and were incompatible with a Catholic university.[197]

How can Ryan the Catholic priest and professor be a proponent of American freedom of speech and other civil liberties

which allow all types of untruths to be propounded against what
is objectively true and good? In Ryan's first writing on the subject, a pamphlet entitled *Francisco Ferrer: Criminal Conspirator*,
a reply to an article by William Archer in *McClure's* magazine in
1910, he does not emerge as a champion of freedom of speech. In
fact, Ryan here proposes the classical arguments against freedom of speech. Not only is it false, but no civilized nation has
ever consistently adopted a theory that a person is free to speak
or write whatever one pleases. Speech or writing is done so that
some action will follow. If destruction of property, anarchy, or
adultery can be restrained by law, so can advocating these things.
If law protects people against adulterated food, one must also
protect people against poisonous ideas. In the United States a
person may not libel a neighbor, send immoral literature through
the mail, or advocate sedition or anarchy. Our author recognizes
that toleration is often more conducive to social welfare than
prohibition, but that matter is a practical problem of judgment
for states. However, here the emphasis is not on toleration as it
would be in Ryan's later writings.[198]

In the 1920s Ryan takes a different approach. All must agree
with the unassailable argument of Pope Leo XIII that unlimited
liberty of thinking, speaking, and publishing is the fountain-
head and source of many evils. Speech and writing are means to
achieve human welfare, the chief constituents of which are truth
and virtue. Whatever exposes people to vice and error is contrary to human welfare and, so far as possible, should be pro-
hibited by the state. In the light of such logic why are the vast
majority of modern people in favor of freedom of expression?
Three erroneous reasons are adduced for freedom of expression.
First, there is a natural right to express whatever one pleases
even if it is false and injurious to human welfare. Such a position is blatantly false. Second, some allege there is no way to
separate truth from error especially in industry and politics, but,
according to Ryan, there are certain fundamental principles
which every government assumes to be essential to the welfare of
its people, such as no destruction of property. Third, some claim
that all ideas should compete in the open market place and that
truth will ultimately triumph. Ryan's concern is the many people who will be hurt in soul and in body before the ultimate triumph of truth.

The Catholic University professor defends unrestricted freedom of expression on the basis of tolerating the evil involved to

avoid the greater evil of provoking continual strife in society by trying to contain error. Freedom of speech for Ryan is a socially practical rule. In addition to avoiding strife such a rule is based on other practical considerations: public repression is frequently unjust or doubtful; legal prohibitions are difficult to frame. Even advocating the violent overthrow of the government can be permitted if there is no clear and present danger of this actually happening. Ryan concludes in favor of freedom of expression except in the case of a few fundamental principles which scarcely anyone questions. Complete liberty of speech and writing, within the limits of public decency, should be permitted and protected in the domain of politics and economics.[199] In defending freedom of expression and civil liberties, Ryan, the politician and pragmatic reformer, not only appeals to the principle of tolerating the lesser of two evils, but he also invokes what might be called the principle of expediency for Catholics. Ryan obviously realizes that many Catholics would tend to disagree with his position, so he appeals to Catholic self-interest to support civil liberties. If the principle is accepted that a state legislature can expel the members of a minority group, party, or religion which it regards as an undesirable element in political and social life, then other groups, especially Catholics who are a minority in this country, should be aware of what might happen to them.[200]

Ryan maintains that one not only can be both Catholic and American at one and the same time but one can also be an American liberal and a Catholic. In this position he has to defend himself both against some Catholics and against some non-Catholic liberals. In the nineteenth century liberalism referred to an anticlerical and anti-Catholic movement which extolled the authority of human reason over God and church and believed in absolute freedom in all areas. Ryan accepts the general definition that a liberal is a tolerant person who is a democrat in politics and who lays strong emphasis upon freedom in speech, in writing, in education, in theological opinion, in civil affairs, and in economic opportunities for the masses. Ryan admits to being a conservative in religion and strongly upholds the authoritative teaching office of the church, but he is a liberal in political and economic matters. For Ryan there is no contradiction in this because each deals with different matters. The Catholic Church has been given a God-granted teaching authority, whereas in political and economic areas the principle of tolerating the lesser of two evils should be applied.[201]

However, there existed particular areas of possible conflicts between Ryan's American liberalism and his Catholicism which had to be addressed. The obvious conflict situation arose in terms of the theory and practice of the relationship between church and state. As mentioned, Ryan solved the problem by accepting the principle of toleration, which can be invoked in a society which is not totally Catholic, even though the ideal calls for the union of church and state and the denial of religious liberty. In Ryan's view the problem was solved. He applied here the same principle of toleration as he did in the question of freedom of expression. Since liberals and many non-Catholics readily accepted his position on freedom of expression, logically they should also accept his position on religious freedom. But things were not that simple. Many liberal non-Catholics accepted the freedom of expression on other grounds and perhaps never realized or even cared how Ryan came to the same conclusion, for they were always happy to have his support in their cause. When Ryan's solution on church and state recognized the ideal or thesis of union of church and state, liberals could not accept either his theory or his conclusion. Despite Ryan's own feeling that he had solved the tension between the Catholic teaching on church and state and the American principle and practice, the problem still remained and awaited a more definitive solution.

There were other tensions between the Catholic understanding of church-state relations and the American theory and practice, but again Ryan tried to downplay and even reconcile apparent differences. Church and state are two independent and perfect societies but with different spheres and purposes, so that there will be no real conflicts if both recognize their own legitimate functions. The major area of tension involves the twilight zone of mixed matters in which both church and state claim competency. Specifically, the church can never compromise its position on marriage as a sacrament, with church laws about marriage, and on the right of all her children to have religious education even in Catholic schools when religion is not taught in other schools. But even on these mixed issues Ryan sees no real conflict. On the matter of religious education the Supreme Court has already upheld the right of private and Catholic schools to exist.[202] Interestingly, Ryan does not mention the more explosive and controversial issue about government support of Catholic schools. One could accuse him of minimizing the possible problems and tensions, but very few people were raising the problem before 1945.

On the question of civil marriage and divorce laws Ryan's thought develops to the point that he claims there is no tension between civil laws allowing divorce and Catholic teaching and laws about marriage and its indissolubility. In 1921 he maintains that the state has no right to grant divorces.[203] In 1924 our author laments the lax divorce laws and procedures in the United States and urges the Irish Free State not to have laws allowing divorce.[204] Later, Ryan suggests that if he were president, he might recommend a uniform divorce law for all the states, which among other things would reduce the number of divorces.[205] In the context of the debates over the Smith election Ryan changes his approach, if not the substance of his understanding. In response to Charles C. Marshall, a New York lawyer, Ryan vindicates the right of the Roman Catholic Church to fix the conditions for the validity of marriages of baptized persons. Ryan recalls that on the question of the validity of marriages different states have different legislation. Other churches have laws which differ from state laws, but no one objects to these differences. Yes, the Catholic Church holds that the state does wrong in granting divorces, but no Catholic priest has ever been arrested for violating the marriage laws of the state.[206] Ryan here hints at the approach to divorce laws he will develop at greater length in 1928 in *The Catholic Church and the Citizen*. Divorce laws are permissive civil laws, but no Catholics are forced to use these laws. The state permits what the church condemns, but there is no real conflict of loyalties because the Catholic does not have to use these laws. In theory there might be some conflict between invalidating statutes and Catholic Church law (e.g., the age required for valid marriages), but there are no practical conflicts because priests invariably try to dissuade their subjects from entering any civilly illegal marriage.[207] Thus, on education, marriage, and divorce there are no conflicts even though both church and state rightfully claim some competence in these mixed matters.

However, tensions and perhaps even inconsistencies arise on the basis of Ryan's position on the dissemination of birth control information and devices. Ryan appeared three times before Congressional committees (1924, 1932, 1934) to oppose the repeal of federal statutes forbidding the dissemination of birth-control information and devices through the mail. Ryan accepts the Catholic position that birth control is intrinsically immoral and has deleterious consequences on both family and society.[208] In another article he even taunts the proponents of birth control with a paraphrase of Tertullian's prophecy about the triumph of Christianity over the decadent Roman civilization of his day.[209] In accord with his own principles Ryan could uphold the dissemination of such information and devices through the mail as the lesser of two evils based on the strife provoked by attempts to suppress such false ideas. On this issue which was so emphasized in Catholic teaching, Ryan not only admits his differences with other Americans but even taunts his opponents and opposes a free dissemination of birth-control information and devices in society.

John A. Ryan argues for a compatibility between the American political system and Catholic self-understanding. He insists, in keeping with the Catholic emphasis on harmony and objective truth, that there can be no real conflict between true loyalty to the state and loyalty to the church or to any other association or society.[210] However, this does not mean that Doctor Ryan is an uncritical proponent of everything American. Indeed, he frequently points out the dangers of an excessive patriotism and opposes both in theory and in practice many inequities in the American system. The loyalties of patriotism are reasonable within certain limits, but all are susceptible of exaggeration and perversion, so that patriotism can unfortunately become the heresy of nationalism. Nationalism exaggerates the obedience and loyalty owed to the state and accepts the thesis of Stephen Decatur—my country right or wrong. Especially in international affairs and war nationalism has had horrendous effects. Since the Catholic Church is international, its members should be expected to have a sane international viewpoint and avoid the dangers of nationalism. Unfortunately, Catholics have not always acted in this way. The object of true patriotism is the common good and not merely the good of one's own country.[211] Ryan's whole life testifies to his willingness to point out defects in the American political and economic system and to try to overcome them. His defense of the compatibility between being Catholic and being American does not make him an uncritical acclaimer of all that is American.

Ryan's approach to the moral obligations of civil law well illustrates his general position on patriotism. Our American Catholic liberal devotes in the 1920s two long articles to the question of civil law and later incorporates them into his books on politics and ethics.[212] Ryan maintains the accepted Catholic teaching, which sees civil law as a reaffirmation of the natural law (statutes forbidding theft, adultery) or as an application which makes determinate what the natural law leaves undetermined (laws decreeing the amount of taxation or traffic regulations). Consequently, civil laws involve a moral obligation because they are based ultimately on the natural law and on the human moral obligation to live together with others in political society. There is in Ryan some tension and even confusion on the role he gives to the intention of the legislator, but such a matter is not of immediate concern here.

Many Catholic moral theologians accepted the purely penal-law theory according to which one is morally obliged either to obey the law or to accept willingly the penalty for disobeying the law. This thesis, according to the renowned moral theologian Father Arthur Vermeersch of the Jesuit Gregorian University in Rome, applies to all laws which are not necessary to safeguard the common good. Ryan, in general, disagrees with purely penal-law theory because of the practical consequences which would follow for the good of society. The citizen could convince oneself that scarcely any law obliges in conscience. The logic of the Vermeersch position would abolish the whole law-making machinery, for citizens would be free to follow whatever in their opinion would be connected with public welfare.

On the other hand Ryan recognizes that the purely penal-law theory attempts to relieve citizens of some unnecessarily burdensome laws, but his positive approach to the problem is different. The traditional Thomistic teaching proposed that an unjust law is no law and does not oblige in conscience. Ryan himself draws the practical conclusions that tariff laws are unjust and are unnecessary, and hence do not oblige in conscience. The same is true of some taxes imposed on the necessities of life.[213] Some Americans are easily disturbed by such an approach because it makes the individual citizen the judge of whether the law is right or wrong. However, the presumption is in favor of the law, and the citizen must carefully examine the question. In addition, the citizen can accept a particular statute as binding according to its spirit and end rather than in accord with its strict wording. Also, epikeia allows the citizen to assume that a law which imposes an unreasonable burden could not be intended to oblige the citizen.[214]

Doctor Ryan developed his theory on civil law in the 1920s in the context of the nationwide debate over prohibition, which ultimately brought him into political debate and disagreement

with President Hoover. The eighteenth amendment to the Constitution, ratified on January 6, 1919, prohibits trafficking in
liquor—the manufacture, sale, and movement of intoxicating liquors. The Volstead Act, passed by Congress, goes further and
even prohibits the possession, manufacture, or transportation of
liquor for personal use. Ryan's consideration of the question always distinguishes these two aspects, the public and the personal, although he is unwilling to accept the purely penal-law
theory as applicable in either case.

Even before the passage of the Volstead Act proscribing
the manufacture and possession of liquors for personal use, Ryan
dismisses this extreme proposal as an unjustifiable usage of legislative authority. Private consumption of alcohol does not interfere with social peace and order, and the freedom of the citizen
should not be abridged in this matter.[215] After the law was
passed, our author describes it as a tyrannical and unjust interference with the liberties and rights of citizens.[216]

Ryan's position on the obligation of the prohibition amendment forbidding the trafficking of liquor evolves over time, as he
himself readily points out.[217] In April 1916 he acknowledges he
was in favor of prohibition on the state level whenever it can
be reasonably enforced. However, before the amendment was
passed, he opposed national prohibition on the grounds that
there is no national urgency and its advocates are guilty of
paternalism. Note that here Ryan employs the concept of subsidiarity. In 1924 and 1925 Ryan acknowledges that the federal
law prohibiting the trafficking in liquor obliges in conscience and
cannot be explained as purely penal law.[218] However, in preparing the 1925 article for publication in his collection of essays
Declining Liberty and Other Papers, Ryan makes a very significant change in his thinking which he clearly acknowledges as
such. After six years of experience and in the light of other possible approaches such as the Quebec Plan, under which in the
United States the federal government would manufacture and
sell liquor in all areas and regions in which there were not local
prohibition laws, Ryan now concludes that the two conditions required for the just character of the amendment are no longer
present. However, he holds this now as an opinion, for the evidence does not yet generate the moral certainty which is necessary to justify acting against the prohibition amendment. Although he will not act on his opinion, Ryan argues that Congress should immediately propose an amendment to the Consti-

tution doing away with national prohibition.[219]

Our author previously accepted the interference in personal liberty in a right (trafficking in liquor) which is only useful and not necessary for individual welfare because of the manifold and grave evils of the liquor traffic and the high degree of probability that the amendment was necessary. Ryan now claims the amendment would be just only if two conditions were verified: first, that national prohibition is the only adequate method of dealing with liquor traffic; second, that it is capable of a reasonable degree of enforcement.[220] Note here that Ryan, without any acknowledgment, has slightly changed his condition to the *only* (emphasis added) adequate method of dealing with the liquor traffic. Earlier his condition was that the amendment was an adequate means of dealing with the liquor traffic and was more helpful than harmful to the community as a whole.[221] He himself does not want to admit this change, for in retrospect he says that he always maintained that national prohibition was justified only if it was the most effective kind of liquor legislation.[222]

In his inaugural address of 1929 Herbert Hoover insisted that citizens cannot break the prohibition law but must observe it, although they have a right to work for its repeal. Ryan attacked the president for usurping the function of the interpreter of the moral law and for an erroneous understanding of legal duty. Hoover responded to Ryan in an address to the Associated Press in New York on April 22, by claiming that no individual has the right to determine if the law should be obeyed or not. Ryan answered by claiming that Hoover had forgotten the moral supremacy of conscience.[223]

Throughout the controversy Ryan appeals to the traditional teaching of Catholic theologians and canonists, but he also ends his first response to Hoover with a rhetorical defense of those who disobey and advocate disobedience to the prohibition amendment as battlers for fundamental democracy, for majority rule, for the banishment of fanaticism, intolerance, and toryism, and for the rejection of all tyrannies that the self-righteous and superior sections of our population would impose upon their inferior fellow citizens. In advocating disobedience to the law Ryan claims to be defending democracy.[224] In discussing this same issue in a later article Ryan finishes with a condemnation of the Protestant churches for having violated our traditional theory and practice of separation of church and state by their advocacy of prohibition. In the process Ryan seems to contradict some of his own

positions by accepting that political activity by churches is generally condemned or at least discouraged unless their own interests are vitally threatened.[225]

In general, Ryan's whole approach to civil law comes from
the traditional Catholic understanding. Civil law is based on natural law and exists to promote the common good of all. Unjust
laws do not oblige in conscience, but the presumption is in favor
of the law. At times the law can tolerate evils, especially in matters of free speech, as the lesser of two evils when compared with
the problem caused in society by trying to suppress such evil. In
all his interpretations and explanations of this theory Ryan tries
to show how it fits into the American self-understanding.

In addition to questions of domestic politics Ryan also took
an interest in international political questions, especially beginning in the 1920s, but these interests never occupied the center
stage in his thought or agenda. Ryan urged Catholics to become
more involved in the work for peace. He himself served for a
number of years on the National Council for the Prevention of
War. From its very beginning in 1927 he was connected with the
Catholic Association for International Peace.[226] Ryan strongly
supported the League of Nations and urged the nations of the
world to overcome their nationalism and work together in cooperation and charity for world peace. Deriving arguments from
charity, realism, and economics, Ryan advocated the cancellation
of war debts and reparations resulting from the First World
War.[227] Ryan, as a Catholic natural-law theologian and a realist,
rejected pacifism and accepted the basic principles of a just-war
theory. However, he agreed with the observation of Theodore
Meyer that, objectively speaking, in war one of the parties is
guilty of objective evil. War can only be justified as a last resort.[228] In the context of this discussion on war Ryan recognized
that the duty of citizens to serve in their country's war admitted
of exceptions based on the Catholic teaching that no one could
paricipate in an unjust war.[229] Ryan even objected to the law
banning citizenship to any person who did not promise before-
hand to take up arms to defend the United States under all circumstances.[230] As the Second World War approached, Monsignor
Ryan spoke out against isolationism, advocated resistance to Hitler, and justified American participation in that war.[231]

Ryan, the social reformer, recognized but did not stress the
problems of minorities living in the United States. In 1929 Ryan
addressed the Conference of the Indian's Rights Association, cri-

ticized the approach of the federal government, and called for two policy goals for native Americans—economic education and the acquisition of sufficient economic resources.[232] Our author wrote comparatively little and showed no creative response to the problem of blacks in the United States, but he was not unsympathetic. In his seminary days he briefly thought about entering the Josephite Fathers who work as missionaries to the American Negro. Ryan successfully urged Father Francis Gilligan in the mid-1920s to write a pioneer doctoral dissertation on *The Morality of the Color Line* and even tried unsuccessfully to have the book published by a commercial press. There were other occasional signs of interest on his part in the problem of blacks, but these were spasmodic and obviously not primary on his agenda.[233]

In commenting upon possible conflicts between Catholic teaching and the American ethos and laws, Ryan mentioned the Catholic acceptance of interracial marriages, whereas some state laws forbade them. His comments on the issue were totally conforming without a hint of the prophetic. Ryan observed that the church prudently urges her pastors to conform to the law.[234] Catholic bishops and priests have exercised such prudence that few if any have ever been accused of violating the civil prohibitions.[235] In 1943 Ryan was invited to speak at Howard University, but his remarks are disappointing. After identifying many of the problems, he calls for active leadership and urged patience, the avoidance of violence, and working with men of good will among the white community. Above all education is necessary.[236] Interestingly there was no mention of government intervention to protect and defend the rights of blacks as there had been in his defense of the workers.

Ryan's attitude toward the role of women and women's equality has already been mentioned. In the 1920s he vigorously opposes the National Woman's Party with its advocacy of an equal rights amendment to the Constitution and the abolition of special labor legislation protecting women. Ryan's natural-law background and cultural conditioning influence his position that women are equal to men as persons, but there are differences and inequalities between men and women which the law should take into account. In Ryan's thought the role of women is primarily in terms of household management and the bearing and training of children. Women should be in the home under ordinary circumstances. As mentioned earlier, equal pay should be given to women who work, but there is no right to a living family wage. Accepting differences between men and women fit in both with Ryan's notion of distributive justice, which is proportional and not arithmetic, and with his reforming approaches to labor legislation. He strongly opposes rescinding protective labor legislation for women, for this legislation is the first step in having such protection for all workers. Ryan admits there exist some injustices and inequalities in terms of women's rights, especially concerning property, earnings, and residence, but he advocates state legislation and not federal amendments to deal with the problem. Again one wonders if Ryan's acceptance of subsidiarity too often happens on those issues which are not so central and significant in his own thinking.[237] Ryan was in favor of women's suffrage but never publicly advocated it before it became law. Although radical groups spearheaded the drive for women's suffrage in New York state, Ryan urges all Catholic women to accept the responsibility to vote. He feels confident that Catholic women and others would not support the radical position but would vote for welfare measures and to support the Christian understanding of marriage and the family.[238]

IV. Critical Assessment of Methodology

Ryan as a moral theologian deals with the theory of social ethics and its practical applications especially in the area of economic and political ethics in the United States in the first half of the twentieth century. In terms of the quality and quantity of his writings, as well as of his significance both inside and outside the Roman Catholic Church, there is no one individual comparable to Ryan at that time. In conclusion, an evaluation of Ryan from the perspective of moral theology is in order. In synthesizing and explaining the Catholic University professor's position on social ethics, some evaluation and critique has been included, but now the assessment will concentrate on the methodology employed.

Ryan uses a natural-law approach. From the theological perspective natural law recognizes that ethical wisdom and knowledge for the Christian are found not only in the scriptures and in Jesus Christ but also in human reason and human nature. Human reason, reflecting on human nature, can arrive at ethical wisdom and knowledge. In fact, Ryan's approach is almost exclusively in terms of natural law, a stance also typical of the papal social teaching at the time. Such an approach, based on human nature and the human reason shared by all, recognizes that the Catholic has much in common with all others. Ryan thus advocates that Catholics work together with all Americans of good will in the struggle for social justice, even though many of these would not share the same Catholic faith. By seeing political and economic life primarily in terms of natural law and distinguished from the supernatural or faith aspect, Ryan could logically stress the compatibility between his Catholic faith on the supernatural level and his daily life as an American on the natural level.

However, the insistence on the natural, as distinguished from the supernatural, has some drawbacks. It is not a caricature to say that Ryan implicitly embraces a two-layer view of human existence—a bottom layer of the rational and the natural with an upper layer of faith and the supernatural. He fails to integrate properly faith and reason, the supernatural and the natural. This failure of integration has many negative effects on his approach. Theoretically, grace, redemption, and the supernatural have almost no impact as such on the social, political, and economic life of human beings.

The practical aspects of Ryan's failure to integrate the supernatural and the natural are many. This failure is not the total cause but remains at least a contributing reason for Ryan's neglecting the importance of the change of heart of individuals as a necessary part of social change. Theological themes such as the presence of grace, the call to conversion, and the recognition of the power of sin lead to a recognition of the importance of a change of heart on the part of the individual if social justice is to be achieved. Sin or selfishness in the hearts of human beings must be overcome before human beings can live together in justice and peace. Yes, change of structures is absolutely essential for social justice, but likewise a change of heart is necessary.

Another negative consequence of Ryan's failure to give enough importance to grace and redemption and to integrate the full Christian vision of reality concerns his understanding of the social mission of the church. Our author sees little or no connection between the kingdom of God and work for social justice. Often he describes the church's role in social justice merely as pointing out to people the correct moral action so that Catholics will be able to do the right action and thereby save their souls and go to heaven. It would be unfair to criticize Ryan for not having a concept of eschatology and its relationship to the kingdom which would only emerge in a much later theology. However, he should have seen some type of more intimate connection between life in this world and the kingdom. In reacting against what at times was a naive social-gospel approach, Ryan goes too far in separating the kingdom or the supernatural from the economic and political aspects of human existence.

Within the Catholic tradition itself in the United States and elsewhere there exist more integrated approaches to the question of social justice. Virgil Michel, the founder of the liturgical movement in the United States, takes a much more integral approach to social justice. There are significant relationships between the change of heart and the change of structures, between the liturgy and the daily struggle for justice, between the kingdom of God and human existence. The more wholistic approach of Michel points up the one-sidedness of Ryan. Michel and others (such as Furfey and the Catholic Worker Movement which will be discussed in chapter four) insist on the importance of the liturgy as the center of the whole Christian life including its ethical dimension.[239] The Eucharist and the struggle for social justice must be linked together, but Ryan in his many writings never develops or even alludes to such an approach.

Ryan's almost total neglect of the scriptures in moral theology is logically connected with his exclusively natural-law methodology. There are many significant questions about how the scriptures are to be employed in moral theology. Problems arise because of the eschatological coloring of the scriptural witness and because of the different historical and cultural circumstances of the times in which the scriptures were written. Some theologians, for example, can be criticized for a simplistic application of the prophetic tradition to the problems of social justice, but such a tradition should have something to say to the Christian and should be incorporated into the methodology of moral theology. Ryan's almost total neglect of the scriptures cannot be an acceptable approach for a wholistic Christian moral theology.

Not only does Ryan fail to integrate gospel and natural law, and the supernatural and natural, but he also makes little or no reference to sin in his theological theory, which again is characteristic of the Catholic theology of the times. In his own writings our author often appeals to realistic considerations, but he never carries out the theological implications of grounding this realism in a recognition of the power of sin in the world. His failure to appreciate the reality of sin and to incorporate it into his understanding also helps to explain the absence of a call for a change of heart on the part of individuals as a necessary part of any social reform.

From the philosophical perspective natural law refers to the way in which human nature and human reason are understood as revealing to us the plan of God for the world and our lives. Ryan often speaks of the eternal, immutable plan of God and the universal principles based on that plan. Likewise, he frequently emphasizes the deductive methodology by which reason arrives at these universal principles. Many contemporary theologians would disagree and give much more importance to historical consciousness and an emphasis on the subject rather than on the "out there" eternal plan of God.

However, Ryan recognizes and even advocates the use of a more inductive ethical methodology in his approach to economic ethics. He insists that Catholic ethics has to incorporate the findings of the sciences, especially economics and sociology; otherwise Catholic theology would continue to be vague and a priori. Unfortunately, he never integrates this creative breakthrough into his more theoretical understandings of natural law. An insistence on a deductive methodology and on eternal, unchangeable principles characterizes his approach to the question of church and state. Ironically, John Courtney Murray ultimately solves that problem for many Americans by using a more historical and inductive methodology. A greater emphasis on historicity and on the role of the subject would argue against the understanding of the natural law as an eternal, immutable plan of God and against a heavy emphasis on deductive reasoning. Also an emphasis on the subject, together with a recognition of the role of sin and grace, would call for more emphasis on the change of heart as an important part in social reform. Ryan's general approach, with its natural-law presuppositions and its failure to emphasize sin, insists on the importance of order and harmony rather than conflict. Such a harmony exists among the different people contributing to production or between the respective roles of church and state. In contrast, other positions would give more importance to the conflict. There are both advantages and disadvantages to Ryan's approach. Although his

basic thrust is on order and harmony, he does recognize in practice at times a realistic tension in human affairs. However,
reality involves more conflict than Ryan admits.

The principle of expediency, insisting that good ethics is
good economics, is perhaps Ryan's most innovative contribution
to methodology, but one that raises many ethical problems. The
principle of expediency fits in with a number of significant characteristics in Ryan's ethics: his general Catholic emphasis on
order and harmony; his inductive methodological approach in
economic ethics; his economic theory of underconsumption; the
downplaying of sin with its clashes and conflicts; the lack of any
call to change one's heart. Especially for a reformer hoping to
bring about needed change as quickly as possible the principle
of expediency is a most potent weapon. However, from a theological and ethical viewpoint there are serious flaws. Ryan's
principle of expediency as applied to economic questions maintains that self-interest and concern for others are in harmony.
Theoretically, such a position at the very least needs to be
nuanced to say that proper love of self and proper self-interest
are in harmony with love of neighbor, especially the poor and
those in need. Practically, Ryan frequently condemns the fact
that a few capitalists control so much wealth and power. At the
very minimum their self-interest is incompatible with social
justice. These capitalists must be willing to give up some of their
material wealth and power. Again, from a theoretical perspective, one must admit possible conflicts between good economics
and good ethics. Ethics is rooted in what is good from the human and the Christian perspective. Economics is only one aspect
of the human. The human can never be totally identical with any
one aspect such as the psychological, the sociological, or the economic. The human and the Christian must govern the economic.
Ethicists frequently point out that ethics must be concerned
with questions of a just distribution and not merely with the
total amount of economic goods produced. The economic problems facing the world today remind us that the rich individuals
and the rich nations of the world must be willing to give up
some of their life-style and wealth. There are no easy solutions
to the problems involving a just distribution of the goods of
creation. Consumerism and overconsumption are very real sins in
our modern world.

Ryan is primarily a reformer. To his credit, and unlike so
many other so-called reformers, Ryan is never satisfied with the

reforms that are achieved. Monsignor Ryan continues to call for ever greater reform in his attempt to bring about more justice. However, being only a reformer also brings with it its own limitations. Ryan the reformer describes his approach as involving two questions: "I ask myself, first, 'is this measure in conformity with right reason and Catholic teaching?' Second, 'is it wise and prudent to advocate the reform at this time?' "[240] Ryan is deeply concerned with being effective in his reform and recognizes the necessity of the emphasis on prudence. However, in trying to be an effective reformer, the temptation is to forget about the deeper issues of injustice which do not seem to allow much hope of immediate change and reform. That attitude partially explains Ryan's failure to deal with some of the more pressing social problems such as the role of minorities in our society.

The presence of the pragmatic and effective, reforming strain in Ryan definitely influences some of his positions and attitudes. Ryan at least never publicly recognizes any tension in the various parts of his own economic program—reform by legislation, a new status for workers, and industry-wide councils. Many who argue for a new status for the worker or for the papal plan for reconstruction claim that their positions are incompatible with the predominance given the role of the state in Ryan's own theory. Ryan's own approaches might not be as internally consistent and coherent as he thinks they are. Practically there is no doubt that the quickest way to bring about change would be through state intervention. The other approaches such as cooperatives would take education and a long nurturing process and even then would affect only a small minority of people. There likewise seems to be no quick way in which to bring about the corporate society. Thus, one can see why Ryan the pragmatic and effective reformer is above all interested in reform by legislation. In addition, it is doubtful that the other changes that he talks about could realistically build on the changes through legislation. Something new and different would really be needed to bring about a greater status for the worker and above all the industry-wide council plans proposed by Pope Pius XI.

It is interesting to note that Ryan seldom disagrees publicly with other reformers who advocate approaches other than his own, even though many would recognize significant differences existing between them. For example, in 1910 Ryan highly praises the work of the German Jesuit Father Heinrich Pesch and his approach of solidarism, but at the very least there is a difference of emphasis, if not a real contradiction, between Ryan's approach at that time of reform by social legislation and Pesch's call for a corporate society.[241] This attitude is best illustrated in a comment Ryan made about Charles Coughlin, the Detroit radio priest, in December 1933. Coughlin has made some mistakes, but between those who are fighting for social justice and those who are fighting against it, Father Coughlin is on the side of the angels.[242] Later Ryan would regret that remark, but the comment well illustrates the mentality of a pragmatic reformer who is not going to divide the forces of change in their struggle against the status quo of social injustice.

Ryan's competent and sympathetic biographer, Francis Broderick, uses the word papalist to best describe Ryan—a term which is more accurate than liberal or progressive. There are many reasons for such a choice. Ryan never publicly disagrees with papal teachings; he changes his own teaching on sterilization of the mentally diseased after the papal encyclical *Casti connubii* in 1930; he defends Leo XIII's teaching on the church and state which would cause many Catholics in the United States great embarrassment; he steadfastly pushes for industry-wide councils only after Pope Puis XI's encyclical in 1931.[243] Yes, all this is true, but almost all Catholic theologians writing in this period could properly be called papalists. Theologians would only later publicly recognize the possibility of dissent in the Roman Catholic Church from authoritative, noninfallible hierarchical teaching. The term papalist is thus too general to distinguish Ryan from other Catholics. In addition, one should point out that Ryan gives more importance to papal teaching as the years went by. The pragmatic reformer uses the papal teaching as a means to get more Catholics involved in working for social justice and at the same time to heighten his own effectiveness by cloaking himself in the papal mantle.

Ryan's methodological acceptance of distributive justice with its heavy emphasis on the criterion of human needs and his central insistence on the common destiny of the goods of creation are two important foundations for his economic ethics. In these areas Ryan makes a lasting contribution to Roman Catholic social ethics. His position on private property is different from that proposed by Leo XIII and anticipated the approach which would be proposed since the Second Vatican Council with its primary insistence on the common destiny of the goods of creation to serve the needs of all.[244]

In addition to theological ethical theory and methodology, the existential problem of being both Catholic and American at the same time greatly influences Ryan's positions. This tension has been discussed at great length in presenting his social ethics. Ryan, the social reformer and accepter of the American political ethos, sees no incompatibility between being Catholic and being American, but this does not make him an uncritical observer of the American scene. He manages, not always with total success, to identify with the American system but also to criticize strongly injustices in it.

Ryan's approach to the substantive issues in social ethics well exemplifies the best of American Catholic social liberalism with its twin emphasis on economic reform and the basic compatibility between Catholic faith and the American ethos. The methodology employed by Ryan closely follows what at the time was the traditional Catholic methodology. The strengths in Ryan's content and methodology are underscored by the role and acceptance he enjoyed in the Catholic community despite some disagreements. However, Ryan's was not the only approach within Roman Catholicism to social ethics in the first half of the twentieth century. The following two chapters will discuss two other positions which were less broadly accepted but which proposed significant alternatives both to the methodology and to the substantive positions proposed by John A. Ryan.

3. THE CENTRAL-VEREIN
AND WILLIAM J. ENGELEN

The largest group of American Catholics involved as such in social reform in the first part of the twentieth century was the
Central Bureau of the Central-Verein, a national federation of
German-American Catholic organizations. In 1909 this group
began publishing the *Central-Blatt and Social Justice,* which still
exists today under the title of *Social Justice Review.* These German-American Catholics were more radical reformers than John
A. Ryan, but at the same time they were also solid conservatives.[1]

I. Historical Background

Ryan the liberal often associated himself with other liberal
Americans in working for the cause of social justice by appealing
especially to the role of the state and of legislation. The German-
American Catholics, on the other hand, were a tight-knit group
characterized by devotion to the German traditions, customs, and
language, as well as by a stalwart, uncompromising Catholicism.
Such a group tended to remain aloof from the mainstream of American political life. In their view the modern world was far from
good; in fact, the primary enemy was liberalism. Ever since the
Middle Ages infectious liberalism had brought about a growing
individualism and selfishness. Capitalism, or economic liberalism, was only the last in a long line of religious, moral, and political liberalisms which destroyed the harmony and peace of the
medieval world.

This theoretical estrangement of German-American Catholics from the modern world with its manifold liberalism was rein-
forced by historical circumstances. Many of these immigrants
had come to the United States in the middle of the nineteenth century to avoid the political liberalism associated with Bismarck in
Germany. Even in their native land they had been somewhat es-

tranged. In the United States they found themselves as an immigrant minority speaking a foreign language. In the American context of the nineteenth century their German immigrant status made them all the more isolated and defensive.[2]

Not only was there a distance and an aloofness from American society in general, but also there was little or no cooperation with other German immigrants. These Catholic immigrants brought with them from Germany their suspicion of Protestant Germans. Also in the midst of the nativist movement in the 1850s, the German Catholics were strenuously attacked by the liberal German freethinkers in this country. Their religion separated the German-American Catholics from many of their fellow German immigrants. In the early part of the twentieth century the Central-Verein rejected direct relationship with the National German-American Alliance, *Deutsche-Amerikanische National-Bund*, whose goal was to bring about unification among all the existing German-American societies in the United States. Although religious questions were to be most strenuously avoided in this alliance, the Catholics feared the influence of the German liberals in the organization. Only with the coming of the First World War did the cool relationship between the two groups begin to change.[3]

The German-American Catholics often found themselves in the late nineteenth and early twentieth centuries in opposition with the liberal wing of the Catholic Church, which was dominated by the Irish. Although there were some Irish in the conservative camp in addition to the Germans, the ideological friction between the Irish and the Germans contributed to their differences.[4]

The basic issue of the compatibility or lack of it between the American ethos and Catholic understanding centered on the Americanization of immigrants. The Germans generally stressed the importance of holding on to their language, customs, and traditions as a way of retaining their faith in an alien land. This basic issue lay behind the nationality question and the demand of the Germans for national parishes. There was some tendency among the second-generation Germans to become more Americanized in all aspects of their life, but many German-American Catholics fought hard to retain the national parishes with all their rights. Peter Paul Cahensly, a devout German merchant, became most interested in the cause of German Catholic immigrants in the United States. In 1891 his St. Raphael Society in Europe requested that each immigrant group have its represen-

tation in the hierarchy. The American hierarchy strongly rejected such a proposal, which they interpreted as a replacement
of territoriality by ethnicity as a basis for episcopal appointment
and rule. The suspicion and lack of trust was to continue for some
time.[5]

Other issues also saw the German-American Catholics take
sides against the Catholic liberals with their emphasis on Americanization. The Germans strongly defended the Catholic school,
for they saw this as one way of retaining their traditions and culture. Some liberals on the school question were trying to find a
modus vivendi with the state schools as illustrated in the work of
Archbishop John Ireland.[6] The Constitution of the Central-Verein,
the most important German-American Catholic society, required
the members of the constituent societies to send their children to
Catholic schools. In 1869 a resolution at the thirteenth convention
of the Central-Verein strongly backed the parochial school and
respectfully requested the bishops to secure the participation of
the Catholic schools in public tax monies.[7] In a similar vein the
German-American Catholics insisted on a strict interpretation of
the Roman condemnations of secret societies, whereas American
Catholic liberals maintained that many of these societies were
primarily fraternal and no threat to the church. For the liberals
even Freemasonry in the United States was not opposed to the
church.[8] Another point of friction involved the temperance movement and especially the crusade, even among Catholics, for total
abstinence. John Ireland, the acknowledged leader of liberalizing
American bishops, was a strong force in this movement. Especially in the light of the general prohibition movement in the United States, the German-American Catholics often found themselves somewhat isolated in defending moderate drinking and
particularly their custom of drinking beer. Under pressure the
German Benedictine monks at Latrobe, Pennsylvania, were forced
to give up their brewery.[9] In sum, the German-American Catholics were a comparatively tightly knit group, often in opposition
to modern society in general, frequently suspicious of and at odds
with other German immigrants, and not even at home with many
other Catholics who were liberal and/or Irish. Such was the historical situation of the German-American Catholics in the beginning of the twentieth century.

The Central-Verein became the most significant organizational presence of German-American Catholics. The organization
held its first convention in Baltimore in 1855 and structured itself

as a national federation of all the local German Catholic organizations, especially benevolent organizations. At first the declared aim was "the mutual support and help in poverty and sickness of the individual members of all German Roman Catholic Benevolent Societies of the United States of North America which belong to the Central-Verein."[10] In the nineteenth century the Central-Verein gradually came to the fore as the central and unifying German-American Catholic society. After reorganization in 1905 the Verein became a more tightly knit union of state leagues, as the principle of subsidiarity was put into practice with a national federal union, state leagues, and the local organizations.[11]

In the first decade of the twentieth century the Central-Verein committed itself to work for the cause of social justice. After an unsuccessful attempt of Nicholas Gonner to establish a Volksverein in America (organized reading circles dealing with social justice), a committee, which was originally called the Committee for Social Propaganda, came into existence in 1907 and focused on social reform as the new thrust of the Central-Verein. This committee reported to the national convention in 1908, and eventually the Central-Verein established a Central Bureau in St. Louis under the leadership of Frederick P. Kenkel to carry out this program of social reform. From the very beginning its emphasis was on education and what might be called today consciousness raising. The *Central-Blatt and Social Justice* began publication in March 1909 as a bilingual journal published every month. The peak circulation of about eight thousand subscribers came in 1913, but the journal has continued down to the present. In 1940 the name was changed to *Social Justice Review*, and the German language, which had become increasingly less used, was dropped entirely.[12]

Kenkel's editorial policy called for comparatively short articles of two to three large pages on questions of social reform in the light of the theory of solidarism. The tone of these articles was of a high caliber, but the approach was neither creative nor scholarly. The journal attempted to educate German-American Catholics about social reform based on the theory of solidarism as proposed in German Catholic social thought, especially by the Jesuit Heinrich Pesch.[13] Kenkel and his associates kept their readers informed about social problems and Catholic attempts to solve social problems both at home and abroad.

Although the journal became the central and most lasting means of propagating social reform, the Central Bureau engaged in other activities. The bureau published and distributed many pamphlets of a popular nature dealing especially with the church and social questions. A news service sent out articles to English-language Catholic papers. Beginning in 1909, summer-school courses were organized to bring the message of social justice to a wider audience. A small speakers' bureau was set up to provide lecturers to speak throughout the country. St. Elizabeth's Settlement was opened in St. Louis as a day nursery school which could serve as a model for practical involvement in reform by the other organizations on the local level. One project which never succeeded was the attempt to form a school for the study of social reform to be called the Ketteler Study House. In these different ways the Central Bureau carried out its aim to educate and work for social reform.[14]

The involvement in social reform was a very creative response on the part of the Central-Verein. Immigration from Germany had fallen greatly in the twentieth century. The attraction of Americanization loomed ever greater for the second generation as more and more Germans readily found themselves at home in the American society. How could the German consciousness, identity, tradition, and even language be preserved? The social question was of great importance for this second generation. Here was an issue that could help deepen their interest and tie them more closely to the thought and traditions of Catholic Germany.

In the first decade of the century socialism made great strides as the Socialist party of America picked up an average of ten thousand new members a year. American Catholics in general reacted strongly to the socialist growth and tried to refute its claims. The German-American Catholics were even more sensitive to the socialist problem because socialism was strong among the Germans and was a constant source of temptation for the German-American working class. Milwaukee was an excellent example of the power of socialism and its strength in the German community. Clearly the best tactic to use against the socialists was to show that the church proposed a social program which called for the reconstruction of society. The church too was interested in the worker. A critique of the American capitalist system also fit in well with the struggle of the German-American Catholics against the liberalizing Americanizers often represented by some of the Irish. The Catholic liberals maintained a basic compatibility between the American ethos and Catholic self-understanding. By attacking the American economic system and calling for reconstruction, the Central-Verein solidified its basic position about the evils of American life and society. Their spokespersons frequently alluded to a remark attributed to Bishop Keane, the rector of The Catholic University of America, that in America we have no social problem. [15]

In the nineteenth century the German Catholics had heavily been involved in the social question as exemplified in the work of Bishop Wilhelm Emmanuel von Ketteler.[16] A Volksverein, organized in 1890 with a very active Central Bureau in München-Gladbach, carried on a great amount of work on social education which was filtered throughout the country. The German-American Catholics would attempt to imitate in this country what the Volksverein had been doing in Germany for the cause of social reform and would base its teaching on the work of these significant German reformers. The movement for social reform would unite German-American Catholics in this country with the Catholics in Germany. No better way could be found to keep the second generation immigrants conscious of their history, identity, and culture.[17]

Decline in the Central-Verein began with the First World War. In the context of a war against Germany only hard times could be in store for a group that tried to create German consciousness and to hold on to their German traditions and identities. After the war the decline continued as more and more of the second and third generations of German immigrants became Americanized. Even after the decline set in, there were still some creative approaches such as support for the Catholic Rural Life Conference and the liturgical movement. In the 1920s and later the editors and writers for the journal were even more alienated from the contemporary life about them.[18] For the last few decades *Social Justice Review* has lost its social interest and primarily protests against many developments in the contemporary world.

Without doubt the guiding genius behind the work of the Central Bureau and *Central-Blatt and Social Justice* was Frederick P. Kenkel, who served as first director of the bureau and editor of the journal from 1910 until his death in 1952. The life and thought of Kenkel have been appraised with historical meticulousness and sensitive criticism by Philip Gleason. Kenkel was not trained as a theologian, and his writings consisted primarily of comparatively short articles on disparate subjects. For all these reasons our study will not focus on Kenkel.

For the purpose of the present investigation of different Catholic approaches to social ethics, the writings of William J. Engelen, S.J., furnish both a more manageable and a more systematic approach to social ethics. Engelen was a Jesuit priest who had been trained in Germany, had a doctorate in both philosophy and theology, and taught in the United States at St. John's College in Toledo and later in St. Louis and at Rockhurst College in Kansas City. He began writing for *Central-Blatt and Social Justice* in 1912 and continued to do so until 1932, five years before his death.[19] The format of Engelen's writings also makes them more appropriate for the type of systematic ethical study being undertaken here. Often he wrote a long series of articles which appeared in as many as twenty different installments in the journal. His series on "Capital and Labor under Solidarism" appeared in seven parts beginning in the November 1914 issue. His last long series on "Social Reconstruction" began in September 1924 and included thirteen different parts with each part usually containing two or more different installments. There can be no doubt that Engelen was one of Kenkel's closest associates. Philip Gleason in his authoritative history mentions Engelen more than any other contributor to the journal except Kenkel, and Gleason uses the Jesuit's address in 1915 to the Central-Verein as a convenient summary of the Central-Verein's social theory.[20] In addition to his writings for the journal and speeches to conventions, Engelen was also a featured speaker at the summer schools held in Springbank, Wisconsin. Our analysis with its more systematic and methodological interests will concentrate on the writings of Engelen but occasionally make reference to others, especially Kenkel.

II. Engelen's Presuppositions

There are three presuppositions upon which Engelen builds his social ethics, even though he does not explicitly refer to them. To understand and evaluate his social ethics these presuppositions need to be examined—his dependence on Heinrich Pesch, his natural-law methodology, and his understanding of contemporary culture.

Dependence on Heinrich Pesch, S.J.

Engelen willingly admitted that his purpose was to educate American Catholics about the social teaching proposed by Heinrich Pesch. On two different occasions Engelen devoted a series of articles to the life and contributions of Pesch.[21] Engelen himself was born, reared, and educated in Germany and proud of the fact that he had studied social philosophical ethics under Father Victor Cathrein, a leading figure in Catholic social thought in Germany. In Germany Engelen also knew Heinrich Pesch and held him in high esteem as a scholar and humble person. In language typical of his own understanding of ethics, Engelen saw his own life in terms of a duty to make Pesch's system known to American Catholics. Occasionally he disagreed with Pesch (the later Engelen would not accept an intrinsic justification for the taking of interest on loans) ; sometimes he arrived at the same conclusion independently of the German solidarist; but he gladly acknowledged Pesch as his guide and gave all credit to him.

Pesch, a German Jesuit, was born at Cologne in 1854 and died in 1926. Fortunately Pesch finished his monumental five-volume work on *National Economy* before he died.[22] According to Pesch, national economy, as an ethical postulate for society, safeguards the prosperity of the entire nation and brings this about through the harmonious cooperation and interdependence of all forces of society. The activity of all in the interest of all and the subordination of all individual and group activity under the common good of social prosperity constitute a duty. His theory of solidarism avoids the individualism of capitalism and the class war of collectivism. Solidarism safeguards both the individual and the social nature of human beings. In his very first article in the *Central-Blatt and Social Justice* Engelen used Pesch to emphasize that society is truly a moral organism which must exist for the prosperity of all.[23]

Natural Law

Engelen bases his social ethic on the natural law. As might be expected from the very nature of his writings, there is no detailed explanation of the meaning, grounding, and extension of natural law. He devotes one installment of a series on "Social Reflections" to natural law. Engelen here briefly repeats the

accepted Catholic understanding and extols the natural law for
protecting the small and the weak from arbitrary power and
tyranny.[24]

The God of wisdom guides all things according to their nature. In irrational nature there is a physical law; in human
beings it is a rational and moral law. Engelen frequently repeats
that the basis of the natural law is the rational and social nature
of human beings. From rational and social human nature he deduces the seven basic principles upon which a just order of solidarism rests.[25] The deductive nature of his ethical methodology
is quite evident in Engelen's first installment of his long series
on "Social Reconstruction," in which he deduces the principles
of his theory of solidarism.[26] He explicitly acknowledges that his
own reasoning is deductive.[27] This deductive approach raises the
suspicion that his methodology does not give great importance to
historical consciousness.

Our German-American Jesuit proudly insists that he uses
the *philosophia perennis* (the perennial philosophy) of the scholastics.[28] Since the natural law is God's law and is based on human nature, the principles of the natural law are eternal, immutable, and unchanging.[29] If the natural law is based on human
nature, then it must be known by all human beings. The ten commandments are merely statements of the natural law. Scripture
tells us that even before God gave the ten commandments to
Moses, the Jews knew about the commandments as illustrated
in the murder of Abel. The pagans too have recognized the precepts of natural law. However, our author recognizes an important role of the church as the authentic teacher of natural law.
Because of the limited mental capabilities of human beings,
mistakes are possible, especially in more complicated matters.
Through revelation, the teaching of the church, and even the positive laws of the state we are instructed in the true requirements
of natural law. Note, however, that the human law of the state
can never go against the natural law, so that the natural law always protects the individual against the tyranny of the state and
its rulers.[30] This divine natural law is made known to us both in
natural and in supernatural ways. For children and the less educated God has laid down in the sacred books of religion in concrete terms the law based on our rational nature. Especially
through the church we are instructed about the natural law. Thus
faith goes hand in hand with reason to instruct us about God's
natural law.[31]

Although Engelen insists on the natural law as the basis for the teaching of social ethics, there are many references in his works to the scriptures and especially to the teachings of Jesus. In his series on "Social Observations" one of his main thrusts is the refutation of liberalism. Here he appeals in separate installments to Deuteronomy and to the teachings of the Sermon on the Mount in the gospels. Part of his purpose in appealing to the scriptures is to avoid repetition, because in many previous articles he has shown how the natural law condemns liberalism. However, these scriptural laws are totally in harmony with the natural law.[32] Unlike John A. Ryan and many Catholics of his era, Engelen even uses the term "social gospel"—a term employed by American Protestant ethicians who did not accept the Catholic insistence on natural law. Engelen describes the Sermon on the Mount as the Magna Charta for a Christian society. However, behind Christ's precepts we discover the stronger and unfailing sanction of natural law. The church has a storehouse of social principles which are as old as our scholastic philosophy and which alone can bring about reform in our world.[33] For Engelen even the Sermon on the Mount teaches us again the eternal, immutable natural law of God of how human beings should live in society. Our author never even alludes to the many problems raised by his grounding of the Sermon on the Mount in natural law. At the very least he uses the scriptures in a proof-text fashion to give authoritative support for a natural law based on rational human nature.

Ethical theories have often been divided into two kinds—teleological and deontological. Teleology views the ethical model in terms of the end and the means by which the end is obtained. The deontological model sees ethics primarily as obedience to duty, law, or obligation. In the Catholic tradition Thomas Aquinas employed a teleological model even though he used natural law as part of his ethics. The manuals of moral theology employed a deontological approach and often followed the schema of the ten commandments. Engelen is firmly in the deontological camp. The moral life is seen primarily in terms of law, with the natural law at its center, and our moral life consists in doing our duty with respect to the law. The German-American Jesuit's favorite moral term is duty. He ends one article with his resolution to the moral problem: "DUTY—SOCIAL DUTY."[34] The insistence on the primacy of duty coheres with his understanding of the contemporary problem. Freedom has been exaggerated. Everyone

speaks in terms of freedom and rights, but this creates problems
for the wider society. Only by accepting our duty will peace and
prosperity prevail.[35]

The centrality of the legal model and the insistence on duty
also explain our writer's interest in the sanctions of the law.
There is a twofold sanction to the natural law—temporal and
eternal. The temporal sanction is temporal happiness, for the
plagues and the miseries affecting modern human life come from
the failure of human beings to live in accord with God's law. If
only human beings would accept our solidaric duty, there would
be true prosperity for all—social prosperity. At times Engelen
paints an almost idyllic picture of what society would be like if
only God's laws were obeyed. Such an understanding of temporal
sanctions logically follows from the fact that natural law is
grounded in human nature and commands what is good for human nature. However, it fails to account for the mystery of evil
and suffering. The second sanction is eternal—eternal reward or
punishment. This is the sanction which Christ has brought to
natural law. By attaching the strong sanction of eternal dam-
nation to the natural law, the Almighty has been able to curb in
human hearts the tendency to revolt against the moral law. Eternal reward is promised by Jesus for the observance of the individual and social natural law.[36]

There is another very important dimension to Engelen's
understanding of natural law which sharply distinguishes his
approach from that of John A. Ryan. Engelen frequently recognizes and implicitly appeals to the traditional Catholic teaching
that the individual is not able to observe the natural law for a long
time without grace. He frequently calls for a change of heart
and spirit which will be necessary to bring about the observance
of natural law and of the solidaric duty which will usher in a new
social prosperity for all. From the beginning human beings discovered in their nature the tablet on which God wrote his law.
Before the fall it was one and the same thing to know the law and
to obey it. But after the fall passion and selfishness rose up a-
gainst the higher self, and the sweet bait of self-satisfaction
brought about the fall of the higher self. Henceforth selfishness
ruled over our better nature. However, the God-given order and
law had not become unknown. For the most part human beings
realized they had broken the law. As a result of sin the human
race was fallen, the family was fallen, society was fallen, religion was fallen. Consequently, both the individual and society

cried out for salvation. And a savior came for the individual, the family, society, and the state. Changes could now take place in society because the gospel had brought back the observance of the natural law. Justice, fidelity, and charity could now become present.

Unfortunately, darkness has once again permeated society because of human pride and revolt. Selfishness now destroys the family through polygamy, immorality, prostitution, and debauchery. Social justice and charity, the strong bonds of society, are severed. Selfish greed raises up nation against other nations. Greed in America has destroyed "the redman." Selfish pride leads to the exhaltation of the absolute state and to the tyranny of rulers. The remedy for the darkness now is the same as then—a return to Christ which will bring back the full truth of the gospel with its reassertion of the natural law over inclination and selfishness. Christ can enable human beings to carry out the natural law and bring peace and prosperity to the earth.[37]

Often Engelen does not speak precisely in terms of sin and salvation but recognizes that social reform demands a change of heart and an awakening of consciousness so that one comes to accept social and economic duty. The church alone, and he means the Roman Catholic Church, can produce all these changes. Reform cannot take place merely through legislation, for only a change of heart will bring back the observance of the natural law and social peace and prosperity.[38]

View of history, culture, and society

On the question of the relationship between Catholicism and contemporary American culture, Engelen stresses the differences and even the basic incompatibilities between the two. Engelen's opposition to contemporary culture is not limited to the American scene but extends to the whole modern world. The golden period in world history was the Middle Ages, but unfortunately the forces of liberalism then took over. Our author often repeats the fourfold aspect of liberalism which infects the modern world—liberalism in religion, morals, politics, and economics. Liberalism is often mentioned in conjunction with individualism and selfishness. In Engelen's view of history the true influence of the church and Christianity on all aspects of life was not reached until medieval times. For the first few centuries the Roman Empire opposed the church. When the empire turned

officially to Christianity en masse, conversion often was superficial and political. The degeneracy of Roman society, especially
the family, shows how little Christianity affected the empire. In
such a weakened condition the empire easily fell to the barbarian
hordes. Symbolic of the lack of Christian influence was the harsh
Roman law which continued to exist at that time.[39]

In medieval times we find the Christian ideal made present—
a social person in an organic society. Selfishness and individualism did not exist. The spirit of liberalism did not permeate the
culture and society. Religiously, all were united in the Christian
faith (the Catholic faith) which pervaded the lives of all. Our
author willingly recognized the hierarchical ordering of medieval
society and the inequalities existing in it, but these were all good.
Princes or kings recognized their obligation to religion and to the
natural law; they were defenders of the poor, the downtrodden,
and the weak. The economic organization of society was marked
by a spirit of solidarity as incorporated in a guild system which
strove for the social prosperity of all and knew nothing of the
individualistic quest for wealth and profit. Labor was not for
monetary gain to acquire wealth but only for earning a comfortable living. Labor was held in high esteem; interest-taking was
forbidden. The guild organized all economic activity and also
supported the spiritual and moral well-being of its members. Society was an organism. Each one had one's own function, but all
worked for the social good of all and not just for personal gain.[40]

Unfortunately, even before the Protestant revolt (Engelen
would never use the word reformation), the spirit of liberalism
began to destroy the beauty and glory of the organic society of
the Middle Ages with its recognition of the importance of religion, the observance of God's moral law, and the existence of a
political and economic organism which, under the influence of
religion and morality, incarnated the solidaric spirit and in an
hierarchical structure looked after the needs of all. The first
opening to liberalism came in the fourteenth century with the
death of Boniface VIII. (Recall his view of society and its relationship of church and state as a good example of an organic,
unified hierarchical structure. All rational creatures should be
subject to the Roman pontiff.) Henceforth the church's influence
on political society came to an end, and political liberalism gradually took hold of Europe. Also, even before the Protestant revolt there emerged the new interest in classical culture and the
pagan antiquities.

With Luther's revolt in 1517 religious liberalism came to the fore. Individual conscience became exalted, and the authority of the church diminished. Engelen was staunchly opposed to all Protestantism and saw its growth as a very important indication of the inroads of liberalism in modern society.[41] Engelen was no ecumenist. In one article he reports that a Methodist conference pointed out the evils of the present economic system, but his response shows his disdain for Protestants. "Must we not fear that their blindness will make a cure impossible; for they above all others are affected with blindness as to their religious liberalism, the root of all liberalism. Their own religious death would be the strongest remedy."[42] Religious liberalism, with its revolt against authority and religious teaching and precepts, vindicated moral liberalism and paved the way for the entrance of liberalism into politics and economics.[43]

Moral liberalism means that the spirit of selfishness and individualism has enticed human beings away from the eternal law of God. Ever since the human mind was blinded by material progress, morality has found new interpreters who are better recognized as very efficient destroyers of true morality. False theories of utility, moral sense, subjectivity, and many other human standards have replaced the immutable law of God. A moral reconstruction in modern life is absolutely essential.[44]

Political liberalism began when secular princes, after throwing off the authority of the church and moral law, began to increase their own wealth and power. They became absolute rulers who wanted to accumulate all glory, honor, and wealth to themselves. The excessive burdens they imposed on their subjects created class antagonisms. Wars and strikes followed.[45] Later on, rulers associated themselves with the rich and failed to help the poor. Once political authority was loosed from its relationship to God and God's natural law, a godless and selfish generation denied the true stewardship of authority of maintaining the place of God and looking out for the poor, the oppressed, and the weak. Democracy has not solved the problem. The worst tyrant is a bigoted majority relying on the strength of its vast following and thereby oppressing the rights of minorities.[46]

Moral and religious liberalism spawned economic liberalism. The spirit of individualistic self-seeking after wealth soon pervaded society and destroyed the old solidaric system. The lords oppressed their vassals. The starving serf suffered most. The guild with its living example of mutual help and social ser-

vice became protective and self-seeking.[47] Wealth and the desire
for wealth generally determined everything. Thus was the spirit
of capitalism born. Wealth monopolized new inventions to the
disadvantage of the middle class and the laborer. The middle
class gradually lost out, and all were at the mercy of the capitalists who controlled the economy. Oppression, antagonism, and
class struggle marked the capitalistic era which arose from
liberalism's injecting its selfishness and individualism into the
economic scene.[48]

As time went on, Engelen and the *Central-Blatt and Social
Justice* became more alienated from the modern world and even
more romantically attached to the Middle Ages. Both the tone
and the substance of Engelen's writings show the ever deepening
suspicion of the modern world and a retreat into the past. His
earlier writings often deal with the practical questions facing
labor and capital, for example, whether or not Catholics can and
should belong to the American Federation of Labor.[49] Later
articles are more removed from the concrete situation and more
global in their condemnation of modern society and all it entails.
The later articles give more frequent citations to Karl von Vogelsang and Albert M. Weiss, who were staunch medieval corporatists opposed to the more moderate reforming elements in Germany in the nineteenth century.[50] In his early series in *Central-
Blatt and Social Justice* on "Capital and Labor under Solidarism" Engelen points out some limitations in the Middle Ages.
He recognizes that in the medieval system there was too much
emphasis on social duty and not enough importance given to freedom. Although feudalism had its problems, contemporary capitalism has many more.[51] In his later writings his criticism dis-
appears and there emerges a romantic picture of the Middle Ages
as a period of true peace and harmony. Life was simple, but
everyone had all that was necessary for a comfortable human
existence. This utopian view of the bucolic Middle Ages is often
contrasted with the present reality of urban society with its
slums, soot, and dirt, together with its morality of individualism
and selfishness, which is seen in the misery and exploitation of
many.[52]

Engelen's later view of contemporary society with its long-
ing for the simpler days of the Middle Ages can best be characterized as an alienated and romantic utopianism. There can be no
doubt that the German-American Catholics were staunchly conservative. However, from this conservative perspective they

were also very strong critics of the existing capitalistic system in the United States and throughout the world.

III. Engelen's Social Ethics

Principles of solidarism

Engelen, in keeping with the general Catholic approach of his day, sees social ethics primarily in terms of the economic question. His answer to the economic problem is called solidarism, which entails a reconstruction of the existing social and economic orders along the lines of an organic society.

In accord with much of Catholic social reform theory, Engelen proposes his solution in the context of the two extremes of capitalism and socialism, but he adds his own distinctive understanding of liberalism as the source of the evils of both capitalism and socialism. In his writing Engelen emphasizes the evils of capitalism because this system is currently reigning in the United States. The German-American Jesuit defines capitalism as the abuse of capital in the exclusively selfish pursuit of profit. The evils of capitalism are great: excessive advantage for a few; all-absorbing desire of enrichment; unjust wages and working conditions for many; existence of monopolies; spirit of selfishness pervading all life; class antagonism; economic and moral degradation of the workers; unfair business practices; an idle, squandering, monied aristocracy; a capitalistic oligarchy which buys the press and the vote, controls legislative processes, and sways public opinion. Personal gain becomes the all-important, ultimate end.[53]

The evil of capitalism is a refrain constantly repeated throughout his many articles. One summary describes capitalism with its liberalistic individualism and selfishness as "the chief disseminator of materialism, the corruptor of politics, the destroyer of the middle class, the ruin of the working class, and the cause of the present class hatred and of the future class war."[54] As will be discussed shortly, such great evils of spirit and structure call for a radical reconstruction and not simply a few haphazard reforms.

However, the very definition indicates that capital in itself is not necessarily evil. Capitalism is the abuse of capital, so there is a role for capital. However, capital must be in the service of national economy, of social, not individual, prosperity, and of the

common good. These terms are frequently used by Engelen to
signify the goal of the economy and contrast his approach with
the individualism of capitalism with its stress on selfish gain and
profit. The economic freedom of capitalism must be countered
with more emphasis placed on social order and the well-being of
all the members of society. Capitalism must distribute magnan-
imously what it has produced.[55] Competition should be eliminated in all areas except the quality of the goods produced. Prices
and the quantities produced should be determined and regulated
by occupational groups, guilds, or vocational groups—all of
which are synonyms for the same reality.[56] In general, solidarism favors smaller industries. There is a place for profit, but only
for a just profit. A minor share of the profit goes to the capitalist
because of the risk involved. In his earlier writings Engelen
even justifies the taking of interest by the capitalist on intrinsic
grounds or titles.[57]

Engelen likewise opposes socialism. Communism entrusts
all property, both consumable and productive, to society. Socialism limits state ownership to all or certain fields of production.
Even the later Engelen cannot find fault with some aspects of a
limited socialism. Socialism is opposed to the position which
Engelen develops on private property and the role of the state, so
that he possesses the logical framework in his thought to condemn socialism as a form of collectivism and even of totalitarianism. Solidarism is a middle ground between the two extremes
of capitalism with its individualistic freedom and socialism with
its collectivism and disregard for individual rights.

Instead of developing only the view that socialism and capitalism are opposite extremes, Engelen emphasizes that socialism is very much related to capitalism because both rest on the
principles of liberalism. The socialist or Marxist society is also
founded on liberalism in religion, morals, politics, and economics. Since there is no recognition of religion and of a higher moral
duty, authority readily becomes absolute and irresponsible. Power is thus abused and used for personal advantage. Engelen
could accept a moderate socialism which recognizes limitations
on the rights of authority, which leaves to individual initiative
what individuals can do, and which respects a limited right of
private property and production. But a society fed on liberal principles knows no restraint either of individuals or of authority.
Socialism is doomed unless it changes its spirit, but if socialism

does change its spirit, it ceases to be socialism and becomes solidarism. Socialism, although it too is based on a pernicious liberalism, is most persuasive and attractive for those who suffer at the hands of capitalism. Socialism will be defeated not merely by refuting its theory but especially by the actual replacement of the present system with solidarism.[58]

The system of solidarism proposed by Pesch, Kenkel, and the writers in the *Central-Blatt and Social Justice* calls for two important realities—a change of spirit and a change of structures. The change of spirit is primary, fundamental, and all embracing; but also corresponding structural changes are required.

The existing spirit of liberalism with its individualism, selfishness, and materialism must be done away with. Acceptance of the moral law and recognition of the social nature of human beings call upon all to work for the good of social prosperity. Political and economic liberalism will be overcome only if moral and religious liberalism are overcome. Here, too, one sees an organic understanding of reality in which all the different aspects of human life are intimately connected. This profound change of heart, which is occasionally explicitly described as going from sin to grace, can only come about by acceptance of morality and religion. Only through the church can such a change occur—and for Engelen the church means the Roman Catholic Church.[59]

Engelen and the Central Bureau rightly insist that the change of spirit, profound and primary as it is, is not enough. There is also required a fundamental change of societal structures. The liberalistic view sees society as composed of many individuals striving in a competitive manner for their self-satisfaction. Solidarism calls for the spirit of social duty to be incarnated in an organic society in which the individuals are organically related through different groupings and work together for social prosperity. In his very first article in *Central-Blatt and Social Justice* Engelen maintains that society is an organism. The moral organism of society is only analogous to a physical organism. A moral organism calls for an interior principle uniting heterogeneous parts into a harmonious order and activity. Society in this view involves more than merely a collection of individuals. The interior unifying principle of the organism of society is authority which is grounded in the natural law and ultimately in God. Society has a life, an interior principle of activity, which is independent of its members. Opponents of socialism must avoid individualism and recognize that society is an organic whole which is restrained by natural law and God from interfering in the legitimate rights of individuals.[60]

Notice the influence of extrinsicism and of a legal model whereby authority becomes the interior principle of the life of society. Here the stress is on the duty to live in society, whereas other scholastics would insist more on the intrinsic character of the obligation as based on the social nature of human beings. The individual by one's very nature needs society. Engelen, while recognizing and stressing that society and the state are natural for human beings, does not emphasize enough the intrinsic grounding of this reality.

In an organic society there is a complex system of order involving coordination and subordination. All have different functions to play in working for the good of the organism. This organic view recognizes the different functions of people and the need for a hierarchical ordering. As a result, solidarism strongly opposes a flat equality of all people and the extolling of freedom to the detriment of order. All are not equal in every sense. Each one has a different function and therefore a different place in society. If all are totally equal and free, then there truly is no organism. An organic society will thus be strongly opposed to liberalism in all its forms. But at the same time solidarism accuses socialism of crushing liberty in a grossly paternalistic state.[61]

Engelen readily admits that solidarism limits freedom and denies the total equality of all. But there are dangers in such a view of society which our author does not discuss. The first danger is that there is very little freedom of opportunity or choice. In a hierarchically and functionally structured society there is not going to be the freedom to move from one role or function to another. The serfs in the Middle Ages according to Engelen were happy with their lot, but there was no chance to change their lot. His view of society is static, immobile, and tending to be inflexible. A second danger which might arise in such a system is totalitarianism. In practice, the fascism of Italy and Portugal have often been used to illustrate the totalitarian tendencies of solidarism or corporatism. Engelen himself never directly addresses the question of fascism, but in theory he has a built-in protection against totalitarianism. The natural law recognizes the rights of individuals and forbids any authority from overstepping its bounds. The solidarism proposed by Engelen in the pages of *Central-Blatt and Social Justice* accepts, without explicitly naming it, the principle of subsidiarity, which calls for the rights of individuals and smaller groups to be respected. This emphasis will clearly emerge in his discussion of how the organic society should be structured. Throughout the writings of the German-American Catholics there is always a great fear of giving too much of a role to the federal government.

The next logical question concerns the exact way in which the solidaristic society should be structured. However, first some consideration should be given to the practical question of the relationship between the present reality of society and the organic society proposed by Engelen.

What is the relationship between the existing society and the solidaristic society? Both a radical change of spirit and a radical change of structure are required. Engelen, unlike Ryan, has no hesitation about calling for reconstruction and not merely reform. His final lengthy series of articles for the *Central-Blatt and Social Justice* is entitled "Social Reconstruction."[62] In an earlier article Engelen criticizes some programs of reconstruction, including in a rather indirect way the Bishops' Program of Social Reconstruction, for identifying the problem primarily with labor reform and for limiting the solution to reform rather than reconstruction.[63] From his earliest articles Engelen warns against temporary, piecemeal, and haphazard reforms which do not go to the heart of the matter and bring about true reconstruction. In today's parlance our author would characterize such reforms as mere band-aids which do not really solve the structural problem. Such warnings are logically consistent with this emphasis on radical reconstruction.[64]

In the light of the call for total reconstruction the question arises about the way in which solidarism can become a reality. Especially in his earlier writings Engelen recognizes and accepts a gradual approach, all the while condemning merely haphazard reform. The German-American Jesuit defends himself against the charge that he is a dreamer. He admits that a complete change of sentiment and perfect reform will not occur immediately. Such a thorough change remains the ultimate answer, but in the meantime we must devote ourselves to enforced reforms until a system begins to be modeled which from day to day becomes a more perfect likeness of the desired reality. In this light he encourages the efforts of the state in trying to overcome the evils of capitalism: intermediate steps such as labor organizations and workingmen's insurance. Capitalism will never evolve by itself. Improvements have been brought about by pressure—the government from above and labor organizations from below. Thus far the progress is essentially sound, although at times there has been the danger of state socialism.[65] This theme of gradualism, while warning against the dangers of haphazard reform or reform without principles, runs through his early, seven-installment series on "Capital and Labor under Solidarism" beginning in the November 1914 issue and finishing in the May 1915 issue of *Central-Blatt and Social Justice Review*. In the last installment Engelen recognizes that it would be imprudent to advocate sudden changes, because every true and lasting reform must be gradual.[66] There is always the insistence upon the need for radical change of spirit and for the new structures of an organic society, but in his first series of articles on solidarism Engelen stresses the gradual approach to bringing about the new structures.

The later writings do not stress the gradualism as much but point out the shortcomings and insufficiencies of what is existing. Labor, for example, has accomplished much good in terms of wages, working conditions, and even some protective legislation. Unfortunately, labor too is still influenced by the liberalistic spirit and has evolved as a defensive reaction of self-protection against capitalism. Organized labor must learn to think in terms of social prosperity and of harmony. Labor has not even taken an interest in the plight of the unskilled and of women workers. Some good things have been done, but the new spirit is required.[67] However, very little is said about how the new society will come about. In fact, Engelen seemed more out of tune with his own society as the years went by because of his romantic yearning for the Middle Ages, his insistence on the middle class and the importance of craftsmen and shopkeepers. His perspective became more utopian, and little was said about how the vision could be obtained in practice in the light of the existing structures of society. The stress was always on the need to change the spirit, but little was said about how the new structures could evolve from the existing ones. As a whole, the Central-Verein feared state intervention and also recognized that labor often functioned on selfish rather than on solidaric grounds. But how changes could be brought about was less and less discussed.

What does the solidaric view of society call for in practice? Justice and charity are the two requirements of the natural law that must govern economic life in society. Justice in economic matters calls for the possibility of material well-being for all. Engelen insists on national economy and social prosperity to stress that the good of society is to provide such a possibility to all and not only to a few. These goals indicate the opposition of solidarism to all forms of individualism. Engelen, even before Pope Pius XI's encyclical *Quadragesimo anno*, employs the term social justice. Social justice refers to all those rights and duties which human social nature concedes to or imposes on individuals or on society. This concept thus includes legal justice, distributive justice, and even some aspects of commutative justice. Social reconstruction according to Pope Leo XIII must be based on social justice and charity, but social justice is primary and essential because it alone can bring about a change of structures. A better structure can and should eliminate poor classes and make the possibility of moderate prosperity available to all, but there will always be those who cannot achieve this, and here lies the field of charity.[68]

Charity has a place, but it alone can never cure the evils of contemporary society. Charity is a true obligation for all, but charity too should have a hierarchical ordering with some things done by individuals, others performed by smaller groups, and, finally, the remaining filled by the role of the state. We must be very careful that the state does not take over all charity. Engelen frequently contrasts charity with philanthropy, which is usually described in terms of the money given by rich capitalists with the motive of trying to maintain the status quo and avoid true reorganization of society.[69] The solidaristic society rests on the principles of social justice and charity, with social justice being primary and dealing with the structures necessary to assure moderate social prosperity for all.

The general thrust of Engelen's solidarism is clear, although details are often scarce. The mode of implementation is missing; tensions arise between the ideal and the present reality; and a romantic, simpler view of middle-class society gives an air of unreality to the whole picture. The solidaric spirit would create structures that are in keeping with it. Functional and hierarchical structures such as characterized the medieval guilds should exist. Individualism, competition, and self-seeking are to be held in check. Order and harmony rather than competition and class struggle should reign. Labor and capital should not be opposed, but all those involved in the same type of work or vocation should be united in vocational groups. These vocational groups, however, must also recognize that they are part of the whole of society and work for the prosperity of all and for civic solidarity. These vocational and occupational groups would set just prices, pay just wages, determine the amount of production, and have some say in management. However, more precise descriptions of these self-governing vocational groups are not given; nor is there any detailed treatment of how they should work or of their relationship to existing organizations. He admits the way in which these groups should be organized cannot be determined by theoretical speculation alone. All these groups representing the various occupations or vocations would then be coordinated through a vocational parliament which would determine all economic questions in the country and have state authority.[70]

Probably the most constant emphasis of the *Central-Blatt and Social Justice* is the insistence on the importance of the middle class. The middle-class person combines both capitalist and laborer in the same person. Both capitalism and socialism are opposed to the middle class. Engelen strongly resists the power of ever bigger industrialization and favors a society of artisans, tradespeople, and shopkeepers. The middle-class virtues of thrift and hard work will be the backbone of the organic society. The evils of industrialism in the city can be overcome in a middle-class society which will check the growth of industry and of the movement of people to the city. Perhaps in the system there will not be as much wealth, but there will be social prosperity for all and a solidaric spirit will prevail. To do away with all industrialization is impossible, but to restore the middle class is an economic, social, moral, and religious duty. After all, Christ himself chose to be a member of the middle class.[71] Engelen's romanticism, utopianism, and historical biases are quite apparent in his insistence on the importance of the middle class.

The role of the state for Engelen stems from the basic structure of solidarism with its opposition, on the one hand, to the laissez-faire state of capitalistic individualism and its rejection, on the other hand, of the all-encompassing state of socialism. For Engelen the state is a natural society, but the state must respect the other intermediary economic structures in society. The state has an important role and function in the reconstructed society, but above all this is performed indirectly. The state gives, as is repeatedly remarked, to the intermediary organizations a limited, subordinated, and superintendent self-government and legislative and judicial power by granting to them public rights, by making them active as well as passive members of the state authority; in short, by making them true social and moral organs of the state. The state should at times intervene to promote both the solidaric spirit and the organic functioning of other organizations. Above all, the state must intervene to suppress all abuses. The Central-Verein leaders opposed haphazard reform that did not mean a true reconstruction involving both the basic change of heart and the reconstruction of solidaric structures. One great temptation involved giving too much importance to legislation and to the role of the state. Reliance on the state would not bring about the reconstruction of society.[72]

Thus, Kenkel and the Central-Verein opposed a federal constitutional amendment prohibiting child labor primarily because it was an unwarranted intrusion of federal power. They were opposed to child labor and even supported state legislation against it, but not a federal constitutional amendment. The danger always existed of taking the easiest solution rather than working for the true reconstruction of society. On this point the Central-Verein was in direct opposition with the position proposed by John A. Ryan.[73]

The relationship between Ryan and the Central Bureau is interesting. As pointed out in the last chapter, Ryan praised the Central Bureau's work for reform in its early years.[74] While still a professor at St. Paul Seminary in St. Paul, Minnesota, Ryan wrote occasional articles in the early issues of *Central-Blatt and Social Justice* and also taught at the summer school run by the Central Bureau.[75] As time went on, the difference between Ryan and the Central Bureau became more obvious. The debate with Kenkel over the child-labor amendment was conducted in a most charitable manner. Engelen himself never expressed his differences with Ryan in print in an explicit manner. However, in personal correspondence with Kenkel, especially during and after the organization of the National Catholic Welfare Conference, Engelen recorded his theoretical differences with Ryan and even some personal pique.[76]

Engelen in his writings never directly addresses the question of the union or separation of church and state, but there can be no doubt about the conclusions that his principles would reach. True reconstruction requires a religious and moral dimension which can only come from the Catholic Church. His organic and hierarchical concept of society necessarily envisions the union of

church and state. At the least, his failure to address the question
at length underscores how little attention he paid to the practical
ways of making the system of solidarism become a reality in the
United States.

Capital and Labor

A further discussion of capital and labor in Engelen's theory
reveals a threefold tension in his thought. First, there is the tension between the gradual change of the present structures and the
solidaric organizations of the future. Second, capital and labor
should on some issues be organically united, but there is also a
place for properly limited organizations of small capitalists and
organizations of laborers. Third, Engelen really prefers, especially as time went on, to limit industrialization, but he has to
recognize there would always be some need for large industrial
enterprises. As a minimum, the importance of the middle class
demands that capitalistic industry should not be allowed to sup-
plant middle-class, smaller producers, provided these are serving the needs of society.[77]

There is place for an organization of small producers based
on a solidaric grouping of all involved in the same industry. He
often refers to these groupings as cartels. Remember that the
major problem of capitalism was the desire for unjust profit at
any cost. He does not want to do away with all capital but to
direct it for solidaric purposes and goals. Big monopolistic trusts
should be suppressed by the state. If necessary, state monopolies
in some areas might be required, but if a truly solidaric spirit
were in existence in society, then there would be no need for state
monopolies. Instead of trusts there should be organizations or
cartels of smaller independent producers which would regulate
prices, production, and competition. Competition would be reduced, as it was in the medieval guild, to competition in work-
manship. These cartels should seek the good of all in their class
and insist on justice for all other classes. Engelen wants the benefit of guild competition without the individualism of the capitalistic system. These cartels must have a solidaric spirit and be
limited by the state if necessary. Such organizations protecting
their own members and working for justice for all other classes
hold out the hope of gradually becoming truly corporative or
vocational groups.[78]

The German-American Jesuit defends the right of private property as a natural right, but its extension is also limited by the natural law. Here too he finds a middle position between the extremes of individualistic liberalism and socialism. There are many abuses of private property existing today in the materialistic accumulation of wealth, but this can be corrected without denying the basic right to private property. The right to private property, according to Engelen's interpretation of Aquinas, is a natural right as opposed to a positive or human-made right, but it is a natural right based on the right of nations (*ius gentium*). Reason grounds these rights on consequences for the individual and society and not on innate human tendencies. Note the similarities with Ryan and Engelen's consistent emphasis on the social aspect of property. Man's rational and social nature calls for this right, but social nature also limits the right. Property retains an ordering for the good of the human race and hence may be limited for social reasons. Inheritances, buying and selling, rates and prices, all admit of restrictions in the light of the social aspect of property. One must respect both the individual and social aspects. Such an understanding calls for a serious reform of modern ideas of private property which are infected with individualistic liberalism.[79]

Engelen's views on interest-taking changed over the years. In his earlier writings he accepts an intrinsic title to interest-taking and denies that Christians must live according to the evangelical counsels.[80] However, later he changes his opinion and now follows Albert M. Weiss and Karl von Vogelsang, two extreme medieval corporatists.[81] Here, without mentioning it, he rejects the position of Pesch, who allows for interest-taking.[82] Engelen understands interest as that which is due someone for the loan or use of money. Catholic teaching always maintained that an extrinsic title—that is, a special reason apart from the loan of the money itself, such as the risk of loss—could justify some return. But interest as such was always wrong. Older scriptural and Catholic teaching had condemned interest, but the majority now argues that in the light of modern business conditions money has changed its nature and become fruit bearing. The giver of the money has the right to the fruit, and therefore interest is intrinsically justified.

Engelen argues against this newer approach. The older teaching gives no indication that it was limited to a certain historical

period. All recognize that capitalism is a false system. How then
can interest be justified if it has come into existence because of
the suspect capitalist system? Interest in itself, and not only
excessive interest, goes against the natural purpose of society
and prevents peace, harmony, prosperity, and fair equality. Ultimately the consumers and others must pay for the interest that
goes to the capitalists. Likewise, interest provides money without
any labor for the capitalist. Our author cites favorably a rhetorical condemnation of banking and investing which compares them
to those shameful practices of money lending or opening a pawn-
broker's shop. What about big business, banking, and our whole
modern economic structure? The practical solution will present
itself in time. Could not the state in one way or other keep some
money in trust, use it in enterprises, and return the profit to the
people in the form of lower taxes? (There could be few solutions
more radical or giving more to the role of the state!) With the
collapse of capitalism and its all-devouring interest Engelen believes chaos and anarchy will not necessarily follow. Perhaps
instead there will arise a more simple and fruitful life—a society
of true cooperation and social prosperity. Although interest-
taking is unjust, the church can tolerate it for Catholics at the
present time because otherwise these Catholics, being in a minority, would suffer too great a burden in their relationship with
other people in society. The condemnation of the present is strong
and sharp, but the shape of the future remains very hazy—and
the ways of arriving at the future are not spelled out.

In general, the *Central-Blatt and Social Justice* gives great
emphasis and dignity to labor. Labor is more than a mere means
of acquiring wealth. Labor is the most fundamental and most
universal duty of every human being. Labor constitutes our humble service to God and is an important moral duty because by it
we sustain our lives. Labor also makes it possible for us to live
in society. Corresponding to this duty of labor is the right of all
to labor, especially as this is necessary for self-preservation.
Through labor one acquires what is necessary to live in this
world.[83] The emphasis on labor as a duty coheres with our auth-
or's deontological approach to ethics.

The primary ethical question concerns the organization of
workers and unions. Engelen upholds the natural right of organization for all, including workers. The historical origin of labor
organizations as self-defensive structures against the forces of
capitalism has often colored the labor movement, so that the

spirit of liberalism continues to be present in labor. It is absolutely necessary for labor to change this spirit and to become more solidaric. The ultimate goal is for cooperation and working together with capital, consumers, and all others for the social prosperity of all. The liberalistic spirit is even more apparent in organized labor's apparent unwillingness to do anything about the plight of the unskilled worker. At times labor's demands can be unjust. Until the new spirit truly pervades labor, the danger of antisocial action remains very real.

However, in the meantime no one can deny the temporary usefulness and necessity of labor's organization and united action against organized and selfish capital. Organized labor has used two generic means to achieve its goals—corporate action and indirect political activity to influence legislation and legislators. Our German-American Jesuit recognizes the danger of abuses but accepts strikes as a last resort. Boycotts are less radical than strikes, though they too can be abused. The closed shop can be tolerated as a necessary measure of self-defense. Engelen does not really develop the morality of these means at any great length but merely alludes to common, although not necessarily universally accepted, Catholic teaching.[84]

A very practical problem centered on the type of labor organization that Catholic workers should join. In the light of Engelen's insistence on an organic society with all parts working together for the good of the whole, on the need for a change of spirit and for a change of structure, and on the necessary role of the church, the conclusion would seem to be that there should be Catholic labor unions. However, the social structure in the United States was such that purely Catholic trade unions in our pluralistic society could not have been effective. Engelen discusses this question in a series involving three installments beginning in January 1913—the first series of articles he contributed to the *Central-Blatt and Social Justice.*

Engelen begins his discussion with the papal encyclical *Singulari quadam* issued in 1912 and directed to the Catholics in Germany. The general question in Germany centered on the possibility of cooperation between Catholic organizations and non-Catholic groups in social and public matters. Specifically, German Catholics were divided on whether German Catholics should form their own labor unions or should join together with Protestants in mixed Christian labor unions. The dilemma centered on the danger for Catholics in mixed Christian unions and the insufficiency and inefficiency of purely Catholic unions. The pope sees dangers in Christian unions: fear of religious indifferentism, failure to recognize the supernatural and the role of the church in social questions which are closely connected with the laws of nature and of divine revelation, fear of class hatred and strikes. In theory Catholic unions are the only ones that are absolutely safe; therefore, they are to be encouraged. However, the encyclical recognizes that in regions of religious pluralism Christian unions can be tolerated provided that certain conditions are met—the dangers are made remote; these unions adopt nothing against Catholic doctrine, teaching, laws, and authority; and Catholics who belong to these unions are also organized into Catholic labor societies presided over by the clergy as representatives of the bishop. Catholic unions are the ideal, but Christian unions are more practical for Germany as the only efficacious means of labor's organization.[85]

What about the American situation? The Pope wrote only to Germans, but his principles can apply to our situation, which is different because our unions are secular and not Christian. Catholic unions and even Christian unions are impractical in the United States. In the light of the dangers mentioned by Pope Leo XIII, Catholics cannot become members of unions founded and directed by socialists for socialist causes. Here Engelen includes not only the International Workers of the World but also the Knights of Labor. The American Federation of Labor has not adopted these pernicious principles, although there are many possible dangers involved in the AFL. At the present time Catholics can belong to the AFL. However, recent events indicate that the dangers may become so prevalent that Catholics would have to leave the organization. This fact furnishes greater impetus at the present time to form Catholic workingmen's associations to which Catholics would belong in addition to belonging to the secular unions. These Catholic groups can be structured either along union lines or independently of union lines. Engelen prefers associations involving all workers of trade or craft industries to be erected in every parish under the authority of the bishop. This type of association is preferred as being more beneficial for Catholics because it will be under the authoritative supervision of the bishops and will not be looked upon as competition to existing unions.[86]

Farmers constitute another important group or vocational class. The *Central-Blatt and Social Justice* always had a great interest in preserving the values and importance of the vocation of farmers, who well exemplify the middle-class person combining the aspects of both labor and capital in one and the same person. Engelen, especially in later writings, contrasts the peace, simplicity, and beauty of farm living with the hustling pace, dirt, and poverty of the city.[87] The Central-Verein was closely associated with the beginnings of the National Catholic Rural Life Conference founded by then Father Edwin V. O'Hara in 1923 and continued working with the conference after it came into existence.[88]

One practical problem concerned the organization to which farmers should belong. Specifically, the issue was Catholic membership in "The Farmers' Educational and Cooperative Union of America," which Engelen addressed in a three-part series in *Central-Blatt and Social Justice* in 1914. Our author evaluates this question in light of the principles laid down by Pius X in *Singulari quadam* and condemns Catholic participation in it. Membership in this organization involves a religious loss without any apparent counterbalancing of an economic gain. If the organization were strictly economic, membership for Catholics would be acceptable, but the existing organization is also social and even has some religious overtones which could be very detrimental to Catholics. Women and even sixteen-year-old girls are admitted to membership and participate in the social activities of the organization. There is a vague religious interdenominationalism about the organization which includes the roles of chaplains, Protestant prayers, and even a ritual that is vaguely Protestant. Also there is a vow of secrecy which indicates the organization is a condemned secret society. In Engelen's view the farmers' union, precisely because, unlike the AFL, it is more than an economic institution, creates insurmountable problems for Catholics.[89]

Some people at this time saw in the growing cooperative societies a substitute for the capitalist system. In general the reader might expect Engelen to be quite positive about the cooperative movement, but such is not the case. He purposely employs a somewhat negative definition of cooperatives—the cooperative society is a free defensive society which is organized by the middle or poorer classes and seeks to eliminate capitalistic oppression by means of corporate activity. The most distinctive form of producers' cooperatives is the self-governing workshop in which workers are owners who share in the profit and management. This is the worst substitute for capitalist industry because it does not do away with the evil seeking of gain, but at the same time it probably cannot possess the good of capitalistic rationalization. Engelen here does not seem to give the real reason behind his judgment of the cooperatives' inability to carry out the good of capitalistic rationalization. In his mind the reason would be the fact that the workers themselves do not have the necessary skills and abilities for management. Engelen constantly insists on the need for hierarchical ordering and structuring based on different functions in society. The self-governing workshop with its emphasis on flat equality denies the existence of different functions. More limited and flexible instances of producers' cooperatives can flourish among farmers and other small producers. These avoid some of the dangers of self-governing workshops. Cooperative banks are also a step forward. Consumer cooperatives, which often flourish in poorer areas, are helpful even if they alone will never overcome capitalism. However, Engelen agrees with Pesch in seeing these consumer cooperatives as a possible threat to the middle-class society. Private cooperation itself will never be enough; public cooperation is needed. In all these activities a renewed social spirit is necessary. Society can be saved without the cooperative system, but not without the reform of spirit.[90]

Political ethics

Although Engelen was primarily interested in the economic aspect of social ethics, he also briefly considered some questions of political ethics. As mentioned, according to Engelen human beings are by nature social and called to live in society. In keeping with his emphasis on organic unity and hierarchical structuring, Engelen in 1925 calls for a world federation of nations. Just as growth made the state necessary on a national level, so continual growth and complexity call for a world federation of nations. Finance and commerce are already international. Only such a structure will avoid the sanctions of want, war, jealousy, and uncertainty. However, Engelen strongly opposes a world empire which is based on the liberalistic desire for preeminent power and supremacy. A world federation calls for self-government on all local levels with the world federation leaving whatever is feasible and possible to the lesser states. This federation of nations, which recognizes that terms such as English, French, and German are all subordinated under "human," would be governed by an institutional council with true but limited authority. Engelen even suggests this council be presided over by or find its last source of appeal in the pope. This worldwide union cannot be realized without the Catholic Church. Our author realizes his proposal is an ideal, but this is what should exist in the future.[91]

The solidaric spirit must also be present in individual nations and states. The state is basically indifferent to a particular form of government. The important reality in the state is authority. The purpose and extent of authority, which is the most significant question, is determined by the natural law; the form of government determines only the distribution of authority (monarchy, oligarchy, republic). If the natural law is kept, the form of government makes no difference. Abuses can exist just as easily in a democracy as in a monarchy. The form of government should be left up to the individual nations. Despite this statement Engelen has his own preferences. The feudal system of the Middle Ages was a combination of republic and of monarchy which excluded the bad features of both. It was monarchic in form but democratic in spirit.[92] Engelen opposes popular or national representation and urges social representation. In other words, he objects to the notion of one person, one vote. Social representation is exemplified in the three estates in France in which nobility, clergy, and citizens met in separate sections to legislate for the good of each class and then discussed in common the effect on the common good. The French Revolution merely resulted in a parliament in which the tyranny of the majority prevailed and there was no sense of social duty. The voice of the people is not necessarily the voice of God. Recognizing the limitations of a theorist, he sketches in very hazy terms a parliament to be based on vocational or class or interest organizations which will make laws for their own group and then discuss with the other classes or vocations questions of common interest. If the economic body cannot agree, then the political body will decide.[93]

The function and limits of the state are set by the natural law. In keeping with his notion of the state as a natural society, its goal is positive. In economic affairs the state seeks the public prosperity, all the while respecting the rights and functions of individuals, of the family, and of the occupational classes or intermediary groups in society. Hierarchical ordering in an organic society requires the state to recognize the rights and competencies of all these others. These intermediary groups are to share in the authority of the state, but the state must be able to enforce cooperation among all the groups.[94] As pointed out earlier, Engelen's theory insists on cooperation between state and church and logically looks to the union of church and state, even though this is not explicitly developed.

The state has a positive obligation concerning the moral life of society. The state must never usurp the rights of others, especially parents and families, but the state should positively stimulate compliance with social duty. Every commonwealth should preserve intact its own public moral life. Everyday life must be free from temptation—especially the press, the stage, films, and amusements. Authority should also insist that Sunday be kept holy. The popularization of false moral standards should not be tolerated; the state should not abet the evil of divorce. Engelen is not a civil libertarian! Here we see once again a paternalistic understanding of the state. Such a position on the moral function of the state coheres with his general theory, since the state is regulated by the natural law and must enforce the natural law. However, for the same reason Engelen can justify the possibility of deposing rulers who go against the natural law or of disobeying authority when human laws are not in keeping with the natural law.[95]

As might be expected, our solidaristic theorist gives great importance to the home and the family, both in themselves and especially in the context of their importance for society. The natural law sees the family as the basic unit of society—the nursery of the state. Without strong homes and families there will be no strong solidaric society, for it is in the family and in the home that religious, moral, and social education occurs in the context of love and affection. With romantic rhetoric Engelen describes the terrible situation of home and family today. The home has been destroyed. The bonds which hold the family together have been severed. Children have been led away from the home by the modern amusements, especially the dance hall and the theater. Divorce has wrought great evil. Easy divorce influences people to enter marriage too lightly and causes even more marriages to break up with most regrettable consequences for the children.

The reconstruction of society depends upon the reconstruction of the family and the home. The modern danger must be combated by cultivating a moral refinement which repudiates low and injurious pleasures and appreciates the higher intellectual and moral pleasures and affections which can only exist in the home. Unfortunately the modern home is not religious; too often religion is relegated to the church on Sunday morning. A Christian atmosphere and Christian charity must pervade the home and everything that takes place in it. Here again reconstruction of society depends on reconstruction of the home and the family, both of which cannot be accomplished without religion.[96]

Engelen touches briefly on other political and social issues. There are occasional references to problems of the blacks in our society. As early as August 1909 *Central-Blatt and Social Justice* published an article on the negro problem.[97] Engelen also briefly mentions the plight of the American Indian.[98] Both Engelen and the journal refer to the dignity of women on many occasions and seek protection for women workers. However, the woman's role is primarily in terms of the home and family. The Central-Verein is against women's suffrage—a point which Engelen makes in passing. Universal women's suffrage is opposed to women's natural and historical position; it is a logical consequence of Rousseau's individualistic state. However, Engelen recognizes that the vote for women will eventually come in our country.[99] A further explanation of this position is given in the *Central-Blatt and Social Justice*. The family is an organic unit with a husband or father as head so that he alone should vote for the family.[100]

IV. Critical Ethical Assessment

There exists a generally accepted axiom that a conservative approach to Christianity in the United States goes hand in hand with an acceptance of the American economic system. Engelen, as a representative of German-American Catholic thinking especially in the first quarter of this century, disproves that axiom. There can be no doubt of the profound conservatism in Engelen's approach, but this conservatism serves precisely as the basis for a strong critique of the existing economic system in the United States. The conservative German-American Catholics were much more radical reformers than the liberal Americanizers represented by John A. Ryan, but they were also quite impractical.

Any ethical theory or approach should be both consistent and coherent, and Engelen scores high marks in these categories. The basic problem in the American society is identified as the multiple forms of liberalism—religious, moral, political, and economic—with its individualism and selfishness. American capitalism, built on such a foundation, seeks unlimited wealth and power for the individual. Competition and the survival and success of the strongest characterize such an approach. The fundamental solution to the problem is twofold—the change of heart or spirit and the change of structures. The all-important change of spirit calls for an acceptance of solidaric duty and putting aside the selfishness that makes individuals seek only their own gain at the expense of others. This basic solidaric spirit must then become incarnated in solidaric structures which enable human beings to work together for the social prosperity of all. The explanation of the problem and the general outlines of the solution are clear and consistent.

Like John A. Ryan, Engelen employed a natural-law methodology, but there are many differences in the way in which both ethicists used this methodology. Engelen, in keeping with his basic understanding that the problem is both one of spirit and structure, strongly insisted upon a traditional Catholic teaching that no one can observe the substance of the natural law for a long time without grace or a change of heart. Engelen did not often appeal explicitly to this theological understanding, but his whole system implicitly rests on it. One could say in more contemporary theological language that the fourfold aspects of liberalism require a fourfold conversion. These conversions are intimately connected, so that change in the economic and political areas will occur only if there is conversion in the moral and religious areas.

The deontological character of Engelen's natural-law ethics also contrasts with Ryan's methodology. This deontological approach coheres with what can be called an extrinsicist rather than an intrinsicist approach to natural law. The Thomistic tradition is generally interpreted to take an intrinsicist stance— something is good because it is a demand of rational human nature itself. The morally obligatory is founded on human nature, and therefore human beings should find their happiness and fulfillment in achieving the morally good. The good is a more fundamental category than right or duty. Something is a duty for the individual because it is based on human nature and is seen as the proper fulfillment of the human person. Engelen seems to make duty more fundamental than the good. Solidaric love and justice are not seen primarily as rooted in human nature itself. There appears to be an underlying tension or even a contradiction in

Engelen. A consistent natural-law approach in the Thomistic tradition is intrinsic and teleological. Engelen wants to ground the obligation in human nature but proposes what ought to be done as a duty and not as the good which is in keeping with innate natural tendencies of human nature.

Ryan, consistent with his grounding of social ethics in human nature, does not require a great change in the human being in order to live out the demands of the natural law, which are the demands of human nature itself. Engelen, with his emphasis on moral duty as so different from what is actually occurring, calls for a change of spirit on the part of individuals. In a sense Engelen's position calling for a change of spirit and Ryan's approach which does not stress the need for a change of heart are both consistent with their different understandings of natural law. I agree with Engelen on the need for a change of spirit, but such a change should primarily be grounded in the presence of sin and the need for continuing conversion in all.

Engelen does not neglect the scriptures in his approach to social ethics, but for him the scriptural teaching remains basically an adjunct to a natural law which is God's law for all human beings. Both the Old and the New Testament support and testify to the demands of the natural law. It seems that the approach should be the other way around. The natural-law approach should be integrated into the understanding of the Christian life as proposed in revelation and in the scriptures as a privileged place of revelation. Engelen too readily uses the scriptures as proof texts to back up and support what the natural law teaches.

Engelen explicitly recognizes the deductive character of his natural-law methodology. By definition such an approach tends to be abstract and universal. He assumes that there can be one approach which is true for the entire world. Such a methodology does not give enough importance to historical and cultural differences. The plan proposed by Engelen has been called romantic and utopian precisely because it seems so far removed from our actual world. A more inductive methodology would avoid such a problem.

Paradoxically, Engelen's deductive methodology, which can be correctly criticized for being too abstract and universal, in reality is not as abstract and universal as he might claim. Natural-law proponents have often failed to recognize that human reason cannot remain unaffected by historical, cultural, and personal particularities. Engelen's deductive reasoning arrives at a conclusion very similar to the historical realities of the Middle Ages. At the very minimum such an appreciation for the medieval world greatly influences his reasoning. His deductive natural law also extols the virtues of middle-class society composed of thrifty artisans and tradespersons, which just happened to be part of the background out of which Engelen and the German-American Catholics came. Human reason is never as abstract and universal as its supporters claim. One can constantly employ some ideological suspicion about the use and abuse of reason.

On the basis of deductive reasoning Engelen arrives at an organic understanding of society with a hierarchical ordering. Such a view stands opposed to the false individualism and liberalism of much of the modern world. However, it seems that Engelen goes too far to the other extreme and does not give enough importance to the freedom, equality, and participation of all in society. His is a paternalistic and static view of society. Everything is so ordered that there is no room for change or growth. The historical model of the Middle Ages well illustrates the paternalistic and static view of society. The serfs could never change their lot, but the rulers in obedience to the natural law were to provide for them.

Engelen, like Ryan and the whole Catholic tradition, recognized the importance of the principle of subsidiarity even though he did not use the name as such. Smaller structures and organizations should be allowed to do all they can on their own level, and the more universal structures and especially the state should intervene only to help the others and not to destroy them or to take over their functions. Engelen, unlike Ryan, insisted on carrying out the principle of subsidiarity and constantly called for intermediary structures and government. His understanding of such structures was more deductive than grass roots, but he correctly insisted that there can be no true social reform without such structures.

Engelen, like Ryan and the Catholic natural-law approaches of the time, has failed to incorporate the realities of redemption and sin into his ethics. The ethical significance of Jesus is reduced to his giving human beings the possibility and the power to observe the natural law. As mentioned, his insistence on the need for a change of spirit could have been more explicitly grounded in the reality of sin and redemption. Once the solidaric spirit does exist, Engelen takes no account of the continuing presense of sin. He assumes that everyone will obey the social duty of the natural law and all will be well. If the natural law is observed, the precise form of government or of authority makes no difference. However, many have proposed democracy as the best form of government because it allows for participation of all in deciding their fate and also because it realistically deals with the reality of human weakness. The division of powers between executive, legislative, and judicial branches of government insures a system of checks and balances which tries to limit the influences of sinful absolutism and of temptations to usurp power.

One important problem, especially from the practical perspective, concerns the implementation of this vision. How is this reform to be brought about? Here Engelen was quite vague. Ryan the practical reformer called for immediate help for the situation, but perhaps his emphasis on short-term change and reform obscured his vision to the need for long-term reform. However, Engelen and the German-American Catholics suffer from the opposite approach. They held out a vision of what the solidaric society should be, but they were quite vague in the details of that plan and even more vague in proposing how such a vision could even become a reality in the United States in the twentieth century.

One might rightly conclude that Engelen was an alienated, romantic utopian. The vision proposed by the German-American Catholics had no chance of ever becoming a reality in the modern world. By their isolation from the rest of American society in general and from other Catholic Americans, their position had little or no real influence outside their own narrow circle. With the death of Kenkel this social vision no longer continued, even among the remnants of the German-American Catholics. However, they deserve great praise for their willingness to criticize the American ethos and its problems. In a very creative way they combined their Catholicity, their conservatism, and their critique of American society. By insisting that social reform involves both a change of heart and a change of structures, they made a lasting contribution to the ongoing dialogue about Christian social ethics in the United States.

4. THE CATHOLIC WORKER
AND PAUL HANLY FURFEY

I. Background

The Catholic Worker has been a small but very significant movement within American Catholicism since its beginning in 1933. The movement in theory and in practice has espoused a radical type of social ethics based on the gospel and thereby distinguishes itself from the approaches already studied. There have been other instances of radical Catholicism in the United States, but none has rivaled the importance of the Catholic Worker movement begun by Peter Maurin and Dorothy Day in 1933.[1]

While sharing much in common, the two founders came from quite disparate backgrounds. Peter Maurin was born of French peasant parents in 1877, was educated by the Christian Brothers, and later joined the brothers. However, he left religious life and became involved in the Sillon, a decentralist Catholic movement in France stressing the role of the church in the reform of society and opposing the rising spirit of nationalism and of militarism. He then left France for Canada, held various jobs, traveled widely from place to place, and apparently had some type of religious experience in the middle 1920s which profoundly influenced his future life. Peter's ideas came from a number of different sources in addition to the thought of the Sillon. He read widely and incorporated into his radical Christian thought a number of other ideas: the anarchism of Peter Kropotkin, the antibourgeois spirit of Leon Bloy, the personalism of Emmanuel Mounier, and the distributist philosophy of Hilaire Belloc and Eric Gill.[2]

Dorothy Day was born in Brooklyn in 1897 but frequently moved as her father acquired jobs in different places in the field of journalism. She, too, read widely as a youngster during a somewhat sheltered childhood and was fascinated with the Russian writers, including Kropotkin, Tolstoy, and Dostoyevsky. She attended college for two years, but there she became preoccupied with the problems of poverty and the poor class and joined the campus socialist club. She then moved to New York, worked for socialist and communist papers, and associated with radicals in the support of such causes as the International Workers of the World. In the 1920s Dorothy Day entered a common-law marriage with anarchist Forster Batterham and had a daughter Tamar in 1927. During this period she became attracted to Roman Catholicism, had her daughter baptized in the Catholic Church, and finally was baptized herself. She was attracted by much in Roman Catholicism but still yearned for active involvement in the cause of the poor. In December 1932 George Shuster of *Commonweal* magazine put Peter Maurin into contact with Dorothy Day. After frequent indoctrinations from Peter, whom she always called the founder of the movement, the Catholic Worker movement came into existence. Dorothy Day remained the central figure in the movement until her death in 1980.[3]

The Worker program is threefold. First comes the clarification of thought through the paper *The Catholic Worker,* which was first published in May 1933, and through roundtable discussions. Their program is based on a gospel radicalism and calls for a heroic life of love exercised through the corporal works of mercy with particular emphasis on voluntary poverty. The paper strongly opposes the present economic order with its emphasis on profit, wealth, and materialism and insists on a personalism stressing the basic equality of all. They oppose nationalism, militarism, race discrimination, and the depersonalization of modern society through coercive government and manipulation. Their personalism takes more concrete form in a Christian utopian communism or an anarchism in which there would be no coercive government. In short, the Catholic Worker wants a personal and communitarian revolution.

A second part of their program calls for houses of hospitality in Catholic parishes, but in reality these houses of hospitality came into existence only in the Worker houses themselves in which the poor and the derelict are fed, clothed, and housed. This apostolate has continued and is the best known work associated with Catholic Worker houses throughout North America.

The third part of the program advocates farming communes where scholars and workers would work and study together on the land in self-sufficient and independent communities. As a matter of fact, the farming communes have never worked and have been a constant source of problems for the Catholic Worker movement.[4]

In keeping with its own radical personalism the Catholic Worker has resisted any attempt to become an organization. It is a movement. Other houses have sprung up throughout the country in addition to the New York house, but there is no formal organization or structure of any kind. The same personalism and fear of manipulation guide the attitude of the Worker people toward the poor, who are never proselytized or forced in any way to accept the Worker program.

In attempting to discuss the theological and ethical theory behind the Catholic Worker there are a number of problems. Neither Dorothy Day nor Peter Maurin was a theologian or an ethicist. Although Peter Maurin read widely and was constantly interested in the clarification of thought, he wrote very little. His *Easy Essays*, which are free-verse essays explaining his thought in a lively and pithy way, were originally published in the paper and later collected in a book.[5] Dorothy Day wrote much, but she was primarily a journalist.[6] Even the paper is not a good source for theory as such because of its very nature as a vehicle of propaganda.

There were also some significant differences of approach between Dorothy Day and Peter Maurin, reflecting their different backgrounds and interests. Especially in the 1930s the paper defended and supported striking unionists, which continued to be a great interest on the part of Day. Maurin, on the other hand, often said that "Strikes don't strike me," because he was fearful that a defense of labor at that time merely perpetuated the present unjust system which must ultimately disappear. Although Peter Maurin was a pacifist, he did not make it as central to the movement as Dorothy Day did, especially in the light of the later circumstances of war, atomic bombs, conscription, and civilian defense drills. Maurin put heavy stress on the farming communes and the impersonalization of the modern world and its work. Through farming communes a new society could be built.

Later editors of the paper added their own emphases, while sharing the basic vision of Dorothy Day. Robert Ludlow in the 1950s concentrated on pacifism, anarchy, and psychiatry, often employing a somewhat deep and theoretical approach which had not been seen previously in the paper.[7] Ammon Hennacy, with his background of secular radicalism, brought a strong pacifism to the paper and encouraged picketing, fasting, and other public signs of protest.[8] In the 1960s Catholic peace activists found the Worker a congenial home as Tom Cornell and others associated with the Worker founded the Catholic Peace Fellowship.[9] The wrong impression should not be given, for there is a basic consistency to the positions taken by the Catholic Worker, but there have been some divergent emphases at different times. However, neither Dorothy Day, Peter Maurin, nor the other editors and authors who contributed to the paper were primarily involved in a systematic and theoretical explanation of their position on the level of Christian social ethics.

The closest thing to a systematic and theoretical development of the radical Catholic approach personified in the Catholic Worker viewpoint can be found in the writings of Paul Hanly Furfey. In his first book on radical Catholicism written in 1936, Furfey makes no claim to originality. His purpose is to express systematically the ideals of the Christian social life found in the New Testament and represented by the thought and action of some movements such as the Catholic Worker. One of the functions of the scholar, especially in the Middle Ages, was to express with clarity and precision the ideas of the group. Such is the purpose Furfey sets for himself in *Fire on the Earth*.[10] Our study will concentrate on Furfey's approach to radical Catholicism.

Furfey brought his own particular interests and background to his exposition of radical Catholicism. He has spent his life as a scholar in the field of sociology at The Catholic University of America. His many writings in the areas of social Catholicism and sociology show the breadth of his scholarly interest. In addition to over twenty books and monographs, he has published articles in a wide variety of scholarly journals in the areas of art, scripture, theology, philosophy, psychology, psychiatry, education, and sociology.[11] Furfey has described his own growth in the 1930s as a change from Catholic liberalism to Catholic radicalism, brought about by a number of factors, especially his relationship with Dorothy Day and Peter Maurin in the early stages of the Catholic Worker movement.[12]

Furfey was ordained a priest in 1922, received a doctorate in sociology from Catholic University in 1926, and spent his entire life as a sociologist teaching and doing research at that university. Catholic liberalism believed social science could achieve the ideal society. Look at the progress made by the physical sciences, especially biology and medicine. The same kind of progress can be brought about through the social sciences. Furfey the sociologist developed and used quantitative tools for measuring development in youth and also a more qualitative case study approach. His publications were numerous and were well received by social scientists even before 1930.[13] During the year 1932 spent in Germany studying medicine, he began to doubt that the social sciences could ever achieve the same results as medicine. Furfey also became very interested in the deeper personal realities found in music and the arts. He was searching for something—and found it upon meeting Dorothy Day in 1934. The answer was simple. Take the New Testament literally; use supernatural and not natural means to achieve the social ideal. Furfey employed his scholarship to further this understanding. His significant book publications during this period included what might be called his early trilogy on radical Catholicism—*Fire on the Earth* (1936), *Three Theories of Society* (1937), *The Mystery of Iniquity* (1944). In addition, at the same period of time he also wrote *This Way to Heaven* (1939) and *A History of Social Thought* (1942). Two books in the late 1960s, *The Respectable Murderers* (1966) and *The Morality Gap* (1969), continued to develop the same basic ideas. During this entire time Furfey also continued his theoretical and empirical sociological work dealing with such questions as the elderly, the deaf, and especially the subculture of the Washington ghetto. In 1978 Furfey, at age 82, published *Love and the Urban Ghetto,* in which he explicitly changed his own position and moved away from Christian radicalism to embrace what he called a Christian revolutionism.

For the most part our concern is the Catholic radicalism proposed by Furfey, especially in his writings in the 1930s and early 1940s, but his change will also be discussed. It should also be recalled that Furfey not only was a theorist of American Catholic radicalism but also was personally involved in aspects of the movement. In addition to his association with the Catholic Worker movement, he was also friendly with the Baroness Catherine de Heuck and her Friendship House movement. Furfey, together with some of his colleagues, lived a life of voluntary poverty and worked with the poor in the Washington ghetto for a number of years. In 1968 he established the Emmaus House as a center for the Catholic antiwar movement in the Washington area.

II. Furfey's Catholic Radicalism

To understand Furfey's theory it is helpful to consider three presuppositions of his thinking on Catholic radicalism—a radical interpretation of traditional Catholic philosophy and theology, a literal interpretation of the New Testament, a supernatural sociology. First, his theology and philosophy are based on the perennial philosophy and the Catholic theology as found in the textbooks of the day, but with a creative and radical interpretation. The supernatural, grace with its distinctions and kinds, and merit are all used by him in systematically explaining Catholic radicalism. At the same time, however, Furfey is ahead of many of his contemporaries in his use of the scriptures, the liturgy, and the social aspect of traditional Catholic theology. In philosophy Furfey follows the Neo-Scholasticism of the times, and in his own position he gives heavy emphasis to the epistemological, metaphysical, and ontological bases of his thought.

The scholastic background of his thinking is well illustrated in his discussion of three theories of society. Our author employs a teleological approach according to which the essential reality in society is the end toward which all members should strive. A positivistic society, which seems to be the understanding of society held by many contemporaries, believes in success as its ideal. Such an approach is neither just nor deeply satisfactory. But the fundamental error is of the intellectual order—a mistake about the ontological ideal of society. The important question is to know the reality on which society should be based.[14]

A second possibility is the noetic society, based on a deeper knowledge and truth about human existence which is available to the human intellect. For Furfey the noetic society is based on the natural law. In Thomistic epistemology Furfey distinguishes two ways of knowing—deduction and noesis, which is the immediate apprehension of truths. We are all familiar with the flash of insight by which we grasp a truth but are unable to express or formulate it very well. In a noetic society the dominant majority of citizens regulate their personal lives and the life of society on the deep truths derived through noesis about the meaning of life and the natural law. However, historically speaking, there has never been such a noetic society existing on a large scale or for an extended period of time. A noetic society in practice is blocked because the majority of citizens cannot sustain the mental labor necessary for noesis, which is the type of knowing that human beings share with the angels. The will of the individual is weakened by the brute force of human passion, which we share with the animals, so that we are unable to sustain a commitment to the more subtle pleasures of the soul. Thus human nature itself shows its duality—a capacity for knowing that is shared with the angels and also the carnal passion which we share with the animals. The noetic society remains an impossibility for human beings within this world. Our only hope is for a savior.[15]

The only alternative is a pistic society founded on faith in the divinely revealed truth. Faith accepts the truth of God's revelation to human beings on the authority of God revealing. The noetic individual examines the motives of credibility—the miracles of Jesus, the prophesies, the beauty of Jesus' teaching, the heroism of the saints—and on the basis of noesis arrives at certitude that the Christian revelation is true. The Catholic Church can be shown to be the one, true Christian church on the basis of the four marks of the church found in the scriptures—one, holy, catholic, and apostolic. The will is also involved in faith, and here our author is quick to point out the supernatural aspect of faith. The supernatural aspect, which stresses the gratuitousness of faith, is employed primarily to show that through faith we gain an insight into reality far beyond that which is available to human noesis on its own. Faith is something absolutely supernatural to which we created or creatable beings have no right. A fully satisfactory human society must be founded on the secure foundation of a deep and penetrating knowledge of reality. Such is the basis for the pistic society, and whoever has this knowledge should never again rely on only human reason and human means which are totally eclipsed by the supernatural knowledge and means available to the Christian.[16]

Such an approach embodies the Roman Catholic theological and philosophical understanding current in that day with its emphasis on ontology, epistemology, and the fact that reason itself is able to prove the credibility of faith. At the same time some creativity and differences are manifest in Furfey's insistence on noesis. Most manuals of philosophy and theology forgot about noesis in their insistence on discursive reasoning, deduction, and the syllogism. But also notice the radical import of Furfey's approach. The pistic society with its supernatural knowledge and supernatural means is quite different from and even radically opposed to the generally accepted positivistic society with its success ideal.

Furfey's ecclesiology reflects the triumphalistic and self-confident Catholic understanding of his day. The Catholic Church is the one true church of Jesus Christ. For Furfey grace and the supernatural are, for all practical purposes, identified with the Catholic Church. Heretics (Christians who do not profess the Catholic faith) and infidels can be saved only on the basis of the fact that their ignorance of the true faith is invincible. The kingdom of God is identified with the Catholic Church but not quite coterminous with it.[17] There are some Catholics who do not have faith and grace, and there are some outside the visible church who do have charity, but the Catholic Church is the social body which preserves and propagates the faith.[18] Actually the sharp distinction in ecclesiology should not be between the layman and the priest, but between the Catholic and the non-Catholic. All Catholics—laymen, priests, and religious—should form a homogeneous group definitely distinguished by their vocation to sanctity from the entire non-Catholic world.[19] Although Furfey admits that the clerical and religious state is higher than the lay state, in keeping with the Catholic theology of the time, he nonetheless creatively anticipates the Second Vatican Council in maintaining the universal vocation of all Catholics to perfection. Later, in the context of the Second Vatican Council, in his preface to *The Morality Gap* (1969) Furfey abandons the triumphalistic ecclesiology of his earlier years and claims that his book describes the Christian social action rather than specifically Catholic social action. In fact, practically everything in the book could be restated also in Jewish terminology.[20] Furfey, however, uses his triumphalistic ecclesiology to call for a radical social ethics distinguishing Catholics from all others.

The Furfey of the 1930s and 1940s also expresses an unqualified acceptance of the various teachings of the church, including the authoritative utterances of the popes and the decisions of the Roman congregations. He even claims that one accepts the whole social doctrine of the church by an act of faith, and this involves the first step in establishing a pistic society.[21] One must accept the whole social doctrine of the church without claiming the privilege of reviewing it.[22] However, again in the late 1960s there is a change in his ecclesiology. Furfey personally supported the priests of Washington who in 1968 disagreed with the papal teaching always condemning artificial contraception.

In addition to his insistence on the universal vocation of all the baptized to follow the call to perfection, Furfey introduces some other somewhat advanced ideas into his ecclesiology. In *Fire on the Earth* he highlights the notion of the church as the Mystical Body of Christ—years before the encyclical of Pope Pius XII on this subject. Such an understanding of the church enables him to recognize the social character of the church and its mission to society and also to stress the important role of the laity in the church.[23] His emphasis on the importance and the role of the liturgy is consonant with his understanding of the church as the Mystical Body of Christ. There were few Catholics at the time who developed this connection between the liturgy and the social apostolate.[24]

No attempt has been made to treat all aspects of Furfey's philosophy, theology, and ecclesiology or even to exhaust the few areas touched upon in this section. The aim has been to illustrate the thesis that Furfey employed the traditional teaching of the manuals of Catholic theology, sometimes being more creative and advanced than his contemporaries, but, above all, he used this theology to support a Catholic radicalism in social ethics.

The second presupposition of Furfey's methodology clearly differentiates him from traditional Catholic approaches. Furfey's radicalism is based on the scriptures and especially the moral teaching of the New Testament and not on the natural law. Such an emphasis follows from what has been said thus far about Furfey's theology and will be even more apparent in developing his principles and strategies. The insistence on faith, grace, and the supernatural means that truly Catholic social action must find its principles and guidance in divine revelation and especially in the New Testament. Furfey constantly appeals to the teaching and example of Jesus as primary for the Christian understanding. Unlike Ryan, the German-Americans, and most of the Catholic tradition, Furfey bases his social ethics not on reason and the natural law but on faith and the scriptures. Catholic radicalism finds its ideal in divine revelation especially as preached by Jesus Christ and developed in detail by the great doctors of the church.[25] All of Furfey's radical writings insist on the centrality of the scriptures as the source for discovering how Christians should act.

In addition, Furfey insists on a literal interpretation of the scriptures and especially the New Testament. His writings constantly appeal to the Sermon on the Mount, the last judgment scene in Matthew 25, the commandment of love and the parable of the Good Samaritan, and the condemnation of the rich, especially the difficulty for a rich person to enter into the kingdom of heaven. These are the Lord's sayings, and they are not to be watered down. We must have the courage to follow Jesus and even to suffer as he did.[26]

In his insistence on the literal acceptance of the New Testament Furfey shows little or no appreciation of biblical hermeneutics and of the eschatological influence present in the New Testament. However, in treating Saint Paul's teaching on slavery he admits that Paul did not push for the freedom of slaves at that time. Paul accepted the moderate approach because the freedom of the slaves was then impractical and agitation for change would have done more harm than good.[27] However, Furfey never applies that or a similar hermeneutic to any of the texts which support his radical approach.

In keeping with his insistence on the scriptures and on a literal interpretation of the New Testament, Furfey himself conducted intense linguistic studies to determine the precise meaning of three important words on which his approach was based— "riches," "worker," and "the mystery of lawlessness or iniquity." In condemning riches Jesus is condemning, not the physical possession of riches, but the bourgeois attitude with its own emphasis on money and profit because of which the bourgeois do not have the necessary detachment to enter the kingdom of heaven.[28] Jesus is described as a worker, and this means one who supports one's self through a particular craft and does not involve absolute poverty or destitution.[29] According to the Second Letter to the Thessolonians (2:7) the mystery of lawlessness is at work. Furfey examines the different theories proposed in the course of time and then expresses as his own that the mystery of iniquity means the malign plan of Satan which is now operating in the world to frustrate the redemptive work of Christ. It is a revealed secret, for even though it is not fully known, the reality can be discovered as working in the world.[30] The scholarly nature of these articles is attested by the fact that all were published in the academic journal for Catholic biblical studies in the United States. Furfey even wrote scholarly articles on the proper way to do the linguistic analysis which he himself then employed in these articles.[31] Note that Furfey's approach to the scriptures was based on linguistics rather than hermeneutics.

A third presupposition of Furfey's radical Catholicism is his understanding of sociology. One constant in Furfey's life has been his work as a sociologist, for he has been teaching and publishing in this field for more than fifty years. The changes in Furfey's approach to social Catholicism have necessarily involved changes in his understanding of sociology. Our author identifies the first stage in his thinking as a period of liberalism or of the scientific approach. The Catholic University sociologist describes his early perspective as almost Comtean—the salvation of the world through science. The physical sciences have given us great control over our material world. The behavioral sciences through exact measurements and mathematical analysis can bring the same kind of scientific rigor and the same kind of results to the study of human behavior. However, doubts began to arise about the ability of science to solve the human ills of society.[32]

Christian radicalism proclaims that only through supernatural means can the ills of society be overcome. In this period Furfey calls for a supernatural or Catholic sociology as being quite distinct from positivistic sociology. The first chapter in *Fire on the Earth* is entitled "Supernatural Sociology" and insists on the need to use supernatural means. Faith, not human means, gives the victory that overcomes the world.

In *The Mystery of Iniquity* Furfey strongly opposes those Catholics who adopt a conformist sociology.[33] Sociology is a systematic study of society, attempting to arrive at broad generalizations which will apply to human group activities. According to Comte, modern sociology has passed through a theological or supernatural stage as well as a metaphysical stage before realizing itself as a positivistic science like the natural sciences of physics or chemistry. On the basis of observing, measuring, and analyzing the data, preferably by mathematical methods, the sociologist can arrive at certain generalizations or laws. Furfey now strongly rejects such an approach, for the data or matter of social sciences is not the same as the matter of physics. The positivist forgets that human acts involve free will, morality, and a supernatural aspect which is the most important of all. Conformist Catholic sociologists thus forget what is the most important and most distinctive aspect in their understanding of human acts in society.

Furfey, in his understanding of Catholic sociology, wants to avoid the two extremes of giving no importance to empirical sociology or of reducing Catholic sociology merely to the empirical. Catholic sociology is the study of human society by the method of observation and experience in the light of principles accepted from philosophy and theology. The Catholic sociologist uses the postulates of philosophy and theology, as accepted from these sciences, along with the empirical data, which are the proper domain of sociology. It is legitimate for a science to accept postulates from other sciences, so the Catholic sociologist is not unscientific. Catholic sociologists will share a great deal with other sociologists because of the common recognition of the empirical level, but the Catholic can never forget what is distinctive and of much more ultimate importance.

Furfey expresses this understanding of Catholic sociology in different ways. For Catholic sociology the major of the syllogistic argument comes from revelation or the teaching of the church, the minor comes from empirical sociology, and a resulting theological conclusion is reached which exceeds the limits of empirical sociology itself and of revelation taken alone.[34] Elsewhere he distinguishes between scientific sociology which works only on the level of the empirical, theoretical sociology which accepts philosophical postulates, and supernatural sociology which incorporates theological postulates.[35] Catholic sociology, while recognizing overlap with empirical sociology, can never deny what is most distinctive and important—the supernatural. Just as Christ was no conformist, so too Catholic sociology should not be conformist.

In the 1950s, with the publication of *The Scope and Method of Sociology,* Furfey no longer uses the terms supernatual or Catholic sociology. Has Furfey of the 1950s become a conformist sociologist? No, but his writings now show a change of terminology and perhaps some change of emphasis. "Sociology" is now restricted to the narrow sense of empirical sociology. Note that empirical science differs from positivism, which itself is a supraempirical philosophy. Furfey still claims a place for supraempirical postulates from philosophy and theology, but they always must be distinguished from the empirical as such. Furfey thus still argues for an integration of the triad of theology or faith, philosophy, and the empirical, but sociology is more clearly distinguished from faith and philosophy.[36] Also in the 1950s and 1960s Furfey himself became involved in much more empirical

sociological work dealing with the elderly, the deaf, poverty, and
the black ghetto. Whatever the ultimate significance of Furfey's
approach to sociological theory and practice in the 1950s, his radical Catholicism is best seen in connection with his insistence on
supernatural or Catholic sociology in his early trilogy.

Kingdom of God versus kingdom of satan

Fire on the Earth, Furfey's first book on radical Catholicism,
describes his approach as supernatural sociology. Grace is absolutely supernatural in the sense of exceeding what is due to the
whole of created or creatable nature. The person who is justified
has attained a new level of existence—the supernatural level of
grace—and the Holy Spirit dwells within one's heart. In *Three
Theories of Society* Furfey develops his fundamental concept in
terms of a pistic society. The Catholic, through revelation and
grace, knows the truths of the supernatural order and has a
strengthened will to live in accord with them. In the light of this
understanding it is unfortunate that Catholic social action has
forgotten these means and uses only natural means. There is no
doubt that Catholics, especially in the United States, have settled
for mediocrity and a moderate approach to social action. We
have professional social workers who are dedicated and use the
latest methods. Our banquets for charity obtain large sums of
money. We have a marvelously efficient organization which tries
to serve the needs of all. But we must be more than a little
ashamed when we compare our social action with the methods of
the saints. Too often Catholics have settled for mediocrity and
have forgotten that we are called to extremism.[37]

Furfey insists that all Catholics are called to holiness. The
position of the moderate, who is content to avoid sin, is not only
false in theory but dangerous in practice, for one cannot be willing to involve oneself in deliberate venial sin for a long time without sooner or later falling into mortal sin.[38] Furfey frequently
distinguishes between two moral codes—the authentic code of
Christian morality based on the New Testament ideal and the
popular code.[39] Too often we have given into social pressure and
have striven to be acceptable and respectable. Throughout his
writings Furfey employs the word respectable in an ironic and
pejorative sense to indicate those who timidly go along with the
popular code and the existing mores of society.[40]

Jesus is our example, and he showed a great heroism in his own life. He stood up to the respectable people in his society and opposed them—the rich, the influential, the Pharisees, and the Scribes. He dared to be different—and was put to death because of it. By appealing to Jesus and to the example of the saints, Furfey calls all Catholics to an extreme and radical approach, but he realistically recognizes that not all will be able to live in accord with this ideal.[41] Despite the fact that Christ and the saints showed heroism, we are afraid to be called radicals or extremists. If we do not live up to this heroic standard, let us not borrow excuses in a hypocritical manner from the respectable and acceptable people in our society, but rather let us humbly acknowledge our weakness and beg for the grace that we too might have a spark of that heroism that makes saints.[42]

Furfey insists on a radical incompatibility between the gospel and the accepted mores of society. If Christ had followed the dictates of prudence, he would have been born into a family of moderate wealth with good connections. He would have studied in all the proper places and would have been on a first name basis with all the influential people in the society. But Christ was no conformist. He identified himself with the disenfranchised poor and antagonized all the privileged classes. He was a social agitator, although in a very different way from the modern leftist radicals. Remember that the wealthy and influential groups of the time put Christ to death precisely because he was a social agitator.[43]

This radical incompatibility between the Catholics and the world in which they live is explained in theological terms. Either one lives on the supernatural level or one rejects the supernatural and grace and lives under the power of sin. Catholic teaching holds that without grace human beings cannot even observe the natural law for a long time. Catholics have both the teaching of revelation to give their intellects the true knowledge of what should be done and the help of grace to enable the will to carry out these beliefs. Thus the opposition experienced in the Christian life and exemplified in the life of Jesus is theologically grounded in the opposition between grace and sin.

Furfey further explains this opposition in terms of the struggle between the kingdom of God and the world. The world is used in the biblical sense as the totality of those who refuse to accept God's revelation and to obey God's law. The world is not simply a conglomeration of forces opposed to Jesus, but there is an underlying unity founded on Satan himself. The devil gives direction and unity to all these forces. Furfey entitles one of his books *The Mystery of Iniquity*, which is derived from St. Paul's usage in 2 Thessolonians—"The mystery of iniquity is already at work." The Catholic looking at the social problem sees something much deeper than the nonbelieving social scientist. The problems are not brought about only by natural causes. The real cause is much more radical—the devil himself, Satan. Satan thus unifies and organizes the assault against the kingdom of God so that one can truly speak of the kingdom of Satan or even of the Mystical Body of Satan. The opposition is clear—the kingdom of God or the Mystical Body of Christ against the kingdom of Satan or the Mystical Body of Satan. Furfey's theological analysis not only spells out the radical incompatibility between the believers in the gospel and the world but also stresses the social aspect of this struggle.[44] Phrased in another way, the church constitutes a pistic society within the larger positivistic society of the modern world.[45]

In general Furfey stresses the radical incompatibility between the kingdom of God and the kingdom of Satan, between the pistic society and the positivistic society, between grace and sin. However, even Furfey at times qualifies this incompatibility and recognizes that it is not total. The world in which we live is not totally identified with the kingdom of Satan, with the positivistic society, and with sin.

In describing our contemporary American society Furfey paints a picture which is not completely negative. Our American state is better than some totalitarian states, but there are still many deep problems existing in our country. Although Catholics enjoy religious liberty, religious indifferentism reigns. The rich and the dominant classes enjoy a privileged position in our legislatures and courts, so that the state aids the preservation of an unjust economic order. The Catholic in the United States is not threatened with martyrdom or persecution. However, in a million subtle ways our society brings pressure to bear on true Catholics. Sometimes one wonders what is more inimical to true Catholicism—the frank hatred of admitted enemies or the blandishments of those who pose as friends. *Fire on the Earth* depicts the helpfulness of the state to the kingdom of God as far from perfect under present-day conditions. However, he explicitly acknowledges that the evil alliance of state and society with the kingdom of evil is never complete. In *Three Theories of Society* Furfey again qualifies somewhat the absolute incompatibilities. Yet, in our society positivism is much more honored than faith. All in all it would not be very far from wrong to say that the world in which we live constitutes a positivistic society.[46]

Theoretically Furfey has a problem because the relationship between supernature and nature is not the same as the relationship between the kingdom of God and the kingdom of Satan. Furfey himself admits that the supernatural-natural distinction is not one of incompatibility and opposition but rather the difference between the minimum standard and the maximum, the moderate and the extreme.[47] Anyone familiar with the Catholic tradition knows that the relationship between the supernatural and the natural is not that of incompatibility. Grace does not destroy nature but builds on it. Furfey's Catholic theology prevents his seeing all reality in terms of the opposition between grace and sin.

Furfey's writings in the 1960s indicate a change whereby he modifies both his insistence on incompatibility between our society and the pistic society and his radicalism. In *The Respectable Murderers* (1966) Furfey no longer distinguishes between the kingdom of God and the kingdom of Satan, the pistic and the positivistic society. Now the distinction is between a moral society and a paramoral society. A paramoral society is not a totally corrupt or evil society but a sick society in which at least a few conspicuous mores are immoral.[48] Not everything in such a society is evil, but sooner or later the Christian will inevitably be asked to follow certain mores which contradict Christian love.[49] Thus even from the beginning, but more so in the 1960s, there is a tension in Furfey concerning the absolute incompatibility between the present society and a Christian society.

Personalist action

Furfey gives the name "personalist action" to the supernatural way in which Catholics should act. Personalist action is grounded in the life of grace in the Catholic. Through grace we now share in the new life of Christ. Furfey was ahead of his time by insisting on the social character of grace. The divine life vivifies not only the individual soul but also the group of all those who are baptized in the church. This social aspect is perhaps best expressed in the similitude of the Mystical Body. According to Saint Paul's letter to the Romans we are one body in Christ (12:5).

God has made Christ head over all the church which is his body. The word "mystical" is used in contradistinction not to real but to physical and visible. Grace in the mystical body in a very real way unites us with Christ as head and with one another. Beyond the evident and visible influence of good or bad example, we can merit grace for one another in the sense that God by his friendship with us is moved to grant the graces which we wish to obtain for our neighbor (merit *de congruo* as distinguished from merit *de condigno*). We cannot add anything new to the superabundant merits of Christ, but we can help in their distribution. A priest in Brazil can be helped by a peasant girl in Belgium who makes a good communion.[50]

Official hierarchical Catholic teaching did not develop the concept of the Mystical Body until 1943, but Furfey creatively uses the somewhat new concept in Catholic thought to emphasize the social dimension of grace and of the Catholic life in general. Our author firmly insists on the social aspect of heaven, which is often seen only in individualistic terms as the fulfillment for the individual soul. Heaven is not only an aggregation of saved individual souls; it is a beatific society—the fellowship of the kingdom, the New Jerusalem. We understand better the pistic society and its social nature on earth when we see it in the light of its consummation in heaven.[51]

The invisible aspect of grace and of the Mystical Body adds an important dimension to Furfey's thought. This aspect clearly differentiates personalist supernatural theory from typical contemporary social thought.[52] Our system emphasizes the invisible rather than the visible, internal rightness rather than external effects, the next world and not just the present world. The saints talked little about efficiency. Our approach will probably have only a minor effect on contemporary affairs. The cross will always be a part of Catholic life. But in the long run this is the only approach which offers the human person the fullness of self-realization and the possibility of elaborating even now a practical social alternative in which Christians would live according to the spiritual and corporal works of mercy and thus constitute a perfect economic microcosm as an oasis within our present materialistic world.[53]

Grace, which incorporates us into the Mystical Body of Christ, is the secret of success for a pistic society in a positivistic world; and the greatest source of grace is the Mass. The Mass is the supreme social act which the Mystical Body performs. The Mass is action, not just something to be said or heard. And it is social action. Furfey associated himself with some of the early pioneers of the liturgical movement in the United States by insisting on the active involvement and participation of all in the Eucharist and also by seeing the intimate connection between the Mass and personalist social action. Those who actively participate in the Mass (Furfey recommended that all of the faithful join in the responses to the priest in a *missa recitativa)* must in their daily lives share the same love of God and love of neighbor which characterized the life and the sacrifice of Christ.[54]

The Mass is the chief means of grace, but it is not the only one. In keeping with the spiritual writers generally accepted at that time, the Catholic University sociologist recognizes the importance of the other sacraments and of liturgical prayer. Private prayer is also very significant and can take the form of vocal prayer, meditation, affective prayer, and contemplation. By prayer we gain intimacy with God, spiritual insight for our intellect, and the strengthening of our will to live out the Christian life. Without prayer and renunciation the Catholic will too readily conform to the spirit of the times, the social mores which characterize positivistic society within which we live.[55]

Our author constantly reiterates the significance of the example of the saints. They have lived in the world with heroic virtue and are models for all of us who are called to abandon mediocrity and accept the extremism of the Cross. He frequently cites the examples of the contemporary saints and calls special attention to the book of his student and colleague Mary Elizabeth Walsh, *The Saints and Social Work*.[56] In this book Walsh describes the lives of modern saints and *beati* who devoted their lives to the care of the poor. The saints are often mocked because they appear foolish and imprudent to human eyes. However, the saints have come to know Christ and in following him have been mocked as was their master. But theirs is a true supernatural prudence, for they know that "the foolishness of God is wiser than men, and the weakness of God is stronger than men."[57]

Personalist action within the pistic society above all consists in living out Christian charity. Charity involves the love of God and neighbor, and the two loves cannot be separated. Charity characterizes the pistic society as opposed to the individualism and competitiveness of the positivistic society. Personalist action motivated by charity upholds the true dignity of all persons. Love for the other is not based on the importance, wealth, or influence of the other. All are loved with the same love, just as God has first loved all of us. Charity takes the form of the spiritual and corporal works of mercy. The prime Christian method of social reform is through the works of mercy. If we Catholics want to right social wrongs, it is vain to rely on worldly wisdom, prudence, or many merely human approaches. In charity and the works of mercy we have weapons far stronger than anything the world has.[58]

To find out in more detail the requirements of Christian charity and the works of mercy the Catholic goes to the sources of divine revelation—scripture, tradition, and the official teaching of the church. Furfey gives primary importance to the example and teaching of Jesus and appeals for literal acceptance of his teaching. The Sermon on the Mount was not preached to a few select souls or to a few rare individuals gifted with uncommon virtues. The Sermon on the Mount was preached to a multitude made up of all kinds. But Jesus in his words was not cautious, careful, circumspect, moderate, and discreet. Do not resist evil. Love your enemies. Do not be solicitous for this life. He summed up his whole message by daring them to be perfect even as the heavenly Father is perfect.[59]

Christian personalism is based on love and calls for the renovation of the individual person on the basis of God's grace and the gospel message. The gentle, and at times seemingly invisible, influence of Christian personalism is aimed at the spiritual and moral reform of individual persons. Furfey's radical personalism thus differs greatly from Catholic liberalism. Remember that personalist action was the way chosen by Jesus. He did not begin with a mass organization trying to change structures but rather gathered around himself a small group of disciples and followers.[60] The early church followed Jesus' approach of personalist social action. Some authors claim there was no social ethics or social action in the early church. They are correct in the sense that there was no organized effort to change the institutions and structures of society, but there was personalist social action. Christians lived in the world, but rather than try to change the institutions of the world, they attempted to build up their own pistic society. Such an approach ultimately bore fruit, for the pagans were attracted by what they saw and accepted the revelation given to Jesus and the church. Personal reform gradually led to social and institutional change. If we follow the example and gospel call of Jesus and carry out the works of mercy, the contemporary pagans, like those of old, will realize how Christians love one another and will hurry to the cause of Christ.[61]

However, from his first writings Paul Furfey recognizes that personalist action with its emphasis on using supernatural means and aiming at the change of heart and moral reform of the individual does not constitute the only or the exclusive way for the Christian to respond in trying to change our society. He never denies the role of organized social action with its use of natural means and its aim at changing structures and institutions, although he definitely downplays and even minimizes political action.

In *Fire on the Earth* Furfey admits in theory that there is a real moral obligation to try for political reform. However, in practice there are formidable difficulties. Catholics cannot agree on the objectives (e.g., child-labor amendment) or the strategies. We as Catholics comprise only one-sixth of the American population, so realistically our influence is limited. We can never use dishonorable means and must be careful of compromising our positions. Political action and the state can only affect externals and cannot reform persons. Political action and legislative activity constitute only a very minor part of our program to reform society. Our program of personalist action remains the heart and soul of all Catholic social and political activity.[62]

The very Catholic social teaching to which Furfey gives such great importance also brings about some problems of consistency on this question. The papal encyclicals call for the reform of institutions through political and legislative action. Recall how Ryan justified his approach on the basis of the encyclicals. Furfey responds to the problem by insisting that according to the papal teaching both institutional reform and personal reform are required, but personal reform is the first, the primary, and the most basic remedy.[63] Notice the tension and possible inconsistency in Furfey's thought on radical personalist action. Just as our author insists on the radical incompatibility between our society and a pistic society but still recognizes some good in our society, so too he insists on radical personalist action, but, when pushed, acknowledges a secondary role for political reform.

Strategies of Christian personalism

What are the strategies that a Christian personalist should employ in living out the life of Christ in the midst of a society dominated by the success ideal? Furfey proposes two basiic and fundamental strategies—separation and nonparticipation, on the one hand, and bearing witness, on the other.

Catholics have their own distinctive doctrine about the ills plaguing society, which is completely and utterly different from the proposals made by unbelieving social scientists and the modern world. Furfey begins his book *Mystery of Iniquity* with these words and ends the book with a chapter entitled "Come Out From Among Them, Be Separated" (2 Cor. 6:17). As Catholics we must stand by ourselves in honorable isolation. We break sharply and clearly with the modern world.[64] The greatest evil for Catholics according to this book is conformism. Christ was no conformist, but unfortunately Catholic conformism has been prevalent in many areas—in sociology, social work, labor problems, race relations, and nationalism. Furfey recognizes that his approach runs counter not only to the mores of society in general but also to the commonly accepted position taken by the Catholic Church in the United States. Conciliation has been the policy of the American Church under a series of great leaders—England, Hughes, Ireland, Gibbons, Spellman, and others. In a sense the Catholic Church in America has seemingly prospered as a result of this strategy. Such an approach sees no basic incompatibility between being Catholic and being American. However, conciliation was not the strategy followed by Jesus Christ, and it has one overwhelming disadvantage—conciliation makes impossible the construction of a new society according to the guidelines of Jesus Christ, for in order to change the present society one must be free to criticize it.[65]

Separation from the positivistic society calls for the strategy of nonparticipation, the first essential in a pistic society. Furfey in his earlier writings recognizes that there will be exceptions to the principle of nonparticipation and degrees of involvement in it, but nonparticipation remains the rule.[66] In his first and most popular work Furfey goes into the degrees of nonparticipation and the forms it takes. One should remember that the situation of the Christian in the world is analagous to the situation of a citizen marooned in an enemy country during wartime. The first degree of nonparticipation is a complete break from the world as illustrated by the religious orders. An attractive possibility is the establishment of Christian village communities which would be self-sufficient in most things and cut off from the compromising world, but Furfey cautions against a literal return to the Middle

Ages. Joining such communities is not feasible even for all earnest Catholics, but all must carry on a form of nonparticipation in terms of the Pauline formula of using the world as if we used it not (1 Cor. 7:31). One should avoid dishonorable vocations, such as working as a stockbroker; and even in honorable vocations, such as law, one could accept only cases in which the lawyer is convinced there exists an injustice. A nonparticipator will not invest in interest-bearing securities, will limit one's income severely, and will avoid the characteristic amusements of modern life. Such a program is not too extreme or too hard, for Christ in the Sermon on the Mount was talking to ordinary human beings.[67]

In the early 1940s Furfey engaged in a fascinating debate with John Courtney Murray on the question of intercredal cooperation. Murray, the Catholic liberal, promoted intercredal cooperation which extols the working together of people of different creeds in the interest of social justice. Furfey, the radical, opposed intercredal cooperation because Catholics must use their own unique supernatural means and not the natural means that are common to all. Here is a practical consequence of Catholic separation and nonparticipation.[68]

In the late 1960s Furfey praised the nonparticipation of David Miller, Tom Cornell, and others who burned their draft cards in protest against conscription and the Vietnam War. Likewise he strongly supported the action of Father Philip Berrigan and others who in February 1967 poured blood over draft records. Those who follow out the strategy of nonparticipation will often not be understood and will be positively opposed by superiors and other fellow believers. On the occasion of the Berrigan incident, the Baltimore archdiocesan chancery office issued a statement deploring the demonstration and calling it disorderly, aggressive, and extreme. Would the Baltimore chancery office have issued the same statement about the action of Jesus in driving the money-changers out of the temple?[69]

The positive aspect of the strategy of personalist action is bearing witness. The Catholic is called to be a martyr, for the root meaning of martyr is to bear witness or to give testimony. Unfortunately tradition has limited the word to the supreme act of bearing witness—the giving of one's life. Bearing witness is a very essential part of the New Testament. John the Baptist saw his life and mission in terms of bearing witness to Jesus. Jesus uses the same description for his own activity. After the resur-

rection Christ handed on to his apostles the duty of bearing witness, and the Acts of the Apostles describes how they faithfully
carried out their duties to bear witness to the risen Lord.

Bearing witness usually involves three things—a clear presentation, a persuasive presentation, and the aid of divine grace.
A clear presentation requires that we know the Catholic social
teaching and use the most modern scientific methods to understand and perceive better the contemporary reality. Second, the
presentation must be persuasive. Testimony is eminently persuasive when it brings us no temporal advantage. Look at the saints;
look at St. Paul. They despised easy methods; they suffered; but
in the process they effectively gave testimony. Third, bearing
witness is done with the aid of grace. Success in bearing witness
does not depend on the immediate results of our endeavors. Those
who bear witness most effectively are those whose lives are most
like the life of Christ—poor in visible results, but rich in grace
St. Paul learned through a special revelation to confess his own
infirmity and to rely on the power of God. Our success rests on
means which appear inadequate to us, for power is made known
in infirmity. Yes, this is a hard method, but if we use it, our own
witness-bearing will be blessed with the marvelous and supernatural significance which marked the work of the saints.[70] Part
of the suffering involved in bearing witness is criticism, name
calling, and the opposition of persons in high places. The Christian bears witness "in season" and "out of season." "In season"
means that the Christian employs all the conventional ways of
preaching the message. But if Christianity is to be socially effective, there must be an abundance of witnesses who are willing to
speak up and oppose the respectable people of society. Furfey
praises the action of the Episcopalian rector in Williamsburg,
Virginia, who pointed out the immorality of the Vietnam War
when President Johnson was in the congregation.[71]

In the late 1960s Furfey emphasizes the importance of nonviolence as a way for the Christian to bear witness. In these more
ecumenical days our author is quick to point out that nonviolence
is not proper only to Christians, but it fits easily into Christian
ideology, and Christians have often used the method with extraor-
dinarily happy results. In his writings in the 1960s there is a
greater emphasis on results and effects than in his earlier writings. Nonviolence is defined as a generic category of actions and
attitudes that deliberately abstains from using force and violence
in situations to which they might be applied. Such was the ap-

proach used by Christ, but this does not mean that Christians should repudiate the use of physical force under all circumstances. The simplest form of nonviolence is the nonresistance which is seen above all in the martyr. Passive resistence as found in strikes and boycotts constitutes a second form of nonviolence. The most difficult, but at the same time a very effective form of nonviolence, is nonviolent direct action. Here the persons involved are not passive noncooperators, but rather the actionists take the tactical offensive as illustrated by the sit-ins in the 1960s.[72]

There can be no doubt that for Paul Hanly Furfey nonparticipation and witness-bearing form the characteristic and distinctive response of the Catholic. However, his understanding of these strategies is influenced and modified by his earlier realizations that the relationship between our society and the kingdom of God is not totally one of incompatibility and that there is some limited room for political and legislative action as well as the primacy of personalist action. Even in the 1930s Furfey acknowledges there are many exceptions to the principle of nonparticipation, but nonparticipation remains the rule.[73] Also Furfey points out different degrees of nonparticipation and does not require a complete break or withdrawal by all from our society. Witness-bearing does not only call for the difficult and the dramatic, but also Christian charity involves the doing of our everyday duties.[74] Catholics must also be ready to participate as citizens in all worldly efforts to pass social legislation, to participate in labor unions, to elect public officials, and to facilitate the routine of just government, but these means are characterized as superficial. Note also that in the matter of nonviolence Furfey is not an absolutist.

The issues

From his first writings as a radical Christian in the 1930s through the 1960s Furfey constantly discussed three issues—poverty and the plight of the poor, race discrimination and the treatment of minority groups, war and the danger of nationalism. Furfey the radical clearly identifies the major problems facing society in the 1930s. These have remained the outstanding problems confronting American society since that time. Many of Furfey's liberal contemporaries were not as aware of these basic problems and tended to gloss over them. All these problems illustrate the conformism of Catholicism to the contemporary mores and its failure to truly bear witness and not participate in these evident evils of society. *The Respectable Murderers* (1966) begins with a long description of four instances of crimes perpetrated in various societies in which the God-fearing have participated and cooperated—American Negro slavery, the slaughter of European Jews, the bombing of noncombatants, and the lot of the subproletariat.[76]

The primary issue and the one that receives the most emphasis in Furfey's writings is the plight of the poor and the unequal distribution of wealth in our American society. There is no issue of social significance which receives more treatment in the scriptures themselves than the problem of riches. As mentioned before, on the basis of a rather intensive study he concludes that the rich who are condemned in the New Testament are the bourgeoisie—the class who are interested in money and totally engaged in the pursuit of wealth.[77]

Furfey the sociologist proves the existence of poverty and the unequal distribution of wealth. He cites the same report from the Brookings Institution used by Ryan to show that in 1929 in the United States the aggregate income of the upper one-tenth of 1 percent of the families was only slightly less than the aggregate income of the lower 42 percent.[78] Unlike Ryan, Furfey seldom mentions the Depression as such. For the radical the economic system itself is unjust and not only the problems of the Depression. Government statistics in 1965 showed that 43.1 million Americans, or 18.1 percent of the total noninstitutionalized population of the United States, were living in poverty.[79] Furfey's description of the contemporary society as a positivistic society dominated by the success ideal also points up the centrality of the question of wealth. Materialistic individualism and competitiveness characterize the positivistic society, which constantly strives for success in terms of wealth and power.[80]

What is the response of the Christian personalist? Answer: voluntary poverty. Furfey's personalist solution recognizes the root cause of the evils of our society in the success ideal and competitiveness, individualism and materialism. To exorcize the mystery of iniquity—or expressed in biblical terminology, the mammon of iniquity—bold measures are necessary. However, voluntary poverty admits of degrees, since it is a form of nonparticipation. Furfey praises the voluntary poverty of those who give up what they have to live among the poor and witness to them. Here he often cites the example of the Catholic Worker and of the Il Poverello House and the Fides House in Washington. But all must practice that voluntary poverty, which may be defined as the position of neither saving nor spending money unreasonably or selfishly.[81]

In keeping with his general approach Furfey stresses the personalist action of the Christian, but he also recognizes the need for a change of institutions and structures at least in the future. All Christians must acknowledge that capitalism in its modern form is evil—our modern economic system is shot through with injustice. All economic systems of the present—capitalist, socialist, and fascist—are evil and must be changed. In three paragraphs Furfey points out that an economic system based on the Mystical Body calls for a corporatism involving an occupational-group system which has been advocated in the papal encyclicals. However, he never really says how this is derived from the Mystical Body; nor does he elaborate on the plan at any length or give any consideration as to how this should come into reality. In fact, he readily admits that his corporatism is not immediately practical. For the present, Christian personalist action is immediately practical. By doing the works of mercy and practicing voluntary poverty Christians can constitute a perfect economic microcosm within our present materialistic world.[82]

The second issue in Furfey's social concern is racial discrimination. From the very beginning of his radical period the Catholic University sociologist condemns the treatment given to blacks in the United States by the country as a whole and also by American Catholics. Catholic attitudes toward slavery can only be described as conformist. Priests, religious, and laity all owned slaves; hierarchical leaders of both the north and the south defended the American practice of slavery before the Civil War.[83] Even in the 1940s Furfey recognizes the plight of other racial and ethnic minority groups in addition to the blacks. We white Americans must examine our consciences in the light of the parable of the Good Samaritan, illustrating for us who is our neighbor. If we do not go out and do likewise, hell will be our portion. How do we treat the Jew, the Oriental, the Mexican, the Indian and the Negro? It is a serious moral obligation—a matter of eternal life or death.[84]

Furfey the sociologist describes well the plight of black Americans. Again many people have said the same thing, but very few were saying it as explicitly and as forcefully as Furfey in the

1930s and 1940s. There is discrimination against Negroes in employment and in job training as is evident from statistics. The housing problem is particularly galling for the Negro. Segregation rears its ugly head in education and in many aspects of life. Long before the famous Brown decision of the Supreme court in 1954, Furfey maintains that as a matter of sober fact, segregation almost in every case involves unequal treatment. Negroes are even deprived of their basic civil rights. Catholics readily conform to these existing mores and do nothing about them.[85]

Furfey's proposed solution to racial discrimination reveals his theory at work. Christian personalist action is primary, fundamental, and immediately possible. In the question of race he does not consider any institutional changes such as laws. He extols those whites who move into black areas to live and work with the people. But all Catholics must practice interracial charity in their relations with minorities.[86]

The third significant issue with which Furfey has been concerned for over thirty-five years is peace. In general, as exemplified in *Fire on the Earth*, he approaches the question of peace and war in the context of the danger of nationalism, which is an exaggeration of the virtue of patriotism. Too often we think that charity should be exercised toward individuals but not toward groups or other nations. In fact, our society invokes patriotism to justify national selfishness together with hatred and distrust of other nations.[87] In *The Mystery of Iniquity*, written in the course of the Second World War, Furfey courageously points out the dangers of an exaggerated nationalism in the United States.[88] *The Respectable Murderers* describes at length two examples of exaggerated nationalism—the slaughter of European Jews and the bombing of noncombatants by the allied forces.[89]

In the course of history the spirit of iniquity was probably nowhere more visibly at work than in the spirit of nationalism. Patriotism is the virtue dealing with the proper love of country and has nothing in common with exaggerated nationalism. The United States has been saved from some of the extremes of nationalism, but the problem is still present. Comformism to exaggerated nationalism becomes a great temptation, as it did especially in the context of the popular Second World War with all the propaganda in its favor. In all his writings our author frequently objects to the maxim—"my country right or wrong." In the light of the Catholic position on just wars there exists the right of the human conscience to review the morality of war. If a

Catholic knows with full moral certitude that a given war is unjust, he is bound to refuse to fight. Unfortunately the Catholic pulpit and press were generally silent about the moral obligation of conscience to review the morality of the Second World War.[90]

In the course of the war itself American policy accepted two postions which are opposed to Catholic teaching and the pronouncements of the popes, but Catholic spokespersons said little or nothing about these realities. The first concerns the bombing of noncombatants. According to Catholic teaching it is clear that the direct killing of innocent persons is always wrong. Bombs should not be dropped on nonmilitary targets. Furfey points out many instances of the bombing of noncombatants in the allied bombing of Germany and Japan: British bombing of the Ruhr in 1943, incendiary bombing to start fires in industrial centers, the fire bombing of Hamburg and Dresden, the attack on Tokyo in March 1943, and finally the dropping of atomic bombs on Hiroshima and Nagasaki. The general silence of the American Catholic Church on this issue is astonishing in the light of the clarity of Catholic teaching. Conformism again won out over principle.[91] Interestingly, in his writings in the 1960s Furfey does not deal with the question of the debate over nuclear weapons, the stockpiling of such weapons, deterrence, and the whole matter of civil defense.[92]

The second issue which Furfey discusses in the course of the Second World War is the moral imperative of a negotiated peace. Pope Pius XII often talked about such a moral imperative. But the Allies called for unconditional surrender, and almost without exception no Catholic voice was raised in protest. Once again conformism triumphed, and rationalization justified the failure to speak out.[93]

Furfey never engages in an in-depth discussion of pacifism and war. During the Second World War he was active in antiwar organizations, served on the board of the National Council for the Prevention of War, and supported Catholic conscientious objectors.[94] During the 1960s he strenuously opposed the American involvement in the Vietnam War and established the Emmaus House in Washington to serve as a center for antiwar activity among Catholics connected with Catholic University.

It seems that in theory Furfey holds a version of the just-war theory. He categorically states that no Catholic may assert a priori that all wars are wrong. Christians do not repudiate the use of physical force under all circumstances.[95] Although Furfey accepts the just-war theory, he apparently sees very few instances of a just war in practice. In attacking the excesses of war he bases his position on papal teachings, which are really derived from natural law and not from a literal interpretation of the Bible.

III. Evaluation and Critique of Furfey's Position

Consistency and coherence

Our perspective has viewed Roman Catholic social ethics in the United States in the light of the question of the relationship between being Catholic and being American. Paul Hanly Furfey identifies himself as a Catholic radical seeing a basic opposition between the Catholic approach and the contemporary culture. For Furfey Catholicism must be an opposition movement employing the supernatural means of personalist action. However, Furfey is not as consistently radical as he often claims to be. Tensions have already been pointed out in his understanding of the incompatibility between the pistic society or the Mystical Body of Christ and the contemporary society or world. At times he insists on the exclusivity of supernatural means and personalist action, while at other times he recognizes the primacy of these means in relation to natural means and political attempts to reform institutions. There is a resultant ambiguity in his stressing the need to build a totally new society as against his recognition of making some efforts to reform the present society. This section will attempt to explain the reasons behind the tension and even the inconsistencies in Furfey's approach. Four reasons contributing to his modification of radicalism will be discussed— his theology, ecclesiology, sociology, and understanding of ethics.

Furfey attempts to base his radicalism on traditional Catholic theology, but traditional Catholic theology and ecclesiology cannot be consistently radical. Roman Catholic theology has traditionally recognized some continuity between grace and nature. The old axiom maintained that grace does not destroy nature but builds on nature. Both Ryan and the German-American Catholics illustrate the traditional Catholic recognition of the goodness of the natural. In this Catholic vision all reality cannot be divided into the opposition between grace and sin or between kingdom of God and the kingdom of Satan. Both Ryan and Engelen and much of the Catholic moral theology of the time can correctly be criticized for not giving enough importance to the power of sin, but the Catholic understanding of continuity between nature and grace argues against the radical incompatibility between the present society and the kingdom of God.

Catholic theology, in a consistent manner, also sees no basic incompatibility between faith and reason, which might be looked upon as the epistemological aspect of the supernatural-natural relationship. Furfey himself recognizes the importance of reason and the role it can play in reforming society. Our author spent his whole life as an academic sociologist studying the social reality. The important role given to reason in Furfey's explanation of the credibility of faith well illustrates such a Catholic approach. Furfey, in an attempt at consistency, realizes that sin prevents our living on the level of the noetic, but still reason is not totally destroyed or corrupted.

The understanding of the term "world" is closely related to the nature-grace question. The world in the Catholic tradition is not always understood as the world in the Johannine sense of that which is opposed to Jesus and the light. The Catholic tradition often insists that the world is the work of God's creation and hence is good. When the world is understood at least partially in relation to creation, there can never be a total opposition between the world and the kingdom of God.

A more positive relationship of continuity, without denying some discontinuity, between nature and grace, between reason and faith, and between the world and the kingdom of God stems from what might be called the Catholic emphasis on mediation. Grace is not opposed to the natural order but is mediated through the natural and the human. So too with faith and reason. No one relying on the Catholic tradition can theologically propose a radical incompatibility between this world and the kingdom of God. To uphold such a radical incompatibility consistently, one needs to modify some significant aspects of Catholic theology.

Furfey's Catholic ecclesiology also mitigates his radicalism. Furfey admits that in Catholicism there has been both an extreme and a moderate approach. Our author opts for the extremist approach, but he cannot deny that the moderate approach (in his pejorative language) has a place within Catholicism. Traditionally, Christian radicals propose an ecclesiology which is based on the sect—a small group of Christians striving for perfection who are separated from the rest of the world. But

Catholic ecclesiology has frequently insisted on its universality—all are called to be members of the church. This universalism and catholicity will not allow the absolute radicalism which Furfey at times calls for. As Furfey himself acknowledges, in Catholic theology one loses grace only through mortal sin.

A thoroughgoing Catholicism, according to Furfey, finds its understanding of social thought in the scriptures, tradition, and the teaching of the church. However, the teachings of the Roman Catholic Church on social ethics, as found in the papal encyclicals, are not radical. Such teaching is based almost entirely on the natural law as made known by human reason and gives a very large place to institutional reform through natural means. Furfey cannot claim to give such importance to the teaching of the church and still be a consistent radical.

Developments in Furfey's ecclesiology over the years strongly militate against his total radicalism. In the 1930s and 1940s there is almost an identity between the Mystical Body of Christ and the Catholic Church. Such an approach results in a very clear-cut demarcation between those who are in grace and those who are in sin. However, by the 1960s he recognizes that his program can be embraced by Protestants and also by Jews. Furfey's older and narrower ecclesiology has the benefit of indicating a very sharp distinction between the realm of sin and the realm of grace. However, Furfey now implicitly admits that God's grace can be found among all human beings. Gone now is the clear-cut distinction between a realm of light and a realm of darkness which serves as the basis for his insistence on radical incompatibilities between the Mystical Body of Christ and the Mystical Body of Satan.

Furfey's lifelong interest in and commitment to academic sociology also rests uneasily with his call for Catholic radicalism. Our author, despite his many personal involvements in different projects, never separates himself from the academic world of sociology. He obviously believes that the science of sociology has something to tell us about a social program. Otherwise it would have been impossible for him to make sociology his lifetime work.

From his earliest radical writing Furfey proposes a methodology in which sociology could be of service to Catholic social action. Scientific investigation helps us to have a better understanding of social problems. As explained in his presuppositions, Catholic social theory can use sociology in a very important way.

Revelation supplies the major of the argument and sociology supplies the minor. This syllogism can result in a new theological conclusion which is something unattainable either by revelation alone or by faith alone. Empirical sociology can and should be used together with the supraempirical postulates of theology and philosophy. Despite long discussions of this theory Furfey himself never puts it into practice in his own understanding of Catholic social thought and action. One looks in vain for his own carrying out of his theory in practice. At best he uses his sociology merely to describe the existing problems.

Why does he not use his own method? It seems that his method as described above is not compatible with his own theological radicalism. His emphasis on separation from the world, nonparticipation, and bearing witness actually pulls one out from the sociological setting rather than positively trying to reform it. His sociology and his social radicalism seem to exist side by side in a somewhat awkward manner because in reality they cannot be readily put together.

In general Furfey's ethical methodology supports a radical position, but even here there are some tensions and modifications. Radical Christian ethics, as illustrated in the left-wing sects of the Protestant Reformation and in some contemporary writings, is deontological. The radical Christian primarily looks to the gospel to determine what is to be done; efficacy and the effects of one's actions are left in God's hands. We do what God requires of us, and God will take care of the rest. Radical Christians, like all deontologists, fear that at times the end or good to be a-chieved will justify the means. Means are determined in themselves as being right or wrong (e.g., nonviolence) and not justified in terms of whether or not they contribute to the achievement of a good goal or end. Too often in the name of effectiveness Christians have accepted means which are opposed to the gospel.

Furfey's approach definitely fits into the deontological category. Furfey often uses the deontological word of rightness or internal rightness as the criterion of action rather than the teleological term of good. The Christian's primary moral obligation is to follow the New Testament literally—not to worry about the achievement of a particular goal or end. The positive strategy of the Christian is to bear witness, which is a very deontological term. The Christian does what God calls one to do and does not worry about the consequences. Our author goes out of his way to insist that success is not something that the Christian should strive for. He opposes the success ideal of a positivistic society. Grace is invisible. The empirical eye cannot tell the difference between an act placed in grace and an act which does not come from grace. The Cross remains a very important symbol for the Christian life and ethics. Success will not crown our works. Like Jesus we will meet with opposition and suffering.

However, aspects of success and efficacy are not lacking in his corpus. Even in *Fire on the Earth* the last chapter is entitled "The Pragmatic Test." The extreme life of heroism represents a human being's deepest self-realization. In heaven we will find perfect self-realization for ourselves and for society. We will have achieved our goal.[96] His two books in the 1960s give much more emphasis to efficacy than the early trilogy. The beginning and end of his discussion of Christian personalist action in *The Morality Gap* illustrates this emphasis. Gone now is all reference to the invisibility of grace. Furfey is much more concerned about efficacy and our obligations to create a better society.[97] The early Furfey consistently buttresses his radicalism with a deontological ethical model. Teleological concerns such as self-fulfillment and efficacy are not totally absent even from his earlier work, but they become more prevalent in the 1960s.

One can rightly conclude that Paul Furfey is not as consistent a radical as his rhetoric might at times lead one to believe. There are significant aspects in Furfey's thought, especially his Catholic theology and ecclesiology, his sociology, and his inability to completely disregard effectiveness, which mitigate against his being a thoroughgoing Catholic radical. Perhaps the most accurate description of his position is the following: Furfey gives as radical an interpretation of social ethics as possible on the basis of traditionally accepted Catholic theology and ecclesiology.

Furfey and the Catholic worker movement

Furfey was chosen to illustrate the position of Catholic radicalism because his express purpose was to explain systematically the spirit of new social movements in the church such as the Catholic Worker movement. As already mentioned, differences existed even within the Worker, so one should not be surprised that there are some differences between Furfey and the Catholic Worker. In general the Catholic Worker is consistently more radical than Furfey.

The Catholic Worker in its paper exhibits a number of different approaches to pacifism and war, but Dorothy Day herself was a total pacifist opposed to all war no matter what the purpose or the goal. Her pacifism especially during the Second World War was not always well received by other Catholics and even by some who had been in the Catholic Worker movement. But such pacifism has emerged as the most significant moral position taken by the Catholic Worker in its history. Dorothy Day had originally based her opposition to war primarily on historical arguments showing the futility of war and that war profited the rich at the expense of the poor. However, by 1940 she justified her pacifism on the foundation of Christian personalist action based on the gospel command of love and saw war as the ultimate objectification of the human person.[98] Recall that Furfey never embraced a totally pacifist position but in practice accepted a limited just-war approach.

A strong theme in the Catholic Worker is the need to build a new type of society on the land and withdraw from the evil industrial society. Furfey tempered such an approach with a call for a realistic recognition that some of the same basic problems exist on the land as well as in the city. It is impossible to turn back the clock to an earlier type of agrarian existence.[99] The Green Revolution associated with Peter Maurin often seemed opposed to technology and the machine as such.[100] However, Furfey objected to such a doctrinaire opposition to technology and the machine. What is required is that the motive of the research worker and the industrial executive be changed.[101]

In his radical period Furfey also criticized Dorothy Day for not giving enough importance to organization. Modern Catholic social work with its emphasis on professionalism, organization, and the use of the latest psychological and sociological methods needs to learn from the example of Dorothy Day and the generous enthusiasm of sharing all with the poor in the following of Christ. There should be some way to combine the enthusiasm and generosity of the Catholic Worker with the order and system of a modern Catholic Charities office.[102]

The Catholic Worker over the years has developed at some length its understanding of the role and function of the state. Here too, the Worker is more radical than Furfey. The Worker often capitalizes "State" to refer to the state when it has become oppressive and idolatrous. Dorothy Day ironically refers at times to Holy Mother the State. Dorothy Day and the movement are opposed to the state because of the coercive authority and manipulation involved in it. In the ideal community all the members are responsible for one another, contributing according to their ability and receiving according to their need. The role of the state is minimal, and coercive authority should wither away entirely. Government, especially in terms of coercion and manipulation, is opposed to the personalism of the Catholic Worker with its emphasis on freedom and responsibility. Within the Catholic Worker movement itself there is no organization or bureaucracy of any kind. The Worker tries to avoid even the suspicion of coercion. Those who receive food, clothing, or shelter are never forced or enticed in any overt way to listen to any propaganda or to participate in the work. The movement fears that institutions are depersonalizing, and the state is the depersonalizing institution par excellence.[103]

In later years Robert Ludlow and Ammon Hennacy used the word "anarchist" to describe the Worker position. There is some confusion over the meaning of the term itself. According to Ludlow anarchists (especially anarchic-syndicalists) are opposed, not to all government, but rather to the State. They advocate decentralized self-governing bodies. Democracy calls for government by representation, but anarchists believe that the whole people comprising a community should take care of what little governing there is to be done rather than have a distant and centralized state do it. Dorothy Day admits she prefers the word "libertarian" because of the wrong popular connotation of anarchism as being synonymous with chaos and disaster.[104] Interestingly, Ludlow later changed his mind about anarchism, whereas Dorothy Day continued to use the term.[105]

In practice the Worker tries to distinguish between different aspects of government to determine what they will support and what they will oppose. Their opposition to the depersonalizing aspects of government is usually justified by the Worker on the basis of the biblical injunction to obey God rather than human beings. There is opposition, for example, to paying federal income taxes. Local taxes are different because these taxes provide community services such as hospitals and the fire department from which all persons in the community benefit. In the light of their pacifism, defense spending and civil-defense procedures are strenuously opposed. The Catholic Worker frequently reminds its readers that people in the movement do not vote. According to the Catholic Worker voting in the present circumstances only contributes to the ongoing existence of the state. The Worker's position on the state is generally more developed and more radical than Furfey's.[106]

The differences between Furfey and the Catholic Worker should not be exaggerated. Furfey, like the Worker, insists on a literal interpretation of the New Testament as the basis of his radicalism and espouses nonparticipation and bearing witness. However, the differences on particular questions are real and point to some deeper methodological divergences between Furfey and the Worker.

The first general area of theoretical differences between Furfey and the Worker corresponds to the concerns discussed under Furfey's consistency as a radical. The aspects mentioned there all influence Furfey's differences with the Worker. Furfey's attempt to base his radicalism in Catholic theology causes him to modify somewhat his radicalism because of the Catholic recognition of some continuity between nature and grace. Catholic ecclesiology does not allow for the sectarian approach which serves as the basis for much Christian radicalism in the Protestant tradition. Our author's insistence on the importance of sociology also makes him somewhat less radical. His even limited acceptance of the need for effective action also undermines an absolute radicalism.

A very significant difference between Furfey and the Worker stems from the latter's development of a philosophical personalism to buttress its radicalism. Catholic Worker personalism insists on the freedom of the person—an aspect not often mentioned by Furfey. To become a person can only happen in freedom. Such freedom is not license but calls the person to work for the development of the self, of others, and of the community. All force or coercion is opposed to the freedom and dignity of the human person. One truly becomes free and contributes to the freedom of the community by recognizing the freedom of others, allowing them to grow, refusing to be threatened by their mistakes, and convincing them by word and example, not by coercion.[107] This emphasis on the freedom of the person serves as the ultimate basis for many of the positions taken by the Catholic Worker—the lack of structure in their own movement; the complete freedom given to the people who receive food, clothing, and shelter in the Houses of Hospitality; the fear of any institutions or bureaucracies which by their very nature seem to threaten human freedom; opposition to technology and work that make the person an object.

Such a heavy emphasis on freedom as an important aspect of Christian personalism is absent in Furfey's writing. Furfey seldom refers to philosophers who espouse such personalism. The different approach to personalism accounts for some of the different emphases between Furfey and the Catholic Worker.

Furfey's radicalism is also somewhat modified by his attachment to other groups in the Catholic Church which are not as radical as the Worker. After 1938 Furfey came into direct contact with the Jocist movement, which had been founded in Belgium by Father Joseph (later Cardinal) Cardijn. The Jocist approach with its threefold methodology of see, judge, and act is not as radical as the Worker.[108]

The reasons proposed explain some of the deeper differences between Furfey's radicalism and that of the Catholic Worker. However, neither the substantive differences nor the underlying explanations of those differences should be exaggerated.

Evaluation of Catholic radicalism

There are very significant strengths in Catholic radicalism. The commitment and dedication of its followers are truly inspiring. Even those who cannot accept such an approach must admire the voluntary poverty and heroic self-sacrifice seen in the Catholic Worker and similar groups. Catholic radicals truly bear witness to their beliefs.

Catholic radicalism brings to bear an explicitly Christian approach to the social problems of the world. Unlike John A. Ryan, the radicals appeal to theological realities such as grace and sin, the importance of the scriptures, and Christian spirituality. The radicals integrate their faith and their social action.

All have to recognize that a very important function of Christian social ethics and activity is to be prophetic. No one can be more prophetic than Catholic radicalism. Furfey, in the 1930s, recognized the deep problems facing our society. Poverty, racial discrimination, and peace have remained very basic issues in our society. Even reading Furfey today, one is struck by how current are his concerns. There can be no doubt that one of the great advantages of the radical approach is the ability to see the problems. Catholic liberals at times might tend to overlook some problems, but the radical possesses a methodological approach which makes one sensitive to the real problems facing our society.

Catholic radicalism, as practiced by the Catholic Worker and Furfey, has made Catholics and others in our society aware of the danger of conformism. At a time when so many Catholics were struggling to be accepted and respectable, the radicals dared to say No and to be quite different.

At the same time there are a number of negative criticisms and/or questions that can be raised against this radical approach. As a matter of fact, the radicalism explained by Furfey and practiced by the Catholic Worker has not really been effective in helping the lot of the poor or the oppressed in our society. Furfey himself later changed his own position precisely because Catholic radicalism with its tactics of nonparticipation and witness-bearing was not effective in bringing about social change.[109] One could respond that effectiveness and immediate solutions are not the only criteria by which such an approach to social justice should be judged. Also, how effective have other approaches been?

Furfey's radicalism has no depth of theoretical development. The radical message is simple—a literal insistence on the following of the New Testament. Furfey's corpus makes easy reading because it involves no penetrating or subtle reasoning. There is no long-involved argument proposed. Furfey's writings tend to be more along the line of proclamation than of systematic study. However, his aim is primarily to change the hearts of average or, at most, educated Catholics. He is not writing primarily for a scholarly audience.

In Furfey there is a one-sided emphasis on the change of heart of the person with comparatively little or no stress on the need for the change of institutions and of structures. Our considerations of liberals like Ryan have pointed out the opposite danger. I would argue that any adequate social ethics must call for both a change of heart and a change of structures.

Within Furfey's system it is very consistent for him to emphasize the need for an immediate personal responsibility which above all is shown by the practice of the spiritual and corporal works of mercy. But both the personal and the immediate aspects of his response indicate only one part of what I think should comprise the total response of the Christian. The response must be personal and institutional, immediate and long-range. The personal performance of the works of mercy alone does not constitute the total Christian response to the social injustice existing in the world.

Furfey's approach is quite vague in terms of details of the pistic society. Perhaps one may ask too much of Furfey, for a prophetic approach will by definition tend to be less specific and concrete than other approaches. Furfey is very clear and insistent on the problems; he insists that the important thing is the change of heart. However, even in Furfey's perspective there is need to say how the pistic society will be structured. What types of economic and political institutions will exist in such a society? At most he vaguely talks about corporatism but gives very few details.

The appeal to the scriptures must be an important part of any Christian social ethic, but Furfey's literal interpretation of the New Testament and especially the Sermon on the Mount cannot be accepted, above all in the light of contemporary biblical and theological scholarship. Furfey seems totally unaware of the hermeneutical problem. In addition, the New Testament ethical teaching is definitely influenced by the eschatological expectations of the times. Furfey gives no consideration to these important aspects. Today the question of the proper way to use the scriptures in moral theology is a matter of great discussion, but at the very minimum contemporary scholarship rejects a literal interpretation of the New Testament ethics.

Any evaluation of Catholic radicalism must consider the issues discussed in the section on Furfey's consistency. Theologically his Catholic radicalism builds on an incompatibility between the present society and the pistic society, or between sin and grace. However, I cannot accept that simplistic or absolute a division between grace and sin in our world. Such an approach fails to give enough importance to the reality of the goodness of creation which is present in the world, overestimates the presence of sin in the world, fails to recognize that grace is already present and to a limited extent redeeming the present, and sees only discontinuity between the present and the eschatological fullness. The same basic problem can be broached from a different angle. Furfey's position posits the existence of a great deal of sin in the world now. How is redemption going to occur so that such sin will be converted into grace? If the redemptive love of Jesus has been present in our world for so long, why has it had so little effect until now and on what basis can one assert that great effects will occur in the future?

Mediation characterizes the Catholic theological approach in my judgment. God's word is mediated in and through the human word. God's love is mediated through human love. Catholic ecclesiology well illustrates the reality of mediation. Our relationship to Jesus is not an immediate private affair but takes place through the visible mediation of the church. So too the divine is mediated in and through the human. Furfey's grace-sin dichotomy explaining the present realities does not recognize the implications of this mediation.

The same failure to appreciate mediation appears in a more practical way in Furfey. He appeals to the ultimate realities of grace and sin to explain the problem and the cure. However, he fails to pay enough attention to the mediating human structures which both incarnate sin and mediate grace. On the other hand, liberals gave so much attention to the mediating aspects that not enough importance was given to the ultimate realities.

A thoroughgoing Christian radicalism also has ecclesiological consequences. At the very least such a radicalism is most congenial with a sect type of ecclesiology, but Roman Catholicism has always argued for a catholic and universal church. However, within the total church there must always be room for a radical Christian witness. Individual Christians, but not the whole church, can be and are called to a radical vocation and witness within the church.

A final question concerns the primary difference between a radical and a reforming approach. Furfey sees the present reality as identified almost totally with sin and therefore incapable of serving as a basis for reform. A view which sees more good in the contemporary situation, which is explained theologically by the goodness of creation and some presence of redemption, has the basis for proposing a more reforming approach. Apart from the more theoretical question there is also the practical question about which approach will be most effective in practice. The basic difference between a radical and a reforming approach and the relative merits of both will always remain a most significant question for all social ethics, including Christian social ethics.

Furfey's change

Radicalism was not Furfey's last word on Catholic social action. In 1978, at age 82, he published *Love and the Urban Ghetto*, which deals with the problem of Christian social action in the context of the problem of poverty in the ghetto. Three of the chapters describe the reality of the conditions of poverty in the Washington ghetto on the basis of sociological studies done by Furfey and his colleagues in the Department of Sociology at the Catholic University over the years.[110] However, the theology of Christian love now proposed by Furfey is Christian revolutionism. The emphasis on the New Testament, the Cross, the heroism of the saints is still present, but gone are the insistence on Christianity as an opposition movement and the characteristic strategies of nonparticipation and bearing witness.[111] Part of the book is autobiographical as Furfey describes his own growth through scientific charity or liberalism, to radicalism, and then to Christian revolutionism.

After describing the reality of social sin as it exists in the poverty and despair of the ghetto, our author views the different Christian solutions to the problem. Christian liberalism is defined as a program of social action that accepts the present system of democracy and capitalism and attempts to achieve social justice within the existing framework especially through political pressure for legislative reform and through social work. Through liberalism the problem of poverty has been assuaged, but liberalism has failed to solve the central problem of the poverty of 25 million people in the United States. In addition, most liberals have no firsthand knowledge of the conditions of poverty.[112]

Christian radicalism, instead of trying to reform the current politicoeconomic system, breaks with it entirely and tries to build the new society based on Christian principles. The work of the people involved in the Catholic Worker such as Dorothy Day is awe-inspiring and of great spiritual beauty, but their program, despite having given birth to the Catholic peace movement, has not been effective. They have concentrated only on the derelicts and have done little or nothing to help the poor of the ghetto to change the conditions in which they live. Even in 1977 the Catholic Worker was still proposing a distributist economy which has not worked and will not work because it is not based on contemporary circumstances but harkens back in a romantic way to an earlier agrarian time.[113]

Christian revolutionism implies the destruction of the existing power structure and the substitution of a different one. Furfey was greatly impressed by the liberation theology movements which he came in contact with during a visit to Latin America in 1974. However, he himself cannot accept Marxism as such and also cautions that violence can only be accepted as a desperate, last resort. As for the American situation, there is no need for violence because here we have the legal and constitutional means for bringing about radical reform in our economic system. Such reform is difficult and will require extraordinary efforts, but it is not impossible. Communism and capitalism are rejected as inadequate alternatives, and a third way is proposed with special reference to the model of Sweden. The means of production still are retained by private owners, but workers and the state become involved in policies so that profit is not the primary motive. He thereby calls for a more egalitarian society to be structured in accord with the Swedish system.[114]

Furfey does not develop his ideal at any great length, nor does he talk about the specific means necessary to bring it about. His proposal raises a number of questions. He appeals to both enlightened selfishness and the Cross for his egalitarian approach, but at the very minimum this must create a tension at the heart of his theory. He calls for a third way, but at this time many Catholic theoreticians have abandoned the practicality of a third way. He accepts a basic reformability in the American political structure, but many others have given up on the political process in the United States. His program comes quite close to the liberalism he attacked especially in terms of liberalism's gradualism and working together with others to change the existing structure. Nowhere does he address the concern that he occasionally expressed earlier about the problem of overcentralization and bureaucracy.

As was pointed out, there were tensions and inconsistencies in his radical theory, and his writings in the 1960s were less consistently radical than his earlier works. In the early 1970s, while still accepting the description of himself as a radical, he acknowledged that he no longer held his earlier position on intercredal cooperation.[115] His newest change indicates above all that the category of effectiveness has become more central in his thinking. One can only marvel at an eighty-two-year old who, instead of being content with the past, is now willing to jettison his own past approach because something must be done and done quickly and efficaciously for the poor. For our purposes Paul Hanly Furfey is important because for two decades he was the most systematic and theological exponent of a radical Catholicism.

5. JOHN COURTNEY MURRAY

This chapter will study primarily the work of the American Jesuit theologian John Courtney Murray. Murray, like John A. Ryan, employed the Catholic natural-law methodology. He paid little attention to economic questions and was basically positive toward the American economic scene. His greatest contribution lay in the area of political ethics and involved creative and significant contributions not only in the area of substantive teaching but also in historical interpretation. To understand and evaluate Murray, some background is necessary.

I. Background

The three approaches to Catholic social ethics considered thus far came into existence in the first half of the twentieth century. During and after the Second World War an important sociological phenomenon occurred. Catholics entered more fully into the mainstream of American life in general and notably into the middle economic class. The immigrant character of the church was changing as Catholics became evermore assimilated into American life.

If one event symbolized this assimilation process, it was the 1960 election of John F. Kennedy as the first Roman Catholic to be president of the United States. This assimilation process took place in many other areas. For example, Catholic higher education in the 1960s no longer saw itself as totally distinctive in relationship to American higher education in general but accepted the basic American understanding of academic freedom and the autonomy of the university or college. The leading figures in American Catholic higher education maintained that colleges and universities could be both Catholic and American at one and the same time.[1]

A significant factor in postwar America was the Cold War and opposition to Russian communism. The United States and the Roman Catholic Church were looked upon as the two great bulwarks in the struggle against the common enemy. Such a cold-war mentality emphasized the area of agreement between the United States and the Catholic Church, which since the 1930s had been a strong opponent of communism. On the domestic front the McCarthy investigations created a climate of suspicion and trampled on the civil and human rights of many. However, it seems that Catholics were not unanimous in their support of the actions of the Catholic senator from Wisconsin. Catholics were as divided as other Americans on McCarthy, but significant Catholic leaders did support his endeavors.[2]

In the midst of the assimilation process the prejudices and persecutions associated with the Nativist and Know-Nothing movements of the nineteenth century no longer existed, but there were still suspicions and fears of Roman Catholicism. It was common political understanding until the late 1950s that a Catholic could not become president of the United States. The organization of Protestants and Other Americans United for Separation of Church and State was founded because of the fear that Catholics were a danger to this basic American principle of separation. Most Catholics looked on this organization as bigoted, but there did exist real tensions in the minds of many between an authoritarian, centralized hierarchical church and the spirit of an open, pluralistic democratic society. There were also some touchy practical issues: Catholics sought government aid for their schools, but many Americans saw this as an abridgment of the first amendment of the Constitution with its call for separation of church and state. Catholics insisted on fighting in some states to preserve the laws against selling, disseminating, or using contraceptive devices—laws which originally were put on the books by Protestants in the Comstock era. Attempts by the American government to appoint an ambassador to the Vatican also met heavy opposition and ultimately were defeated. Thus the postwar period witnessed a greater assimilation of Catholics into the mainstream of American life, but at the same time tensions and suspicions about the compatibility of Catholicism and Americanism remained.

In terms of economic ethics John F. Cronin, a Sulpician priest, a teacher and writer, and an assistant director of the Social Action Department of the National Catholic Welfare Conference, was the successor of John A. Ryan. The postwar economic conditions were greatly changed. The problems of the Depression no longer existed, although they had been solved in an artificial way through the war economy. Workers now began to be part of the middle class, with automobiles and homes of their own. Unprecedented prosperity marked the American economic scene in general.

Father Cronin wrote on Catholic social principles and Catholic social action. His best known book, *Social Principles and Economic Life* published in 1959, was often used in Catholic colleges and seminaries as a textbook. An earlier version in somewhat different form had been published in 1950 and a later revised version in 1964 incorporated the teaching of the two important encyclicals of Pope John XXIII—*Mater et magistra* and *Pacem in terris*.[3] Cronin was also acknowledged by the American bishops as their expert on communism.[4]

Although Cronin in many ways is the successor of John A. Ryan in the mainstream of American Catholic social ethics, there are significant differences between Ryan and himself. Cronin shows a much heavier dependence on authoritative papal and hierarchical church teaching. It is true that the later Ryan appealed more to such teachings, especially at times to justify and defend his own positions. In his widely used textbook Cronin begins each chapter with long excerpts from appropriate papal and episcopal teachings.

Cronin is much more optimistic about the American economic scene and does not see the need for great changes. In the 1950 version of his textbook the Sulpician strongly defends the papal program of Pius XI and Pius XII for a somewhat radical reconstruction of the social order based on the program of the organic or corporate society. However, after 1954 Pope Pius XII himself seldom referred to this plan, and his successor, John XXIII, gave only brief mention to his predecessors' plan in his own encyclicals in the early 1960s. The later Cronin also abandons the call for reconstruction.[5] Cronin recognizes the need for some reform and specifically points out three troublesome areas—the persistence of poverty in certain sectors, the increasing challenge of automation, and the stubborn fact of unemployment. However, basically Cronin accepts the existing system and sees these problems as ongoing challenges, for our living standards are unquestionably high and more Americans have moved into the middle class. In terms of material prosperity Cronin is basically content with the existing system and its ability to deal with the ongoing challenges, but the Sulpician economist reminds his students that material prosperity can never be the ultimate goal of society. At times Cronin is quite defensive and apologetic about the American system. Competitive individualism is no longer the dominant form in our society, and great changes for the better have occurred in our economic structure.[6]

Perhaps the biggest substantive difference between Cronin and Ryan concerns the role of the state in social reform. Cronin describes the American state as moving toward some approximation of statism by becoming overcentralized and absorbing functions which should be committed to lesser powers and groups.[7] The practical involvements of Ryan and Cronin well illustrate the differences existing between them. Ryan was labeled by some as a socialist. He championed for a long time many of the social reforms that ultimately came into existence with Franklin Delano Roosevelt, while some of his progressive social proposals have never been put into practice. Ryan was associated and identified with the Roosevelt administration and the New Deal, as was well epitomized in the title of his biography —*Right Reverend New Dealer.* John Cronin was acknowledged as the American bishops' expert on communism. He became associated with Congressman Richard Nixon and shared with Nixon and others his knowledge about communist activity and possible spying in atomic espionage rings and in the State Department, even naming names such as Alger Hiss. From 1953 to 1960 Cronin was a speech writer—the only speech writer—for Vice-President Nixon. However, Cronin, because of his position at the National Catholic Welfare Conference, did not actively participate in the presidential campaign of 1960 and after that time had no further contact with Nixon.[8]

The truly pioneering work done in Catholic social ethics in the post-Second World War era was that of the Jesuit John Courtney Murray. Murray addressed head on the question of the compatibility between Catholicism and American democracy and tried to prove the thesis that Catholicism had nothing to fear from American democracy and American democracy had nothing to fear from Catholicism.

Roman Catholics, with emphasis on the Roman, were somewhat suspicious of American pluralism, freedom, and, especially, of the separation of church and state. Catholic teaching until the Second Vatican Council maintained that in the ideal order the state, since it is a creature of God and owes worship to God, should support the one true church, thus advocating the union of church and state. However, in practice the Catholic Church tolerated the system of separation of church and state lest greater evils result from trying to enforce the ideal. The genius of John Courtney Murray was to confront the former Catholic position and show that a development of Catholic teaching in the light of historical circumstances could fully accept the American system of separation of church and state and espouse religious liberty. The Declaration on Religious Freedom of the Second Vatican Council crowned his work with success.

Murray also contributed to the other side of the problematic. Many Americans, even after the Second World War, remained suspicious of Catholicism and its commitment to the American understanding and ethos. The American Jesuit proved that Catholic Americans could wholeheartedly support the American political system. In fact, the basic principles of equality and the right to life, liberty, and the pursuit of happiness are not only compatible with Catholic understanding but are actually based on a natural-law view which has been developed and championed by Catholic thought. Ironically, many secularists and Protestants in the United States no longer accept the basic philosophy of natural law, so that it is only the Catholic tradition which now supports the philosophical grounding of the American political system and the basic rights of human beings. Catholics are not only committed to the American political system, but they alone have a philosophy which adequately supports the basic truths on which the system rests. However, Murray is no uncritical observer of the American scene, and he candidly and clearly points out various flaws. Murray's accomplishment was to solve the problematic that confronted American Catholicism from its very beginning—Could one be both Catholic and American at one and the same time?

John Courtney Murray was an academic person, more so than any other author considered in this study. He was not connected with any particular movement or organization, although he did have a great influence on the life and times of American Catholics. Murray was born in New York City in 1904, joined the Society of Jesus, and after the usual Jesuit training and education was ordained a priest in 1933.[9] He earned a doctorate in theology at the Gregorian University in Rome and taught theology, specializing in the areas of grace and of the Trinity, for thirty years at Woodstock College in Maryland until his death in 1967. He was the editor of the Jesuit theological journal *Theological Studies* (since 1941), which under his editorship became the most highly respected Catholic theological journal in the United States. Our author also frequently contributed articles to the more popular Jesuit magazine *America,* on whose staff for two years (1945-1946) Murray was an associate editor. In the 1940s he was not always sure that he should continue teaching theology at Woodstock, but he remained there until his death. His research interests and writings were primarily in the area of church and society and took the form of long scholarly articles.[10] However, his short book *The Problem of God Yesterday and Today* showed the more systematic side of his theological interests.[11] He was a visiting professor at Yale in 1951-1952 and later received honorary doctorates from many American universities in recognition of his work on the question of religious liberty and on the Catholic presence in American democracy.

Murray's writings on church and state in the 1950s brought him into intellectual discussion and conflict with many others in the Catholic Church. In the United States Murray was continuously involved in debate with Joseph Clifford Fenton, the editor of the *American Ecclesiastical Review,* and other writers in that journal. His position sharply contrasted with that of Cardinal Alfredo Ottaviani, the influential head of the Vatican Congregation of the Holy Office, which defends and protects theological orthodoxy. Ottaviani himself was an ardent supporter of the union of church and state as an ideal. In 1955 Murray was silenced by Rome through Jesuit superiors and forbidden to write on the topic of church and state. Murray was not even able to publish his final article on the interpretation of Pope Leo XIII's teaching on church and state which was at that time in galley proofs for publication in *Theological Studies.* He obediently accepted the command of his superiors and turned his attention to aspects of American culture itself and to the presence of the Catholic Church in that culture.

In 1962 the Second Vatican Council began, but Murray had no input into the preliminary drafts of the council on the subject of religious liberty and was even "disinvited" from attending the first session. However, he was invited to the second session of the council as the personal theologian of Cardinal Spellman of New York. Recall that the question of religious liberty was a very important matter on the agenda of the American bishops. Spellman and the other American bishops were eager to show that the

American system was not second best or something merely to be
tolerated. Murray's sophisticated defense of religious liberty was
known to them, though they had not publicly defended him in his
earlier struggles. Murray later became an official theological
peritus (expert) and was most influential in drafting various ver-
sions of the document on religious liberty and in shaping the final
positions.[12] Then, ten years after his silencing, Murray was vindicated by an ecumenical council of the church whose teaching
he had influenced in a most significant way. Two years later he
died at age 62.

II. Murray's Presuppositions

In keeping with the emphasis on methodology in this study
and in order to appreciate better the substantive positions taken
by Murray, this section will concentrate on the methodological
presuppositions of his work. Looking back after the acceptance
of religious freedom by the Second Vatican Council, Murray
maintains that this new teaching is due to the Catholic Church's
acceptance (but not in a blind or uncritical way) of two great
movements that began in the nineteenth century—the secularity
of society and the state along with historical mindedness.[13] This
observation provides us with a clue for understanding what appears to be the two most important presuppositions in Murray's
own work. Murray accepts the secularity of society and the state,
but even more fundamental and more pervasive in all his writings
is his acceptance of natural law. The second presupposition of
Murray's efforts is precisely the matter of historical consciousness.

Natural law

The basis for Murray's entire approach is natural law in both
its theological and philosophical aspects. From the theological
perspective natural law recognizes in the epistemological order
that reason is able to arrive at ethical wisdom and knowledge for
the Christian, so that faith and scripture are not the only sources
of ethical wisdom. The epistemological aspect rests on the ontological or metaphysical reality of the natural order as distin-

guished from the supernatural order. According to Catholic teaching the natural order remains valid even within the order of grace.

From his earliest writings Murray insists on the significant distinction between the supernatural and the natural, the order of grace and the order of nature, the realm of the spiritual and the realm of the temporal. On the basis of the natural law and what is common to all human beings, we can find agreement with those of other faiths and those who profess no faith. There may be greatly different motivations, but there can be basic agreement both on goals and on the means to obtain them in the temporal or the natural order. Although the distinction is based on an abstraction from the experiential order, it still retains its truth.[14]

Such a distinction paves the way for Murray's approach to many of the questions and problems he faced. The life of the church and the unique and distinctive importance of the Catholic Church lies on the level of the supernatural or grace. On the level of the natural the Catholic shares much more with all other human beings. Within such a perspective it is easy to see how Murray could propose his positions that in the temporal order Catholics can and must cooperate with all people of good will to bring about the common good and social peace, that there can be a legitimate separation between church and state, and that Catholics might be able to assent fully to a democratic government that calls for the separation of church and state. Murray readily admits that the distinction between the sacred and the secular order of human life is the first principle in his coming to grips with these questions.[15]

Although Murray clearly distinguishes the supernatural order of the church from the natural order of civil society and of the state, he does not want to accept a complete separation between them. Before our author became involved in the debate over church and state, he was interested in the wider problem of the church's relationship to society. Murray strongly condemned the secularism and materialism of our age.[16] In the theoretical realm he spoke out against the danger of that false liberalism which, as a militant secularism, denies any place to religion in human social life.[17]

Murray wants to avoid the two extremes of failing to distinguish the two orders, on the one hand, and of secularism, on the other hand, by insisting on the broader understanding of Catholic action as it was known at that time. Yes, Murray recognizes a sharp distinction between the spiritual and the temporal order;

each order has its own distinct finality and purpose. The City of God is not the City of Man. The organic connection and the mediator between the two orders and the two cities is the laity. The ministerial priesthood mediates God in the supernatural order and gives nourishment and guidance to the Christian people. The function of the laity is to go into the temporal order and society in order to Christianize them.[18] Religion, faith, and the supernatural cannot be excluded from human existence. Through the laity there is a mission of the church to the temporal order and to the society in which we live. There are two reasons for the church's involvement in the temporal order through the ministry of the laity. First, involvement in the temporal sphere brings about those conditions which are favorable to the eternal and thereby helps our eternal destiny. Second, the perfection of social being is an end willed by God, even though it is not an ultimate end but only an intermediate one. The unity of the City of God and the unity of the City of Man are two different realities. However, charity motivates us to become involved in the techniques of politics to work for the peace and good of the City of Man.[19]

Murray espouses what he calls an incarnational humanism. Although there is a radical discontinuity between the order of grace and the order of nature, nature does not become irrelevant to grace. Incarnational humanism has a place for all that is natural, human, and terrestrial. Nature does not stand in a relationship of causality to grace, but it is both dispositive and disponible in regard to grace. The work of human society in using reason toward positing justice to achieve a proper civilization and humanization is a *praeparatio evangelica*. The Christian and the community of the church are helped in their Christian life by being in such an atmosphere. Also, the creation of a temporal order of justice and of civic fraternity has been a humanistic aspiration connatural to the Christian heart.[20]

In the light of such an understanding of the two orders, Murray speaks about the temporal order and earthly society on the basis of human reason, which is common to all inhabitants of the City of Man. Murray employs his natural-law approach in dealing with questions of the common good of society—peace and war, censorship, civic unity. Murray never appeals to scripture in his theological considerations of political ethics. In fact, our author on one occasion cavalierly dismisses the contention that the Sermon on the Mount has guidance to give to foreign policy.[21] He opposes an approach to religious freedom which comes to the same conclusion as his because its approach is too scriptural and theological and fails to give enough importance to the political and puridical dimensions of the question.[22] Murray is not unaware of the Catholic teaching that one cannot observe the substance of the natural law for a long time without grace or a change of heart and even mentions it early in his writings, but such a teaching does not enter into the heart of Murray's understanding.[23] There are occasional references about the need to return to God and God's law in order to change society, but such reform remains on the periphery of his thought.[24] The temporal order is governed by reason and natural law which are common to all human beings.

The acceptance of natural law by Murray also includes the philosophical aspect of natural law. Once one recognizes that, on the basis of common human nature and human reason, one shares with others what is required for living in society with its temporal finality, then the question shifts to what is meant by human reason and human nature. Our author makes no apologies for his Scholastic and Thomistic concept of natural law as being a part of the tradition of reason and constituting the *philosophia perennis*. Murray ends his 1960 book of essays *We Hold These Truths* with two chapters on the natural law. In "The Doctrine Is Dead" Murray laments the fact that in America the natural-law ethic, which launched Western constitutionalism and gave essential form to the American system of government, has now ceased to sustain the structure and direct the action of this Christian commonwealth. However, in the final chapter Murray maintains "The Doctrine Lives." There are very significant decisions which must be made in our contemporary world by our society, but Murray asserts that even more important than the individual decisions are the structural foundations of the political, social, and economic orders. Natural law gives us, not a blueprint for all of society, but rather a skeletal law to which flesh and blood must be added by competent, rational political activity.

There are four premises of natural law which seem quite abstract, but in reality they are the elaboration by the reflective intelligence of a set of data that are ultimately empirical. First, natural law presupposes a realist epistemology that asserts the real to be the measure of knowledge and also maintains the possibility that intelligence can reach the real—the nature of things. Second, natural law implies a metaphysics of nature. Nature is a teleological concept, and the "form" of a thing is its final cause—the goal of its becoming. There is a natural inclination in human beings to achieve the fullness of one's own being. Third, natural law supposes a natural theology acknowledging that there is a God who is eternal reason, the author of all nature who wills that the order of nature be fulfilled in all its purposes. Fourth, natural law presupposes a morality. Since human beings are rational, the order of nature is, not an order of necessity to be fulfilled blindly as it is by animals, but an order of reason and freedom. Human reason discovers this ordering, and the human will freely conforms to it.[25]

Such a natural law is both immanent and transcendent. Thomas Aquinas has described natural law as the participation of the rational creature in the eternal law. The natural law is rational but not rationalistic. It is not the work of autonomous human reason as a self-sufficient reality in itself but is transcendentally related to the eternal law as the plan in the mind of God. However, since the natural law is also immanent, it can be related to the eternal law without any tyrannical heteronomy, for reason discovers the natural law in human nature itself. There is room for a proper historicity in the natural law because of its immanent aspect, which in changing historical circumstances admits the possibilities of new orderings and new human institutions. But the transcendent aspect founded in the reason of God assures that the new orders conform to the order of reason which is structured by absolute and unalterable first principles. History does not alter the basic structure of human nature nor affect basic human destiny and experience, but history changes human reality and brings about new situations.[26]

There are different operations or ways in which human intelligence grasps the moral reality. First, intelligence grasps the ethical a priori, the first principle of moral consciousness, not by argument but merely by being conscious of itself. Good is to be done and evil is to be avoided. Second, after some basic experience of human existence, intelligence can grasp the meaning of good and evil in basic human relationships and situations. Third, as human experience unfolds, simple human reason can arrive at the derivative natural-law principles generally associated with the ten commandments. These three rational operations are within the range of all, for they require only common human experience and a modicum of reflection and reason. A fourth achievement open to human reason involves the requirements of rational human nature in complex human relationships and amid institutional developments in the progress of civilization. Here we deal with what was traditionally known as the more remote principles of the natural law which require greater knowledge, experience, reflection, and dispassion. These are not the province of all but rather of the wise. Murray willingly acknowledges that he is an elitist. On the fourth level, the role of the wise people and of the university comes into play to develop and promote the common consensus.[27]

Murray rejects the many misunderstandings which have arisen about the natural law. Properly understood, the natural-law theory cannot be accused of abstractionism, intuitionism, legalism, immobilism, or biologism. He also quickly rebuts the charge that the natural law is not Christian. Natural-law theory only attempts to give a philosophical account of moral experience and to indicate the way to being human, not to being a saint. Moreover, the gospel invitation never pulls us totally out of the human, for the followers of Jesus are called to perfect our own humanity.[28]

Human rights are derived from the natural law. The human individual is regarded as a member of an order instituted by God and subject to the laws of this ordering. The human individual is essentially social by nature. Objective law grounds human rights because law is the foundation of human duties. Too often people talk about human rights, but they forget to recognize that human rights are ultimately anchored in a natural law which also talks about human obligations and duties.[29]

Murray makes very strong claims for natural law, a stance which will be developed later. It is the only way in which to defend Western constitutionalism, the American proposition, and the general consensus that is necessary for our society today. Murray argues for the truth of natural law and its superiority over other existing systems. He singles out three particular theories for extended discussion and rejection.

First, he considers the law of nature proposed in the Enlightenment, which is much different from the natural law of the *philosophia perennis*. Locke's theory of the law of nature is deficient because of its rationalism, individualism, and nominalism. Above all such a theory suffers from an individualism which sees the person as an atom and reduces all society to the level of the contractual, for there are no objective social bonds which bring us together into human and political society. There is no reality upon which the theory is based but only a fictitious state of nature and a disembodied idea of the human.[30]

Murray gives attention to two approaches associated with American Protestant thought. Although our author never mentions the names most often associated with these two theories, it is obvious that he is speaking about the social-gospel school whose principal figure was Walter Rauschenbusch and the later school of Christian realism personified by Reinhold Niebuhr.[31]

The social-gospel school held sway in the nineteenth and early twentieth centuries. Its style was voluntarist, not intellectualist, for it appealed primarily to the will of God. The will of God is above all found through somewhat fundamentalist appeals to the scriptures. Such a morality is subjectivistic, emphasizing especially a morality of intention and giving little or no importance to the objective. Its whole spirit is individualistic in the sense of rejecting authority outside the individual and in focusing on individual, interpersonal relationships as the ethical standard and criterion even for complex social problems. Christian perfectionism becomes a societal requirement. All societal problems would be done away with if Christians would just love their neighbor. Murray dismisses as utterly naive those who ask what the application of the Sermon on the Mount has to do with American foreign policy.

Christian realism has criticized such a simplistic approach and now is supplanting it. Complexity and ambiguity, especially because of the presence of sin in the world, are the hallmarks of such an approach. Pragmatism and consequentualism are given great importance. This approach sees things as so complex that making a right or wrong moral judgment is impossible. The self-righteousness of the older approach is replaced with a recognition that social responsibility calls for us to accept the guilt of sin and stand under the judgment of God. Murray's discussion of these approaches is quite superficial and, in reality, somewhat of a caricature.

These two theories to a great extent form the context or the basis for much of American foreign policy, but neither can deal adequately with three basic problems—the relationship between individual and social morality, the national interest of the nation-state, and the understanding of power. These two approaches vacillate between a naive biblical perfectionism or a Realpolitik. What are problems for the Protestant moralist, either of the older approach or the newer, are really only pseudoproblems and in fact no problem at all for those who follow the tradition of reason and of natural law. There is no dichotomy between moral man and immoral society, for human beings are by nature social. The imperatives of political and social morality are derived from the very order of political and social reality itself with its fivefold structure of obligatory political ends—justice, freedom, security, the general welfare, and civic unity or peace. Since human beings are by nature social, there should be no such dichotomy between the individual and the social. Nor does national self-interest create a problem if properly understood in the light of the tradition of natural law. National self-interest has a relative and proximate status as an end of political action, but political action must also in some minimum measure realize the fivefold structure of obligatory political ends. National self-interest, rightly understood, is successfully achieved only at the interior of the growing international order to which the pursuit of national interest can and must contribute. Nor is power a real problem. The tradition of reason distinguishes between force and violence on the basis of teleology. Force is the measure of power necessary and sufficient to uphold the valid purposes and ends of both law and politics. Violence is that which exceeds this measure and destroys the order both of law and of politics. Murray thus confidently proposes his natural law theory as the tradition of reason and the *philosophia perennis,* which alone can serve as a guide for human political endeavor.

Historical consciousness

A second presupposition of Murray's thought, which came to light over the years, is historical mindedness. There are three important ramifications of historical consciousness in Murray's own work especially as related to religious liberty—a hermeneutic of papal teaching, the development of doctrine, and the philosophical consequences of historical mindedness.

Murray was confronted with many papal documents, especially from Pope Leo XIII in the nineteenth century, which advocated the confessional state and the union of church and state. In advocating a new approach to religious liberty Murray had to deal with these authoritative texts which proposed as an ideal or thesis the rejection of religious liberty. An historical hermeneutic would have to distinguish in these teachings what was permanently valid (Murray often used the term transtemporal) and what was historically and polemically conditioned. Such a hermeneutic had to be adopted by Murray if he wanted to propose a different teaching in the Catholic Church. At that time it was not a viable possibility for Murray to propose that the past teaching might have been even partially in error. Our author successfully and brilliantly applied such an historical hermeneutic to the teaching of Leo XIII.[32]

Intimately connected with an historical hermeneutic is the question of the development of doctrine in the Catholic Church. Is it possible for the Catholic Church to maintain one position in the nineteenth century and another position in the twentieth century? At the Vatican Council it was very evident that the primary question involved in the matter of religious liberty was this deeper question of the development of church teaching.[33]

The recognition of historical consciousness in these areas logically leads to an understanding of how historical mindedness affects one's philosophy. In later years Murray, recognizing his dependence on Bernard Lonergan, briefly discusses the question in terms of the shift from classicism to historical consciousness. Classicism understands truth as objective truth "existing out there" apart from history and formulated in verbally immutable propositions. Truth remains unchanged even in its formulations but can find different applications in different historical circumstances. Historical consciousness wants to hold on to the objective nature of truth, but it is also concerned with the historicity of truth and with progress in the grasp and penetration of what is true by the subject. In the nineteenth and early twentieth century the movement to historical consciousness resulted in the extreme of modernism which actually destroyed the notion of truth with its objective character, its universality, and its absoluteness. The Second Vatican Council embraced a sane historical consciousness characterized by concern for the truth not simply as a verbal proposition to be repeated but as a possession to be lived. Historical consciousness gives importance to the subject seeking truth and to the historical reality itself.[34]

In the light of these presuppositions it is easier to understand Murray's approach to the substantive questions he faced. The first question addressed by Murray in the 1940s was the problem of intercredal cooperation. Although this discussion took place early in Murray's career and did not perdure, his first writings set the stage for his later work. The two most significant issues addressed by Murray in his more mature scholarship were the relationship between church and the state with its more particular aspect of religious liberty and the relationship between Catholicism and the American political system. These three areas will now be studied in depth.

III. Intercredal Cooperation

From our perspective one of the most fascinating aspects of Murray's discussion of intercredal cooperation is the debate between himself and Paul Hanly Furfey on this issue. The problem of intercredal cooperation arises from the fact that Catholicism understands itself as the one true church of Jesus Christ, but it exists in a pluralistic society. The Catholic is both Catholic believer and citizen in a religiously pluralistic and even de-Christianized society. The two important realities are the unity of the Catholic Church with its claim to be the one true church of Jesus Christ and the social peace and unity of the temporal society in which Catholics live with many others.

Murray contends that in order to bring about a greater realization of social justice and peace, especially in the midst of the Second World War and after the war, organized cooperation is necessary. The efforts of individuals will not be enough to bring about the necessary changes. Organized cooperation on the part of all people, especially Christians, is required. Intercredal cooperation for Murray involves an alliance of effort between Catholics and non-Catholics with some organizational framework on the basis of some pre-existing agreement of minds and wills for the effective application of Christian and ethical principles to the right ordering of the sociotemporal life of humanity. Such organized cooperation is called for by the crisis of the times in which we live.[35]

The organizational form of such united action is not proposed in terms of a superstructure or a bureaucratic organization. By organizational cooperation Murray means that Catholics and non-Catholics work together in organized activity on the basis of some common ground to accomplish their purpose in the sociotemporal sphere. Murray especially commends the Catholic Sword of the Spirit Movement in England and the Anglican Religion and Life Movement, which promised to work through parallel action in the religious field and joint action in the social and international field. This organized cooperation will be headed by lay people and will not involve Catholic groups directly under the jurisdiction and pastoral authority of the bishop. The individual members as Catholics are under the hierarchy, and the expediency of such cooperation in general is left to the judgment of the bishops, but the movements themselves and the organizations are interconfessional.[36]

Such organized cooperation is described by Murray as "religio-civic action." The crisis our world faces is a spiritual crisis, but in the temporal order. There is need for a spiritualization of the temporal order of society so that a new world order might come about and social insitutions will come into existence which reflect this new ethos. The various religions share much in common about the temporal order and how it should be structured. This cooperation is not merely civic nor is it purely religious. It is a question of civic unity because it is formed for the pursuit of the common good in the social, economic, and temporal orders, but it transcends the merely civic because its bond is religious— faith in God and the love of his law.[37]

From his general background and from his extensive reading of the contemporary literature on the subject, John Murray is aware of the arguments that can be used against him. The Catholic Church is the one true church of Jesus Christ. She, therefore, does not recognize the ecclesial realities of other churches, is opposed to any *communicatio in sacris* (sharing in holy things or in faith and in worship), and is ever vigilant about any intercredalism which smacks of indifferentism. Our author solves the problem by his distinction between the supernatural order and the natural, the City of God and the Earthly City, the supernatural order and the temporal, the church and the world. Intercredal cooperation involves unity on the second but not on the first of these orders, and the basis of such intercredal cooperation in the temporal sphere is the natural law, which the Catholic Church shares with all human beings. Yes, Catholics and others might bring different motives to what they do in the temporal order, but they are working for the common good of the temporal order on the basis of a shared agreement of what is good for the temporal order grounded on natural law.[38]

Murray clearly distinguishes his approach to intercredal cooperation from that held by some Protestants. The theory of cooperation proposed at the 1929 Stockholm conference on "Life and Work" is definitely at variance with Murray's concept. The Stockholm meeting and many Protestants see the common activity in the interest of peace, justice, and brotherhood as an ecclesiastical movement whose cooperation now brings about in an incipient form the unified church of Christ, which we are all trying to bring into existence. For the Catholic, Christian unity already exists and has a visible face in the one true church of Jesus Christ, the Catholic Church. According to Murray there are two different approaches to this question of intercredal cooperation. The liberal Protestant takes hold of the religious end of the problem and asks for agreement on certain fundamentals of Christian theology—an approach which solves nothing but creates a false unity on the religious level. The Catholic takes hold of the social end of the problem and finds unity on the social plane and in the temporal order based on agreement on the natural, religious, and moral principles of social unity and peace (the natural law). Liberal Protestants err by seeing this cooperation and unity as related to the supernatural and ecclesiological levels, whereas conservative Roman Catholics such as Francis J. Connell,[39] professor of moral theology at The Catholic University of America, err by ruling out cooperation in the temporal sphere because of the danger of indifferentism.[40]

Murray willingly admits shortcomings in his solution, but these result from the tension of the reality itself. The solution is not ideal. Agreement on the natural-law principles alone is not enough, but it is the most that can be obtained, granted the present situation. The Catholic believes in the enduring validity of the idea of nature within the order of grace even if this is not the total picture. Yes, there might be some danger of indifferentism for Catholics, but the importance of working for the common good of society in the midst of the present-day crisis overcomes these problems. In addition, the problems of overcoming indifferentism can be reduced to the scandal of the weak with the obvious solution of educating the weak.[41]

Paul Hanly Furfey entered into debate with Murray on this question of intercredal cooperation in late 1943.[42] The short discussion between the two centered on two issues—the substantive question itself and the interpretation of relevant papal documents. The substantive differences between Furfey and Murray stem from their different overall positions—Furfey the radical and Murray the liberal.

Furfey strongly opposes intercredal cooperation understood as an organizational unity that is both spiritual and interconfessional, based on common ground shared by all and not under

direct authority of the hierarchy. Furfey does not object to cooperation, but cooperation should mean that non-Catholics and
others should cooperate with us and not the other way around. He
believes that in Murray's scheme we Catholics would lose what is
most distinctive and most important in our social action. The
mind of the church insists that every true and lasting reform has
proceeded from the sanctuary. The Catholic solution for the problems of society is supernatural. The Catholic approach recognizes the importance of natural means such as labor unions,
social legislation, efficient social work, and public-health measures, but these are subordinate to the supernatural. Unfortunately, there is little Catholic social action in our country in the
sense of the supernatural means stressed by the popes. Where is
the crusade of prayer and penance prescribed by Pope Pius XI as
the only remedy for the evil which torments humanity? How
often have we preached detachment from worldly goods as a
defense against communism? How often have we pointed to the
Eucharist as the only remedy for the class struggle? Intercredal
cooperation would deny our most important and effective means
of social action.[43]

Much of the discussion between Murray and Furfey involves
the interpretation of authoritative papal teaching, especially
Pope Pius X's *Singulari quadam* (1912) and *Notre charge* (1910).
In *Singulari quadam* Pius X settled a dispute which arose in Germany by tolerating the fact that Catholics could belong to intercredal Christian trade unions, even though this was not ideal.
Murray emphasizes the need for an historical hermeneutic in
studying *Singulari quadam* and accuses Furfey of being unhis-
torical. According to Murray Pius X's thought is controlled by
two important principles—the unity of the church recognizing
the danger of indifferentism and a social concern for the common
good of society. On the basis of the social concern for the common
good, Pius permitted Catholic participation in such Christian
trade unions despite some possible dangers. Today the popes
give even more emphasis to the concern for the common good of
the temporal society as illustrated in many recent papal statements. Intercredal cooperation, consequently, is justified and
necessary today.[44] Furfey sees the action of Pius X as a mere
toleration of an evil involving serious hazards to faith. The Holy
See does not encourage such mixed trade unions any more than it
encourages mixed marriages.[45]

Pius X, in *Notre charge* in 1910, condemned the French social movement called *Le Sillon,* which had been founded by Marc Sangnier (recall that Peter Maurin was involved in this movement in France after he left the Christian Brothers). After 1905 the movement had begun to espouse an intercredal cooperation calling upon all Christians to unite to work for the reform of civilization. Murray claims that this is a type of intercredalism to which he is opposed precisely because it confuses the supernatural and the natural.[46] Furfey interprets the condemnation of intercredalism of *Le Sillon* as based on the fact that Catholic members of such groups cannot use the full social doctrine and teaching of Catholicism. The Catholic must check one's Catholicism at the door so as not to shock one's comrades.[47]

There are two weak points in Murray's consideration which will continue to be of importance and interest in his subsequent writings. First, he presumes that at least among other Christians there exists agreement about the natural law. Second, and perhaps more significant, although Murray bases his approach on a sharp distinction between the supernatural and the natural order, he also is forced to recognize that the Catholic tradition acknowledges some closer union between the two. Catholic doctrine holds that the integral observance of the natural law is impossible for human beings without the aid of grace. It is precisely this aspect of Catholic teaching which Furfey constantly stresses and which results in his emphasis on grace as that which is primary and absolutely necessary. Murray's response in 1943 recognizes the insufficiency of the natural law alone to achieve even the perfection proper to its own order, but what is insufficient is not therefore useless.[48]

Murray's substantive position and methodological approach to the question of intercredal cooperation can be looked upon in retrospect as paving the way for much of his future work. The problem centered on the role of the Catholic church with its self-understanding as the one true church of Jesus Christ and its relationship to the temporal order in the context of religious pluralism. The relationship between the church and social peace and unity would be at the forefront of his concerns in the future. He would always be dealing with the dual reality of the same person as a Catholic in the supernatural order and as citizen in the temporal order. Already some methodological approaches were developing which would also serve as the basis for his future work—the distinctions between the order of grace and the order of nature, between the sacred and the secular, the natural law as something held in common by Catholics and other Christians, the recognition that social justice and peace in the temporal order does not imply a unity of faith. In addition, Murray brought to his understanding of older papal documents an historical hermeneutic and emphasized the need to sort out the doctrinal principles from the contingent historical aspects of the question. The stage is thus set for Murray's future work.

IV. Religious Liberty

The general question of the relationship between church and state and the more specific question of religious liberty have always been present within the Catholic tradition. The genius of John Courtney Murray was to propose a new theory that would accept religious liberty and a certain separation of church and state as proposed in limited constitutional government. To understand Murray's contribution, it is necessary to know what had been the official teaching of the hierarchical magisterium and the teaching generally found in the theology and canonical textbooks before the Second Vatican Council. Recall that it was Ryan's acceptance of the older position that occasioned much controversy in the United States. Throughout his attempt at formulating a new approach Murray was at odds with the contemporary defenders of the older position, especially Joseph Clifford Fenton, Francis Connell, and George Shea, all of whom wrote in the *American Ecclesiastical Review*.[49]

In keeping with a significant strand in the Catholic tradition, the older position gives primary importance to objective truth. A sincere but erroneous conscience is endowed with individual, internal, personal freedom. Such a conscience or person can never be forced to change one's belief or religious faith. However, such a conscience, since it is not objectively in conformity with the truth, has no right to external, social freedom within society, for the propagation of such falsehood goes against the good of the state. Error has no public rights. The concept of the state supposed in the older position recognizes that the state deals only with the temporal order of human existence, but the temporal always remains subordinate to the spiritual or the supernatural realm. Since the state is a creature of God, the state has an obligation to worship God. In addition, there is the hypothetical natural-law obligation to worship God in the way in which God reveals he should be worshipped. Now, since God has revealed the Catholic Church as the true church of Jesus Christ, the state must worship God in accord with the teaching of the Catholic Church. The state in such an approach has both a religious and an ethical function. According to its ethical character, which might even be called its paternal character, the state must repress error—above all religious error. In repressing error the state is not doing injury to anyone's rights, for error has no public rights. The state has the positive function of caring for the common good, but religious error is harmful for the good of other citizens whose possession of the truth is threatened.

However, what has been presented here represents the thesis or the ideal which should be present in a Catholic society. John A. Ryan went out of his way to give as liberal an interpretation as possible by saying there probably was not such a Catholic country existing in the world at that time—not even Spain. Others talked about the ideal as existing only when Catholics constituted a majority of the population. The traditional approach thus distinguished between the thesis or ideal and the hypothesis. In circumstances other than the ideal, Catholics can tolerate a situation in which all religions have religious freedom. This toleration is ultimately based on what is for the common good. If it is impossible or harmful to the common good to deny religious liberty to all others except Catholics, then the religious liberty of all can be tolerated. However, the ideal always remains—only the Catholic Church as such has a right to religious liberty. Religious liberty of others is merely tolerated because in the existing circumstances any other solution would be harmful to the common good.[50]

Concept of religious liberty

Murray gradually developed and defended his theory of religious liberty over a period of years beginning in the early 1940s. Thomas Love and others have already traced with meticulous accuracy the evolution and changes in Murray's thought as he gradually came to his position and then defended it against attacks. Our exposition will be more synthetic, although certain key points involved in Murray's development will be mentioned.

First, it is necessary to know what is meant by religious liberty. Rights can be understood as empowerments or as immunities. The right to religious liberty is an immunity existing in

civil society and involves a twofold immunity. No person can be
forced to act against one's conscience in religious matters, and no
one may coercively be restrained or impeded from acting in accord with conscience.[51] Since religious liberty is primarily an
immunity in civil society, there is no direct connection between
religious liberty and freedom in the church. However, behind the
notion of religious freedom as an immunity in civil society there
stands a recognition of the dignity and freedom of the individual
human person. This same dignity and freedom of the human
person also has some repercussions in the theory and practice of
authority in the church.[52]

There are various aspects involved in the free exercise of
religion. Ecclesial, or corporate, religious freedom is the right of
religious communities to corporate, internal autonomy within
society. Freedom of association and freedom of religious expression are both integral parts of religious freedom.[53]

Murray, from his earliest writings on the subject, has insisted
that religious freedom is more than only a theological and an ethical concept. In 1945 he realized that the problem is threefold—
theological, ethical, and political.[54] At the time of the Second
Vatican Council Murray insisted that religious freedom is formally a juridical or constitutional question which has foundations in theology, ethics, political philosophy, and jurisprudence.
Some theologians and bishops at the council who were in favor of
religious liberty did not agree with Murray's concept because it
was too political and did not give enough importance to the theological and the ethical. Yet Murray pointed out a number of defects in an approach which employed only the theological, with
its emphasis on the freedom of the act of faith, and the ethical,
with its support for the rights of conscience.

According to Murray religious freedom is not formally and
primarily a theological and ethical concept. Such an argument is
abstract and says nothing about the concrete historical context
which has varied greatly. Historical mindedness calls for a more
concrete approach. From such a theological and ethical perspective the result is an ideal, but traditional philosophies of politics,
law, and jurisprudence do not recognize an ideal instance of constitutional law. Such a limited perspective sets afoot a futile argument about the rights of the erroneous conscience. The public
powers are not competent to judge if the conscience is true or
erroneous or if the person is in good or bad faith. Moreover, a
theological-ethical approach cannot deal with the important prob-

lem of the limits of religious liberty.[55] Can the state or should the state ever interfere with religious liberty? What if certain religious groups propose child sacrifice, polygamy, or celibacy? For Murray the question must be seen primarily as a juridical or constitutional concept which has foundations in theology, ethics, political philosophy, and jurisprudence. To understand Murray's concept it is therefore necessary to appreciate his notion of the state.

Murray's concept of the state

Specifically, Murray understands the contemporary state in terms of constitutional government—a government of limited powers. The mature Murray posits four basic principles for a proper understanding of constitutional government. The first principle is the distinction between the sacred and the secular orders of human life. The whole of human existence is not absorbed by our temporal and terrestrial existence. Each human being has a transcendental and supernatural end which is beyond the power and competency of government. Murray's recognition of the natural or the temporal order as distinguished from the supernatural or spiritual is the basis of this distinction.[56]

In his writings on the narrower question of church and state he constantly emphasizes the dyarchy—there are two societies and they cannot become confused. The distinction can be denied from both aspects of the dyarchy. The church wrongly intrudes into the realm of the temporal in any number of ways. For example, the church can use the temporal and terrestrial power for its own spiritual purposes. The terrestrial or temporal order can also overstep its bounds and allow no room for the sacred order. According to Murray the most recent example of such a position is Continental liberalism, which insists on the autonomy of individual reason and the omnicompetence of the state. The sacred or supernatural order is denied any place in human society.[57] Murray advocates a distinction between the two orders and upholds the autonomy of the temporal. Recall that the two are organically united, as mentioned above, through the conscience of the individual who is both Christian and citizen.

The second important distinction is between society and the state. The state is an agency with a limited role within society. This distinction plays a very important part in Murray's thought and was not present when he first wrestled with the problem of religious freedom in the middle 1940s. In struggling against liberalism and secularism Murray insists that human society must recognize the sacred order and its implications for human existence. Without a distinction between society and the state it is necessary for Murray and the older Catholic position to affirm the obligation of the state with regard to God and God's law. The state is a creature of God and has a natural-law obligation to worship God in the way he wants to be worshipped. Murray correctly recognizes that the relationship of the civil society or the state to God is the basis for the older Catholic teaching on the union of church and state. In this understanding, public religion and public morality are also part of the common good and hence come under the care of the state. The early Murray is not able to come up with a different approach to religious liberty precisely because of his understanding of the obligation and role of the state.[58]

Our author first recognizes the distinction between society and the state when he addresses in 1948 the question of governmental suppression of heresy—the rights and obligations of a Catholic government to suppress by legal measures the public expression of heretical opinions.[59] In this article Murray makes a break with his former position. The state aids the church only through the exercise of its own native power, which is human in its origin, temporal in its finality, and limited in its competence. The civil power is limited and is not to be considered an auxiliary function of the church to be used for the church's own ends. Murray here affirms the autonomy and the limited competency of the state. The state is no longer the subject of an obligation to worship God in the way in which God wants to be worshipped. Just as the state has no power to define the church, so it has no power to impose the definition of the church, as accepted from its citizens, on those of its citizens who do not freely by their own personal act of faith embrace the church. Such an imposition would be beyond the competency of the state. In this same section Murray asserts that the maxim that error has no rights is not an operative political principle precisely because of the limitations of the state. For Murray the important thing is that the state grant and protect the freedom of the church, but a constitutional situation of the religion of the state is not required.[60]

Murray's position was carefully examined and found wanting by George Shea, who even quoted the early Murray against the later Murray and asserted that the state finds the church indirectly through the medium of the Catholic citizenry.[61] Shea made some telling points in his 1950 article, and Murray responded in 1951 with an article in which he tried to synthesize his own position and state it as clearly as possible.[62] For our present purposes this important article has bearing on the distinction between society and state. Here Murray changes and clarifies the definitions he made in 1948. The purpose behind the clarification is quite clear—to recognize the autonomy and limited competency of the state. Murray now distinguishes civil society, political society, the state, and government. Civil society designates the total complex of organized relationships on the temporal plane which arise either from nature or from choice. Political society designates civil society as politically organized. The state is not the body politic, which is the same as political society, but that particular, subsidiary, functional organization of the body politic. It is not a person but a set of institutions whose functions are not coextensive with the functions of society. Its functions are limited to the fact that it is only one, although the highest, subsidiary function of society. In accordance with the subsidiary function, the axiom obtains: "As much state as necessary, as much freedom as possible."[63] Murray claims that Shea has an hypostatized concept of the state, whereas Murray's own notion is functional. There are many questions about Murray's distinctions, but his purpose is entirely clear.[64] The state is seen primarily in terms of a limited function and therefore has no competence in the area of faith and religion. In general Murray indicates that society signifies an area of personal and corporate freedom, whereas state signifies the area in which coercive power may legitimately be applied.

The third principle in Murray's understanding of constitutional government is the distinction between the common good and the public order. The common good includes all the social goods —spiritual, moral, and material which human beings pursue here on earth. Public order, whose care devolves upon the state, is a much narrower concept and embraces those goods which can be achieved by the power of the state—public peace, public morality, and justice. The power of the state is limited to the public order in this threefold sense. The public order thus becomes the criterion which controls and justifies the intervention of the state in all matters including the area of religion. This criterion constitutes the limits of religious liberty and justifies state curtailment and interference.[65]

The fourth principle is both a substantive political truth and the primary rule of political procedure. It is the principle and rule of freedom under the law. Murray often stresses that freedom is the political method par excellence and the highest political goal.[66] Murray contends that the secular exegete may well consider the most significant section of the Vatican document on religious liberty to be the statement that the freedom of human beings be respected as far as possible and curtailed only when and insofar as necessary. Murray sees this basic principle of the free society as having origins in the medieval tradition with its distinction between society and the state, but also as containing an element of blessed newness. Catholic thought has constantly maintained that society is based upon truth, directed toward justice, and animated by charity. In *Pacem in terris* in 1963 Pope John XXIII added the missing fourth term: freedom. Freedom is an end or purpose of society and is the political method par excellence.[67]

Murray's concept of the state accepts the principle of limited constitutional democracy. Democracy today, he wrote in 1951, presents itself with all the force of an idea whose time has come.[68] In keeping with historical mindedness Murray recognizes the most important characteristic of contemporary consciousness is the emphasis on personal and political freedom. We are dealing now with an adult state. No longer can the people be described as the unlettered masses—the term often used by Leo XIII. Leo also described the rulers as *principes*. But today in an adult state free individuals participate in their own government and are not merely the subjects of the paternal care of their rulers. In the light of this contemporary political and personal consciousness Murray proposes his understanding of the state. Recall that Murray sees a tremendous difference between limited constitutional democracy and the liberalism of the nineteenth century.[69]

Murray's position on religious liberty is greatly influenced by his understanding of the role and function of the state. Religious liberty as such can be viewed from two different perspectives. In one sense religious liberty is a *sui generis* right because it raises the issue of human beings' relationship to God and the transcendent, whereas all other civil rights deal only with relations to other human beings and to society. However, in a very true sense religious liberty is also related to all other rights because of its grounding in the nature of the state and in the dignity and rights of the individual person. In defending religious freedom the church now also defends the basic right to freedom of all human beings. So in this sense the right to religious freedom is intimately connected with all the other basic human rights.[70]

The church

To appreciate Murray's position we have examined his understanding of the role of the democratic state. Logically the next step involves Murray's understanding of the church and especially the relationship of the church to temporal society and to the state. The broader question of the relationship between the supernatural or spiritual order and the natural or temporal order is one question, while the specific question of the relationship between church and state is another question. In dealing with the state our author insists on the independence and autonomy of the state. Now he wants to defend the primacy of the spiritual in general and the church in particular and to show how these understandings of the role of the church are compatible with the autonomy of the state.

Murray dealt with the problem of the orderly relationship between the two powers—church and state—in a number of articles published in 1948 and 1949.[71] Specifically, Murray here considers the question of the power of the church in temporal affairs. In keeping with his methodological presuppositions the American Jesuit proceeds from an historical viewpoint. Murray considers three older theories of the power of the church in the temporal order.

The theory of direct power interpreted the primacy of the spiritual to mean that the temporal power is included in it as an emanation from it. The hierocratic theory maintained that Christ who was both priest and king, delegated to Peter and his successors a direct jurisdiction over temporal affairs as well as over spiritual affairs. According to the metaphor of the two swords, the pope ordinarily uses only the spiritual sword and delegates the temporal sword to the prince, but if the prince is delinquent, the pope can and should take over the temporal sword. Murray agrees that on the basis of Christendom such an approach was true. However, the position was never an abstract ideal thesis, but a hypothesis based on the hierocratic hypothesis of the origin and end of political power. In this social hypothesis heresy was treason and treason heresy, and in this political hypothesis the unity and good of the state (if one may use the word state of Christendom) were identically the unity and good of the church.

However, the contemporary political, social, and juridical orders have changed radically so that such a theory is no longer true. Catholic faith is no longer constituent of citizenry, and religious unity is no longer an integral element of the common good. There is no longer just the one society with two powers in it.[72]

Robert Bellarmine, a Jesuit theologian in the Counter-Reformation, proposed what he called the theory of the indirect power of the church. Bellarmine borrows from Aquinas the distinction between the spiritual and the temporal orders, but the temporal is subordinate to the spiritual. He especially defends the primacy of the spiritual against royal absolutists proposing the divine right of kings and denying a legitimate role to the spiritual. The temporal power is not derived from the spiritual power as in the hierocratic theory. The church must always act for spiritual reasons and spiritual ends. Its power extends to everything which helps or hinders the spiritual good of the kingdom of God. The spiritual has no direct power over the temporal, but there is indirect power because of the relationship of the temporal to the spiritual. For spiritual reasons, the pope can depose the ruler.

Murray views Bellarmine's approach as being somewhat transitional. Although the two powers are distinct and in a sense independent, Bellarmine does not recognize that he is dealing with two societies and not just with two powers in the one society. In reality Bellarmine proposes a restricted direct power, for the church can directly produce temporal effects provided it is done for a spiritual purpose. Murray recognizes that Bellarmine in his circumstances rationalized a situation of fact with its contingent juridical exigencies. However, what Bellarmine asserted cannot be a thesis or an ideal for all times.[73]

Murray finds himself much more in agreement with the indirect power theory of John of Paris, a fourteenth-century Dominican theologian. John proposed his theory as a middle way between the theory of the curialists, who exaggerated the role of the spiritual power in temporal things, and the regalists, who extolled the temporal power and downplayed the spiritual. John insisted on the independence of the temporal power on the basis of Aristotelian-Thomistic philosophy. However, there is an indirect subordination of political society to the spiritual society because of the higher end of the spiritual. John stresses that the spiritual power is singly and solely spiritual in character. The church has no direct power in temporal realities and in temporal jurisdiction. The primacy of the spiritual power results in an indirect power over the temporal, but not to the destruction of the independence of the temporal power. The spiritual power by definition must terminate in spiritual realities; in itself and in its manner of exercise the spiritual power of the church must always remain spiritual.

The crucial case here is the deposition of kings and emperors. The ecclesiastical censure in its entirety is spiritual, consisting in excommunication, suspension, and interdict; beyond this the church has no power except indirectly and *per accidens*. The church can excommunicate the king, but not depose him, for its power involves only the moral jurisdiction over the conscience of both king and subjects. However, the subjects can depose the king. John interpreted all the historical facts of the medieval times in accord with his basic principles—the power of the church and its jurisdiction terminate in the consciences of its members and not directly in any temporal effect such as the deposition of the king. John in his discussion saw the problem of church and state in terms of, not two powers or two functions within a unitary society, but rather two societies.[74] Murray points out that John of Paris said, not that the church has "an indirect power," but that the church "indirectly has a power." The church does not have two powers, one direct and one indirect. The church has only one power which is purely spiritual but which indirectly operates temporal effects.[75]

Our author then raises the question of applying the thought of John of Paris to the modern problem. In modern governments the church no longer confronts the temporal power in a concentrated and centralized way such as in the person of the king. Modern political development has brought about a dispersion of the temporal power by adding both the principle of political responsibility of the government institutionalized in the system of free elections and other civic freedoms to the principle of the legal limitation of government which is now institutionalized in modern forms of constitutionalism. The church today does not immediately confront temporal power in the sense of government or the legal order of society. The church comes into relationship with the state only mediately through the citizens. The same person is both Christian and citizen. It is through the conscience of the citizen that the purely spiritual power of the church has repercussions in the temporal order. In a sense the whole system for Murray pivots on freedom. There is the free obedience of the Christian conscience to the magisterial and jurisdictional

authority of the church; second, there is the free participation
of the Christian citizen in the institutions whereby the processes
of temporal life are directed to their proper ends. Murray concludes his analysis of the spiritual power of the church by showing the striking similarities between this understanding and the
role of the state in a limited constitutional government.[76]

Murray's transtemporal principles

What should be the relationship between church and state?
In 1951, in response to Shea and on the basis of his study of the
history of the problem and of the pertinent magisterial documents, Murray attempts a systematic statement of his position.[77] The permanent purpose of the church in her relation with
the state is to maintain her teaching of juridical and social dualism under the primacy of the spiritual against the tendency to
juridical and social monism under the primacy of the political,
which is always a tendency of the state whether it be pagan,
Christianized, or secularized. The church asserts three transtemporal principles rooted in the nature of things which are
applicable in all different circumstances. These three transtemporal principles spell out the meaning of the social and juridical dualism involving both the autonomy and independence of
the temporal and the primacy of the spiritual. Murray states
them very succinctly, and our exposition will basically be a paraphrase and almost an exact citation of his explanation.[78]
    The first principle of the freedom of the church is rooted in
the very nature of the church as a spiritual power and a supernatural society, independent of the state in origin and in function,
which claims primacy over the order of human terrestial life and
all its social forms. The formula of the freedom of the church has
two senses. There is the freedom of the church understood as her
spiritual power—the freedom to teach, rule, and sanctify. Then
there is the freedom of the church understood as the Christian
people—the freedom to hear the teaching of the church and to
obey her laws, to receive the sacramental ministry of grace, and
to live out supernatural lives within the world. The church is
immune from any politicization or subordination by the state.
The church alone defines herself and her activities; the state
accepts the church as "being there," the same way it recognizes
the freedom of the individual as "already there."
    The second principle is that of the necessary harmony be-

tween the two laws which govern human existence and between the whole complex of social institutions and the exigencies of the Christian conscience. This harmony establishes a unity of order in human social life based on its acceptance of the distinction between the two societies and on the primacy of the spiritual. This principle is grounded in the nature of the human individual existing at the present time who is at one and the same time a Christian or a member of the church and a citizen. The individual has a right to demand that the two orders act in harmony in order to protect the integrity of one's personality, spiritual freedom, and the full possibilities of self-fulfillment.

The third principle is the necessity of cooperation of church and state—a cooperation that is ordered and bilateral. The church in its way cooperates with the state, and the state in its way co-operates with the church. Each acts toward its own distinct end which is ultimate in its own order. Since these two ends are ends of human beings, there must be cooperation between the two in order to achieve the ordered human good. This third principle springs from the nature of civil society as a naturally necessary sphere of human life developing toward the perfection of the human personality. Generally speaking, the Christian life is difficult and even morally impossible apart from those conditions of the temporal society such as freedom, justice, and a sufficiency of material goods and of cultural opportunities to whose creation political society and the state in its own way are committed. On the other hand the creation of these conditions of social order is impossible without religion and the church. But remember that it is not the direct function of the church to create a social order any more than it is the direct function of the state to save souls. The contribution of each to the work of the other is indirect but indispensable. The church creates a Christian spirit within the temporal order, and the state aids in creating a temporal structure that may be a milieu conducive for the life of the spirit.

Now the problem for Murray is the application of these trans-temporal principles to the concrete historical circumstances of different times and cultures. Here we find his historical mindedness at work. Church-state relationships follow the vital law of adaptation which ultimately has its grounding in the very nature of the state. The state is variable and has taken on many different styles in history—monarchical, patriarchal, dictatorial, democratic, and so on. The church applies her principles to all

these different circumstances, while recognizing there will never
be an ideal application. There will always be compromises of one
type or another. Murray thus rejects the whole distinction between thesis and hypothesis which had become a central part of
the textbook treatment of church and state. Although the general
approach is clear, there is some confusion because at times
Murray himself invokes the distinction of thesis and hypothesis.
Sometimes the distinction refers to the transtemporal principles
and their historical applications,[79] but in some writings he seems
to include some historical and political aspects in his notion of
thesis.[80]

Murray also strongly insists that the American democracy is
not the basis for establishing a new thesis.[81] Throughout his
writings the American Jesuit never condemns the situation of
religious freedom existing in Spain.[82] At the time of the Second
Vatican Council Murray insists there is no such thing as an ideal
instance of Catholic constitutional law. The categories of ideal
and tolerable, thesis and hypothesis, are invalid categories for
the discussion of constitutional law.[83] Murray even refers to the
"sound Anglo-Saxon and basically Catholic principle of the relativism of political forms."[84]

Murray on a number of occasions examines the historical
development of the various church-state relationships. In so
doing he is attempting to show that none of these can constitute
an ideal or thesis. All are in some sense an hypothesis. Murray
uses his interpretation of the various church-state relationships
in the course of history to prove his own point that there is no such
thing as an ideal or thesis that has been historically incarnated.

The American Jesuit gives great importance to and frequently cites the classic statement of the church's fundamental doctrine as formulated by Pope Gelasius I in 494. This text explicitly
states the doctrine of the two powers but implies the distinction of
the two laws and the two societies. Gelasian dualism sets forth
what should be the basis for Catholic understanding of the church-
state relationship. In this case the pope was attempting a radical
dedivinization of the temporal sphere of the power of the emperor.
The state is not ultimate nor the only society; there is also the
supernatural society of the church.[85]

There were a number of different types of relationships
present in the Middle Ages. Pope Gregory VII, the famous Hilde-
brand, formulated the poignant phrase *libertas Ecclesiae* (the

freedom of the church). The temporal care of religion was limited by the principle of the freedom of the church—the immunity of the church from imperial intervention.[86] However, in the late Middle Ages after a series of strong popes the power of the papacy was expanded into the theory of direct power having the pope holding both swords. The secular was seen as an arm of the church. Such an approach was obviously an hypothesis which came into existence as a result of immaturity proper to a particular age of civilizational development. This theory arose in the hierocratic hypothesis of the origin and end of political power, in the political hypothesis in which the unity and good of the state involved the unity and good of the church, and in a social hypothesis in which heresy was treason and treason heresy. No one can call this the perfect solution. It was occasioned by the disorder and immaturity of the state at the time. There was no other way to keep the ruler just and to insure against tyranny.[87]

Another significant historical development which had great importance in the church was the confessional state. Murray devotes great attention to the historical reality of the confessional state because the defenders of the older opinion saw this as the ideal or thesis of the relationship between church and state. For Murray it is merely an adaptation to the particular historical circumstances of the given time.

The most important historical condition was the rise of the nation state, followed later, after the Protestant Reformation, by the acceptance of the territorial principle *cuius regio, eius religio* —the religion of the ruler becomes the religion of the people. At first the Catholic Church only tolerated such a position. Since the true church is one and universal, it ought not to be the state church or the church of a limited territorial entity. Only later with the rise of Protestantism did this position become accepted as a way to defend the one church, which is true. Acceptance of this positon only turned into a positive defense of it in the much later nineteenth-century polemic against the liberalistic proposition according to which religion is only a private matter, irrelevant to public affairs, while the state is atheistic. The state acknowledges no *officium religionis* regardless of the traditional faith of the nation, and the secular power is entitled to define the status of the church in society.[88] The state church did not come into existence as the triumphant product of an enthymeme: the Catholic Church is the one true church; therefore, it should be the

state church. In truth, the institution arose in historical circumstances, and the church's attitude toward it changed over time
beginning with mere toleration, then acceptance, and finally
defense.

With the rise of constitutional democracy we have a new political development. Like any political development, this one has
been ambiguous in its origins and effects especially on the European Continent where it was a product of liberalism. However,
in the Anglo-Saxon tradition the liberalistic underpinnings were
not present. The new development of constitutional democracy
has been increasingly revealed as corresponding to the demands
of human nature. However, even here Murray wants to talk
about, not ideals or thesis, but the application of the transtemporal principles to the democratic reality. Murray himself succinctly summarizes what such an approach should be. The church
should accept, as an application of its principles to the legitimate
idea of democratic government and to the historically developed
idea of the people, a constitutional system of church-state relations with the following characteristics:

> (1) The freedom of the church is guaranteed in a guarante
> to the people of the free exercise of religion; (2) the harmony
> of law and social institutions with the demands of the Chris-
> tian conscience is to be effected by the people themselves
> through the medium of free political institutions and freedom
> of association; (3) the cooperation between church and state
> takes these three forms: (a) constitutional protection of the
> freedom of the church and all her institutional activities;
> (b) the effort of the state to perform its own function of jus-
> tice, social welfare, and the favoring within society of those
> conditions of order and freedom necessary for human devel-
> opment; (c) the effort of the church, through the action of
> laity conscious of its Christian and civic responsibilities, to
> effect that Christianization of society in all its dimensions
> which enable and oblige the state, as the instrument of so-
> ciety, to function in a Christian sense.[89]

In the midst of the Second Vatican Council Murray attempts
to state the issues which distinguish his position from the older
theory. In the process our author gives a summary of his theory.
For Murray the state of the question is altered in the light of the
different historical circumstances. The basic concept of the public care of religion is concerned, not with the exclusive rights of
truth, but with the freedom of the church as essentially allied

with the freedom of the civic people. There is no such thing as an ideal or thesis in the public care of religion and of constitutional law. The competency of the public power with regard to religion is limited to the freedom of the church and the demands of public order. The Catholic confessional state owed its origin not to the transtemporal principles but to historical circumstances.[90]

Teaching of Leo XIII and development

After Murray had prepared and defended his theory in the early 1950s, he still met quite a bit of opposition which often centered on citing the teaching of Leo XIII against Murray. From 1952 to 1954 Murray published five articles (a sixth was about to be published when Murray was silenced) in which he explicitly dealt with the teachings of Pope Leo XIII.[91] Murray brilliantly interpreted the papal teaching as being in accord with his own position by distinguishing the polemical, the historical, and doctrinal elements in Leo's teaching. At the time of the Vatican Council this historical spadework served him in good stead, for it was necessary to deal with the important issues of the development of church teaching and to show how there had been no contradiction in such teaching. Perhaps the primary concern in the whole discussion of religious liberty at the Second Vatican Council was this question of the development of doctrine.

To understand Leo's position with his defense of the confessional state and the denial of religious liberty, one must understand the circumstances of the time. Leo was fighting against Continental liberalism. This theory maintained the absolute autonomy of individual human reason. Human beings were no longer related to God and God's law. Human conscience was totally free and based only on itself. In the political sphere Continental liberalism espoused a totalitarian democracy. Its basic premise was a thoroughgoing monism—political, social, juridical, religious. There was one sovereign, one society, one law, and one secular faith. The Christian dualism of societies and powers —the spiritual and the temporal—was denied. The church was reduced to the realm of the private. The separation of church and state really meant the removal of the church and the spiritual from public society as such. Its only role and function could be private. Public life was atheist.[92]

For Leo the primary problem was the broader question of the relationship between the spiritual and the temporal, between faith and society, rather than the narrow issue of church and

state. Against the liberalistic approach Leo strove to put together
what human beings had torn asunder. Leo defended the sovereignty of God who rules over all human beings and all human
existence. God cannot be separated from the individual nor from
society. Leo's emphasis on the importance of the moral order
also caused him to neglect the reality of the juridical or legal
order and to see the state primarily in ethical terms. Leo, reacting against those who insisted on the rights of man, stressed
the rights of God and the role of God in private and political life.
But by insisting on the rights of God he did not adequately develop the rights of human beings.[93]

Against totalitarian monism Leo rightly insisted on the Gelasian dyarchy, but as a matter of doctrinal principle and not of
historical accommodation. Leo more clearly than anyone in the
Catholic tradition recognized that the dyarchy involves not two
powers but two different societies with two different orders of
law. Murray examines the seven major texts in which Leo developed his Gelasian dyarchy.[94] Leo's doctrine can be briefly
summarized: civil society and the political authority that rules
it are from God through nature; the church and her spiritual
authority are from God through Christ.[95] There can be no stronger
statement of the dualism of the two societies and of the independence and proper autonomy of the temporal. Leo here accepts
that the state is lay in a proper understanding of the term lay and
as distinguished from the totalitarian "laic" state of nineteenth-
century liberalism.

Equally as central as Leo's emphasis on the dyarchy was his
insistence on the freedom of the church (*libertas Ecclesiae*).
The phrase freedom of the church or its equivalent appears
eighty-one times in some sixty Leonine documents. The essential vice of the liberalist state was to deny this freedom. Freedom
is the first claim that the church makes in the face of society and
the state.[96] The freedom of the church follows from her trans-
cendence as a spiritual and supernatural society in her own right.
She must be free from subordination to the powers and purposes
of the state. But the church must also be free to enter by her
proper spiritual action into the area of temporal affairs. Some
have referred to this freedom as the indirect power of the church,
but Leo appropriately does not use this term. One could best describe Leo's teaching as the primacy of the spiritual. This primacy involves two basic assertions. First, in the temporal life of
human beings there is something sacred—the doctrine of the *res*

sacra in temporalibus. Second, the church must be free to enter into the temporal sphere and authoritatively lay its hands on these sacred elements.[97]

It is precisely in explaining the meaning of *res sacra in temporalibus* that Leo has worked out his principle of harmony (*concordia*) between the two societies. The church and the state meet in the conscience of the individual person who is both a member of the church and citizen. This is the new aspect found in Leo. In the medieval conception the root of the necessity of an orderly relationship came from the fact that one and the same society was both church and state. Now the orderly relationship is derived from the fact that the same person is both Christian and citizen.[98] Based on his restatement of the Gelasian dyarchy and his emphasis on the freedom of the church and the relationship between the two societies grounded on the individual who is both Christian and citizen, Leo has proposed what Murray calls the transtemporal principles which should govern church-state relations—the primacy of the spiritual with the freedom of the church, the necessary harmony between the two, and the necessary cooperation between church and state. Murray maintains that Leo's understanding and explanation of the Gelasian dyarchy contained implicitly the teaching ultimately made explicit in the conciliar Declaration on Religious Freedom of 1965.[99]

As a matter of fact, Leo did not come out in favor of religious liberty but rather espoused the confessional state or the religion of the state with the consequent denial of religious liberty for all others. However, Leo did not propose the confessional state as the ideal or thesis, but rather he argues for it on the basis of certain historical facts existing at the time. Murray does not suggest that Leo's defense of the confessional state was an error. In fact, Leo's position is reasonable and prudent in the light of the circumstances of the times.[100]

There were two very significant historical circumstances. First, as mentioned above, Leo was involved in a polemic with totalitarian democracy. The only type of religious liberty that he knew was the type determined by and infected with liberalism. Sectarian liberalism aimed at the apostasy of the masses, the destruction of the traditional Catholic culture, and the establishment by the power of the state of a new order with a purely naturalistic morality, totalitarian political structure, and an atheistic conception of society. Second, in the traditionally Catholic countries of Europe with which Leo was dealing, there existed the

phenomenon of the illiterate masses (*imperita multitudo*)—a
term frequently used by Leo to describe the people at that time.
Illiteracy rates were extremely high in those countries—61.9
percent in Italy, 72 percent in Spain, 79.1 percent in Portugal,
31.4 percent in Belgium, and 28.1 percent in France. These illiterate masses were obviously also very weak in understanding
their faith and in need of protection.[101]

Leo's defense of the confessional state arose in these circumstances. He adopted the theory of the ethical society-state. Leo
did not clearly distinguish between society and the state except
in *Rerum novarum.* The society-state was built on a conception
of the common good. The total care of the common good was
given to the *principes,* the rulers who ruled and guided the illiterate masses. The social order was constructed from the top
down by the action of the rulers. The citizen was a subject whose
single duty is obedience. In such a view there is no distinction
between society and the state. Only with a growing emphasis on
personal and political consciousness did the notion of a limited
constitutional government become a possibility with its concept
of the juridical state as opposed to the ethical understanding of
the state supposed by the pontiff. The ethical concept of the state
employs the analogy between domestic and civil society. The
ruler is like the head of the family who governs in a kindly fashion
and with fatherly love. The subjects are like children in their
obedience and respect. The ruler protects and guides the children.
Leo also accepted an adaptation of the territorial principle of the
post-Reformation era. In the one city only one faith should publicly be professed. Leo's premise here was historical—the traditional unity of faith in the Catholic nations of Europe. The Catholic
faith should enjoy the favor of the law and the protection of the
ruler as part of his political care for the common good and for the
total welfare, including the spiritual welfare of his subject children. Leo the realist saw that the church had to depend upon the
heads of state. However, religious liberty could be tolerated to
avoid a greater evil or to obtain a greater good.[102]

Leo XIII tried to respond to his historical circumstances and
to resist the evils of his time by recourse to an historical understanding of government charged with a direct duty toward the
supreme good of the human spirit, which is true religion, and a
consequent obligation publicly to suppress religious error. In his
circumstances the recourse to this approach was a necessity.
There was no other way. But this conception is in contradiction

with Leo's development of the Gelasian theory, which is a more fundamental reality and involves pure principles which are not historically conditioned.[103] By distinguishing the historical, the polemical, and the doctrinal Murray is able to justify Leo's acceptance of the confessional state in his time but also to call for religious liberty today in the light of the heightened personal and political consciousness which has resulted in limited constitutional governments with a juridical rather than an ethical concept of the state.

Murray also tries to show how this development continued in the later popes, especially Pius XII and John XXIII. The development above all consists in the acceptance by these popes of a juridical concept of the limited state. Murray summarizes the development by maintaining two essential junctures of ideas which occurred. The first juncture is between the two correlative exigencies of the personal and political consciousness—between limited constitutional government protecting basic human rights and the concept of religious freedom as a general, civil, and human right claiming the protection of the juridical order of society. The second juncture is between the ancient historical defense of the freedom of the church and the newly necessary defense of the freedom of the people against totalitarian exigencies. Today the freedom of the people of God is inseparably linked with the freedom of the peoples of the world.[104]

Vatican II and afterward

Murray was silenced in 1955 and did not write on the subjects of church and state and religious liberty again until the Second Vatican Council.[105] Our earlier discussions have incorporated these later writings of Murray's, but a brief word should be said about Murray's relationship to the final document proposed by the Second Vatican Council.[106] Murray had no input into the preconciliar drafts on the subject and was not invited to the first session of the council, but, as has been said, Cardinal Spellman personally invited Murray to attend the second session of the council as an expert.

The first schema or draft text on religious freedom was presented at the second session of the council on November 19, 1963. This schema constituted chapter five of the document on ecumenism and based its acceptance of religious liberty on the ethical theory of the freedom of conscience. The second schema, which was discussed by the council fathers at the third session of the council, September 23-25, 1964, followed basically the same ethical approach. After the conciliar debate a subcommittee with Murray as "first scribe" was commissioned to prepare a new draft. The third draft, written primarily by Murray, was now a fullfledged declaration in its own right and was no longer attached to the schema on ecumenism. But more importantly, the third schema proposed religious liberty as a formally juridical concept in accord with Murray's own understanding.[107] Recall that Murray's 1964 article "The Problem of Religious Freedom" tried to spell out the reasons for adopting such an approach as compared to the ethical approach based only on the rights of conscience. However, there was opposition to the new approach in methodology especially from some French bishops, who thought that a conciliar document should not begin with a limited concept such as a civil right but with what scripture and theology say about human freedom in general and religious freedom in particular. The subsequent drafts and the final texts made some modifications in the text of the third schema, which was also primarily the work of Murray.

How does the final document on religious liberty adopted by the Second Vatican Council relate to the thought of John Courtney Murray? There can be no doubt that the Declaration on Religious Freedom vindicates Murray's position and incorporates much of his thought. For example, Murray's definition of religious liberty as a twofold immunity is accepted (par. 2). The four important principles for understanding the role of the state are readily found in the final document—the distinctions between the sacred and the secular, between society and the state, between the common good and the public order, the jurisprudential principle of as much freedom as possible and as little constraint as necessary. The role of the state and the criteria of state intervention are discussed in the light of these principles (par. 7). Murray's insistence on the freedom of the church is embodied in the declaration: "The freedom of the church is the fundamental principle in what concerns the relations between the church and the government and the whole civil order" (par. 13). From its very beginning the document acknowledges the importance of historical consciousness. Murray's explanation of the teaching of Leo XIII and his understanding of the development of doctrine paved the way for conciliar acceptance of the new teaching.

However, interestingly enough, the final document does not

accept Murray's basic grounding of the right to religious liberty in a formally juridical and constitutional approach. The final document is a compromise, and it proposes a number of reasons for religious freedom. The argument from the right and duty to seek the truth and freely embrace it gains primacy in the final document. The formally juridical argument based on constitutional principles (Murray's approach) is present but not primary as it was in the third draft. Also, a subsidiary place is given to the argument based on the right and duty to follow conscience and to the argument from scripture which constitutes the second chapter of the final text.[108] Thus the final document does not incorporate as primary the precise juridical argument proposed by Murray as the basis for religious freedom.

In his commentaries on the declaration Murray does not explicitly call attention to the fact that the final document does not base its teaching primarily on the juridical and constitutional argument. Murray even claims that the doctrinal line proposed in the third schema remains substantially the same in the following drafts and in the definitive declaration itself.[109] However, many other commentators rightly point out the fact that the final document does not give primacy to Murray's constitutional grounding of religious liberty. Francis Canavan, an American Jesuit political scientist, writing in a symposium edited by Murray, maintains it is regrettable that the final document does not make the acceptance of constitutional government the major basis for its acceptance of religious liberty.[110]

In general, Murray's commentaries and discussion of the declaration tend at times to be apologetic and even defensive. For example, many commentators object to the statement found in the declaration that the Catholic Church is the one true church and all people are bound to seek this truth. The objection is, not to the truth of the statement for a Catholic, but to the propriety of inserting it in a document on religious liberty which is primarily addressing itself to all people living together in the civil order.[111] However, Murray defends the inclusion of these paragraphs on the grounds that human beings live in the religious order as well as in the secular order and that truth demands that Catholics state their position very candidly on what the religious order demands.[112] However, in the final analysis no one can deny that Murray was the most important single influence on the declaration, and the conciliar document marks the vindication and ultimate triumph of Murray's work and ideas.

V. The American Political Experience

There are two aspects in Murray's work of reconciling Catholicism and Americanism. First, he must prove to Roman Catholics that religious liberty and the American concept of the separation of church and state are compatible with Catholic understanding. Second, the Jesuit theologian must show to his fellow
citizens that Catholics can wholeheartedly accept the American
political system. Catholicism and Americanism are compatible.
However, Murray insists that the question must be phrased properly: Is American democracy compatible with Catholicism?
The religious order of values is always supreme, and therefore
the question has to be phrased in this manner.[113]

The American reality can briefly be described. American
democratic principles rest on the tradition of Western constitutionalism with its respect for basic human rights, recognizing
the individual person as a *res sacra in temporalibus*. However,
the American experience has never known a religious unity.
There is a civic unity with religious pluralism but without the
banishment of religion from public existence. Murray refers to
four "conspiracies"—Protestant, Catholic, Jewish, and secularist; but he wants to understand conspiracy according to its
etymological root of breathing together—united action for a
common end about which there is agreement. His purpose is to
limit the warfare between these groups and enlarge the dialogue.
Here again Murray's distinction between the sacred and the secular, the spiritual and the temporal, comes into play. Religious
pluralism is against the will of God, but it is the human condition.
Despite that religious pluralism there can and should be civic
unity.[114]

Murray sees the basis of the civic unity of the United States
in terms of the American proposition, or, as it is otherwise called
with nuances of meaning, the public consensus or the public
philosophy of America. Murray is a strong intellectualist. The
most important American reality is the American proposition—
the truths we share. It is classic doctrine that our nation was
brought forth dedicated to a proposition. The American proposition is both doctrinal and practical. As a doctrine it lays claim to
intellectual assent, but it is also an organized political project
that aims at historical success.[115]

According to Murray the American proposition or consensus
refers to two realities—the political unity we share and an ap-

proach to religious pluralism. First, consider the political unity we share. The first truth to which the American proposition appeals is the sovereignty of God over nations as well as over human beings. We are, as the Declaration of Independence states it, one nation under God. This insistence on the sovereignty of God as the first principle of political organization distinguishes the American self-understanding from the Jacobin tradition of Continental European liberalism. From his earliest writings Murray emphasizes the difference between American democracy and Continental liberalism which proclaims a militant secularism and makes religion a totally private affair denying it any public and social life.[116]

The American proposition, in keeping with the liberal political tradition of the West, believes in a free people under a limited government. Constitutionalism, the rule of law, the notion of sovereignty as purely political and limited by law, government as the rule of law and not of human beings, are all basic ideas going back to medieval times. The great American contribution to this constitutional tradition, found especially in Britain, is the Constitution as a written document. The Constitution embodies the consensus of the people and stands as a charter of freedom and a plan for political order. The principle of consent wedded to the principle of popular participation in rule results in a new synthesis—government by the people. The American government is limited both by the rule of law and by the consent of the people. The American consensus includes an act of faith in the capacity of the people to govern themselves.

The free institutions of American society, such as free speech and the free press, do not rest on an individualistic basis which was present in nineteenth-century liberalism. They have two different bases. First, such institutions are necessary and essential for the conduct of free, representative, and responsible government. Second, the important distinction between society and the state recognizes the incompetency of the government in the area of opinion. Freedom of communication and freedom of the academy are immunities which constitute civil rights of the first order essential to the American concept of a free people under a limited government. The American ideal of freedom recognizes that only a virtuous people can be free. The success of democracy depends upon the virtue of the people, for political freedom is endangered as soon as the universal moral values incorporated in personal and social responsibility are no longer vigorous enough to restrain the passions and shatter the selfish inertia of human beings. The Bill of Rights in the American Constitution recognizes certain inalienable human rights which belong to all, antecedent to one's status as a citizen. These inalienable rights are proximately grounded in human nature and have their ultimate source in God. The Bill of Rights is not based on rationalistic individualism but on the natural law.[117]

In explaining the truths we hold about civic unity in government Murray constantly emphasizes two points. First, the American system is quite different from the democracy proposed by Continental liberalism in Europe. Second, the American system is in continuity with the medieval political understanding. The medieval political tradition, for example, also recognized the distinction between the state and society. Even the medieval inquisition respected the distinction of the orders and recognized that opinion as such can never be a crime.[118]

What is the relationship between the unity in the civic order and the pluralism in the spiritual or religious order? This relationship is governed by the first amendment to the Constitution which assures religious freedom to all through the instrumental companion doctrine called (not felicitously) the separation of church and state. The first amendment guarantees the freedom of religion and prohibits the establishment of any religion.

Murray points out three false understandings of the first amendment which cannot be accepted by a Catholic—the Protestant theological interpretation, the American secularist theory, and the understanding of Continental liberalism.[119] In all his writings Murray does not hesitate to state his opinions very strongly, and at times he even ridicules the position of his adversaries. Nowhere is this characteristic of Murray's writings more evident than in his disagreements about the basis of the first amendment. He claims that "the Protestant mind is itself natively confused, endemically unclear in this whole matter."[120] Murray sees the attacks of Paul Blanshard on the Catholic Church as a form of a new nativism illustrating the profound anti-Roman bias which exists in the American republic.[121]

The Protestant theological interpretation sees in the first amendment a principle embracing a liberal ecclesiology. There is no true church of Jesus Christ; all religions are equal before God; the church is a voluntary society to which people freely give their adherence. Murray objects that the first amendment does not endorse a Protestant concept of the church. It is neither an article of faith nor a theological doctrine about the church. No Catholic could accept such a theology of the church.[122]

American secularism, like Continental liberalism, also provides a false basis for a proper understanding of the first amendment. According to Murray, Blanshard's position is based on such a secularism and naturalism. The church is limited to the sacristy. The democratic state is supreme over all with its majoritarianism. All reality must be subject to the scientific method. Blanshard really proposes a social monism of the political process and of the scientific method. The American secularist approach closely resembles the monism of a Continental liberalism which has no place for God or religion in public life.[123]

Murray, who frequently objects to the formula "separation of church and state," understands the first amendment not as articles of faith but as articles of peace—and as such they are totally acceptable to Roman Catholicism. They are articles of peace because they are matters of law and political principles—not matters of faith and theology. They speak about the role and function of the state. The first amendment developed in the light of the historical circumstances peculiar to the American situation, but it also rests on good ethical principles about the role and function of government. Religious liberty and the separation of church and state came into existence in response to four historical realities—the great mass of the unchurched especially on the American frontier, the multiplicity of denominations, economic factors, and, to a lesser extent, the widening of religious freedom already occuring in England. This social necessity brought about these institutions as articles of peace necessary for a religiously pluralistic society to live together in civic accord.

Murray does not want, however, to give the impression that these institutions are based solely on expediency. Behind the will to create civil peace there stand important principles which are a part of the classical and Christian tradition—the dyarchy and the freedom of the church. The classical tradition accepted the dualism between the spiritual and the temporal, the church and the state. The American impetus toward freedom and limited self-government led to a new emphatic affirmation of the traditional distinction. The American theory thus greatly differs from that of Continental liberalism. The theory is simply political and not philosophical or theological; the state is limited and not juridically omnicompetent; one of the limits of the state is the distinction between the state and the church. The American solution also commends itself to the Catholic intelligence and conscience because it recognizes and upholds the freedom of the church. It is legally recognized that there exists an area outside the competence of government in which the church exists and is fully independent to structure itself and to carry on its mission.

The American experience has also affirmed the validity of the American approach. Political unity and stability are possible without religious uniformity. Stable political unity is even strengthened by the exclusion of religious differences from the government's area of endeavor. Religion itself and, in particular, the Catholic Church have flourished in the American ethos. Thus, for many reasons, the Catholic intelligence wholeheartedly accepts the religious liberty and the separation of church and state as found in the first amendment of the American Constitution.[124]

Catholics can and should accept the American consensus because ultimately this public philosophy is based on the natural law. "Catholic participation in the American consensus has been full and free, unreserved and unembarrassed, because the contents of this consensus—the ethical and political principles drawn from the tradition of natural law—approve themselves to the Catholic intelligence and conscience."[125]

However, the question is: Does the American consensus or public philosophy still continue to exist in the United States?[126] Murray maintains that at the present time it seems that the public consensus no longer exists either on the level of the people at large or on the level of "the clerks"—the intellectuals. However, today more than ever there is need for the American consensus or political philosophy. Our vacillating and unsatisfactory approaches to foreign policy, to the use of force, and to our response to communism, all prove the need for a new moral act of purpose and a new act of intellectual affirmation comparable to that which launched the American constitutional experience.

Murray's contention is that "only the theory of natural law is able to give an account of the public moral experience that is the public consensus.[127] Recall that at great length he refutes the approaches of the law of nature proposed in the Enlightenment, of the social-gospel school, and of Niebuhrian realism. Only the natural law can serve as a basis for the American consensus. The doctrine of natural law has no Roman Catholic presuppositions about it. Unfortunately, the American universities no longer accept it, but Murray confidently ends the last chapter in *We Hold These Truths* with the assertion that there are resources in natural law that would make the dynamic of a new age of order by providing the skeleton and the structural foundations of the political, social, and economic orders necessary for life in the contemporary world.[128]

In relating the consensus to its natural-law basis Murray recognizes that the principles and rules of the consensus belong to what are called the remote precepts of the natural law, which bear on complex human relationships and institutional development. The operation or achievement of human reason on this level does not belong to the work of the people at large but is the task of the wise. The wise and the intelligent must develop the consensus and the application of it and thereby inform the generality of human beings. Once all human beings have been instructed by the wise, the generality of human beings can accept this consensus on the basis of the innate dynamism of the natural law present in all human beings. Murray in theory and in practice rejects a flat equalitarianism but recognizes that in addition to basic human equality common to all, there are special gifts and functions to fulfill in society. The wise and intelligent have the role of articulating and applying in ever new circumstances the American consensus or the public philosophy—the truths by which we live and to which we as a nation are dedicated.[129]

In summary, Murray makes a very audacious proposal. Our governmental system is based on the American consensus—the truths we hold. Catholics can readily accept the American political consensus including the first amendment guarantee of religious freedom and the separation of church and state because it is based on natural law. Unfortunately, today, when it is most needed, the consensus no longer exists. The only solution is to rebuild the consensus on the basis of natural law. Not only can Catholics accept the principle of the founding fathers of our nation, but today the Catholics are the only ones with the ability to rebuild and to rearticulate the consensus.

Murray is particularly concerned that American policy on a number of important issues is theoretically erroneous and practically harmful because of its failure to be based on the truths of natural law. He deals with a number of questions of contemporary significance including the American reaction to communism, the use of force in war, federal aid for Catholic schools, and censorship. A brief explanation of his positions will be given.

Our author addresses the problem of American foreign policy vis-à-vis communism. Murray sees communism as an enemy

trying to put an end to the history of the West. Communism is not
a legacy of Western history, nor a Christian heresy, but an apostasy from the West building on the Jacobin notion of the juridically omnicompetent state. American pragmatism, the social
gospel, sentimentality, and political realism have all failed to
recognize what is the communist doctrine or dogma which determines their practice. Russia today has a fourfold uniqueness—as
a state or power which is a police state of new proportions and
unique efficacy denying the true rule of law, as an empire based
on a revolutionary doctrine, as an imperialism with nearly half
of its citizens as really colonial people, as an inheritor of czarist
imperialism and of mystical panslavic messianism. Communism
seeks to inaugurate a new epoch in history. The pragmatic American mind finds it difficult to understand that the Russians always act on the basis of their doctrine. We should never confuse
negotiations with foreign policy, for negotiation is simply a way
of getting what your doctrine proposes. The Russian doctrine is
inherently aggressive—it admits of no disengagement. Therefore, our policy must be one of continuous engagement at every
point and on all levels of action. But such a policy of continuous
engagement with communism does not only involve a policy of
hostility, contraction, and opposition engaged in primarily on the
military level. The engagement can be positive, cooperative,
and constructive. Today more than ever a doctrinal response is
required—a doctrine of reason about the very meaning of freedom, justice, and human rights. Doctrine can and does have very
important practical effects in this matter. Yes, there is a Cold
War, but our mistake has been to see it primarily and almost
exclusively on the military level. Murray is still a cold warrior,
but in a modified and more intellectualist way.

However, one cannot neglect the question of force in war.
Here Soviet theory dictates a policy of maximal security and
minimal risk. Historical evidence confirms this position. Where
there is little risk, as in Hungary in 1956, aggressive policies
will be carried through. Communism wants to avoid major
nuclear collisions, for they cannot advance their cause. Survival
is one thing that the Soviets will never risk in war. Our policy in
response should involve a minimum of security and a maximum
of risk in order to counteract their policy.[130]

Murray discusses the problem of force and war in the light of
the natural-law teaching on the just war. The just-war theory
avoids the false dilemma of sentimental pacifism often associat-

ed with the social-gospel school and of cynical realism proposed by the Niebuhrians and others. The just-war theory also rejects the simplistic fallacy which sees only the extreme alternatives of red or dead—surrender to communism or universal atomic death. The just-war theory avoids all such extremes with its triple traditional function of considering war as evil, limiting the evils it entails, and humanizing its conduct as far as possible. Limited war can be morally acceptable as a last resort.

Murray develops the doctrine of just war which must guide our policy in the light of the teaching of Pope Pius XII. War at times can be justified on the basis of the needs of justice itself. In the light of the modern reality all wars of aggression are morally proscribed. A defensive war to repress injustice is morally admissible both in principle and in fact. Such a war can even involve atomic weapons, but four conditions are necessary. The war is imposed by a grave injustice. War is always an *ultima ratio*, or a last resort. The principle of proportion must be present between the evils caused by the injustice and the evils caused by the war, with the solid probability of success being included as a factor. The fourth important principle of limitation is surprisingly not emphasized that much by Pope Pius XII. This principle of limitation forbids the direct killing of noncombatants. In keeping with the importance he gives to doctrine, Murray insists that policy must be set and prudently carried out in the light of these principles.[131]

Near the end of his life John Murray became involved in the question of selective conscientious objection. As a member of the Marshall commission—the National Advisory Commission on Selective Service—he dissented from the final report which came out against selective conscientious objection. Shortly before his death he explained his own position on selective conscientious objection. The presumption of justice lies in favor of the judgment made by the political community. But the political community must respect the conscience of its members. Murray well recognizes the dangers of possible chaos and anarchy and the perennial problem of the erroneous conscience. However, selective conscientious objection can work if there is abroad in the land a sufficient measure of moral and political discretion which is based on moral and political intelligence.[132] Note again the importance he gives to doctrine and intelligence.

One of the most divisive issues between Catholics and other Americans was the question of federal aid to Catholic schools.

Murray addresses this question more frequently than any other particular issue.[133] Murray supports some federal aid for Catholic schools (he never delves into the question of precisely how much aid should be given to Catholic schools) on both moral and legal grounds. The principle of distributive justice requires that a proportionately just measure of public support be available to schools which insure the public care of popular education, whether these schools be specifically religious or not. Contemporary sociological conditions in the United States also call for such support precisely because we are a religiously pluralistic country, and religious pluralism must be respected.

What about the legal aspects in the light of the nonestablishment clause of the first amendment of the Constitution? From his earliest writings Murray insists that the nonestablishment clause of the first amendment is not the primary clause or even an independent clause in itself. This clause is subordinated to the primary clause of religious freedom for all. The phrase "separation of church and state" can give the wrong impression if not properly understood. There is no iron curtain, for there is some common ground between church and state. Here again Murray sees the child, like the individual citizen, as both a child of God and a citizen of the state.

One can read into the separation of church and state a philosophy of hostility to religion. However, the Supreme Court in the *Zorach* case asserted that government respects the religious nature of the people and accommodates the public service to their spiritual needs. The principle of accommodation is an extension of the general principle that government exists for the people. Two outstanding examples are government support of military chapels and chaplaincies and the granting of tax exemptions to religious institutions. The principle of accommodation or cooperation can and should be applied in the area of education. Education is a public concern, and religious schools fulfill the public purpose of education. Undoubtedly there will be practical difficulties in applying this principle and distinguishing between constitutional accommodation of public service in the aid of religion and unconstitutional aid to religion itself. But we have the intelligence and courage to apply these principles. However, very early in his writings on this subject Murray expressed the fear that the day will come when such aid will be declared unconstitutional. Then schools will have become churches, and we will have forgotten that all schools fulfill a public purpose.[134]

With his acceptance of limited constitutional government Murray upholds the basic American freedoms. However, his justification of such freedoms does not rest on individualistic and subjective grounds. A virtuous people is a necessary presupposition of freedom. Our author strongly supports the jurisprudential principle of as much freedom as possible and as little constraint as necessary. The criterion for government intervention is the public order—an order of justice, of public peace, and of public morality.

Murray explicitly addresses the problem of censorship in the light of these principles. It is necessary to distinguish between law and morality and between public morality and private morality. The function of coercive law is very minimal and must be upheld by some type of consensus among the people.[135] Murray does not consider at length other questions of law and morality, but his basic principles, especially as enunciated in the context of government interference in religious matters, are quite clear.

VI. Evaluation and Critique

There can be no doubt that John Courtney Murray is the most academic and creative author considered in our study. However, even Murray the scholar sees his work as having very important practical ramifications. One can only admire both the lofty goals he set for himself and the achievements he accomplished. He stands at the apex of that long line of predecessors who tried to voice in the development of Catholic teaching on religious liberty. show that Catholicism and the American political ethos are compatible. Without doubt, Murray was the most significant single Murray's apology for full Catholic acceptance and participation in the American political system received a sympathetic hearing not only from many Catholics but also from other Americans.

Murray was one of the first Roman Catholic theologians to recognize the importance of historical mindedness and to employ such a concept in his methodology. This perspective gives him a hermeneutical tool for dealing with past Roman Catholic teachings as illustrated especially in his creative interpretation of Pope Leo XIII. Such a perspective also makes it possible for him to propose a concept of development acceptable to the fathers of the Second Vatican Council.

However, Murray's work is also open to criticism. The American Jesuit observes in referring to Pope Leo XIII that all are influenced by the historical circumstances in which they exist and by the need to contend with opposing positions.[136] In my judgment this is also true of Murray's approach, for the circumstances and polemics of the moment cannot help but have some influence on one's teaching. This general comment will be verified in a number of the specific criticisms raised in the following paragraphs.

A major point in Murray's approach is the distinction between the spiritual and temporal orders and the sacred and secular orders of human existence. This serves as the basis for the Gelasian dyarchy—the dualism and the distinction between church and state. The distinction in Murray's writing corresponds to the traditional Catholic distinction between the supernatural order and the natural order. In Murray's day such a distinction served as a basis for much Catholic theologizing. Murray himself recognizes that there must be an integration between the two orders and no clear dichotomy. The individual person who is both Christian and citizen is the integrating factor in the church-state relationship just as the individual and corporate activities of the laity are the integrating factor between the spiritual and the temporal orders.

However, many contemporary theologians call for a more integral approach.[137] The distinction between the natural and the supernatural does not exist as an historical reality. At best the concept of the natural as distinguished from the supernatural is only an abstraction and a remainder concept. The natural as such and as distinguished from the supernatural has never historically existed.

The Second Vatican Council attempts a better integration of the natural and the supernatural, although not always successfully. Some of the objections from the French bishops and theologians to Murray's failure to be more theological point in the same general direction. There can be no doubt that Murray does not give enough significance to the role of the gospel and of the mystery of Christ in the political and social orders of human existence The gospel, grace, and Christ must have something to say about all worldy realities. At the same time it is important to point out the opposite danger of denying any autonomy to political science, economics, sociology, and psychology by simplistically reducing all reality to faith and grace.

Murray can also be criticized for failing to recognize the reality of sin and its influence on human existence in the temporal sphere. Again, such a failure comes from a narrow view of seeing the political, social, cultural, and economic aspects almost univocally in light of the natural. However, sin affects all of reality. Although Murray does not theoretically recognize the role and influence of sin, he has an innate sense of realism which comes through in his discussion of many issues and in his personal correspondence.[138] However, such realism in Murray lacks any theoretical grounding in the presence of sin.

Seeing all reality, even the political, social, and cultural aspects of human existence, in the light of the full Christian mystery and not only on the basis of the natural results in a different understanding of the social mission of the church. The gospel itself is more directly related to the temporal order than Murray admits. Murray justifies the church's involvement in the temporal order on two grounds—because we create conditions favorable to our eternal destiny and because the perfection of social being is an end willed by God.[139] But if the gospel itself calls for us to become involved in the transformation of the world, then one can and should see such transformation and involvement in the world as a constitutive dimension of the gospel.

In the polemics of the situation Murray is struggling against various forms of monism which failed to recognize the distinction between the spiritual and the temporal. However, because he interprets the distinction primarily on the basis of the distinction between the natural and the supernatural, he fails to see how the gospel and the full mystery of Jesus must affect the Christian's relationship to the world.

Intimately connected with Murray's understanding of the relationship between the spiritual and the temporal is his failure to give any importance to the need for a change of heart on the part of all individuals in order to bring about peace and justice in our world. Murray emphasizes the need for structures and institutions, but he does not call for personal conversion. In this approach Murray follows in the footsteps of Ryan rather than of Furfey. From the perspectives of both theology and of social ethics I see the need for both a change of heart and a change of structures.

I also question Murray's bold assertion that the American consensus is ultimately grounded only on natural law. Murray recognizes that civic unity exists together with religious pluralism. However, he bases his civic unity on an epistemological and metaphysical unity! One has to accept the natural law with its philosophical underpinnings in order to accept logically the American proposition! At least one might maintain that there are certain values and ideals held in common without claiming that one must accept one philosophical grounding of these commonly held values. Our society exists not only with a religious pluralism but also with a philosophical pluralism. Few if any Catholic theologians today would insist on the need for an acceptance of natural law with its epistemological and metaphysical presuppositions as the only foundation for the American proposition.

In this context an important question arises. The Christian believes that the gospel and the mystery of Christ are relevant to our life in the world. However, we live in a world with many who are not Christian. How then are we as Christians to try to address all others and work together with them? At the very minimum it would seem that Christians among themselves should appeal to explicitly Christian warrants in determining how they should act in society. However, there then arises the strategic question of whether Christians should appeal to others in society on the basis of Christian warrants or on the basis of warrants which would claim to be less particular and more universal.[140] For Murray, there is no problem or dilemma on the level of strategy. In principle the Christian approaches the temporal order only on the basis of reason and of natural law.

Murray creatively employs historical consciousness to solve a number of different problems, but there are significant questions that arise in the light of his understanding and use of historical consciousness. Perhaps the most fundamental question is the compatability between his understanding of historical consciousness and his understanding of natural law. At the very minimum many have attacked the static notion of being connected with traditional natural law precisely in the name of historical consciousness. Murray does call for a dynamic understanding of natural law, but still one wonders if he logically should give more importance to the historicity of being and thereby change some of his basic metaphysics and ontology. At the very minimum historical consciousness calls for a more inductive and less deductive methodology.

On the other hand, Murray can be criticized for going too far with his historical consciousness. The American Jesuit argues strenuously against the thesis-hypothesis understanding of church-state relationships, which uphold the union of church and state as an ideal. For Murray there is no such thing as an ideal form of church-state relations, for constitutional law never speaks in terms of ideals which are true in all historical circumstances. There are absolute transtemporal principles, but the institutionalization of these shows enormous variations. The notion of the ideal or the optimum form of government is perilous and opposed to the "sound Anglo-Saxon, and basically Catholic, principle of the relativism of political forms."[141]

Even in his writings at the time of the Second Vatican Council Murray makes the same basic point. Religious liberty is a demand of the natural law at the present moment of history.[142] The state under today's conditions of growth in personal and social consciousness is competent only to promote the religious freedom of people.[143] According to Murray the institution of intolerance and establishment must be judged *in situ* and might well be valid *in situ*, for the function of law is to be useful to the people.[144]

Both theoretical and practical problems arise from Murray's historicism. From a theoretical viewpoint, and contrary to his own assertion, the Catholic natural-law theory has tried to say that some forms of government are better than others. A theory of regimes with evaluative judgments has always been a part of natural law. Here again there exists a tension between Murray's historical mindedness on these issues and the natural-law background. Edward A. Goerner, a political scientist, seems to be correct in making this criticism,[145] but as John Rohr, another political scientist, points out, this does not mean that Murray cannot and does not criticize some unjust types of government.[146] In Murray's defense it might be pointed out that the popes themselves avoided saying that one particular form of government is best.

On the practical level Murray's position means that circumstances could arise in which religious liberty would not be required. In response to an explicit question he dismisses the possibility that the sacred society could ever come into existence again, but he never changes his basic historicism on this question.[147] Goerner explicitly refers to Murray's position as situationist.[148]

What explains Murray's position? Again I see his polemic and historical situation as influencing him. He opposes the thesishypothesis approach of the older school. Our author fears that what has happened in the past could happen again—what is historically acceptable in certain circumstances would become an ideal for all times and all places. In addition, especially in the

1950s he never directly attacks the existing Spanish system of church-state relations. Murray obviously knows that his position would be even less acceptable if he maintains that the Spanish solution is not only not the ideal but is wrong. Such a position also makes it easier for him to deal with the teachings of Leo XIII. In no way can he be forced to say that Leo's position was wrong— it was right in the light of the circumstances of his day. Here again the polemical aspect of Murray's teaching might have predominated.[149]

The explanation for the Jesuit theologian's historicism proposed above leads into a criticism of his theory of development. Murray's theory of development, especially with its historical analysis of Leo XIII, is ingenious, enabling its adherents to affirm religious liberty without having to repudiate the teaching of one of the more recent popes. However, one wonders if the theory of development is not somewhat skewered by the theological considerations of the time. In Murray's day there were practically no Catholic theologians publicly maintaining that the official hierarchical teaching could and did make mistakes. Murray's theory neatly side-steps the problem by explaining all in terms of historical differences. In my judgment such an explanation both in theory and in the particular case of religious liberty does not do total justice to the reality involved. There can be and has been error in some official teaching, and there was some error (as will be noted later) in some of the positions taken by Leo XIII in the matter of religious freedom. However, again, Murray was living in his own time (the possibility of error in official church teaching is much more widely recognized today), and he never would have been successful with any other approach.

The use of historical consciousness and the question of development are also present in another context in Murray's writings—his understanding of God and of dogmatic definitions concerning the Trinity and Christology. In this context Murray understands the development between the scriptural approaches and the dogma of the Council of Nicea as a move from what is prior in the order of experience to what is prior in the order of being. The conciliar definitions are immutable because they describe the realities as they exist in themselves and not as they might appear to us at a particular time.[150] Many contemporary Catholic theologians would give greater emphasis to the historicity of the conciliar definitions themselves. Murray's approach to historical consciousness and to development in his discussion of conciliar definitions about God and Jesus appears to be somewhat different from his approach in the question of religious liberty.

Within the same general area of historical consciousness one can also question Murray's historical analysis. It seems that his own prejudices have entered into his historical interpretation in a number of different areas. Murray's interpretation of Pope Leo XIII is ingenious in its distinction among the doctrinal, the polemical, and the historical aspects of the pope's teaching. By deftly sorting out these three aspects Murray is able to show the development because of which his own theory is truly in continuity with Leo XIII. However, I do not think that Leo XIII would have recognized himself in the picture drawn by Murray! There are many indications that Leo would not have accepted his defense of the confessional state as merely belonging to the polemical and/or historical aspect of his teaching. Murray has been criticized by some of his adversaries for leaving aside those texts which do not support his position—especially Pope Leo XIII's Apostolic letter *Longinqua oceani*.[151] In this letter Pope Leo praised the progress of the Catholic Church in the American situation, but he then stated that the church in the United States "would make far greater gain if, in addition to freedom, she were to enjoy the favor of the laws and the patronage of the public power." In a footnote in 1952 Murray claims that Leo is making a statement of fact, not of doctrine, and that the precise content of the proposition requires a careful and prolonged investigation.[152] However, such an investigation is never made by him, although he returns very briefly to the subject in his last article on Leo XIII which he was never allowed to publish.[153] Even here there is no in-depth investigation. Murray merely asserts that Leo XIII is not talking about an ideal that would be even more beneficial for the church in the United States, but rather he has in mind the theoretical error of those who wish to make the American constitutional situation a generalized and universal principle.

In addition, Murray could have been more critical of Leo XIII. In his later writings there are some hints about this, but they are never systematically developed. At the very minimum it can be pointed out that Leo did not recognize the differences between the liberalistic theory of separation of church and state proposed in Europe and the constitutional system proposed in the United States. In Leo's time there were alternatives other than the religion of the state and monistic liberalism.

Throughout his writings Murray insists on the continuity between Western constitutional democracy and the Middle Ages. At the very minimum this insistence appears a bit one-sided. As a matter of fact, the Anglo-Saxon tradition of limited constitutional government did not arise from the medieval experience. The medieval experience of a limited understanding of government practically had little or no historical effect on the development of constitutional government. Limited constitutionalism did not flower in the Catholic countries with their medieval heritage. Perhaps there is some continuity between the Catholic medieval experience and limited constitutional government, but at the very minimum there also exists great discontinuity both in history and even in terms of theory.

Murray is also open to the charge of reading into the minds of the founding fathers of the United States a natural-law mentality. Again there might have been some influence of the natural-law tradition on the founding fathers, but generally speaking the latter did not accept the epistemological and metaphysical presuppositions which Murray sees as the basis for natural law. Some might want to rescue Murray from such criticism and justify him on the basis that he merely attempts to give a Catholic interpretation of the American proposition.[154] However, at the very least his somewhat apologetic and polemical purpose too readily colors his proposals. Thus Murray's interpretation of a number of important historical realities is open to serious challenge. He too readily sees in history the realities that support his own positions.

I also disagree with Murray's interpretation and justification of some realities on the American scene. In his strong defense of the American political system Murray does not explicitly call attention to the fact that many Americans have a view which emphasizes the wall of separation between church and state and comes to different conclusions on practical questions. Our author does refute their approaches, but he seems unwilling to admit that the American system is open to interpretations different from his own.

In his attempt to show compatibility between being American and being Catholic, Murray too often accepts uncritically the American realities and approaches. The best example of this is

the American economy. Murray never deals with economic problems in any detail. One cannot be criticized for not dealing with
every question, and Murray's writing is directed almost exclusively to the political aspect of social ethics. However, he shows
no awareness of any economic problems in the United States. One
brief reference to the American economic scene seems to accept
the unique American claim to have abolished the problem of
poverty. There still exist some depressed areas, but the means
for the solution of the problem exist and are known.[155] Even in
Murray's day there was evidence that the problem of poverty
was not solved in the United States. Murray fails to realize the
reality and the extent of the problem.

Our author too easily accepts the American ethos in his support for the Cold War and in his position toward communism.
Although Murray is critical of some aspects of American foreign
policy and of the Cold War mentality, he still aligns himself with
the general thrust of that policy. The failure to be critical of the
American ethos is also seen in his approach to peace and war,
especially nuclear war. At the very minimum Murray fails to
appreciate the horror of nuclear war and all that is involved in it.
To cross the atomic threshold could open up the possibilities of a
nuclear holocaust.

Murray's uncritical attitude toward aspects of the American
ethos finds some grounding in his methodology. From a theological perspective the lack of sin and grace in his approach robs
him of a more critical stance vis-à-vis the existing American
realities. The danger of Furfey and the Catholic Worker is to
equate the natural with the sinful. The danger of Murray is to
forget the sinful and to accept the existing reality as an expression of the natural which is not infected by sin. From a philosophical perspective the American Jesuit puts great stress on
reason, order, and harmony. However, human problems are
rooted not only in the intelligence but also in the will. It is not
enough merely to know what is the right thing to do. His overly
intellectual approach, together with his failure to stress grace,
helps to explain the failure to stress the need for a change of
heart on the part of all if there is to be true justice and peace in
our world. Likewise, his highly rational approach does not give
enough importance to the realities of power and conflict in all
their ramifications.

Murray's notion of the state can also be questioned. Again,
from his perspective Murray wants to emphasize the limited

nature of the state, so that the matter of religion lies beyond the competency of the state, while there is still room in society for the religious aspect of life. He strongly opposes the totalitarian state in all its forms. However, as a result Murray appears to overly restrict the role of the state. His criterion of public order is quite limited. He sees no economic problem that calls for greater state intervention. In my view the state must have a greater role to play in economic affairs, even while it adheres to the principle of subsidiarity. There can be no doubt that Murray is a political conservative with a view of a very limited state. In contrast, John A. Ryan is a political liberal, for he expands the role of the state especially in terms of its function with regard to social justice. Note that there is some consistency in Ryan, who also calls for a greater role of the state in religious questions. However, I believe that one could still see an expanded role for the state in economic matters without denying Murray's position about the role of the state in religious matters. During the course of the debate on religious liberty at the Second Vatican Council some bishops feared that the concept of the state in the Declaration on Religious Freedom favored a Manchester liberalism and individualistic capitalism.[156]

Serious criticisms can and should be made against Father Murray's approach, and from the contemporary understanding of theological ethical methodology he is particularly vulnerable. However, Murray's creative genius has made him the most outstanding Catholic theologian in the United States in this century.

6. THE CATHOLIC PEACE MOVEMENT AND JAMES W. DOUGLASS

The late 1960s saw a new social movement in the United States—
what was called by the media the Catholic Left. This quite amor-
phous group was committed to nonviolence but used direct action
raids, especially against the draft boards in various cities of the
United States, as a means of protesting the war in Vietnam. The
people involved referred to themselves as action communities.
The names most commonly associated with this group were
Daniel and Philip Berrigan.[1] The present chapter will discuss
the Christian social ethics which serves as an explanation of and
a basis for a nonviolent resistance movement.

I. Presuppositions and Context

This volume has consistently insisted on the importance of
both historical circumstances and of methodology in influencing
various approaches to Catholic social ethics. These influences
very clearly had great impact on that comparatively small but
quite well-known group of Catholics who were committed to
non-violence and used direct action raids to protest the war in
Vietnam.

First, the historical circumstances. No sooner had John
Courtney Murray proved there was no incompatibility between
being American and being Catholic than the Berrigan brothers
and their cohorts came to almost the opposite conclusion. Their
Catholic faith made them very critical about aspects of American life, especially the war in Vietnam. There were a number of
significant historical developments in the 1960s that made all
Americans, including Catholics, more critical of their country.
However, these Catholic radicals of the 1960s were also con-

sciously influenced by their preceding generation who, in the
1930s, recognized the deeper problems of race, poverty, and war
which existed at that time and surfaced with much greater force
in the 1960s. The inequalities between black and white and the
racial discrimination against blacks became evident for all Americans in the decade of the 1960s. No longer was racial discrimination a phenomenon which people could claim existed only in the
south. The riots in many of the northern cities indicated how deep
and widespread the problem of race was in our society. Discrimination in jobs, housing, and unions was deeply ingrained in the
American ethos and culture. America claimed to be the land of
equal opportunity, but this was a living lie in view of the plight of
the blacks in our society. In the early 1960s Martin Luther King,
Jr., developed the tool of nonviolence as a way of improving the
lot of the blacks. Marches, boycotts, and sit-ins were all strategies employed with some success. Whites also participated in
many of these nonviolent strategies to overcome racial injustice.
However, at the time of King's death in 1968 some black leaders
and others did not think nonviolence had achieved its purpose.
Any objective American had to admit that racism existed in all
parts of the United States, even though some approaches were
being employed to overcome it.

American consciousness was also raised about the problem
of poverty in the United States. After the Second World War the
United States experienced an unprecedented prosperity which
served to mask for a time the continuing presence of the poor,
the unequal distribution of wealth, and the continuing wide gulf
between the haves and have-nots in our society. In the late 1960s
and early 1970s the problem of poverty took on a worldwide
dimension with much criticism of the United States for its economic colonialism and for the unbridled power of multinational
corporations. However, the most divisive issue in the United
States was the Vietnam War. At first most Americans apparently
believed in the war, but opposition to it quickly grew on all sides.
As the government tried in many different ways to convince the
American people of the legitimacy of the war, confidence in
government and in our political insitutions eroded.

The problems that loomed so large before 1960 were no longer
the real problems of that tempestuous decade. The economic
problem no longer focused primarily on the worker and the rights
of the worker. The primary social problem was no longer how
there could be civic unity in the midst of religious pluralism. A

generation who had been trained to think of America as the citadel of freedom, equality, fairness, and peace now began to see the great disparity between these ideals and the realities of the 1960s. In this climate many citizens became quite critical of American institutions and policies. Catholics also shared in the discontent and criticism which probably reached their greatest intensity in opposition to the war.

In the 1960s a newer methodology emerged in Catholic social ethics as exemplified in the work of the Second Vatican Council. In general the Second Vatican Council, which began in 1962 and ended in 1965, insisted that scriptures had to be the soul of all theology.[2] The Decree on Priestly Formation called for special attention to be given to moral theology. Its scientific exposition should be more thoroughly nourished by biblical teaching, and the noble vocation of all Christians to bring forth truth and charity for the life of the world must be stressed.[3] These directives attempted to counteract a methodology of the manuals of moral theology which had been based almost exclusively on natural law and human reason. The manuals can rightly be characterized as minimalistic, individualistic, and legalistic with their primary emphasis on distinguishing what is sinful from what is not sinful and what is mortally sinful from what is venially sinful.

One of the most significant documents of the council was the Pastoral Constitution on the Church in the Modern World. Interestingly, of the seventy schemata prepared for the council by the preparatory commissions, only one dealt with the social order. However, at the instigation of Cardinal Leo-Joseph Suenens of Belgium, and with the support and help of the pope, the council fathers saw the need to address not only the life of the church *ad intra* but also *ad extra*—the presence of the church in and to the modern world.[4] The final document acknowledges that the split between the faith which many profess and their daily lives deserves to be counted among the more serious errors of our age.[5] The church has the task of scrutinizing the signs of the times and of interpreting them in the light of the gospel.[6] Now the emphasis is placed on the gospel rather than only the natural law.

The first part of the constitution deals with the general questions of anthropology, human community, and human activity in the world in the light of creation and of the mystery of Christ. The second part of the document considers some problems of special urgency "in the light of the gospel and of human experience."[7] The centrality and importance of the scriptures, of the gospel, and of the mystery of Christ are thus emphasized, but reason and human experience still have important roles. The contrast with the older natural-law approach is quite striking, for the former approach is based exclusively on a human reason and human nature common to all human beings. In general the insistence on the gospel as the criterion indicates a more critical approach to the existing structures and institutions of human society. The gospel emphasis on perfection and its radical moral demands call more readily into question the existing structures and what is by definition the more moderate standard of a common human nature. It also follows that in the light of the gospel the Christian is called to change and transform these structures. Thus both the historical circumstances and the changing methodology in Catholic moral theology and social ethics in the 1960s combined to create an atmosphere conducive to a critique of the American ethos.

The Second Vatican Council addressed the specific question of peace and war. As mentioned in chapter one, the existence of an official church teaching also characterizes Catholic ethics. The whole topic was made even more actual by the existence of atomic and nuclear weapons and by the arms race. The council's deliberations on this question provoked discussion both within and outside the council itself.[8]

Chapter five of part two of the Pastoral Constitution on the Church in the Modern World insists upon the importance of peace, the Christian and human basis for peace, and the need for all to work at the Christian vocation of being peacemakers. The document affirms the need to undertake an evaluation of war with an entirely new attitude. Qualified praise is given to those who renounce the use of violence. However, Christians cannot be denied the right to legitimate defense once every means of peaceful settlement has been exhausted. The council also affirms the right of conscientious objection to participating in war and calls for laws to allow such objection provided some other form of service to the human community is provided. Total war is condemned by stating the traditional principle of discrimination prohibiting direct attack on noncombatants—any act of war aimed indiscriminately at the destruction of entire cities or of extensive areas along with their population is a crime against God and humanity. Such action merits unequivocal and unhesitating condemnation.[9]

The arms race is characterized as an utterly treacherous trap for humanity, and one which injures the poor to an intolerable degree. Many regard the stockpiling and possession of nuclear weapons as an effective way to maintain peace of a sort at the present time, but this so-called balance is not a sure and authentic peace. The arms race is not a safe way to preserve peace. It is the clear duty of all to work for the complete outlawing of war by international agreement through some universal public authority acknowledged by all. In the meantime efforts must be made to end the arms race through disarmament, proceeding according to agreement and backed up by authentic and workable safeguards. However, unilateral disarmament is not required.[10]

The official Catholic teaching on peace reluctantly acknowledges the possibility of war and legitimate self-defense but limits the conduct of war. Some have claimed that the constitution at least partially rejects the just-war theory.[11] It is more accurate to say that the just-war theory is still acceptable in official Catholic teaching, but it is no longer the exclusive Catholic position. Pacifism is now an officially acceptable Catholic position.[12]

In the United States in the middle and late 1960s and in the early 1970s the country experienced the agony of the Vietnam War. There was growing opposition to the war from many segments within American society. American Catholics in their reaction were not that different from Americans in general. One poll showed Catholics slightly more inclined than other Americans to support the war, but the differences in percentage were quite small. The vast majority of American bishops favored the war in the middle 1960s. Cardinal Spellman, archbishop of New York, was the leading spokesperson for this group, but there were a few episcopal voices raised against indiscriminate bombing and killing by the United States in Vietnam. In 1966 the American bishops as a whole maintained that, on the basis of the facts as known at that time, it is reasonable to argue that our presence in Vietnam is justified. In 1968 the bishops raised the question whether the war had reached the point where its continuation was no longer justified. By 1972 they had answered their own question. The ending of this war is a moral imperative of the highest priority.[13]

Catholic opposition to the war took many forms and was based on a number of different theoretical positions. Many Catholics employed a basic just-war position and condemned the war for a number of different reasons—lack of a just cause, violation of the principle of discrimination with its insistence against the direct killing of noncombatants, lack of proportion between the evil involved in the war and the good to be attained by it. Others objected to the war on the basis of their commitment to nonviolence.

There have been a number of movements in the history of American Catholicism connected with peace. As already mentioned in chapter two, in April 1927 John A. Ryan was one of the founders of the Catholic Association for International Peace. In general this group espoused the just-war theory, worked for peace in the context of this theory, and later justified American participation in the Second World War. In the 1960s this organization continued in this course and opposed efforts of the Second Vatican Council to propose a totally pacifist or nonviolent position applied to nuclear weapons. John Courtney Murray was associated with this group, and his policies and theories reflected the general direction of the group.[14] Chapter four pointed out that the Catholic Worker under Dorothy Day espoused pacifism during the Second World War and became the best-known supporter of pacifism in the Catholic community. The pacifists and nonviolent movements which came to the fore in the 1960s owed much to the Catholic Worker.[15]

One important figure in the Catholic pacifist movement who has not been mentioned before is Gordon C. Zahn. Zahn was a conscientious objector in the Second World War. He earned a doctoral degree from the Catholic University after the war, doing his dissertation under the direction of Paul Hanly Furfey on Catholic conscientious objectors.[16] Gordon Zahn is by far the best known and most widely published Catholic exponent of pacifism. One of his studies is a fascinating analysis of German Catholic reaction to the Second World War.[17] Zahn has remained a consistent and articulate voice for Catholic pacifism down to the present era.

In the early 1960s Eileen Egan, a Catholic Worker and close friend of Dorothy Day, founded *Pax*. This group, directing its efforts primarily to working within the church, began publishing a quarterly magazine *Pax* in 1963. Especially in the Second Vatican Council a three-person group from *Pax* (Eileen Egan, Gordon Zahn, and James W. Douglass) lobbied for a nonviolent approach to the question of peace and war.[18] In the summer of 1964 James Forest of the Catholic Worker, James Douglass, who was then studying theology in Rome and was working on peace issues, and Daniel Berrigan, who was on sabbatical in Paris, conceived the idea of a Catholic Peace Fellowship modeled on the pacifist Protestant organization called the Fellowship of Reconciliation. Daniel and Philip Berrigan, with Catholic Workers James Forest, Thomas Cornell, and Martin Corbin, cooperated to form the new peace organization. This self-consciously Catholic group devoted to peace and nonviolence under the umbrella of the Fellowship of Reconciliation was dedicated to opposing the draft and stopping the war in Vietnam.[19]

Catholic Workers had also been prominent in the burning of draft cards as a sign of their resistance to the war in Vietnam. On October 15, 1965, David Miller, a young Catholic Worker, burned his card and was later arrested and convicted under a new law passed by Congress and signed by President Johnson in 1965 that made draft-card burning a crime and punishable by a fine of $10,000 and/or five years imprisonment. Others at the Catholic Worker and elsewhere followed his example. Thus was born "the resistance" which ultimately was successful because so many draft cards were burned that the Rivers' law was unenforceable.[20] In addition, the Catholic Worker was involved in other protests which received great attention in the media. Thus, civil disobedience, protest, and resistance by performing an illegal act were now accepted strategies by some who were opposed to the war in Vietnam. Other Catholic opposition followed more conventional and less radical ways of protest. *Pax* now tried to work for a change in the law which would allow for selective conscientious objection. The Catholic Peace Fellowship with its basically pacifist thrust continued more in the Catholic Worker vein of protest by working from outside the existing institutions of church and state.[21]

In 1968 the spotlight shifted to a new form of Catholic opposition to the war—small groups involved in direct-action raids. Father Philip Berrigan and three others from the Interfaith Peace Mission in Baltimore were searching for a new form of creative nonviolent protest and found it in the symbolic pouring of blood on draft records. In late October 1967 the Baltimore Four staged the first draft raid—a tactic which was to become the hallmark of what was popularly called the Catholic Left in the next few years. However, many Catholic antiwar activists, including Daniel Berrigan and James Forest, did not agree with the tactic when they first heard about it.[22]

In May the Catonsville Nine, made up of all Catholics, including both Berrigans, took files from the draft board, burned them with homemade napalm, and waited in prayer for arrest while the media observed and recorded the entire action. The trial in October brought hundreds of sympathizers to Baltimore as a support group. The trial itself gave the group an opportunity to publicize their stand on the war. Thus was a pattern established which spread throughout the country as other action communities were formed in different places, and a great number of "actions" occurred, beginning with the Milwaukee Fourteen in September 1968. The D.C. Nine in March 1969 raided the Washington offices of Dow Chemical, thus expanding both the object of the raids and the reasoning to include a strong anticorporate and anti-imperialist theme. Innumerable actions took place in the period from 1969 to 1972. What characterized these actions was a form of felonious nonviolent direct action to protest the war in Vietnam. Charles Meconis in his book on the Catholic Left has identified 232 people involved in these actions.[23]

The best-known figures in the movement were the Berrigan brothers, who participated together in the Catonsville Nine.[24] Philip Berrigan went to jail shortly thereafter for his involvement in the Baltimore Four action. Both were sentenced to prison after the Catonsville trial. However, Daniel decided to go underground and managed to elude the FBI from April 1970 until August 11, 1970, during which time he wrote many articles, held interviews with the press, and even preached a sermon at the First United Methodist Church in Germantown, Pennsylvania. By late August both Berrigan brothers were in jail, but ironically their movement was about to receive even greater publicity.

J. Edgar Hoover in a Senate hearing, in November 1970, hinted at the existence of an East Coast Conspiracy to Save Lives which he claimed was planning a kidnapping and bombing. In January six persons were indicted on charges of plotting to blow up the heating system in government buildings in Washington and to kidnap Henry Kissinger. Shortly afterward a new prosecutor was named, and a superseding indictment was issued that made it easier to prove the conspiracy charge against what was now eight defendants—Father Philip Berrigan, Sister Elizabeth McAlister, Eqbal Ahmad, Father Neil McLaughlin, Father Joseph Wenderoth, Anthony Scoblick, Mary Cain Scoblick, and John Theodore Glick. Daniel Berrigan had been dropped from the list of coconspirators. Thus began the Harrisburg conspiracy trial. There was much publicity in the media. Defense committees again functioned in support of the defendants, who had outstanding legal defense but could not agree among themselves on the approach to take to their defense. Their principal attorney, Ramsey Clark, a former attorney general of the United States, made a one-sentence statement for the defendants, and then the defense rested its case. The verdict was a hung jury—ten for acquittal and two against. In the eyes of many theirs was a political trial to harrass those opposed to the war and government policies.[25]

Although the trial of the Harrisburg Seven (Glick was separated from the other defendants when he chose to defend himself against the conspiracy charges) generated great publicity and resulted in acquittal for the defendants, the trial also marked the decline of the Catholic Left. Some action communities continued to function, but the importance of the movement and its prominence in the media quickly waned.

There are many factors that help explain the downfall of this movement.[26] The movement itself was not large and was never well organized but consisted of a number of grass-roots groups sharing similar ideas. There was no real leadership. The debate over the way to conduct the defense of the Harrisburg Seven indicated some of the problems of organization and leadership within the movement. Some of the defendants wanted to work within the system to try to get an acquittal for themselves, while others wanted to take on the whole system itself.

External factors influenced the decline of the movement. The whole American peace movement declined once troop withdrawal began in Vietnam and a final end of the war appeared imminent. FBI surveillance and the political trials took their toll against not only the defendants but also against other members of the group. There were suspicions and mutual incriminations. Imprisonment removed many of the members from their communities. Also relationships with the other aspects of the American peace movement often resulted in various types of misunderstandings. The Catholic Left was accused of being too open and too naive by many of the secular peace activists.

There were also elements of fragmentation within the movement which came more and more to the fore. Some were disillusioned over the announcement of the secret marriage between Philip Berrigan and Elizabeth McAlister. The draft raids which had originally given them great publicity, no longer attracted the attention of the mass media once they became more common events. Some became gradually more disillusioned with American society and adopted more revolutionary rhetoric and strategies. There were debates within the movement itself as to whether or not nonviolence was the proper approach to take in the light of the entire contemporary situation. The movement itself also became greatly divided over the feminist question. The women rebelled against the sexism which had been a part of many of the action communities. Thus for a number of reasons the radical Catholic peace movement, which had been called the Catholic Left by the media, ceased to exist. However, in a broader sense the Catholic peace movement has continued to exist.

The action communities and the Catholic peace radicals of the 1960s differed somewhat from the older pacifism associated with the Catholic Worker and especially with Gordon Zahn. These differences centered primarily on the question of tactics, with the underlying fear on the part of older pacifists that too great an importance was given to effectiveness or efficacy rather than witness. The newer approaches with their emphasis on direct action and the use of at least some symbolic violence against draft-board files were adopted precisely because the older forms of protest were no longer effective. Some even talked about the draft-board raids as a way to interfere with or at least delay the government's ability to wage war. The new peace radicals used the media to publicize their efforts, but in so doing, charges of manipulation were often raised—the peace radicals manipulating the media and the media manipulating them by continually calling for greater escalation. The decision to go underground and to avoid arrest on the part of Daniel Berrigan involved a decided change in the traditional tactic of accepting arrest both as a witness and as a sign of one's recognition that civil disobedience is a very specific and well defined reality not to be confused with revolution or the general rejection of the legitimacy of government. Gordon Zahn, while personally admiring the witness of the direct-action communities and sympathizing with their course, questioned some of their tactics because of the reasons just mentioned.[27] Similar questions had also been raised by Thomas Merton after the Catonsville draft-board raid.[28]

Our primary interest is in the systematic and theological explanation of the position taken by those involved in Catholic nonviolent resistance. In the eyes of the media the most significant people in the movement were the Berrigan brothers. They have also written much about their involvement, and much has been written about them. Since neither Daniel nor Philip Berrigan has written primarily from the viewpoint of theological ethics, their writings are not that directly pertinent to our study.

One very significant writer and theologian who influenced the Catholic nonviolent resistance movement in the 1960s was the Trappist monk Thomas Merton. Merton began actively writing on the issues of war and peace in 1961. He eventually proposed a position of Christian nonviolent resistance which he saw as something different from both the just war and absolute pacifism. The nuclear weapons debate and the Vietnam War constituted the historical context within which he developed a biblical and eschatological Christian approach. For Merton nonviolence is justified theologically, not just tactically. Nonviolence is primarily a matter of truth and witness, not of power and pragmatism. Nonviolent resistance is aimed at conscience, not at revolution. Merton also points out the dangers of self-righteousness on the part of those involved in resistance.[29]

There can be no doubt that both in person and in writing Merton exercised quite an influence on the Catholic nonviolent resistance movement in the 1960s. In November 1964 Merton brought together a small group of Catholics and Protestants, including the Berrigan brothers, James Forest, Thomas Cornell, and others, to his hermitage for a retreat on the topic "The Spiritual Roots of Protest." Merton remained in close contact with these people, but he publicly expressed some reservations about the draft-board raid at Catonsville in 1968. Merton died on December 10 of that year, and there were no direct contacts with the peace-movement activists during the interval between Catonsville and Merton's death.[30]

However, for a number of reasons Merton is not the most apt person to study in this volume. The Trappist monk did not write any systematic works on nonviolence and resistance. He was never personally involved in the direct-action communities and even expressed some reservations about the tactics of direct action in the form of the raids on draft boards. In addition, others have already examined Merton's thought in some detail.

II. James W. Douglass and Nonviolence

Our theological-ethical discussion will concentrate on the works of James W. Douglass, who was greatly influenced by Merton. Douglass has published three books developing his understanding of Christian nonviolent resistance—*The Non-Violent*

Cross: A Theology of Revolution and Peace (1968), *Resistance and Contemplation: The Way of Liberation* (1972), and *Lightning East to West* (1980).[31] Douglass has also been involved in direct-action and nonviolent resistance throughout the seventies—after many others abandoned the approach and after the mass media ceased to publicize such methods as much as they had during the time of the Vietnam War.

Douglass is a dual citizen of Canada and the United States, having been born in Canada of American parents in 1937. In college Douglass had been interested in becoming a weapons researcher but dropped out of the University of California at Berkeley and enlisted in the army. In a course at the University of Santa Clara he was first introduced to the thought of Dorothy Day and the Catholic Worker movement. In the pages of *The Catholic Worker* in 1961 he first saw the work of Thomas Merton on peace. Our author earned a master's degree in theology from the University of Notre Dame in 1962 and studied theology, with emphasis on the question of peace, at the Gregorian University in Rome from 1962 to 1964. During the Second Vatican Council he worked with *Pax* and lobbied the bishops at the council on the issue of peace. He has taught at Bellarmine College (where he frequently visited with Merton in 1965) and at the University of Hawaii, where he formed the Hawaii Resistance in 1968-1969 and spent his first two weeks in jail. Since that time he has devoted his life to contemplation, writing, and resistance.

Since 1975 Douglass has continued to work in a campaign of resistance against the Trident submarine and missile base being built in Bangor, Washington. In 1978 he moved, with his wife and son, to the Ground Zero Center for Non-Violent Action, an action community located next to the Trident missile base. Together with his wife and others he has continued resistance against the Trident project through leafletting, education, and direct action usually in the form of going over the fence into the base to protest and to point out the horrors of nuclear war. His actions have brought him and wife Shelley several arrests and jail terms.[32] His writings, illustrated by his practical involvements, will furnish the basis for our discussion of Catholic nonviolent resistance.

Theological perspectives

Douglass' approach to nonviolent resistance is Christological and eschatological. He shows the influence of Merton in his appeals to Gandhi and to eastern religions and also by insisting on the need for interior conversion or change of heart.

The eschatological aspect of the times in which we live sets the stage for the discussion and understanding of nonviolence. The nuclear age is the eschatological age. Human beings now have the power to destroy themselves and their world. The pursuit of security and peace through superior weapons and destruction has led to the insecurity of threatened existence.[33] The title of Douglass' last book indicates the eschatological reality in which we live. In Matthew's gospel Jesus says that the coming of the Son of Man at the end of the world "will be like lightning striking in the east and flashing far into the west" (Mt. 24:27). Jesus' image reminds us of a nuclear blast. The lightning east to west in the sky can be either a nuclear holocaust with its destruction or the coming of the kingdom with the victory of truth and love in history.[34] Douglass often mentions Albert Schweitzer's opinion that Jesus himself expected the end would come soon.

Whatever one might think about that particular opinion, at least all must recognize that Jesus lived and expressed himself in a world of apocalyptic thought forms in which the myth of the end of the world was common. In response to the crisis of his time Jesus proposed in the Sermon on the Mount and lived out on the Cross a way to transform an otherwise end-time into a new beginning for the world.[35] Our author's eschatology is apocalyptic; we are living in "an end-time." Although there are frequent references to eschatology and especially the apocalyptic crisis of our nuclear age, there is also some development of a different understanding of eschatology. In the last chapter of the last work Douglass points out that Christians hold in common a hope in an ultimate justice and peace. The most popular interpretation holds that the kingdom will come at the end of time or beyond time and that God alone will bring it about with only the human instrumentality of the returning Christ. A second view sees the kingdom or new earth as occurring somewhere in time as a culmination of human struggle through the power of God. Perhaps the view of Jesus lies in the combination of these two understandings—the vertical and the horizontal.[36] However, Douglass usually stresses the eschatological notion of the contemporary time with its impending chaos and catastrophe through nuclear destruction. The understanding of these times in which we live is similar to the understanding of eschatology that was in the air at the time of Jesus.

Douglass' Christological approach is seen in the full title of his first book—*The Non-Violent Cross: A Theology of Revolution and Peace.* The basic meaning of Jesus' life is suffering love as exemplified on the Cross. In his earlier writings Douglass inveighs against milieu Catholicism, which too readily accommodates to the prevailing ethos and culture. The scandal of western Christianity is the denial of its own truth. Too often Christians have not incarnated the truth about who Jesus is. Militarism in Germany and racism in America show how cultural interests have overcome the church's witness to Jesus. There are many popular incarnational heresies today. The question for modern Christians today is the same as the question posed by Jesus in Mark's gospel (8:27-29) : "Who do people say that I am? Who do you say I am?' We must cut through the veneer of so-called Catholic culture to answer that question.

To know truly Jesus as Lord we must pass over to the subjective standpoint of Jesus the man. Douglass in his earliest book calls for an existential Christology—what is often called today a Christology from below. Through the gospels Douglass sees Jesus' understanding of himself in terms of the *ebed Yahweh*—the suffering servant of the Lord as found in Isaiah. Basing his analysis on the works of the Protestant scripture scholar Oscar Cullmann, Douglass shows how Jesus' own self-understanding was affected by the concept of the *ebed Yahweh*. The words attributed to God in the baptism of Jesus by John in Mark's gospel are the citation of the opening line of the *ebed Yahweh* poem in Isaiah 42. John (1:29) calls Jesus the lamb who will take away the sin of the world. Although Jesus prefers the description Son of Man, the vocation of the *ebed Yahweh* becomes the context of the Son of Man's earthly works, as illustrated by numerous scriptural references. Essential to the definition of Christ is suffering, rejection, and a sacrificial death.[37]

Jesus, the suffering servant of Yahweh, was a revolutionary. Some authors, especially S.G.F. Brandon, have thought that Jesus was a Zealot. The Zealots were a revolutionary party who advocated violent resistance to Rome. Jesus' most inner circle of disciples included at least one Zealot and probably several others, perhaps even Peter. The Roman state condemned Jesus as a Zealot. However, Jesus himself was not a Zealot. He regarded the Zealot program of violence as his greatest temptation. But Jesus was a revolutionary—a nonviolent revolutionary.[38]

The Cross is truly the crisis of history. In the midst of the injustice of the world and of history there must be revolution. How do we as Christians overcome the evil and injustice of the world?

The suffering servant's love is the power to redeem evil. Some sensitive contemporary people find it hard to believe in God after Auschwitz and the evil of the Holocaust, but we have forgotten the true presence of God in our world—the redemptive presence of suffering love. The Cross of Jesus stands as testimony of the true power of suffering love to overcome the power of evil. Jesus on the Cross reveals a profound union between himself and all human beings, for the crucifixion unites Jesus with all sufferers of violence and injustice and also with the executioners. The victim of violence and of injustice on the Cross through the power of suffering love becomes the redeemer—the one who overcomes violence, injustice, and death itself. Christ becomes present everywhere as he was present—in suffering servanthood and crucifixion. The way, the truth, and the power of Jesus involve suffering love.[39]

Just as the Cross of Jesus and his suffering call for nonviolent resistance on our part in the face of evil and injustice, so too the logic of nonviolence leads into the mystery of the suffering Christ. Nonviolent resistance seeks to move the oppressor to recognize the humanity of the oppressed through the power of the voluntary suffering of the oppressed. Nonviolent resistance motivated by suffering love is redemptive—it can bring the aggressor to the recognition of the humanity of the oppressed and thus bring about reconciliation. The Cross of Jesus stands as the symbol and the reality of suffering love and nonviolent resistance to evil.[40]

Douglass does not, however, propose a narrow Christology. He sees the same basic reality in other places—especially in Gandhi and in the religions of the east. Undoubtedly our author here follows the inspiration of Thomas Merton. Throughout his writings there are constant references to Gandhi. The scandal of western Christianity is its failure to bear witness to its own basic truth about Jesus. On the other hand, the Hindu Gandhi can be described as the most living belief in the incarnation given in our time.[41]

Gandhi entitled his autobiography *The Story of My Experiments with Truth,* because satyagraha, or truth force, is that power which can overcome any injustice on earth. The Hindu leader came to the conclusion that God is truth. This truth is the power of nonviolent resistance and suffering love. Acceptance of suffering in love for the sake of a higher good is the absolute weapon of truth.[42] Gandhi and his followers ultimately triumphed over the English oppressors by offering their bodies and their lives. The purpose of nonviolence is to move the oppressors to see the humanity of those they are oppressing. Recognition is brought about through the power of voluntary suffering. The logic of nonviolence is the logic of the crucifixion and of suffering love.[43] Douglass thus implies that the recognition of truth and the power of suffering is available to all human beings and not just to Christians.

In his later writings Douglass indicates how an existential Christology and Gandhi's own experiments with truth point to the fact that all human beings can come to the same recognition of the truth and of the power of suffering love. Gandhi's secretary, Pyarelal, has described Gandhi's discovery of reality in relation to Einstein's discovery. Einstein discovered that once an infinitesimal particle attains the velocity of light, it acquires a mass which is infinite. The corresponding law governing the release of spiritual energy is to be found in Gandhi's formula—when an individual has realized the fullness of *ahimsa,* that person becomes filled with the power of love, soul force, truth force, or the godhead within us, to which there is no limit and before which all opposition and hatred must cease.[44]

Gandhi describes his own experiments with truth, but Douglass maintains Jesus too experimented in truth. What the gospels give us is the end result of these experiments, but we want to discover what Jesus did and what he came to see so that we can help ourselves to discover the new reality. The gospels do not tell us how Jesus came to discover the absolute truth—the truth behind the reality of the Sermon on the Mount, and especially the admonition to seek first the kingdom of God and all other things will be given as well. The spiritual constant analogous to the speed of light which brings about the physical transformation of the atom is the self-emptying love for the sake of the other which is found at an inconceivable depth in ourselves. Both Gandhi and Jesus were forced by public and private experiments to experience the deepest powerlessness, self-emptying, and poverty—they discovered the self-emptying love that can transform the world. Jesus describes this reality in the paradox of losing one's life in order to find it, whereas, according to Gandhi, the satyagrahi realizes the nature of truth force only when one has reduced self to zero. This objective reality is a possibility for all of us, and like Jesus and Gandhi we can find the reality through experiments in truth.[45]

Jesus was not originally what he became. He discovered this deeper reality which he became. Our acceptance of Jesus the man who discovered the reality is closer to our lives and much more threatening to our security than our confession of him as Christ. Douglass attempts to explain what Jesus discovered, what Gandhi discovered, and what all of us must discover in the light of Jung's understanding of the human psyche.

According to Jung the shadow is the unconscious self containing all that I refuse to recognize about myself. If a person can acknowledge the shadow and make it conscious, one can become whole—in contact with truth and reality which constitute the source of great psychic energy. Without the power of becoming whole, the autonomous eruptions of the shadow bring about self-destruction and the collective evils of modern totalitarianism. There is a close relationship between personal and cosmic wholeness. This crucial, personal process of acknowledging the shadow initiates a conscious tension of opposites. The clash of opposites brought about by the recognition of the shadow first appears to be only of a private nature, but the subject's conflict is an instance of the universal conflict of opposites. This confrontation brings about the truly graceful production of symbols of unity—a unity derived from the reality of the Self, or of God.[46]

The gospels tell us that the preparation for Jesus' public life involved his going into the wilderness and experiencing there the temptations. We usually think of these temptations as coming from the outside, but the Jungian model of the human psyche suggests a profoundly interior interpretation of the temptations. Jesus' temptations were in the form of messianic power—economic (bread to the hungry), political (all the kingdoms of the world), and spiritual (triumphal religious authority over the people). Jesus recognized himself in these temptations. He encountered the depth of his own self. The shadow of the psyche involves the person in a deepening self-recognition which acknowledges the bottomless void within the self. Jesus underwent these temptations alone in the wilderness in the situation of ultimate powerlessness and recognized their roots in his own emptiness. Jesus acknowledged the shadow in himself which went to an inconceivable depth but finally broke through to ultimate reality and wholeness—his identification with the sins and sufferings of all to the point of accepting personal responsibility for them. The temptations reveal to us Jesus' experiments with the truth; thus

Jesus was liberated for his work. Gandhi came to the same realization through his experiments in truth. In the psychic depth of reality, in the shadow common to all of us, each person is to blame for everyone and for all things.[47]

Douglass thus proposes his transformation hypothesis that every living person is in contact with the same shadow and the same reality of oneness as were Jesus and Gandhi. For all of us the shadow in our individual consciousness with its pride and its pretended control over reality keeps us from being present to the one world in truth. The possibility of transformation rests on my ability of being present to pain—my own and others. Through experiments in truth, by entering into the shadow and the darkness, we begin to come into contact with truth and the possible oneness of our world. The self-acting energy of reality is unconscious to us, but the way into it is through a sacrificial union. The individual psyche realizes soul force, the overwhelming force of wholeness in the world, only when it has established a conscious unity with all psyches. The kingdom of reality will be like lightning striking in the east and flashing far into the west when that hidden, latent energy of the unconscious self, which is God and humanity, has been opened by sacrifice and is allowed to surface into a conscious flash of truth, a force of oneness manifested in a spiritual chain reaction.[48]

Douglass earlier explained the anthropological grounding of his theory in a somewhat different way. Violence is ultimately based on the Cain instinct—the drive to kill and disrupt community. The Cain instinct denies the truth of our basic human brotherhood and sisterhood and consequently is inhuman. The Cain instinct is aggression distorted by sin and unredeemed. Douglass wants to distinguish violence from aggression. Violence is the usual expression of aggression, but aggression need not and should not take the form of destructive violence. The aggressive instinct must be transformed by the power of the Cross—the power of suffering love. There is a truly aggressive aspect about the nonviolence of Jesus. The nonviolent aggression of the Cross challenges our own self-resistance to the personal self-surrender which is forgiving love.

The Cross is a double symbol. On the one hand, the crucifixion of Jesus stands as the apparent triumph of sin, violence, and the forces of destruction. On the other hand, Jesus' active redemptive acceptance of the Cross in suffering love is the triumph of life over death and suffering love over violence. We must transform the Cain instinct in all of us by moving from one side of the Cross to the other. To accept Christ we must move from death-dealing violence to suffering love and thereby transform and redeem the aggression in us which has been distorted by the Cain instinct. The Cain instinct is present in varying degrees in all of us, and we must try to overcome it. Nonviolent Christian resistance based on suffering love does not deny aggression, but it transforms aggression into this Christic form.

However, Douglass wants to avoid the dangerously simplistic solution which would reduce all violence to the Cain instinct. Violence can occur in many different ways and for many complex reasons. Violence embraced by people oppressed by poverty and racism cannot be reduced simply to the Cain instinct in them. However, the need, through grace, to transform the Cain instinct in us and then to direct properly our aggression is the challenge which we are all called to follow.[49] In this analysis the radical transformation is firmly grounded in the reality of sin or the Cain instinct, whereas sin is not explicitly mentioned in the Jungian analysis. However, the Jungian shadow could be understood on the basis of sin. Without explaining himself, Douglass asserts in his discussion of the Cain instinct that Christology and anthropology are ultimately one.[50]

Douglass' theory of nonviolent resistance and self-sacrificing love can only be understood in the light of his eschatological, Christological, and anthropological perspectives. What Jesus experienced and learned in his temptations and lived out on the Cross is available to all of us human beings. Just as the eschatological end-time is made possible with the nuclear bombs which can bring destruction, so too human beings can find the power for a psychic transformation. The atomic and nuclear bombs are based on physical laws, but there is also a psychic law, or structure to our being, which we can use to bring about a transformation of ourselves and of the world—a psychic energy stronger than the physical energy of the atom. The hidden, latent energy of the unconscious self, which is God and humanity, has been opened by sacrifice and has surfaced in a conscious flash of truth. The revolution proposed by Jesus and Gandhi is available to all of us.

Ethical considerations

The theological background with its consideration of eschatology, Christology, and anthropology sets the stage for an evaluation of the more strictly ethical aspects of Douglass' approach.

His approach can best be described as a call for revolution or a radical transformation. Peace and justice will never become a reality in this world without such a radical transformation. Look at the world in which we live—a world of nuclear proliferation, of global poverty, of big-power imperialism, and of Third-World nationalism. Our world is characterized by a constant undercurrent of intrigue, exploitation, and a violence which threatens to destroy the world itself.[51] These are eschatological times. There is need for a new beginning, or there will be an end. The radical revolutionary change must affect humanity itself. Unfortunately, in the course of history humanity has become conformed to structures and institutions radically incapable of serving the needs of the human family. Our contemporary institutions of war and private wealth must change radically.[52]

What is the basis of this radical transformation? The primary ethical reality is truth or self-emptying and suffering love, which is above all made manifest and incarnated in the Cross of Jesus Christ. But, as noted above, this suffering love can be lived out by all and was especially present in the life of Gandhi. Self-emptying and suffering love is the way of truth and liberation for both the oppressed and the oppressor. The temptation of the oppressed is to return evil for evil and violence for violence. The oppressed who overcome that temptation rely on the powers of truth and love. They have delivered themselves from reliance upon power and violence. Self-emptying love for others—all others—is the radical means of liberation for all, especially the oppressed themselves. The possibility of human beings acting in this way is available because of the liberating gift of God's love to us.[53]

But suffering love also has the power to free and to transform the oppressor. Gandhi's greatest accomplishment was the liberation not of the Indian but of the English. The English came to power by relinquishing it. The logic of nonviolence and of suffering love is exactly the opposite of the logic of power, war, and violence. The proponents of power and violence believe that we overcome the enemy through our power. This was the American strategy in Vietnam. We tried to change the enemy's mind through our military and economic might, which brought about suffering and should ultimately bring them to surrender. But the logic of military and economic power forgets about the more significant reality of the power of suffering love. All our mighty military and technological techniques could not bring us victory in Vietnam.

The power of the Vietnamese to endure and suffer was stronger than all our military might. The purpose of nonviolence is to transform the hearts and spirits of the aggressors to perceive as human beings those whom they are opposing. The goal of human recognition is achieved through the power of voluntary suffering. War appeals to brute force and violence and denies the basic humanity of the other. Nonviolence appeals to spirit and truth and calls for the true conversion of the oppressor, which involves a recognition of the basic humanity of all of us. The suffering love of nonviolence is the way to truth for both the oppressed and the oppressor. Only through this love can true human communities come into existence.[54]

The Cross is a paradoxical symbol, and Douglass frequently employs paradoxes in his ethical thinking. He insists on the paradox of power. Suffering love and its incarnation in nonviolent resistance are totally opposed to power. In fact, we must be redeemed from all power over human beings, for this is the power of domination and sin. Suffering love, as the way of truth, seeks a power *for* and not *over* humanity—a power to serve, to care, to love, and to build a human community. To enter into the Cross and the self-emptying love of Jesus one must first recognize one's own powerlessness. This is what Jesus experienced in his resistance to the temptations. Note the dialectical or even the oppositional relationship between power as it is usually understood and the power of truth and love which can only come to be through an admission of one's own powerlessness.[55]

Throughout his major works Douglass often agrees with Jacques Ellul's strong critique of technology. Technology involves power that dominates and manipulates. Our technological civilization has resulted in the domination of machines over human beings, of standardization over spontaneity, and of means over ends. In this context we must critically raise the question of truth.[56]

Intimately connected with this understanding of power and of technology is Douglass' strong warning about effectiveness and the desire for visible fruits of success. The approach of Jesus, like that of Gandhi, was based not on effectiveness but on faith. To the eyes of the world Jesus was a failure and the Cross was a defeat, but to the eyes of faith the Cross was a success story and the ultimate triumph of life and love.[57]

The great temptation for us is to meet the state's technique and power with an evermore effective technique and greater

power. The way of effectiveness and the philosophy of calculation
are the opposites of self-emptying love. My desire for success and
for the fruits of action drags me further and further down into
myself. Technique ultimately imprisons the person and the self.
As frustration mounts, this philosophy has only one response—
escalation toward more forceful means. The whole history of the
American involvement in Vietnam well illustrates this reality.
Ironically, the result of this emphasis on effectiveness leads to
greater bondage for the self and ultimate futility. Nuclear weapons are again a good illustration. Now through the technique of
these advanced weapons, fed by the desire for more effectiveness,
we are at the brink of destruction and death. The ultimate act of
effectiveness is global destruction. But again there is the paradox
and irony of the Cross. Self-emptying and suffering love which is
so technologically ineffective is spiritually explosive. In the long
run what appears as failure will result, to the eyes of faith, in
true success.[58]

Douglass' ethic well illustrates a deontological ethical model,
but our peace activist and writer never explicitly uses this term
to interpret his own work. A deontological approach is distinguished from a teleological approach that puts emphasis on the
goals to be attained. These two ethical models are very broad and
include many different and nuanced approaches under their respective umbrellas, but the differences between the two do furnish
some important ethical insight. A teleological approach sees ethical reality in the light of the good or the end to be attained and
justifies means on the basis of their relationship to the end. A
deontological approach stresses an independence of means and
claims that some actions are always wrong no matter what the
consequences or the good that will come from them. Douglass'
emphasis on bearing witness illustrates a deontological method.
Our responsibility is to act as Jesus acted; God will take care of
the consequences. We are called to bear witness, not to achieve
the good.

The deontological character of Douglass' ethic (again recognizing that he never explicitly employs the term) is also readily
apparent in his discussion of the relationship between means and
ends. The emphasis in our society on technique has resulted in the
domination of means over ends. Unfortunately our technique and
our means have become autonomous. We like to think that our
means are directed to some noble end, but in reality technique
has created its own ends. Every means by its very nature tends to

create its own end. The end itself must be incarnate in the means. There is the same connection between means and ends as there is between the seed and the tree. Certain means such as violence are always wrong and can never be justified by proposed ends.[59] In a Catholic newspaper column Douglass quotes the famous phrase of A.J. Muste, a long-time American, Christian pacifist—the way to peace is peace.[60] Douglass describes Gandhi's approach as an ethic of ultimate ends which insists that the means must always be pure and one can never accept anything less than such pure means.[61] Thus Douglass' position definitely fits into the category of a deonotological ethic with his primary emphasis on bearing witness to the suffering and self-emptying love of Jesus and his insistence on the need for an independent evaluation of means so that they can never be justified because of the ends which they seek to achieve.

The issue

The primary issue for Douglass centers on peace and nonviolent resistance. Occasionally other topics such as poverty and racism are mentioned, but these other issues receive no substantial development. Douglass opposes war and proposes nonviolent resistance as the means to overcome injustice. Much of his discussion of war is in the context of nuclear war and nuclear power. There are only occasional references to revolution and to wars of liberation, but our author remains opposed to all war.

The basic argument against war and violence follows from the centrality of self-giving and suffering love as exemplified and incarnated in the Cross. War's central action of inflicting suffering and death is directly opposed to the example of Christ in enduring these same realities. The church must repent for having allowed itself from the time of Constantine to accept an ethic of just war which condones that which conflicts with the essence of the gospel.[62]

Douglass proposes another way of looking at the relationship between war and the Cross. Rather than beginning with the Cross and condemning war as a violation of the Cross, the procedure can be reversed by beginning with a phenomenological analysis of war. What values is war capable of bearing? As Hemingway pointed out in *For Whom the Bell Tolls*, killing, if done by a person who has not forgotten one's own humanity, must always be experienced as an inhuman act. In modern warfare our technology changes this experience somewhat by distancing us from the face of the enemy, so that now we no longer even see the enemy. But killing remains the central reality of war.

However, there is another aspect to war in addition to this killing. War also involves suffering. The warrior runs the risk of having injury inflicted upon him. The soldier in war suffers greatly. Such a person is therefore both Pilate and Christ. Since the soldier also suffers, there is the possibility of redemption which can rescue the soldier from the killing. There is an intolerable contradiction in war between the genuine redemptive suffering within a particular army or fighting group and the murderous weapons directed at the enemy on the other side. There is a magnificent human community and bonds of care and concern uniting the comrades in arms. There is an aspect of the Cross and of suffering love in war, but it is limited to one's own comrades and contrasts with the killing of others. But war can finally be redeemed by the Cross, which exists in an incipient way even in the trenches of war. William James has called for humanity to develop the moral equivalent of war which could have its good points without its violent destructiveness. The evil of war is a complex manifestation of the Cain instinct imbedded in the sinful side of the Cross. The moral equivalent of war, of the Cain instinct, and of the Cross as murder, is the Cross of suffering love incarnated in nonviolent resistance. A phenomenological consideration of war looks to the possibility of its being redeemed through the suffering love of the Cross and transformed into nonviolent resistance.[63]

Douglass, operating within the Catholic tradition, has tried to show how his position relates to that tradition. One of his heroes is Pope John XXIII. One chapter in *The Non-Violent Cross* considers the nonviolent power of *Pacem in terris*. John XXIII issued this encyclical in 1963. Distinguished theologians and ethicists such as Reinhold Niebuhr, Paul Tillich, and John Courtney Murray criticized the encyclical for being overly optimistic, unrealistic, and naive in its treatment of peace and war. Douglass staunchly defends the document as endorsing a nonviolent commitment to the entire human family which is one under the Fatherhood of God. The encyclical repudiates the use of force: "It is hardly possible to imagine that in the atomic era war could be used as an instrument of justice." Based on human dignity, Johannine nonviolence is a natural-law imperative. Like Gandhi, John emphasizes the power of truth. The need for truth is congenital to human nature and is never extinguished. *Pacem in terris* is unrealistic only to those who understand power in terms of military force and who forget the power of truth.[64]

However, there is an important element of Gandhi's approach that is missing in *Pacem in terris*—the acceptance of suffering in love for the sake of a higher good. Although *Pacem in terris* does not explicitly mention suffering love, the document itself is still the fruit of the personal suffering love of John XXIII which is revealed in his own life as described in his spiritual diary *Journey of A Soul*.[65]

In my judgment some critical comments are in order. Douglass recognizes that John XXIII does not mention suffering love in the encyclical. This ommission points to a much deeper difference with Douglass' own thought. Our peace activist has a strong Christological and eschatological basis for his approach. Both these aspects are missing in John's *Pacem in terris*. The pope does not employ a Christological or a scriptural methodology but instead insists on a natural-law approach grounded in human nature and human reason which all human beings share on the basis of creation. Creation, and not redemption, forms the basis for John's total approach. Christological love is never mentioned by John. Nor does the pope propose the eschatological perspective that forms an important backdrop to Douglass' own theory. There is no methodological basis in *Pacem in terris* for grounding a theory of self-emptying and suffering love.

In addition, a very strong case can be made for the fact that John XXIII did allow for some war and violence in extreme circumstances. I believe Douglass is wrong in his interpretation. The Catholic peace activist bases his position on the general thrust of the encyclical toward peace and on the specific quotation mentioned above: "It is hardly possible to imagine that in the atomic era war could be used as an instrument of justice." However, there is some dispute about the proper translation. Only in a footnote in the following chapter does Douglass even refer to the problem. He bases his translation on "the original Italian" and the Vatican polyglot translation.[66] However, the official Latin is different: "In this our age which glories in atomic power, it is foreign to reason that war is an apt means to repair rights that have already been violated."[67] On the basis of this official Latin text the pope does not exclude the right to use war in the case of self-defense against actual injustice.

The context also argues against Douglass' interpretation.

It is somewhat inconceivable that John would have dismissed the whole Catholic tradition with its acceptance of the possibility of some just wars in one ambiguous sentence. Douglass is aware of such arguments but rejects them because they would indicate that John is not saying anything really new in this encyclical. He points out that in the context John has just finished referring at length to the immense suffering which the use of these armaments would bring to the human family. However, the Second Vatican Council pointed out the immense evils and sufferings of war and of the arms race but did not exclude the right to limited war as a last resort in self-defense. Pope Paul VI, for example, could say to the United Nations "war, never again," but at the same time he recognized that arms could be used for defensive purposes.[68] Neither the council nor Pope Paul VI thought they were contradicting John XXIII. In my judgment Douglass has read too much of his own theory into John, who never developed an eschatological, Christological theory of suffering love and did not adopt a totally pacifist position with regard to war.

Douglass also describes the teaching on war proposed by the Second Vatican Council and discusses some of the debate within the council. Recall that he was in Rome lobbying the council fathers for the cause of peace during the council. In the light of his interpretation of Pope John XXIII our author is disappointed with the results and the work of the council. The council made some significant achievements in the area of peace: a clear and unqualified condemnation of total war, support of the legal right of conscientious objection, affirmation of the primacy of conscience, and even a qualified endorsement of nonviolent resistance. However, there are some weak points and debits: governments cannot be denied the right to legitimate defense, nuclear deterrence is not condemned, unilateral disarmament is not required. In our author's judgment the council both succeeded and failed in its statements on peace and war.[69]

In the light of the text and context our author maintains that the council included in its condemnation the fact that one cannot intend to use the nuclear weapons which one is morally obliged not to use. However, deterrence itself was not condemned because the council fathers were not able to know and judge the particular intentions of practicing statesmen. We do not know if the preparation for indiscriminate warfare (which is the policy of both the United States and of Russia) necessarily involves the morally evil conditional intention to carry out the use of such weapons.[70]

As for the statement of the Constitution on the Church in the Modern World about unilateral disarmament, Douglass accepts the translation and comments offered to him by Bishop Christopher Butler of England with whom he corresponded on the issue. The text should read: "That disarmament should really begin (and) proceed not indeed unilaterally but by equal stages and by agreement." Therefore, Douglass concludes that the text in particular and the document in general do not exclude unilateralism and do not justify the possession of nuclear arms. I, with other commentators, disagree. The specific text even in the Butler translation does not call for total and complete unilateral disarmament. Also by not condemning deterrence and by not demanding total and complete unilateral disarmament, the document at least implicitly justifies the possession of nuclear weapons.[71]

For Douglass all modern war (he usually is referring to nuclear war when he uses the term modern war) either involves the intention to become involved in total war or risks escalation into total war by accident or miscalculation. If we wish to take seriously the council and its central declaration, in spite of the council's own evident hesitancy to face that declaration squarely throughout its statements, we must declare the just war dead. The council has brought down the curtain on just-war doctrine.[72]

I disagree with Douglass' thesis that the theory or doctrine of just war was cast aside by the council. On the basis of just-war theory one could come to many of the same conclusions as Douglass did above. There are nuclear pacifists who have come to this conclusion on the basis of the just-war teaching. Also the just-war theory coherently explains many of the teachings of the council— what Douglass describes as the achievements as well as the debits. On the basis of just-war theory one could accept the condemnation of total war and the endorsement of selective conscientious objection while still allowing defensive war and not necessarily condemning deterrence. The council did not bring down the curtain on just-war doctrine. The major development of the Second Vatican Council was not the denial of just-war theory but the acceptance of pacifism and just war as legitimate Catholic approaches.

Douglass studies the just-war teaching in a deeper and more nuanced way in a later chapter in *The Non-Violent Cross*. He admits that the just-war theory is most often used by Catholics today as a point of reference for those who wish to go beyond it. Many Catholic theorists employ this teaching to condemn as unjust all warfare in the nuclear age. This chapter examines in detail the just-war theory of Paul Ramsey, the American Methodist from Princeton University who has written extensively on the subject in the last two decades. Ramsey throughout his writings has insisted on the principle of discrimination which prohibits the direct killing of innocent people. However, he has throughout the years escalated the destructive potential of a discriminate weapon, so that now thermonuclear weapons are not necessarily indiscriminate. Although Ramsey maintains that one can never intend massive retaliation or countercity warfare, he has over the years expanded his understanding of legitimate deterrence to justify much of our existing system. Douglass dubs Ramsey's approach a theory of nonresponsible deterrence. The Princeton professor acknowledges in theory the possibility of selective conscientious objection, but he rejects it in practice. Ramsey seems willing to go a long way before he would take a stand in conscience against the leaders of the government or the military.

For the Catholic peace activist there is one important question to raise to Ramsey: When does the just-war theory compel the nation to accept the Cross and apparent defeat or when does it ask the individual Christian to adopt the Cross of conscientious objection? Where does the just-war doctrine embrace the Cross in opposition to national and personal interests? Ramsey seems reluctant to do this. Military necessity and national survival always seem to win out at the expense of the Cross. In fact, the Princeton professor has no moral alternative to war. Justice, peace, and order in this world can be preserved only by clothed or naked force according to Ramsey. A suffering resistance to injustice has no value for him. Only a warring resistance can accomplish this purpose. For Ramsey there is really no alternative to war in our world.

Douglass asks if the just-war doctrine itself, as distinguished from Ramsey's development of it, must in every case lack the theological strength to support the Cross of nonviolence or of conscientious objection? Some people have been conscientious objectors on a just-war basis. For Douglass there is a basic flaw in the theory itself. The theory has always insisted on the ultimate criterion of justice. But in the light of the nuclear age justice no longer can accept violence and war. The theory must be transformed by the basic recognition that violence in our age cannot be a form of justice. The theory does not accept the moral value of suffering love as the way to overcome injustice. The just-war theory must be transformed into a theory of just resistance which accepts the Cross with its suffering love. Today the just-war doctrine is fast becoming a relic for the Christians of the Johannine church, the believing community of Christ crucified which is committed to living out the fullness of the gospel.[73]

The way

The reality of the world in the 1970s was such that nonviolent resistance was not accepted by nations. However, individuals were called to practice nonviolent resistance as a protest. Douglass maintains that the people practicing such nonviolent resistance will be a minority and will need strength and conviction to carry out their resistance against the many forces opposed to them. In additions, as the 1970s began, there was a feeling among some former adherents of nonviolent resistance that violence was necessary to overcome the enormous injustices of our world. These circumstances formed the background for Douglass' second book, *Resistance and Contemplation: The Way of Liberation*, which might be called a spirituality for the nonviolent resistor.

Resistance alone is not enough. There must be something deeper and more radical which nourishes the resistance, keeps it alive, and gives the resister the courage to continue. Violence itself always remains a real temptation to the resister who does not go deep enough. Liberation has two dimensions—freedom from the bondage of the individual self, as in Zen, and freedom from the extended self of social oppression, as in liberation movements in Latin America and in Southest Asia. Neither dimension of freedom, personal or social, can be had without suffering. We all always begin on the far side of the flaming sword, the purifying fire of revolutionary suffering. We are enslaved to ourselves and to the social bonds of exploitation and war. The way of liberation passes through fire and is the fruit of crucifixion.[74]

The full truth of liberation is like the *Tao*, or the Way, realized through a *yin-yang* movement in all things. In Taoist mysticism *yin* and *yang* are complementary aspects of a single Reality as seen in the polarities of active-passive, bright-dark, firm-yielding, etc. *Yin* and *yang* are meaningless in themselves, but the union of their differences yields the wholeness in which the *Tao* (the Way) is known. The *yin* is receptive, yielding, life-giving water, the cloud, the dark side of the mountain—contemplation. The *yang* is creative, firm, the power of command, the banner moving in the sun, the light side of the mountain—resistance. In this book he begins with a commitment to resistance which logically calls for the deeper need for contemplation. Liberation consists in the *yin-yang*, contemplation and resistance.[75]

Our proponent of nonviolent resistance has also described how in his personal experience he came to see the need for both contemplation and resistance. *Lightning East to West* includes more autobiographical material than any of Douglass' other works. He experienced the contemplation aspect especially when residing at his original home in Hedley, British Columbia. This town is situated between towering red-tainted rock bluffs at the entrance to a canyon. Here, communing with nature, Douglass often struggled with the meaning of his own commitment to nonviolent resistance.[76]

The example of Jesus reminds us that contemplation must come first. Before Jesus was tortured and executed for resistance, before he confronted the power of the Sanhedrin, before he knocked over the tables of the money-changers in the temple, before he publicly flayed the righteousness of the Pharisees, before he called human beings to pick up their own crosses and come along—before all this, Jesus went into the desert. In the desert in contemplation and solitary struggle he renounced the temptation of power for the sake of resistance and liberation into the kingdom.[77]

The biblical concept of *metanoia* describes well the meaning of this internal change. *Metanoia* is the absolute demand made on every human being to turn from self—to repent—and to turn toward the One who can finally become present only through the emptiness of human self-surrender. Those who want to follow Jesus must renounce themselves, take up their cross, and follow him. Whoever wants to save one's life will lose it, whoever loses one's life for Jesus and the gospel will save it. The Zen equivalent of metanoia is *Satori*, or "awakening." *Satori* is the outcome of an inward struggle to be free from an autonomous ideal of the self and of all the frustrated cravings of a self-contained world. This type of profound inner change and of liberation is the only basis for a truly liberating social change.[78]

Douglass is calling people to go to the depths of liberation both in its personal and its social aspects. One example of not going deep enough into the reality of personal self-change is psychedelic contemplation. Psychedelic drugs expand consciousness into the luminous experience of an all-embracing reality and appear to free people from the current technological society with its materialistic environment which cripples the human personality and psyche. However, in the last analysis, such contemplation is not only shallow but is the ultimate sellout to technology itself. True liberation demands a self-surrender in the depths of one's own existence which is brought about only through fire and suffering, and which leads to resistance for the sake of others. As the *Bhagavad Gita* taught Gandhi, contemplation, if it is to sustain nonviolent resistance, must be a dark night of inner renunciation liberating the soul into a light deeper than any perception. In Christian terms, there is need for the basic change of heart—to die to self in order to rise in the newness of light and life.[79]

Such a radical and disciplined *metanoia* as the constant inward dimension of the struggle for justice is the key to opening up the otherwise impossible way of nonviolent liberation in our end-time. The lack of such an inward dimension is the explanation not only of our present inability to confront a doomsday reality but also of the unfulfilled nonviolence of the past. Many people use the lack of success of nonviolence in the past as a reason for not accepting nonviolence today. Rather, we must take a more careful and critical look at past nonviolent campaigns, especially those of Martin Luther King, Jr., and Gandhi. These two men were definitely heroes to Douglass, but he says in a rather cryptic sentence that attention must be given to the question of how fully King met the radical demands of *metanoia* in himself and to what extent he disseminated those demands to a wider community. There is also need for a critical attitude toward Gandhi, particularly from a feminist standpoint.[80]

There are indications that Douglass has some appreciation of conversion or *metanoia* as an ongoing process for all. Resistance is a struggle against the world, but the mystery of evil engages myself on the level of complete coresponsibility. The mystery of evil can never be external to myself. What I am resisting began as a clearly defined social imperialism but later emerges with sharp clarity as my own imperialism toward every member of the human race. *I* am a major source of the power of the persons of this world to kill others. If my resistance is real, it must continue to go into deeper levels of reality, uncovering new dimensions of evil and responsibility for change within myself. My love must deepen to the point of risking my life in the struggle for truth.⁸¹ In his own life Douglass recalls how he has discovered this evil in himself—especially in the area of sexism.⁸² We are constantly called to make experiments in truth.

Only a deep inner *metanoia* can sustain nonviolent resistance, but just as contemplation at times does not go deep enough, so too resistance can be somewhat short-circuited and not go to the depths of nonviolent resistance. There are some ambiguous forms of liberation—more ambiguous than the Cross of Christ. One can admire the resistance of the National Liberation Front in Vietnam, of Castro, of Camillo Torres. They too have gone through the fire and have been tried in poverty, powerlessness, and suffering. Despite all the important lessons in resistance we can learn from these people and others like them, there remain a deep contradiction and an enormous danger in their pattern of resistance. However, there exist more authentic and unambiguous illustrations of the Cross, especially in forms of nonviolent resistance communities built from the bottom up by people like Cesar Chavez in the United States and Danilo Dolci in western Sicily. Resistance must go to the depths and embrace the truth and the soul force—the Cross which incarnates the suffering and self-emptying love of Jesus.⁸³ Liberation theology today profoundly confronts suffering humanity's need for freedom from oppression but unfortunately forgets the need for peace. In our end-time there is a twofold moral imperative— to resist both the means of oppression and the means of war. This is the depth of resistance which is required today.⁸⁴

Douglass' first book dealt primarily with nonviolent resistance. However, his own experience and the reality of the intervening years brought him to appreciate the need for an inner spirituality as the basis for the radical response which is required in this end-time. Especially in the West we lack a spirituality with a radical enough critique of reality to sustain a theology of revolutionary transformation.⁸⁵ In his two later books Douglass develops in some detail what this basic *metanoia* entails.

The way of resistance grounded in such a *metanoia* involves solitude, trial, prison, and the risk of death itself. True liberation can be found only in solitude, where the individual discovers the reality of one's own powerlessness and how unfree one is. Too often the movement politics of the 1960s sheltered its adherents from this lonely and deep encounter with the self. It is only in the desert experience that one can truly be transformed.[86]

They experience the reality of trial who resist in the name of truth and suffering love. Jesus was put on trial; Gandhi was put on trial; nonviolent resisters have been put on trial. To stand before judges and give witness to the truth is our calling. But first we must undergo that trial in the solitude of our own contemplation.[87] Douglass in his own personal life has been on trial for his civil disobedience on a number of occasions. His sentencing statement on March 28, 1980, indicates his personal response and witness at this time. After comparing the different logic of war and of nonviolence, Douglass promises to love and pray for the judge even when he is in jail. The judge is a good person, but our activist also promises that he and his family will continue to go over the fence at the Trident base in their efforts to stop nuclear war.[88]

In our contemporary society a nonviolent commitment based on suffering love will not only constitute a protest against society but will ultimately face trial and prison. The Way involves going to prison. From the viewpoint of technical efficiency prison seems to be a defeat for anyone involved in resistance. But what is technically ineffective can be spiritually explosive. Gandhi, Bonhoeffer, the Berrigans, and thousands of young American war resisters, by living out the truth behind bars, have changed their own lives and others. From the perspective of technical effectiveness prison seems to be a total negative, but the Way of truth, love, and the Cross is through prison.[89]

The Way of the Cross involves more than solitude, trial, and imprisonment; it also entails the risk of death. But here, too, there exists the paradoxical aspect of death. The radically liberating experience involves a self-emptying love for all others. As resistance increases to the point of risking my life in the struggle for truth, death now reveals its force as a potentially life-affirming end through a final gift of self to the love which gave me life. Death becomes the ultimate liberating act which overcomes evil. Evil is resisted and overcome by a force of truth which depends on the progressive liberation of myself to zero.[90] In the midst of civil disobedience against the Trident missile base Douglass experienced the reality of risking death for his action.[91] Direct action alone is not enough. True liberation can only come from a self-emptying love which experiences solitude, trial, prison, and even the risk of death. Such is the Way of Liberation.

Tactics

The distinctive aspect about Douglass' approach is the heavy emphasis on interior personal transformation. In his publications there is no detailed ethical or theological defense of the tactics to be used by the nonviolent resister. Obviously, violent means of resistance are not acceptable. Instead of an analysis of the tactics of nonviolent resistance there are descriptions of the various movements with which Douglass has been associated and the types of direct action, usually in the form of civil disobedience, employed by these groups. These autobiographical aspects of his personal involvement can be found especially in *Lightning East to West*. The lack of a discussion of tactics is even more surprising in the light of Douglass' admission that he changed his own mind about direct action and civil disobedience. In 1968-1969 after the publication of *The Non-Violent Cross* our author was teaching a seminar on "Theology of Peace" in the Department of Religion of the University of Hawaii. The Hawaii Resistance group was then formed. Some members burned their draft cards in protest. Douglass argued strenuously all one night against a proposed direct action in the form of civil disobedience by the Hawaii Resistance, but a day later he joined in this demonstration by sitting in front of a troop convoy. This resulted in his trial and a jail sentence. The second part of *Resistance and Contemplation*, describing the Way as involving trial, imprisonment, and death itself, is dedicated to the members of the Hawaii Resistance, especially those who endured prison and exile for the sake of liberation.[92] Despite the apparent struggle within himself he never discusses the tactics of direct action and of civil disobedience.

In 1969-1970 the Canadian-American peace proponent was appointed the first visiting professor in the "Program for the Study and Practice of Nonviolence" at the University of Notre Dame.[93] Our author was again teaching at the University of Hawaii in 1972 and became involved in a nonviolent resistance community called Catholic Action of Hawaii. On March 2, 1972, the group planned a leafletting invasion of the Pacific Air Force Headquarters building in Hawaii. Douglass and James Albertini carried blood with them on the almost inconceivable chance that they might come across top-secret papers. This is exactly what happened. They were arrested and trial was set for August 1972. Having learned from the experience of other similar trials, the defendants planned to ask to examine the bloodied files. The files could then be shown to contain evidence of the United States Air Force's use of antipersonnel weapons directed against civilians, thereby violating both international law and the United States Constitution, which makes all treaties signed by the government, including the Geneva and Hague conventions on the rights of civilians, the supreme law of the land. At a pretrial hearing their motions were denied. The defendants refused to cooperate with the judge. At the trial a new judge allowed the planned testimony. The Pentagon refused to hand over the bloodied secret files to anyone, so the charges against Douglass were reduced from a felony to a misdemeanor. He was found guilty, put on a year's probation, and fined $500; but he refused to go along with the penalty. As a result of his refusal to cooperate, he was ultimately arrested by the F.B.I. in 1975 while giving a talk at Immaculate Heart College in Los Angeles and was returned to Hawaii for sentencing. The judge gave him a suspended sentence, thanks to widespread public support for his cause.[94]

Since 1975 James and Shelley Douglass have been involved in a nonviolent campaign of resistance against the Trident submarine base at Bangor, in the state of Washington. The Trident II missile will be the ultimate counterforce weapon and will give the United States first-strike capability. The Trident Campaign was begun in 1975 by a group of Canadians and Americans who have employed a number of tactics—public education, attempts to influence legislators especially in Canada, and, above all, nonviolent direct action which has been the spearhead of the campaign. Many times Douglass, his family, and others have gone over the fence of the base to protest, have occasionally been arrested, tried, and imprisoned. In 1977 a group bought a plot of land adjacent to the base and established the "Ground Zero Center for Nonviolent Action." Note the Gandhian basis for the name, which reminds all of the need to reduce ourselves to zero as the way of entering into the life-force which alone can liberate. The community also employs tactics such as fasts which, from the viewpoint of productivity and effectiveness, seem useless. In reality, fasts have been sources of forming community and strengthening the life-force within the members. Also the

Ground Zero community tries to maintain good relations with those who work at the Trident base. No one really believes in Trident. It is being built out of fear, profit, and passive cooperation. On the other hand the power of life-force is unlimited. If we persist ever more deeply in the truth of life-force, there is no way that Trident can overcome it. If Trident can be stopped by a grass-roots movement involving nonviolent direct action, then one can believe that any destructive force, including the nuclear age itself, can be turned around. The Trident Campaign in its nonviolent approach, transnational character, and seemingly impossible goal is a communal experiment in faith and hope which can open up a whole new world.[95]

From the description given by Douglass in his writings there has been no destruction or symbolic destruction of the weapons themselves. However, his direct actions have included the pouring of blood on files and the cutting away of the fences surrounding the Trident base as well as many other forms of trespassing on the property to plant gardens or to pray. In general our author gives no real ethical analysis and justification of the means used in the direct action except for the fact that they are nonviolent and can be justified in terms of his understanding of law. In this area his writings are primarily autobiographical and descriptive.

Some opponents have criticized the Catholic peace movement for its self-righteousness. Douglass does not explicitly discuss the charge, but his theory and practice are such as to provide a strong defense against the dangers of self-righteousness. Especially in his later two books the emphasis is on the sin and mystery of evil in each of us. Personal liberation is all important. The truth is that there is no intentional evil or sin which we can be certain of except our own. It is thus our own sin which is the metaphysical key to the apparent sin of all.[96] No negative judgments are made about the people who work for the Trident base. They are good people.[97] Even in statements to judges Douglass tries to avoid any hint of self-righteousness.

A politics of nonviolence

In his life and especially in his later writings Douglass has emphasized the concept and reality of nonviolent resistance as a form of protest and dissent. But there arises an important question about whether politics or the state can accept nonviolence. Can there be nonviolent politics, a nonviolent rule, or non-violent states? The Canadian-American writer addresses this question in two essays incorporated into his work *The Non-Violent Cross*. But these essays themselves show some inconsistencies and tensions. In the light of his life and interests in the last thirteen years it is not surprising that Douglass has not returned to this topic.

Chapter eight of *The Non-Violent Cross*, "Christians and the State," begins by describing the attitude of Jesus to the state and depends quite heavily on the work of the Swiss Protestant theologian Oscar Cullmann. There are two aspects in Jesus' relationship to Rome. On the one hand there is his death under its authority and his nonviolent revolution against the state's suppression of the Good News. On the other hand there exists his apparent indifference to the state as such during his lifetime. At first Paul's advice to the Romans in chapter thirteen might seem contradictory especially to our modern mentality. Even though the state does exactly the opposite of what the Christian is to do by taking vengeance on the one who does evil, nevertheless the Christian is to be subject to the governing authority. These words were addressed to nonviolent Christians with no thought given to the fact that they might ever be administrators of the government. Paul does not really justify the state's use of coercion. The governing authorities, in the prophetic tradition followed by Paul, carry out their work in a history over which God rules, but God does not justify their work anymore than God justifies sin and wars which are also a part of that histoy. Even after Christ's victory over the powers the Apocalypse reminds us that the rulers of this world will rise up in a desperate final attempt to defeat the Cross which in effect has already defeated them. The New Testament describes a basic and irreducible tension between the nonviolent Christian whose ethic transcends national loyalties and the national absolutism of the sword-wielding state.

But with Constantine a great change occurred. The Cross had won its victory by forcing Constantine to accept the Cross, but Constantine nullified the victory by joining the Cross to the sword. Christians cannot take up the state sword without compromising the savior's Cross. The Christian lives a permanent revolution toward the state, hoping that the state will take a step further toward the Cross. But the Christian never expects the governing authorities to embrace the Cross, and, like Paul, the believer remains subject to them in all that is just. However, the Christian knows that it was Caesar's Cross on which the Lord of Glory died. The Christian, too, may have to render Caesar a Cross rather than a denarius.

How, then, should one understand the relationship between the Christian community and the state? What are the ecclesial implications of this approach? Ernst Troeltsch distinguished two different Christian approaches—the church which meets the world in a socially responsible way but therefore has to accept some violence and destruction, and the sect which lives the full life of Christian discipleship but in withdrawing from the world and the state. From the critical perspective of the New Testament the horns of the church-sect dilemma as proposed by Troeltsch are equally unacceptable.

H. Richard Niebuhr in *Christ and Culture* adopted a conversionist model of Christ the transformer of culture in which the saving power of God tries to change and convert earthly reality, including the state. Although less domineering than Troeltsch's church approach, Christ the transformer of culture still implies a too early and easy triumph over the powers which in the New Testament are seen as crucifying both Christ and his followers until the end of time. Niebuhr has overemphasized the resurrection and detoured around the Cross.

The founder of Christianity did not promise that the church would convert the world but that it would endure until the end of time as a sign of contradiction. The community of Christ is neither triumphant by converting and dominating the world nor sectarian by withdrawing from it. Douglass accepts an understanding of the church of the diaspora as living in the world the form of Christ's confrontation with that world—a Cross of suffering, redemptive love. The Christian community should live out the enjoinder of Paul. You Christians, distinguished from and even alienated from the state which bears the sword, you should nevertheless be subject to it, but in being subject to it, remember that love does no wrong to a neighbor. There will always remain these two realms, for nowhere in the gospel does Christ envision such a transfiguration of the world that the tension between the way of his followers and the ethics of the state will be eliminated. The church is to be a suffering and not an established church. The state's particular realm of conduct is not therefore justified; it is simply inevitable given its independence from Christ. There can be no direct Christian responsibility for the state.[98] Our author does not systematically draw out the very significant practical ramifications of such an ecclesiology, but it seems that Christians then cannot function as authorities in the state.

However, there seems to be a different approach in chapter ten, "Is There a Politics without Violence?" Reinhold Niebuhr contended that the Christian can remain a politician because the gospel primarily signifies justification by faith of sinful human beings. Gandhi was scandalized that a person of faith could continue to sin in one's own effort and then rely on Jesus to save one from the consequences of one's own sinful action. For Gandhi the only responsible political ethics is an ethic of ultimate ends. The end of peace is realized by the presence of peace in the means themselves. There is no absolute dichotomy between a politics of protest or dissent and a politics of rule or government. The predominantly nonviolent state (Gandhi did not think it could ever be totally free of coercion) can come into existence only through a nonviolent revolution—an enormous spiritual transformation brought about by the prolonged suffering of thousands of satyagrahi revolutionaries. The result would be a nonviolent democratic state marked by service, equality, and sacrifice. Gandhi did not expect to see this vision fulfilled in his lifetime and refused to go into details about it. The nonviolent state police force will make a minimum use of coercion. Foreign aggression will be minimized by the nonaggressive character of the state. If aggression does come from others, it will be met by nonviolent resistance. However, Gandhi insisted that this would never come in his lifetime. Douglass assures the reader that at this point in history nonviolence is connected not with rule but with protest rising from the disinherited of the earth. A radical change of hearts and structures is required before a nonviolent politics of rule becomes possible.

In addition to a politics of dissent and protest one can ally oneself with a global institution like the United Nations to overcome the nation-state with its tendency to violence. The United Nations has prevented some violence. Even when the United Nations has sent in emergency peace-keeping forces armed with weapons, their effectiveness has not really depended on their weapons. Perhaps these forces can be transformed into a totally nonviolent presence without even their now largely symbolical arms. The global politics of belief found an adroit leader in Dag Hammarskjöld, who was truly a successor to

Gandhi. Hammarskjöld, too, was committed to truth and the Cross in an attempt to strengthen the bonds of trust among nations.[99]

Douglass' proposals in this chapter are somewhat inconsistent with his earlier approach. To the final question of whether it is possible for human beings to practice politics without violence, his answer is an imperative. If humanity is to live, there must be a politics without violence.[100]

III. Evaluation and Critique of Douglass

Douglass has given personal witness to his belief in nonviolent resistance. He has been tried, convicted, and put in prison, but still remains committed to continue the struggle. His own life well exemplifies his theory, and the harmony between theory and practice speaks an eloquent testimony to fellow believers.

On the level of nonviolence as resistance there is a basic consistency about his theory with its grounding in the power of truth and of self-emptying and suffering love. With self-emptying and suffering love as incarnated in the Cross as the fundamental ethical value, nonviolent resistance is the logical consequence.

There are many positive aspects about Douglass' approach. He is dealing with one of the most significant issues of our time —violence and especially nuclear force. Unfortunately there has not been enough attention given to these issues in contemporary Catholic theological ethics. The methodology employed is a distinctively Christian approach unlike the natural-law methodology employed by Murray. Catholic moral theology in the future will have to incorporate these scriptural, eschatological, and Christological aspects which are a part of Douglass' approach. One can disagree with Douglass, but these aspects must find a greater place in Catholic ethics. In a time when people are looking for a Christian identity, Douglass proposes one in terms of the Christian's commitment to nonviolence and the willingness of the Christian to say No to every attempt of coercion and force. At times Christianity can and must say No to the contemporary culture and society. The description of the American Catholic scene in the United States in this book reminds us of the perennial danger of conforming the gospel to culture and society. Douglass' countercultural position clearly indicates the difference that being a Christian can and should make. However, as attractive as all these aspects are, they are not beyond criticism.

The Catholic peace activist's writings have contributed a very important aspect to nonviolent resistance—the need for a spirituality involving a deep personal *metanoia* which begins with the recognition of one's own powerlessness. A nonviolent resistance based on such a radical personal transformation will have the strength to withstand and resist in the midst of great suffering and opposition. People formed in such an approach will not be tempted by the superficial allure of technology and of quick results which short-circuit the power of deep personal change that is required for any true liberation with its twin aspects of both contemplation and resistance. The radical call for transformation of the individual makes one much less dependent on the need for external successes. The nonviolent resister needs this strong internal power, what Douglass often calls life-force, in order to continue the struggle.

In his discussion of nonviolence as rule or government, as distinguished from nonviolence as protest, there appears to be a lack of consistency. In fairness it should be remembered that our author has not devoted much of his writing to this question and has not discussed it since the 1960s. The historical situation is that of nonviolence as protest, and he rightly has spent his personal efforts and his theoretical and writing interests in this area. However, as pointed out above, there is an inconsistency in the two chapters appearing in the same book. The chapter based primarily on Christian considerations of the role of the state indicates that the state can never be expected to embrace the Cross. Its conduct is not justified but only inevitable.[101] The chapter relying more heavily on Gandhi indicates that human beings must be able to practice politics without violence if humanity is to live. In this chapter there is the indication that one can move step by step in this direction, especially by opposing exploitative nationalism through some world agency such as the United Nations. To come into existence the nonviolent state would require the radical transformation of hearts and of structures. Even then one can never expect the state to be totally nonviolent, for any state must depend on some coercion. The nonviolent state would be a predominantly nonviolent state.[102] There is not a complete contradiction between the two chapters, but there is at the very least a very different emphasis which would make it quite difficult to reconcile the two.

Although the possibility of nonviolence as applying to rule and the state is not the primary concern of Douglass, the tensions and different emphases in his discussions of this issue are indicative of a deeper problem that is involved in Douglass' presentation. The problem centers on the universality and the efficaciousness of nonviolent resistance. First, consider universality. If nonviolence will always be a resistance movement, then it is not destined for everyone. Some people in the Christian tradition propose such a resistance movement on the basis of what is unique to Christians who are so different from all others. In many ways this was the approach proposed by Paul Furfey in the 1930s. However, Douglass explicitly denies such a Christian uniqueness. He insists that Christology and anthropology are ultimately one.[103] There is no uniquely Christian foundation for nonviolence, since nonviolence is based on a common anthropology. It is a truth power which is available to all human beings as human. His frequent use of Gandhi and of eastern religions also indicates the more universal call to nonviolent resistance. There is thus a tension between emphasizing the resistance and protest aspects of nonviolence and the universal grounding in a common anthropology.

A second related tension in Douglass' thought centers on the efficaciousness of nonviolence. The Canadian-American peace activist strongly disagrees with an emphasis on effectiveness which is based on power, manipulation, and technology. The pursuit of such effectiveness is a shallow short cut of the call to the fullness of liberation, especially in its deep personal aspect of *metanoia*. However, nonviolent resistance not only can, but even must, be effective; otherwise we will all perish. The nuclear apocalypse will occur unless we embrace the way of nonviolence.

This theoretical tension between nonviolent resistance and its universality and efficaciousness also has practical parallels. Why are so few people attracted to nonviolence? Why has nonviolent resistance not been successful? It is interesting that Douglass wants to claim a number of people for his nonviolent approach who are not ordinarily connected with nonviolence. He has many heroes—John F. Kennedy, Pope John XXIII, Teilhard de Chardin, and Dag Hammarskjöld are often referred to very favorably. They are not believers in total nonviolence, but Douglass apparently sees that these people were on the way to nonviolence. Here, too, he seems willing to accept growth toward nonviolence. However, it should be noted that the praising of the individuals mentioned above is found primarily and almost exclusively in his first book. The practical problem about the efficaciousness of nonviolence is directly faced by our author. For Douglass it is now the only effective alternative to nuclear destruction. As for the lack of success of nonviolent movements in the past, even in the case of King and Gandhi our author blames not the reality itself but the practitioners of the movement.

There generally exists in Douglass' thought a very consistent basis in his theological and ethical presuppositions for his nonviolent resistance. In this nuclear end-time we are called upon to live out the suffering and self-emptying love of the crucified Christ. However, I disagree with his theological and ethical presuppositions precisely because they are too one-sided and ignore the complexity which I think belongs to these aspects. On occasion there also appears to be some tension or inconsistency in his own thinking. These theological and ethical presuppositions will now be examined in a critical manner.

The eschatology proposed by Douglass assumes that we are in an end-time just as Jesus thought he was in an end-time. This apocalyptic eschatology calls for the radical ethics proposed by Jesus. Such an apocalyptic perspective makes the matter much more urgent and radical, thereby calling for the self-emptying and suffering love of Jesus.

However, problems exist about the consistency of this eschatology in Douglass. Near the end of *Lightning East to West* there is a different approach to eschatology. Jesus' view of eschatology, according to our author, probably includes a combination of both the vertical and the horizontal coming of the kingdom—that is, the coming of the kingdom somewhat in history and also somewhat outside history.[104] But in such a view the future is not yet here, and meanwhile we must live short of the fullness of the eschaton. The lamb and the lion have not yet laid down together, even though we must try to make the end-time reality more present in our world. This type of eschatology fits in better with the conversionist model proposed by H. Richard Niebuhr and rejected by Douglass. It is also the eschatological approach I favor. The kingdom has already begun, but its fullness will only come at the end of time. Meanwhile, we are called to make that kingdom more present in our world, all the time realizing that the fullness of the kingdom will be God's gracious gift at the end of time. Continual conversion rather than radical transformation fits in better with this eschatological understanding. There are indications that Douglass himself at times leans toward such an approach. The experiments in truth done by both Jesus and Gandhi at times seem to involve continual growth and even incremental growth. Our author's own call for *metanoia* often has the connotation of gradually going deeper into our change of heart and is not just a radical call for total transformation. We are an imperfect and sinful people, living this side of the fullness of the kingdom, always striving to make the kingdom more present.

The radical transformation in an apocalyptic age does not seem to account for the fact that the kingdom has already begun. Our author seems to imply that until now there has been little or nothing of the kingdom but that its fullness will now be present through a radical transformation. This might be true of some individuals, but I do not think it is true of the world as we know it. Douglass criticizes H. Richard Niebuhr for seeing too much of the resurrection already present. I hold to more of the resurrection already present than Douglass wants to admit. The resurrection reality of Jesus is already present in our world, but its fullness will only come at the end of time. Meanwhile, we are called to make that kingdom evermore present.

The most innovative aspect of Douglass' Christology is the emphasis on a Christology from below, which indicates how Jesus himself experimented in truth until he came to the point of the Cross. However, the dominant aspect of this Christology is the Cross. The Cross fits in well with the resistance aspect of the ethical position and with what is best described as the dialectical and paradoxical paradigm necessary for the radical transformation which is at the heart of the Christian life. The Cross is truly paradoxical. The Cross is the result of sin and the victory of evil in putting Jesus to death, and, at the same time, through suffering love it is the sign of redemption and the victory of Jesus. The Cross as paradigmatic reminds all of us of the need to give of ourselves and to suffer—in dying we live and in our powerlessness we find our true strength.

However, the Cross alone is not a symbol of the total reality of Jesus. There is not only the Cross but also the resurrection. Those who have been baptized into Christ Jesus now truly share in the newness of the life of the resurrection. In my judgment the conversionist or transformationist approach of Niebuhr is more appropriate than the paradoxical perspective of Douglass. Our author is aware of the differences and rightly recognizes that a greater emphasis on the resurrection would bring about a change in his own position.

In anthropology the paradoxical element also receives the emphasis—only by dying, by giving, by admitting our own powerlessness, by suffering, can we become radically changed. From the perspective of grace and anthropology I do not see the divine-human relationship totally or exclusively in paradoxical terms: that is, God's power is made known in human weakness, receiving in giving, joy in sorrow, and life in death. Sometimes God's love is known and manifested in human love, God's beauty in human beauty, God's power in human power. Sometimes there is the paradoxical element, but it is not the only element. A conversionist motif allows for some paradoxical aspects but does not explain the divine-human relationship only in paradoxical terms. We share even now in life, love, joy, peace, and victory of the Risen Lord; but these are only the first fruits. The fullness will only come at the end of time.

In my view Christian ethics looks at the human reality in the light of the fivefold Christian mysteries—creation, sin, incarnation, redemption, and resurrection-destiny. Such a stance is much more complex than the apocalyptic eschatology assumed by Douglass. We all share in the goodness of creation. However, sin infects but does not totally destroy our world. Incarnation and redemption mean that individuals and the world already belong to the kingdom in its beginnings, but its fullness will only come at the end of time as God's gracious gift. Such a perspective does not support a totally paradoxical view of human anthropology. We live between the two comings of Jesus and will always experience the tension of living in these in-between times. But apocalyptic eschatology, a Christology of the Cross alone, and a paradoxical Christian anthropology are, in my judgment, too one-sided approaches. In fairness it should be recognized that my ethics will not be as radical as the ethics proposed by Douglass.

Douglass gives very little consideration to ecclesiology, mostly in the context of his early discussion of the relationship of Christians to the state, but this incipient ecclesiology is consistent with his general eschatological, Christological, and anthropological emphases. The church in his diaspora model will never transform the world but will be a sign in the midst of the world of suffering love. In my judgment this is too narrow a view of ecclesiology and of the social mission of the church. The gospel which the church proclaims calls for Christians and the church to try to transform and improve the world in which we live. The role of the church vis-à-vis the world is not always or only that of resistance and suffering love. However, since the fullness of the kingdom is God's gracious gift at the end of time, the world in which we live will always be marked by finitude, sin, and a lack of eschatological fullness.

Douglass consistently and logically makes self-emptying and suffering love as incarnated by the Cross the primary ethical value. From my perspective love is a more complex reality and involves more than self-emptying. Love is truly a multifaceted reality and should bring together aspects of self-surrender, of mutuality, of reciprocity, of friendship, and even, in some ways, of self-fulfillment. Love is a complex reality and involves more than suffering. There are also joy, peace, reconciliation, and many other aspects connected with Christian love. In terms of the Christian symbols of love the Cross is important but, again, is not the only symbol. Here, too, one must always see both the Cross and the resurrection. In addition, there are other Christian symbols of love, especially the Trinity. Whereas the love shown on the Cross is primarily self-sacrificing love, the love symbolized in the Trinity is primarily relational, reciprocal, and communal. Here is the love of union, not the love of sacrifice. So my understanding of love and of the Christian symbols includes more than just self-emptying and suffering love.

Douglass' implied ethical theory is also consistent with his theological perspectives and with his practical conclusions. A deontological ethic calls for us to bear witness to Jesus and maintains that some actions (e.g., violence) are always wrong no matter what the consequences. Currently there is a significant debate taking place in Christian ethics about methodology and moral norms which is often discussed in terms of a deontological versus a teleological ethic. My own position tries to find a third, or mixed, position which I prefer to call a relationality-responsibility approach. Within such a perspective it is more difficult to maintain that some actions such as violence are always and everywhere wrong. The relationality-responsibility model is more prone to see ethical values in relationship to one another and does not absolutize any one value.[105] The concentration on suffering love and on deontology absolutizes nonviolent resistance. In my perspective peace or nonviolence exists together with many other values such as justice and freedom. It is possible that in the name of justice one might have to use violence as a last resort.

As for Douglass' specific analysis of war, my disagreements with his analysis of Pope John XXIII and of the Second Vatican Council have already been mentioned. Douglass' analysis of a just war raises a very significant question: When will the theory ever be used decisively to say No to our nation's policy? Douglass could have made his point even stronger by showing historically how the just-war theory has almost inevitably been used to justify *our* wars. There are also other weak aspects of the just-war theory that were not pointed out by Douglass. Often just-war theorists accuse pacifists and proponents of nonviolent resistance of being naive and overly optimistic because they forget about human sinfulness. However, there is an aspect of naiveté and overoptimism in the just-war theory itself, especially in that part which concerns the limitations on the conduct of war as set forth in the principle of discrimination. War, according to this principle, can never be total but is always limited by the fact that noncombatants can never be directly attacked. Countercity warfare is the total war condemned by the Second Vatican Council. With modern weapons' technologies there have been many violations of this principle. Is it realistic to think that in the crisis of war itself nations will limit their technology and their weapons systems? Is it not the human tendency to do everything we can do technologically to achieve our purpose of victory? Is it not naive to think that if nations go to war in the first place, and thus cannot recognize the demands of justice in the dispute, that they will now adhere to the rules of justice in the conduct of war? There are, in my judgment, a number of difficulties connected with just-war theories, even though I basically accept the theory.

Our author's discussion of war centers on two areas—war involving nuclear weapons and nonviolent resistance with special emphasis on opposition to nuclear war. It seems that Douglass is definitely opposed to all wars and revolutions, but wars of liberation and revolution are not discussed at any great length by him. One cannot expect Douglass to cover all areas, but such a discussion would at least help to flesh out his total approach.

Part of the problem is that one can be opposed to nuclear war and still not accept nonviolent resistance as an absolute. There is a legitimate position of nuclear pacifism or at least of a rejection of all indiscriminate nuclear weapons. One does not have to embrace nonviolent resistance in order to be opposed to the use of nuclear weapons. Douglass himself seems to be aware of this reality when discussing the various means which are now being used to protest the Trident missile project. Direct action is described as the primary approach but not the only one. Education, appeals to legislative changes, and appeals to individuals who work on the project have all been employed. He even asserts that no one really believes in Trident.[106] To oppose Trident and to use some of the means mentioned above, one does not have to accept the approach of totally nonviolent resistance based on the suffering love of the Cross.

The problem of war and violence is a most important question for our lives as Christians. I have disagreed with the theological and ethical presuppositions on which Douglass has based his approach and also have some differences with his practical conclusions. Justice and peace do not always go together in this imperfect world in which we live. As a last resort I see the possibility of violence—more so even when it is used in a limited way by the weak against the strong as in the case of liberation and revolution. However, one must be conscious of the dangers involved in even a limited acceptance of violence—the danger of a facile justification of violence, the danger of a romantic acceptance of violence, and the danger of escalation. I am opposed to the use of nuclear weapons. Indiscriminate weapons violate the just-war principle of discrimination. However, in my judgment the use of any nuclear weapons is wrong because it would usher in a nuclear age and open the door to all-out nuclear war. As for nuclear deterrence, there is a moral imperative for disarmament. Some first steps can and should be taken in a unilateral way, but full disarmament can be accomplished only through agreements and with the proper safeguards.

The spirituality and interior change of heart which form the basis for nonviolent resistance in the social area are developed well by Douglass and are very consistent with his basic thesis. This emphasis also enables him to guard against the danger of self-righteousness which has often been charged against radical Catholic peace activists. However, there are two significant omissions in his discussion of spirituality—community and liturgy. Douglass himself has been associated with many communities, but his writings never really discuss this aspect of his spirituality. Perhaps the emphasis on the need for deep personal change has been so strong that the communal aspect of spirituality, especially as lived out by small groups in community, has been lost sight of. The lack of a liturgical dimension to spirituality is surprising, especially in the light of the emphasis on liturgy in Furfey and in the Catholic Worker.

As for tactics, nonviolent direct action in the form of civil disobedience is accepted without any attempt at prolonged justification. The moral justification of the destruction of property is never explicitly raised, let alone proved. According to his actions and his writings Douglass sees trial and imprisonment as a necessary part of the resistance movement. However, he reports in an approving manner Daniel Berrigan's four-months underground fleeing from arrest.[107] From the viewpoint of civil society nothing is said about civil disobedience, about action raids, or how these should be dealt with by society. How does society differentiate this particular form of civil disobedience from other forms of civil disobedience? What about civil disobedience done by the Ku Klux Klan? Douglass cannot be blamed for not having discussed all possible aspects of nonviolent direct action, but one is somewhat surprised at some of the omissions.

In conclusion, Douglass has developed an ethic which in its general approaches to eschatology, Christology, anthropology, ecclesiology, love, Christian ethics, and spirituality consistently supports his admirable personal commitment to nonviolent resistance, especially in the context of nuclear warfare. I have expressed some disagreements with his theological and ethical approaches as well as with his conclusions. It is important to note that his generally consistent theory supports a somewhat complicated reality, namely, resistance and nonviolence in the contemporary nuclear context. One could logically opt for nonviolence but not necessarily for resistance. Also one like myself could be totally opposed to the use of nuclear weapons and at the same time accept the possibility of some limited use of force.

Even though I do not accept a total pacifism, I think Douglass' position gives too restricted a place to nonviolence precisely because it is limited to nonviolent resistance. I want to see more scope given to nonviolence in terms of politics. The politics of government in our contemporary world can never be totally nonviolent (a point accepted by Douglass in *The Non-Violent Cross*), but it can be more nonviolent than it is now. As a last resort violence in self-defense, including especially the possibility of justified revolutions, remains a possibility in our contemporary world. The primary obligation of Christians and of the church is to make God's peace more present in our world. This means that peace or nonviolence cannot be restricted merely to a resistance movement. Christians must work together with all people of good will to develop the poltiical approaches and structures which will make peace and justice more present in our world. Neither Christian social morality nor the Christian call to peace should be restricted to resistance movements.

Recall that in Douglass himself there is some tension and perhaps even inconsistency between his acceptance of a universal anthropology and a universal call to nonviolence with his restriction of nonviolence to a resistance movement. However, to buttress an understanding of nonviolence in government, one has to change many of the somewhat narrow and one-sided theological and ethical considerations proposed by Douglass. Eschatology must be more than apocalyptic eschatology. Christology must be more than the Cross. Anthropology needs to include more than suffering resistance. Love is more than self-emptying and suffering love. Ethics is more than a deontological bearing witness to the Cross. The church must be broader than a community of suffering and resisting love.

My understanding of ecclesiology and of the social mission of the church is broader than the role of suffering, nonviolent resistance briefly sketched by Douglass. Within my broader ecclesiology, however, there must always be an honored place for those who live out a personal vocation to nonviolent resistance in the face of evil. James Douglass has enriched American Catholic social ethics by providing a systematic and generally consistent theory of such nonviolent resistance.

EPILOGUE

The purpose of this volume has been to analyze, discuss, and criticize five significant approaches to American Catholic social ethics in the twentieth century. As such, that work has now been done. The purpose of this epilogue is to consider two questions which are logically but not necessarily connected with the primary purpose of this book. The first part of the epilogue will try to draw together in a more positive and synthetic fashion my own approach to social ethics. The second part will take a brief glance forward toward the future development of American Catholic social ethics.

In evaluating and criticizing the five different approaches I have obviously been basing my critique on my own methodological approach to Catholic social ethics, whose basic outlines it is now appropriate to explain briefly.

This study has singled out the problem of the relationship between being Catholic and being American as the primary question raised to Catholic social ethics in the American context. In general my approach avoids the two extremes of either complete identification of the two or of total opposition. The relationship between the two is dialectical. At times the Christian perspective must criticize and protest against the American, but at other times the church can learn and profit from the American experience. In areas such as racism, nationalism, and care for the poor the church in the past has often had to protest against the American ethos. However, the American experience has taught the church especially in the areas of freedom and human dignity. The general understanding of freedom in the American ethos is not without some problems especially in terms of individualism and a failure to appreciate the need for social justice. However, John Courtney Murray's work on religious liberty and the relationship between church and state attests to how the American Catholic Church has learned from its Ameri-

can experience. On the other hand, the trenchant criticisms made
by the German-American Catholics, the Catholic Worker movement and Paul Furfey, and the Catholic peace movement in the
1960s and 1970s remind us of the need for the church to be constantly vigilant and ready to criticize abuses on the American
scene. History thus seems to indicate there has been this dialectical relationship between being Catholic and being American
with the need for the believer and the believing community to
be ever vigilant both to criticize abuse and to learn from the
good that can be present in our society.

My reading of the historical reality of the reciprocal relationship between Catholic and American is grounded in a theological understanding. My stance for moral theology sees all
reality in terms of the fivefold Christian mysteries of creation,
sin, incarnation, redemption, and resurrection destiny. Whatever God created is good and still shares in the basic goodness of
God's gift. However, sin has affected everything human even
though it never totally destroys the goodness of human creation.
Incarnation and redemption with their healing effects also touch
all reality. Resurrection destiny reminds us that the fullness will
never be present in this world. My theological stance can appreciate the existence of good in the world in general and in the
American ethos in particular because of the presence of creation,
incarnation, and redemption; but finitude, sin, and radical incompleteness still mar all human existence.

The proposed theological stance involves an eschatology
which sees the Christian as living between the two comings of
Jesus. This position differs from a realized eschatology which
overstresses the presence of the kingdom here and now, an eschatology which sees all as future in the next world, and an
apocalyptic eschatology which emphasizes the opposition between the existing world and the kingdom. Within my eschatological approach the Christian strives to make the kingdom more
present in this world, but the fullness of justice and peace will
never be here. I maintain there can be some truly human progress
in history, but such progress is ordinarily slow and painful with
penultimate victories outnumbering the recessions which will always mark our human existence. Such an eschatology grounds
a realistic anthropology which recognizes the human possibilities
to bring about some greater peace and justice but is also aware
of the sinfulness and radical incompleteness which characterize
human existence in this world. Believers and the church are

called to work together with all people of good will to protect and promote human good. This theological perspective influences my approach to peace. Christians are called to make peace more present in our world. There is a need to create all the different structures which make peace more possible to attain. However, in this imperfect world violence at times might be necessary as a last resort. Unfortunately, sometimes in our imperfect world the existing peace might only be a pretext for continuing injustice. However, the resort to violence in the pursuit of justice can only be justified as a last resort and within severe limits.

The theological stance grounds my approach to the Catholic and/or American question and also serves as a basis for the evaluation of what might be called the theological aspect of the natural-law question. On the basis of this stance the understanding of the natural as found in Engelen, and especially in Ryan and Murray, can no longer be acceptable. Their approach was in keeping with the Catholic manualist tradition which separated the realm of the supernatural from the realm of the natural. Whatever happened in the world including the areas of justice and peace pertained only to the natural as distinguished from the supernatural. Catholic theological developments in the last few decades have rightly insisted on overcoming the separation between the realm of the natural and the realm of the supernatural, between daily life and the gospel. Perhaps the most conspicuous illustration of a change in Catholic social ethics is found in the difference between the natural-law approach of the papal encyclicals before the Second Vatican Council and the liberation theology methodology proposed especially in the Latin American context.[1] Liberation theology insists that the gospel and what might be called the supernatural must affect our daily life. The gospel not only frees persons and souls from sin but also frees human beings from the oppressive social, political, cultural, and economic situations existing in the world. There are no two planes or levels—the plane of the supernatural and the plane of the natural; and no two histories—salvation history and secular history. Salvation embraces the whole world and the one history of God's relationship with human beings. This is not the place for a full-scale exposition and evaluation of liberation theology. I am in general agreement with the basic thrust to overcome the separation between the supernatural and the natural, provided that in this process the future aspect of the full-

ness of the eschaton is not denied. Also there is the need for
social ethics through reason and the social sciences to mediate
from the gospel message to the concrete social realities.

The overcoming of the artificial separation of the natural
realm from the supernatural realm has important methodological ramifications. All the realities mentioned in the stance are
present in the world in which we live. A theological ethic must
understand and reflect on these realities in explicitly theological
terms recognizing all the aspects of the stance and incorporating a corresponding Christology and anthropology. An ethical
approach based exclusively on creation, the natural, and human
reason is incomplete. Christian social ethics as such is a theological discipline and must be explicitly theological in its method
and reflection on social reality. However, the positions arrived
at in Catholic social ethics are rationally understandable and
defensible. I have maintained that there is no distinctive content
to Christian social ethics that can claim to be exclusively Christian and not available in some way to all other human beings.
Many other contemporary Catholic theologians hold similar
positions.[2]

Catholic or Christian social ethics as a second-order discipline must reflect on reality in a theological way. However, such
teaching can also be proposed to others without the theological
aspect and thus rely on sources and approaches that are not distinctively Christian. The argument has been made that the use
of distinctively Christian sources takes away from the universality of approach to social ethics needed in a pluralistic
society. I believe there is some truth in such an assertion, but,
on the other hand, within a pluralistic society there should be
room for different perspectives and viewpoints. Our existence
within a pluralistic society does not mean that we as Christians
cannot think about and reflect on our society in the light of an
explicitly Christian and theological understanding. Also, from a
philosophical perspective one can point out that all viewpoints
tend to be particularistic in one way or another. In retrospect,
both Ryan and Murray did not have to face the dilemma as we
understand it today. For them a natural-law approach based on
human reason alone without explicit theological reflection was
theologically justified because of their poor understanding of the
distinction between the realm of the natural and the realm of the
supernatural. Such an approach with its apparently universalistic
perspective was also open to broad reception by the general pub-

lic. As a matter of fact, both Ryan and Murray did have a significant impact on the broader American community perhaps precisely because of the way in which they proposed their teaching. In conclusion, there can be room for two approaches. Christian social ethics as such should reflect on social reality in the light of explicitly Christian concerns, sources, and understanding. Such an approach can also be used to address the broader society. However, that same teaching and understanding can sometimes be presented to the religiously pluralistic human community using sources, reflections, and approaches which are common to all and not distinctively Christian.[3]

The respective strengths and shortcomings of the five approaches studied indicate the need for a social ethic which stresses a change of heart and a change of structures. Both are necessary. The more radical groups in the Catholic tradition as exemplified in the Catholic Worker movement and in James W. Douglass' approach to peace and nonviolence rightly stressed the need for a profound change of heart, but they failed to give enough importance to the need to change institutional structures to bring about greater justice in society as a whole. On the other hand, Ryan and Murray rightly emphasized the need to change institutional structures, but they forgot that justice and peace also call for a change of heart and a continuing change of heart on the part of all, especially those who are in power or who possess more of this world's goods. The gospel-centered approach of the former and the natural-law approach of the latter also influenced the position on the change of heart and/or change of structure question. History as well as contemporary theology reminds us of the need to stress both aspects. The need for structures was emphasized in response to Douglass' approach. Nonviolent resistance is a very noble and laudable vocation for a few, but it can never be the totality of the Christian quest for peace. Institutional and governmental structures on both national and international levels are necessary to make peace more present in our world and to secure it for the future.

The German-American Catholics and John A. Ryan, in keeping with the Catholic tradition, insisted on both the individual and the social aspects of human existence. A contemporary Christian ethic must continue to recognize the importance of both aspects. The dignity of the individual and the rights of the human person form the basis of an adequate social ethic. The individual cannot be sacrificed for the good of the state or the totality. However, one can never allow the emphasis on the individual person to degenerate into a false and narrow personalism. Human persons are also social by nature, and human community, including the political aspect of the state, is a necessary and integral part of truly human existence in this world.

In light of this emphasis on the social aspect of human existence the state or political society has a positive role to play in human affairs.[4] In contrast with those theories which see the state only or primarily in terms of sin, my approach understands the political order relative to all aspects of the stance, and as thus having a positive function in the quest for social justice and peace in our world. No one can deny the reality of sin influences and affects the role of the state, but it is only one influence and not the most important or significant.

Holding on to both the dignity of the individual person and the social and communal nature of the human person will always involve some tension. The state exists to secure and promote the common good which redounds to the good of individual persons. The proper structuring of society and the roles of various groups and individuals within society—family, private institutions such as schools, churches, businesses, labor organizations, and the political role of the state on different levels—involve the tension of insisting on both the individual and social aspects of the person. The principle of subsidiarity rightly insists that the larger groups in society should only do what the individual and smaller groups are incapable of doing. In the light of complex modern existence this principle must be seen in the context of socialization—the complex reality of human existence which recognizes the need for intervention and direction by the central authority in the state when this is necessary for the common good. Historically, the dispute between the German-American Catholics and John A. Ryan centered over the interpretation of the principle of subsidiarity. Ryan saw a need for state involvement as the only feasible way to bring about justice, whereas Engelen feared that such short-term gains from state involvement would ultimately stifle more radical changes. Especially in the context of the contemporary world I favor Ryan's understanding and approach which insists on the need for state intervention, but the principle of subsidiarity prevents such state intervention from overriding the legitimate rights of individuals and of smaller groups and avoids the danger of an overcentralized bureaucracy.

Intimately connected with the need to hold on to both the

individual and the social aspects of the human person is the importance of both political freedom and social justice in society. John Courtney Murray stressed political freedom but unfortunately failed to give enough importance to the role of the state in securing social justice for all its citizens. Ryan emphasized the role of the state in trying to bring about social justice, but his approach to freedom was not theoretically accepted on the American scene. The relative strengths and weaknesses of the two authors are intrinsically related to their notion of the role and function of the state. Murray's concept of the public order as the end of the state is acceptable on questions primarily involving freedom and individual private actions, but a broader concept of the role of the state is necessary to deal with questions of social justice. Ryan's understanding of the state, while providing for a positive function of the state in promoting social justice, did not properly safeguard the basic human freedoms. The historical debate between capitalism and socialism mirrors this same problem of emphasizing either individual freedom or social and economic justice. Some contemporary modifications of these two approaches such as democratic socialism try to account properly for both aspects.

A very significant methodological problem for Christian social ethics involves what can be called mediation. How does one go from the gospel or biblical vision to the concrete social reality? What mediates this vision to the structures and institutions which should be present in society and to concrete policy decisions? John A. Ryan employed the concept of distributive justice as a way to mediate and make more specific the general call for justice in the distribution of goods in this world. Distributive justice puts heavy emphasis on the category of need and sees these human needs as grounding basic human rights such as the right to food, clothing, shelter, health care, and such. Distributive justice with its highlighting of human needs can well serve as a way of mediating and making more particular the gospel message.

The human sciences are also a necessary part of any mediation. Here much work needs to be done in Catholic social ethics. There should be greater dialogue between social ethics and all the social sciences, including especially political science, economics, and sociology. The problems in this dialogue are many and complex, but social ethics needs such an interdisciplinary approach. Among the authors considered in this volume, John A. Ryan stands out as the one who most effectively used the social sciences, especially economics, in developing his social ethics. However, Ryan's use of economics shows the hazards involved in such an enterprise. His underconsumption theory fit very well in the context of growth and expansion on the American economic scene, but on the world scene today the underconsumption theory and its grounding in continual growth can no longer be acceptable. The need for the social sciences is great, but much work remains to be done on the theory and practice of incorporating the social sciences into Christian social ethics. The recognition of the significance of the social sciences also underscores the importance of a more inductive and more historically conscious methodology for social ethics.

In connection with the distribution of goods and with the recognition of the importance of both the individual and social aspects of human existence, Catholic social ethics can learn from Ryan the importance of the social dimension of property. Private property or any human system of distribution must be governed by the basic principle that the goods of creation exist to serve the needs of all. No matter what system of economic distribution is accepted, this basic principle must remain the controlling criterion.

In addition to theological and ethical considerations, there are also ecclesiological presuppositions involved in the criticisms proposed in this volume. In general there should be a consistency among the theological, ethical, and ecclesiological aspects of one's approach to Catholic social ethics. The fivefold theological stance definitely has ecclesiological implications. The first consequence of such a stance is a recognition of the importance of the social mission of the church. The gospel and the Christian church have a social mission and must work for peace and social justice. The gospel cannot be relegated merely to the realm of the supernatural, but the gospel is ultimately destined to have some effect on all human reality, although we can never forget that the fullness of the kingdom will only come at the end of time. Second, such a stance implies that the church cannot be defined only as an opposition movement. The world can never be totally identified with sin so that the church and the gospel are always opposed to it. Not even as radical a thinker as Furfey could systematically and consistently see the church always in terms of an opposition movement. The world is affected by all the elements of the stance including the goodness of creation and the redeeming and healing aspects of incarnation and redemption. The mission and role of the church is seen in terms of the transformation of the world. The social mission of the church strives to make the gospel aspects of love, justice, and peace evermore present in our world.

Christian ethics has frequently talked about the famous typological distinction between the sect and the church.[5] The sect is understood as a small committed group of believers generally existing in opposition to the world around them. The church is a larger gathering of believers less radical in its demands and more accepting of aspects of the wider society in which it lives. In general I accept the church understanding and even insist on "a big church" with room for disagreements and pluralism on specific moral issues. Anyone within Roman Catholicism who accepts the possibility of dissent from official, authoritative church teaching on specific moral matters must of necessity recognize the room for a pluralism and diversity of approach on specific ethical issues. The five figures examined within this volume point out the pluralism existing in what many thought was a very monolithic Roman Catholic Church. The Catholic Church has always recognized a pluralism in social ethics which extends to both substantive issues and to social ethical methodology itself.

My ethical methodology helps to explain the pluralism which can exist on specific social and moral issues. The gospel message and vision must be mediated in and through other realities, especially utopias, reason, and the social sciences. However, as one descends to specifics, one cannot claim that the conclusion mediated through the social sciences has the same degree of certitude as the gospel vision itself. The lack of certitude in the area of many specific approaches means that the church will often live with pluralism and diversity about how best to deal with the social problems of the day. The Christian church community must be encompassing enough to have room for these disagreements and diversities which are necessary precisely because of the complex nature of specific social problems. Very often the prophetic role of the church will be exercised in terms of a denunciation of the existing evils in society. The problem of how to counteract these evils in a positive way frequently allows for a diversity of interpretation and of means. Often I as an individual Christian will think that some of the other proposed approaches are incorrect (e.g., the German-American Catholics' understanding of subsidiarity), but I cannot claim that such particular positions put one outside the church of Jesus Christ. Christians often can and will disagree on the specific ways of overcoming social injustice.

There is also another type of diversity or pluralism that can and should exist within the church. Certain individuals or smaller groups can follow a special vocation to bear witness to one particular virtue or way of acting. In the past, religious life in the Catholic Church has exemplified this type of approach by its bearing special witness to the virtues of poverty, chastity, and obedience. In addition, there are and should be many others who feel a call to live out a vocation to bear witness to one particular aspect of the Christian life, such as poverty or peace. It is precisely this type of vocation which is seen in the life of the Catholic Worker and in the commitment to peace of people such as James W. Douglass. I do not think that all Christians in the church are called to such a life of voluntary poverty or to a life of nonviolent resistance. However, as a member of the church I am very grateful that God calls such generous individuals and groups to bear witness to these important aspects of the Christian life. In my judgment the total church cannot be absolutely pacifist or committed to total poverty, but individuals and prophetic groups within the church bearing witness to these virtues are very important and significant for the life of the whole church. This generic insistence on the need for pluralism and diversity must always be balanced, of course, by a recognition of legitimate limits within which such diversity can exist. Here is not the place to attempt a discussion of such limits, but their existence must be brought to mind.

This overview has tried to give a more synthetic understanding of the theological ethical methodology which I use and which undergirds the evaluation and criticism of the approaches discussed in this volume. This completes the first part of the epilogue and serves as a transition to the second part.

The focus of this volume on American Catholic social ethics has been historical. The five most significant approaches in the twentieth century have been discussed and evaluated. However, Catholic social ethics in the United States must also look to its future. One of my hopes in writing this book is that it will increase the interest in and appreciation for the area of American Catholic social ethics.

Unfortunately, there has been comparatively little work done recently in American Catholic social ethics. One can think, for example, of the publications of David Hollenbach, J. Bryan Hehir, and John A. Coleman.[6] In the future there should be and hopefully will be more publishing in this particular field. Within Roman Catholicism there is a growing awareness of the importance of the social mission of the church. The 1971 Synod of Bishops reminded Catholics that "action on behalf of justice and participation in the transformation of the world fully appear to us as a constitutive dimension of the preaching of the gospel, or, in other words, of the church's mission for the redemption of the human race and its liberation from every oppressive situation."[7] Such emphasis on the social mission of the church should help stimulate American Catholic social ethics as the theological reflection on this action on behalf of justice and peace. The specifically American aspect of the social mission and of social ethics has also been stressed recently in official church documents. Pope Paul VI, in *Octogesima adveniens* in 1971, insisted on the need for social reflection on the local level. The pope makes no attempt to put forth solutions that have universal validity. "It is up to the Christian communities to analyze with objectivity the situation which is proper to their own country, to shed on it the light of the gospel's unalterable words and to draw principles of reflection, norms of judgment, and directives for action from the social teaching of the church."[8]

Hopefully the present volume will be able to make some slight contribution toward this future development. We can all learn from the way in which those who have gone before us have tried to deal with the problems facing their generation. My own theological methodology for social ethics as sketched above has obviously profited from an analysis of the people studied in this volume. However, there are other factors which must also be taken into account in striving to develop a contemporary American Catholic social ethics.

The historical realities existing today are definitely different from those existing at the time of the writers discussed in this book. A contemporary American Catholic social ethics must deal with the historical circumstances of our own scene. There are a number of significant realities which must be taken into account. The social problem has now become worldwide and cannot be looked at in narrow nationalistic perspectives. The fact that the

United States is the richest country in the world presents us with highly significant responsibilities and obligations. Problems of violence and war are even more acute in the light of the nuclear capability of our age. Nuclear disarmament is a moral imperative which must find a practical solution. The ecological and population questions make modern human beings much more conscious of our limitations. A heightened consciousness of the role of women exerts an important influence on all contemporary thought.

There have also been developments in theological ethical methodology in the last few years that must be considered and incorporated into a contemporary American Catholic social ethics. The practical need to work together with others calls for an ecumenical aspect to Catholic social ethics. The official church teachings show an evolution toward a greater appreciation of freedom, equality, and participation. The social aspect of human existence receives much greater emphasis today in official church documents as indicated in more nuanced approaches to private property in the light of the universal destiny of the goods of creation to serve the needs of all. The official church reaction to relations with Marxism and Marxists has also changed from one of anathema to dialogue. Some contemporary theological ethics highlight the importance of critical reason and of praxis. Liberation theology in Latin America and in black and feminist contexts in the United States has come to the fore. Emphasis on an inductive methodology underscores the importance of dialogue with the sciences of economics, anthropology, sociology, psychology, and political science. The church's social mission will be effective only to the extent that the church in its own life incorporates the principles of justice and lives out its option for the poor and oppressed. All of these theological ethical factors must be considered in developing a contemporary American Catholic social ethics.

It is within these historical and methodological parameters that a contemporary American Catholic social ethics must be built. The work of producing such a social ethics is the responsibility of the present generation. A knowledge of the past tradition is helpful in developing such an ethic. Above all, we of the present can learn from the tradition the importance of doing in our time what the figures studied in this book did in their times.

NOTES

1. Setting the Stage

1. William F. Drummond, *Social Justice* (Milwaukee: Bruce, 1955); Thomas J. Harte, *Papal Social Principles* (Gloucester, Mass.: Peter Smith, 1960); Joseph Husslein, ed., *Social Wellsprings*, 2 vols. (Milwaukee: Bruce, 1940, 1942); Virgil Michel, *Christian Social Reconstruction* (Milwaukee: Bruce, 1937).

2. John F. Cronin, *Social Principles and Economic Life* (Milwaukee: Bruce, 1959), pp. vii, viii. A revised edition incorporating the two important encyclicals of Pope John XXIII was published in 1964.

3. John F. Cronin, *Catholic Social Principles: The Social Teaching of the Catholic Church Applied to American Economic Life* (Milwaukee: Bruce, 1950), pp. 603–726.

4. For the classical article on this subject, see John Tracy Ellis, "American Catholics and the Intellectual Life," *Thought* 30 (1955): 351–388. See also Walter J. Ong, *Frontiers in American Catholicism* (New York: Macmillan, 1957); Thomas F. O'Dea, *American Catholic Dilemma: An Inquiry into the Intellectual Life* (New York: Sheed and Ward, 1958).

5. There have been significant contributions made by historians both in terms of general histories and in discussions of particular persons. In the light of the perspective adopted here the most significant historical contribution, which also touches on some of the ethical and theological aspects, is David J. O'Brien, *American Catholics and Social Reform: The New Deal Years* (New York: Oxford University Press, 1968). For a pioneering and still valuable work, which at times is too apologetical and uncritical, see Aaron I. Abell, *American Catholicism and Social Action: A Search for Social Justice 1865–1950* (Garden City, New York: Doubleday, 1960; paperback reprint: Notre Dame, Indiana: University of Notre Dame Press, 1963). For a book of selected readings on the subject, see Aaron I. Abell, ed., *American Catholic Thought on Social Questions* (Indianapolis: Bobbs-Merrill, 1968).

6. For a practical illustration of this focus, see Abell, *American Catholicism and Social Action*, pp. 137–285.

7. John A. Coleman, "Vision and Praxis in American Theology: Orestes Brownson, John A. Ryan and John Courtney Murray," *Theological Studies* 37 (1976) : 3–40.

8. For a Catholic reaction to McCarthy, see Donald F. Crosby, *God, Church and Flag: Senator Joseph R. McCarthy and the Catholic Church, 1950–1957* (Chapel Hill, North Carolina: University of North Carolina Press, 1978). There is no definitive work on Coughlin because of lack of access to his archives and to the archives of the Archdiocese of Detroit. For a laudatory and uncritical account, see Louis B. Ward, *Father Charles E. Coughlin* (Detroit: Tower Publications, 1933). For a more critical evaluation, see Charles Joseph Tull, *Father Coughlin and the New Deal* (Syracuse: University of Syracuse Press, 1965).

9. John Brophy, *A Miner's Life* (Madison: University of Wisconsin Press, 1964), p. 100.

10. John Tracy Ellis, *American Catholicism* (Chicago: University of Chicago Press, 1956), p. 148.

11. For the definitive study of this development, see Robert D. Cross, *The Emergence of Liberal Catholicism in America* (Cambridge: Harvard University Press, 1958). For the acceptance and application of such an understanding in the realm of American Catholic social thought, see Abell, ed., *American Catholic Thought on Social Questions*, pp. xxiii–xxvi and "Part Three: The Emergence of Catholic Social Liberalism," pp. 143–262.

12. Archbishop John Hughes, "Liberty and Enlightenment Not Obstacles to Catholic Growth," in *American Catholic Thought on Social Questions*, ed. Abell, pp. 3–19. For a recent biography of Hughes, see Richard Shaw, *Dagger John: The Unquiet Life and Times of Archbishop John Hughes of New York* (New York: Paulist Press, 1977).

13. James E. Roohan, "American Catholics and the Social Question (1865–1900)" (Ph.D. diss., Yale University, 1953), p. 70.

14. On the question of German immigration, see Colman J. Barry, *The Catholic Church and German Americans* (Milwaukee: Bruce, 1953).

15. Ellis, *American Catholicism*, pp. 67–68.

16. In addition to the summary treatment by Ellis, *American Catholicism*, pp. 85–117, see Ray Allen Billington, *The Protestant Crusade, 1800–1860* (New York: Macmillan, 1938); John Higham, *Strangers in the Land: Patterns of American Nativism, 1860–1925* (New Brunswick: Rutgers University Press, 1955).

17. Abell, *American Catholicism and Social Action*, pp. 15–18.

18. There are numerous studies on Brownson; Arthur M. Schlesinger, Jr., *Orestes A. Brownson: A Pilgrim's Progress* (Boston: Little, Brown, 1939); Theodore Maynard, *Orestes A. Brownson, Yankee, Radical, Catholic* (New York: Macmillan, 1943); Thomas R. Ryan, *Orestes A. Brownson: A Definitive Biography* (Huntington, Indiana: Our Sunday Visitor, 1976).

19. Walter Elliot, *The Life of Father Hecker* (New York: Columbus Press, 1891); Vincent F. Holden, *The Early Years of Issac Hecker (1819–1844)* (Washington: Catholic University of America Press, 1939). David J. O'Brien has been commissioned to write a new biography of Hecker.

20. Biographies of all these important figures in the American Catholic hierarchy have been written. Frederick J. Zwierlein, *The Life and Letters of Bishop McQuaid*, 3 vols. (Rochester, New York: The Art Print Shop, 1925–27); John Tracy Ellis, *The Life of James Cardinal Gibbons, Archbishop of Baltimore, 1834–1921* (Milwaukee: Bruce, 1952); James H. Moynihan, *The Life of Archbishop John Ireland* (New York: Harper, 1953); Patrick H. Ahern, *The Life of John J. Keane, Educator and Archbishop, 1839–1918* (Milwaukee: Bruce, 1955); David F. Sweeney, *The Life of John Lancaster Spalding, First Bishop of Peoria, 1840–1916* (New York: Herder and Herder, 1965); Robert Emmett Curran, *Michael Augustine Corrigan and the Shaping of Conservative Catholicism in America, 1878–1902* (New York: Arno Press, 1978). Many of these institutional biographies suffer from a touch of Catholic triumphalism and a lack of a critical perspective.

21. For an account of this controversy, see Henry J. Browne, *The Catholic Church and the Knights of Labor* (Washington: Catholic University of America Press, 1949).

22. Browne, *The Catholic Church*, pp. 365–378, reprints the entire memorandum and also points out slight but nevertheless significant differences between the French version, which was sent to the congregation, and the English version, which ultimately appeared in the United States.

23. Ellis, *American Catholicism*, p. 105.

24. There is no definitive biography of McGlynn, but he is mentioned by almost all of the historians dealing with the major figures in American Catholic history at this time. For a very favorable and somewhat partial account, see Stephen Bell, *Rebel, Priest and Prophet: A Biography of Dr. Edward McGlynn* (New York: Devin-Adair, 1937). See also E. H. Smith, "McGlynn, Edward," *New Catholic Encyclopedia*, IX, pp. 18–19.

25. Henry George, *Progress and Poverty* (San Francisco: W. M. Hinton and Co., 1879). After the publication of Leo XIII's *Rerum novarum* in 1891, George wrote an open letter to the pope in which he defended his position against the charge of being socialistic: Henry George, *The Condition of Labor: An Open Letter to Pope Leo XIII* (New York: United States Book Co., 1891).

26. Abell, *American Catholicism and Social Action*, pp. 100–117.

27. For the background and condemnation of Americanism, see Thomas T. McAvoy, *The Great Crisis in American Catholic History, 1895–1900* (Chicago: Henry Regnery, 1957); published in paperback under the title *The Americanist Heresy in Roman Catholicism* (Notre Dame, Indiana: University of Notre Dame Press, 1963).

28. Ellis, *The Life of James Cardinal Gibbons,* II, p. 71. One contemporary scholar maintains that there truly were some doctrinal and ecclesiological issues in the Americanist controversy: Margaret Mary Reher, "The Church and the Kingdom of God in America: The Ecclesiology of the Americanists" (Ph.D. diss., Fordham University, 1972).

29. Dorothy Dohen, *Nationalism and American Catholicism* (New York: Sheed and Ward, 1967), p. 82.

30. Philip Gleason, "The Crisis of Americanization," in *Contemporary Catholicism in the United States,* ed. Philip Gleason (Notre Dame, Indiana: University of Notre Dame Press, 1969), p. 30.

31. Paul Blanshard, *American Freedom and Catholic Power* (Boston: Beacon Press, 1949).

32. For an accurate and concise history, see Franz H. Mueller, "The Church and the Social Question," in *The Challenge of Mater et Magistra,* ed. Joseph N. Moody and Justus George Lawler (New York: Herder and Herder, 1963), pp. 13–154. For the background to Leo's encyclical *Rerum novarum,* see pp. 66–80. For a more detailed history of the development of Catholic social thought especially in Europe and the United States, see Joseph N. Moody, ed., *Church and Society: Catholic Social and Political Thought and Movements* (New York: Arts, 1953).

33. For a frequently used English translation, see Etienne Gilson, ed., *The Church Speaks to the Modern World: The Social Teachings of Leo XIII* (Garden City, New York: Doubleday Image Books, 1954), pp. 200–244. Citations will be to the paragraph numbers in this translation.

34. *Aeterni patris,* in *The Church Speaks to the Modern World,* pp. 29–54. In my opinion such an emphasis on Aquinas in the nineteenth century, while having many beneficial effects, was basically a conservative move to establish a perennial philosophy and prevent any real dialogue with contemporary thought.

35. For a more comprehensive treatment of natural law, see Charles E. Curran, *Themes in Fundamental Moral Theology* (Notre Dame, Indiana: University of Notre Dame Press, 1977), pp. 27–75.

36. These and other important documents may be found in Joseph Gremillion, ed., *The Gospel of Peace and Justice: Catholic Social Teaching Since Pope John* (Maryknoll, New York: Orbis Books, 1976); and in David J. O'Brien and Thomas A. Shannon, eds., *Renewing the Face of the Earth: Catholic Documents on Peace, Justice and Liberation* (Garden City, New York: Doubleday Image Books, 1977).

37. Peter Hebblethwaite, *The Christian-Marxist Dialogue: Beginnings, Present Status and Beyond* (New York: Paulist Press, 1977).

38. Fr. Refoulé, "L'Église et les libertés de Leon XIII à Jean XXIII," *Le Supplément* 125 (Mai 1978): 243–259.

39. Celestine Joseph Nuesse, *The Social Thought of American Catholics 1634–1829* (Washington, D.C.: Catholic University of America Press, 1945), p. 283.

40. Joseph D. Brokhage, *Francis Patrick Kenrick's Opinion on Slavery* (Washington, D.C.: Catholic University of America Press, 1955), especially pp. 17–53; Richard A. Lamanna and Jay J. Coakley, "The Catholic Church and the Negro," in *Contemporary Catholicism in the United States*, pp. 147-153.

41. Abell, *American Catholicism and Social Action*, pp. 27–53.

42. Ibid., p. 29.

43. Joan Bland, *Hibernian Crusade: The Story of the Catholic Total Abstinence Union of America* (Washington, D.C.: Catholic University of America Press, 1951).

44. Roohan, "American Catholics and the Social Question," pp. 218–239.

45. Abell, *American Catholicism and Social Action*, p. 47.

46. Roohan, "American Catholics and the Social Question," chapter five; for a scholarly account of the whole dispute, see Wayne G. Broehl, *The Molly Maguires* (Cambridge, Mass.: Harvard University Press, 1965).

47. John A. Ryan, *Social Doctrine in Action: A Personal History* (New York: Harper and Brothers, 1941), pp. 18–23.

48. Roohan, "American Catholics and the Social Question," pp. 388–425.

49. Mary Harrita Fox, *Peter E. Dietz, Labor Priest* (Notre Dame, Indiana: University of Notre Dame Press, 1953).

50. Philip Gleason, *The Conservative Reformers: German-American Catholics and the Social Order* (Notre Dame, Indiana: University of Notre Dame Press, 1968).

51. John F. O'Grady, *Catholic Charities in the United States* (Washington, D.C.: National Conference of Catholic Charities, 1931).

52. Abell, *American Catholicism and Social Action*, pp. 137–204.

53. John B. Sheerin, *Never Look Back: The Career and Concerns of John J. Burke* (New York: Paulist Press, 1975).

54. "The Bishops' Program of Social Reconstruction," in *American Catholic Thought on Social Questions*, pp. 325–348. For this statement and a book-length commentary on it, see John A. Ryan, *Social Reconstruction* (New York: Macmillan, 1920).

55. Francis L. Broderick, *Right Reverend New Dealer: John A. Ryan* (New York: Macmillan Co., 1963), pp. 104–108.

2. John A. Ryan

1. The definitive source for Ryan's life is Francis L. Broderick, *Right Reverend New Dealer: John A. Ryan* (New York: Macmillan, 1963). Also, see Ryan's own autobiography, John A. Ryan, *Social Doctrine in Action: A Personal History* (New York: Harper and Brothers, 1941).

2. Ryan, *Social Doctrine in Action*, p. 12.

3. Broderick, *Right Reverend New Dealer*, p. 19.

4. For a complete bibliography of Ryan's works and works about Ryan, until the time of its publication, see Theodora E. McGill, "A Bio-Bibliography of Monsignor John A. Ryan" (M.S. diss., Catholic University of America, 1952). The principal books published by John A. Ryan are the following (in chronological order):

A Living Wage: Its Ethical and Economic Aspects (New York: Macmillan, 1906); rev. ed., 1920.

Morris Hillquit and John A. Ryan, *Socialism: Promise or Menace?* (New York: Macmillan, 1914).

Distributive Justice: The Right and Wrong of Our Present Distribution of Wealth (New York: Macmillan, 1916); rev. ed., 1927; 3rd ed., 1942.

The Church and Socialism and Other Essays (Washington: The University Press, 1919).

Joseph Husslein and John A. Ryan, eds., *The Church and Labor* (New York: Macmillan, 1920).

Social Reconstruction (New York: Macmillan, 1920).

John A. Ryan and Moorhouse F. X. Millar, eds., *The State and the Church* (New York: Macmillan, 1922).

Declining Liberty and Other Papers (New York: Macmillan, 1927).

The Catholic Church and the Citizen (New York: Macmillan, 1928).

Questions of the Day (Boston: Stratford Co., 1931).

A Better Economic Order (New York: Harper and Brothers, 1935).

Seven Troubled Years, 1930-36: A Collection of Papers on the Depression and on the Problems of Recovery and Reform (Ann Arbor, Michigan: Edwards Brothers, 1937).

John A. Ryan and Francis J. Boland, eds., *Catholic Principles of Politics* (New York: Macmillan, 1940).

Social Doctrine in Action: A Personal History (New York: Harper and Brothers, 1941).

The Norm of Morality Defined and Applied to Particular Actions (Washington, D.C.: National Catholic Welfare Conference, 1952).

5. These paragraphs have briefly summarized the important aspects of Ryan's life as a social reformer, which are developed at length in the autobiography and in Broderick.

6. Francis L. Broderick, "The Encyclicals and Social Action: Is John A. Ryan Typical?" *Catholic Historical Review* 55 (1969): 1–6.

7. *Social Doctrine in Action*, pp. 116–117.

8. Ibid., pp. 214–216.

9. Broderick, *Right Reverend New Dealer*, pp. 156–162.

10. Ibid., pp. 230–236.

11. "Dedication," in *Declining Liberty; Social Doctrine in Action*, p. 223.

12. O'Brien, *American Catholics and Social Reform: The New Deal Years*, pp. 70ff.; George Q. Flynn, *American Catholics and the*

Roosevelt Presidency (Lexington, Kentucky: University of Kentucky Press, 1968).

13. John A. Ryan, "Some Ethical Aspects of Speculation" (S.T.L. diss., Catholic University of America, 1900), p. 1.

14. *Seven Troubled Years,* pp. 110, 111.

15. *Norm of Morality,* pp. 3, 4.

16. *Catholic Principles of Politics,* pp. 4, 5; *Norm of Morality,* pp. 24ff.

17. *Norm of Morality,* pp. 29–63.

18. *Catholic Principles of Politics,* p. 9; *Norm of Morality,* pp. 29–44.

19. *Norm of Morality,* pp. 10, 11; 45–63.

20. Ibid., pp. 17, 18.

21. Broderick, *Right Reverend New Dealer,* pp. 29–31.

22. *Distributive Justice,* p. 252.

23. Ibid., pp. 7; 48.

24. *Catholic Principles of Politics,* pp. 13–27; *Living Wage,* pp. 43–66.

25. *Distributive Justice,* pp. 56–69; *Norm of Morality,* pp. 56–63.

26. *Catholic Principles of Politics,* pp. 13–15; *Living Wage,* pp. 45–48.

27. *Catholic Principles of Politics,* pp. 19–27; *Living Wage,* pp. 52–66.

28. For the most complete treatment of Ryan's theory of the state, see John W. Gouldrick, "John A. Ryan's Theory of the State" (S.T.D. diss., Catholic University of America, 1979).

29. *Catholic Principles of Politics,* pp. 29–41; 102–107.

30. *State and Church,* pp. 195–207, with the two citations on p. 207; *Catholic Principles of Politics,* pp. 102–107, with the two citations on p. 106; *Social Doctrine in Action,* p. 44.

31. Franz H. Mueller, "The Church and the Social Question," in *The Challenge of Mater et Magistra,* ed. Joseph N. Moody and Justus George Lawler (New York: Herder and Herder, 1963), pp. 96, 97.

32. *Catholic Principles of Politics,* pp. 127–139.

33. Ibid., pp. 108–117.

34. John A. Ryan, "A Program of Social Reform by Legislation," *The Catholic World* 89 (July 1909): 433-444; (August 1909): 608–614.

35. *Declining Liberty,* pp. 133, 134; 194–208.

36. E.g., *Seven Troubled Years,* pp. 201–205.

37. *State and Church,* pp. 217–220.

38. *Catholic Principles of Politics,* pp. 120–126.

39. For a systematic exposition and critique of Ryan's economic theory, see Patrick W. Gearty, *The Economic Thought of Monsignor John A. Ryan* (Washington, D.C.: Catholic University of America Press, 1953).

40. *Living Wage,* pp. 153–189.
41. *Socialism: Promise or Menace?* p. 39. Note the similarity with the three defects pointed out in the Bishops' program as mentioned in chapter one.
42. *Seven Troubled Years,* p. 259.
43. *Living Wage,* pp. 68–71; *Distributive Justice,* p. 358.
44. Reginald G. Bender, "The Doctrine of Private Property in the Writings of Monsignor John A. Ryan" (S.T.D. diss., Catholic University of America, 1973), p. 85.
45. *Distributive Justice,* p. 252.
46. *Living Wage,* p. 248; *Distributive Justice,* p. 357.
47. *Distributive Justice,* 3rd ed., 1947, pp. 97–99; see also *Seven Troubled Years,* pp. 174–176.
48. *Social Doctrine in Action,* p. 136.
49. *Seven Troubled Years,* p. 59.
50. *Living Wage,* p. 312.
51. Ibid., pp. 328, 329.
52. *Socialism: Promise or Menace?,* p. 58.
53. Ibid., pp. 152–154; 175, 176; 184, 185.
54. Ibid., p. 260.
55. *Distributive Justice,* pp. 376, 377.
56. Ibid., pp. 408–423.
57. John A. Ryan, "The Dignity of Labor and the Duty of the State," *Catholic Charities Review* 10 (1926) : 212–215.
58. *Living Wage,* pp. 169–172.
59. Without mentioning Hobson or the theory by name, Ryan incorporated it into the Bishops' program. See *Social Reconstruction,* p. 228. The theory is not developed in *Distributive Justice.*
60. *Better Economic Order,* pp. 1–30; *Seven Troubled Years,* p. 38.
61. George G. Higgins, "The Underconsumption Theory in the Writings of Monsignor John A. Ryan" (M.A. diss., Catholic University of America, 1942).
62. *Questions of the Day,* p. 208.
63. *Distributive Justice,* pp. 323–355.
64. *Living Wage,* pp. 99–122; *Distributive Justice,* pp. 356–378.
65. *Living Wage,* pp. 123–150.
66. *Distributive Justice,* p. 379.
67. Ibid., pp. 381–399.
68. *Living Wage,* p. 120; *Distributive Justice,* p. 274.
69. *Living Wage,* p. 108.
70. Ibid., p. 120.
71. For the most complete discussion of this issue, see Bender, "The Doctrine of Private Property in the Writings of Monsignor John A. Ryan."

72. Ryan's position on private property was in general agreement with the theory proposed by James Kelleher, *Private Ownership: Its Basic and Equitable Conditions* (Dublin: Gill: 1911), which Ryan claimed to be on many accounts the best book written in English on the subject. See, John A. Ryan, "Private Ownership and Socialism," *The Catholic World* 94 (January 1912) : 497–504.

73. *Distributive Justice*, pp. 48–51.

74. E.g., Ibid., pp. 152–170.

75. Ibid., pp. 53, 54; Ryan, "Henry George and Private Property," *The Catholic World* 93 (June 1911) : 289–300; "The Ethical Arguments of Henry George Against Private Ownership of Land," *The Catholic World* 93 (July 1911) : 483–492. See also R. V. Andelson, "Msgr. John A. Ryan's Critique of Henry George," *American Journal of Economics and Sociology* 33 (1974) : 273–286.

76. *The Church and Labor*, p. xii.

77. Bender, "The Doctrine of Private Property," p. 159.

78. Gearty, *The Economic Thought of Monsignor John A. Ryan*, p. 136.

79. *Distributive Justice*, pp. 74–133.

80. Ibid., p. 68.

81. John A. Ryan, *The Church and Interest Taking* (St. Louis: B. Herder, 1910).

82. *Distributive Justice*, pp. 171–186.

83. Ibid., pp. 187–208.

84. *Seven Troubled Years*, pp. 252, 253.

85. Ibid., p. 164.

86. *Distributive Justice*, p. 3.

87. *Seven Troubled Years*, p. 252.

88. *Distributive Justice*, pp. 254–319.

89. *Socialism: Promise or Menace?*, pp. 140–147.

90. *Social Reconstruction*, p. 3.

91. John A. Ryan, "The Church and the Workingman," *The Catholic World* 89 (September 1909) : 782.

92. John A. Ryan, "A Democratic Transformation of Industry," *Studies* 9 (1920) : 383–396; *A Better Economic Order*, pp. 148–174.

93. *Declining Liberty*, p. 226.

94. *Seven Troubled Years*, p. 275.

95. John A. Ryan, "A Program of Social Reform by Legislation," *The Catholic World* 89 (July 1909) : 432-444; (August 1909) : 608–614.

96. *Declining Liberty*, pp. 240, 241.

97. *Seven Troubled Years*, pp. 289–291.

98. Broderick, *Right Reverend New Dealer*, pp. 230, 231.

99. *Seven Troubled Years*, pp. 150; 163; 214; *Better Economic Order*, pp. 65–67.

304 *Notes to Pages 52–57*

100. John A. Ryan, "The Supreme Court and Child Labor," *The Catholic World* 108 (November 1925): 213–219; *Social Doctrine in Action*, pp. 222–227; Broderick, *Right Reverend New Dealer*, pp. 156–162.

101. *Declining Liberty*, pp. 101–114.

102. Ibid., pp. 202–208.

103. *Social Doctrine in Action*, p. 72.

104. *Seven Troubled Years*, p. 35.

105. *Better Economic Order*, pp. 68, 69.

106. John A. Ryan, *Can Unemployment Be Ended?* (Washington, D.C.: American Association for Economic Freedom, 1940), p. 12.

107. *Seven Troubled Years*, pp. 221, 222.

108. *Distributive Justice*, 3rd ed., 1942, pp. 221, 222.

109. *Social Doctrine in Action*, p. 110.

110. "Some Ethical Aspects of Speculation," p. 82.

111. John A. Ryan, "The Ethics of Speculation," *International Journal of Ethics* 12 (1902): 347.

112. *Social Doctrine in Action*, p. 69.

113. *Distributive Justice*, p. 214; *Church and Socialism*, p. 39.

114. *Better Economic Order*, pp. 160–176.

115. *Declining Liberty*, pp. 224–238.

116. *Socialism: Promise or Menace?*, p. 41. Belloc had a real influence on Ryan at this time according to Gearty, *The Economic Thought of Monsignor John A. Ryan*, pp. 271, 272. However, Ryan never accepted the more radical distributist theory proposed by Belloc. See, John A. Ryan, "Hilaire Belloc as Prophet of Woe," *The Catholic World* 119 (June 1924): 321–325.

117. John A. Ryan, *Social Reform on Catholic Lines* (New York: Columbus Press, 1913), reprinted in *Church and Socialism*, pp. 35–56. For the point in question, see pp. 41ff.

118. *Distributive Justice*, pp. 214–233.

119. Ibid., p. 425.

120. *Social Reconstruction*, pp. 141–181.

121. Ibid., p. 176; *Declining Liberty*, pp. 225–238; *Better Economic Order*, pp. 148–174.

122. *Better Economic Order*, p. 161.

123. Ibid., pp. 162–174.

124. *Seven Troubled Years*, pp. 42ff., 72ff.; *Better Economic Order*, pp. 175–190.

125. Gearty, *The Economic Thought of Monsignor John A. Ryan*, pp. 287–297.

126. Karl H. Cerny, "Monsignor John A. Ryan and the Social Action Department," (Ph.D. diss., Yale University, 1954), pp. 213; 244–283.

127. O'Brien, *American Catholics and Social Reform*, p. 143.

128. *Church and Socialism*, pp. 147, 148.

129. Ibid., p. 39.

130. Ryan's address on the occasion of his seventieth birthday celebration, as cited by Gearty, *The Economic Thought of Monsignor John A. Ryan*, p. 296.

131. Cerny, "Monsignor John A. Ryan," pp. 186–213; Mark A. Miller, "The Contribution of the Reverend Raymond A. McGowan to American Catholic Social Thought and Action, 1930–1933" (M.A. diss., The Catholic University of America, 1979).

132. *Better Economic Order*, pp. 177–190.

133. *Distributive Justice*, pp. 303–318; *Seven Troubled Years*, pp. 68, 69.

134. E.g., *Church and Socialism*, p. 209; *Declining Liberty*, p. 328.

135. Robert M. Preston, "Towards a Better World: The Christian Moralist as Scientific Reformer" (Ph.D. diss., Catholic University of America, Washington, D.C., 1969), pp. 147–149.

136. *Church and Socialism*, pp. 39–43.

137. John A. Ryan, "Morality of the Aims and Methods of the Labor Unions," *American Catholic Quarterly Review* 24 (1904): 326–355.

138. *Social Reconstruction*, pp. 121–140.

139. *Declining Liberty*, pp. 203–212.

140. *Social Doctrine in Action*, pp. 72, 73.

141. *Church and Socialism*, pp. 148–151; *Social Reconstruction*, pp. 138–140.

142. *Declining Liberty*, pp. 213–223.

143. *Church and Socialism*, pp. 37, 38.

144. *Living Wage*, pp. 291–296; *Distributive Justice*, 417–425.

145. *Distributive Justice*, p. 420.

146. Broderick, *Right Reverend New Dealer*, pp. 234, 235.

147. E.g., *Seven Troubled Years*, pp. 61–87.

148. Mueller, *The Challenge of Mater et Magistra*, pp. 93–97.

149. O'Brien, *American Catholics and Social Reform*, pp. 58–60.

150. *Seven Troubled Years*, pp. 122; 281.

151. Ibid., pp. 47; 77.

152. *Better Economic Order*, p. 118.

153. *Seven Troubled Years*, pp. 124ff.

154. *Socialism: Promise or Menace?*, pp. 247, 248.

155. *Seven Troubled Years*, pp. 125–127.

156. Ibid., pp. 280, 281.

157. *Socialism: Promise or Menace?*, pp. 186–199.

158. *Distributive Justice*, p. 145; *Socialism: Promise or Menace?*, pp. 103–122.

159. *Socialism: Promise or Menace?*, pp. 254, 255.

160. Ibid., pp. 143–154.

161. *Distributive Justice*, pp. 152–170; *Socialism: Promise or Menace?*, pp. 48–69; *Better Economic Order*, pp. 126–137.

162. *Distributive Justice*, pp. 162–167.

163. *Better Economic Order*, pp. 137, 138.

164. *Seven Troubled Years*, pp. 87–91.

165. *Better Economic Order*, p. 135.

166. *Declining Liberty*, pp. 180, 181.

167. *Church and Socialism*, pp. 152–155.

168. *Declining Liberty*, pp. 181–184.

169. *Church and Socialism*, pp. 157–162; *Seven Troubled Years*, pp. 33–39; *Social Doctrine in Action*, p. 107.

170. *Church and Socialism*, pp. 55, 56.

171. *Socialism: Promise or Menace?*, pp. 194, 195.

172. "The Church and the Workingman," pp. 776–778.

173. *State and Church*, pp. 32–39. Note that Ryan developed his thought in the context of a commentary on *Immortale Dei*, the encyclical of Leo XIII called in English "The Christian Constitution of States."

174. *State and Church*, p. 38.

175. Despite all the controversy that Ryan's position occasioned he never departed from this teaching. In his 1940 *Catholic Principles of Politics*, Monsignor Ryan incorporated the same earlier chapter and only slightly changed the sentence about how constitutions can be changed. It now reads: "Suppose that the constitutional obstacle to proscription of non-Catholics has been legitimately removed...." *Catholic Principles of Politics*, p. 320.

176. Broderick, *Right Reverend New Dealer*, pp. 170–185.

177. *Catholic Church and the Citizen*, pp. 30–36.

178. John A. Ryan, "A Catholic View of the Election," *Current History* 29 (1928): 377–381; republished in *Questions of the Day*, pp. 91–99.

179. *Social Doctrine in Action*, pp. 231, 232. The article cited here is mentioned in note 178.

180. Will Herberg, "A Jew Looks at Catholics," *The Commonweal* 58 (May 22, 1953): 174, 175; John C. Bennett *Christians and the State* (New York: Charles Scribner's Sons, 1958), p. 264; Paul Blanshard, *American Freedom and Catholic Power* (Boston: Beacon Press, 1949). Blanshard cites Ryan's position on religious liberty (p. 52) but also refers to Ryan as "the most liberal leader American Catholicism has produced" (p. 159).

181. John A. Ryan, "Catholic Doctrine on the Right of Self-Government," *The Catholic World* 108 (December 1918): 314–330; (January 1919): 433–442. This early position also became Ryan's final position because he incorporated these two articles into *Catholic Principles of Politics*, pp. 72–101.

182. *Catholic Church and the Citizen*, pp. 13–22.

183. Gouldrick, "John A. Ryan's Theory of the State," pp. 48–57.

184. *Catholic Church and the Citizen*, p. 21.

185. Ibid., pp. 85, 86.
186. John A. Ryan, "Assault Upon Democracy," *The Catholic World* 128 (March 1929): 641–647; "An Assault Upon Democracy," *The Commonweal* 40 (October 13, 1944): 608–611.
187. "Assault Upon Democracy," *The Catholic World* 128 (March 1929): 647.
188. Most Rev. John Ireland, "Catholicism and Americanism," in *Catholic Principles of Politics*, pp. 343–359. This article by Ireland had been included in the earlier *State and Church* but not as the final chapter.
189. Pope Leo XIII, *Libertas praestantissimum*, nn. 19–37. For an English translation and commentary on Leo's encyclicals, see Etienne Gilson, ed., *The Church Speaks to the Modern World: The Social Teachings of Leo XIII* (Garden City, New York: Doubleday Image Book, 1954), pp. 70–79.
190. *Social Doctrine in Action*, pp. 159–176.
191. John A. Ryan, "Freedom of Speech in Wartime," *The Catholic World* 106 (February 1918): 577–588.
192. John A. Ryan, "The Political Prisoners," *Catholic Charities Review* 6 (1922): 191; *Social Doctrine in Action*, pp. 139, 140; 159–173.
193. *Declining Liberty*, pp. 4–19.
194. *Social Doctrine in Action*, p. 169.
195. *Declining Liberty*, pp. 3–42.
196. Gouldrick, "John A. Ryan's Theory of the State," pp. 125–127.
197. *Social Doctrine in Action*, pp. 173–176.
198. John A. Ryan, *Francisco Ferrer: Criminal Conspirator* (St. Louis: B. Herder, 1911), pp. 80, 81.
199. *Declining Liberty*, pp. 38–42.
200. *Social Doctrine in Action*, pp. 165, 166.
201. *Declining Liberty*, pp. 64–69; *Questions of the Day*, pp. 247–255; *Catholic Principles of Politics*, pp. 161–168.
202. *Declining Liberty*, pp. 121–125.
203. John A. Ryan, "The State and the Family," *America* 25 (July 9, 1921): 217.
204. *Declining Liberty*, pp. 295–306; originally published as "Divorce Legislation in the United States," *Studies* 13 (1924): 513–524.
205. *Declining Liberty*, pp. 138, 139.
206. John A. Ryan, "Church, State and Constitution," *The Commonweal* 5 (April 27, 1927): 680–682; reprinted in *Questions of the Day*, pp. 57–65.
207. *Catholic Church and Citizen*, pp. 28–30.
208. Gouldrick, "John A. Ryan's Theory of the State," pp. 127, 128.
209. *Declining Liberty*, p. 314.

210. *Catholic Church and the Citizen*, p. 23.

211. Ibid., pp. 71–84; *Catholic Principles of Politics*, pp. 200, 201.

212. John A. Ryan, "The Moral Obligation of Civil Law," *The Catholic World* 114 (October 1921): 73–86; reprinted in *State and Church*, pp. 244–259, and, with one slight change on penal law, in *Catholic Principles of Politics*, pp. 179–193; Ryan, "Binding Force of Law," *Catholic Charities Review* 12 (1928): 17–21; reprinted in *Catholic Church and the Citizen*, pp. 47–57.

213. *Catholic Church and the Citizen*, pp. 62–64.

214. Ibid., pp. 54–57.

215. John A. Ryan, "Undemocratic Prohibition," *Catholic Charities Review* 2 (1918): 101–103; Ryan, "Intolerant Prohibitionists," *Catholic Charities Review* 3 (1918): 165, 166; Ryan, "Prohibitionist Tyranny," *Catholic Charities Review* 3 (1919): 40, 41.

216. John A. Ryan, "Are Our Prohibition Laws Purely Penal?" *American Ecclesiastical Review* 60 (1924): 404–411.

217. *Questions of the Day*, pp. 29–36; *Social Doctrine in Action*, pp. 177–190. In these places Ryan explains his own evolution and development.

218. John A. Ryan, "Are Our Prohibition Laws Purely Penal?" *American Ecclesiastical Review* 60 (1924): 404–411; Ryan, "Do the Prohibition Laws Bind in Conscience?" *The Catholic World* 121 (May 1925): 145–157.

219. *Declining Liberty*, pp. 56–68.

220. Ibid., p. 56.

221. "Do the Prohibition Laws Bind in Conscience?", p. 157.

222. *Questions of the Day*, p. 34.

223. Broderick, *Right Reverend New Dealer*, pp. 187–189. For Ryan's own account of the controversy, see *Questions of the Day*, pp. 3–12.

224. *Questions of the Day*, p. 10.

225. Ibid., p. 52.

226. Broderick, *Right Reverend New Dealer*, pp. 103, 104; 135–138; 159, 160.

227. *Declining Liberty*, pp. 148–159.

228. Ibid., pp. 160–170, especially 162.

229. *Catholic Church and the Citizen*, pp. 65, 66.

230. John A. Ryan, "Patriotism vs. Conscience," *Catholic Charities Review* 14 (1930): 34.

231. See Ryan Papers, "Statements on the War and Hitler." These papers are found in the archives of The Catholic University of America.

232. John A. Ryan, "Basic Economic Facts in the Condition of the Indian," *Catholic Charities Review* 13 (1929): 85–88.

233. Broderick, *Right Reverend New Dealer*, pp. 117; 262.

234. *State and Church*, p. 51.

235. *Catholic Church and the Citizen*, p. 28.

236. John A. Ryan, "The Place of the Negro in American Society," *The Catholic Mind* 41 (July 1943) : 13–22.
237. *Declining Liberty*, pp. 101–114. For a critique of Ryan's position, see Arlene Swidler, "Catholics and the E.R.A.," *Commonweal* 103 (September 10, 1976) : 585–589.
238. *Church and Socialism*, pp. 236–245.
239. Paul Marx, *The Life and Work of Virgil Michel* (Washington, D.C.: Catholic University of America Press, 1957).
240. *Social Reconstruction*, pp. 213, 214.
241. John A. Ryan, "A Great Catholic Work on Political Economy," *The Catholic Fortnightly Review* 17 (1910) : 289–293.
242. Broderick, *Right Reverend New Dealer*, p. 223.
243. Francis L. Broderick, "The Encyclicals and Social Action: Is John A. Ryan Typical?" *Catholic Historical Review* 55 (1969) : 1–6.
244. J. Diez-Alegria, "La lettura del magistero pontifico in materia sociale alla luce del suo sviluppo storico," in *Magistero e morale: Atti del terzo congresso nazionale dei moralisti* (Bologna: Edizioni Dehoniane, 1970), pp. 211-256.

3. The Central-Verein and William J. Engelen

1. For the definitive historical study of this movement, see Philip Gleason, *The Conservative Reformers: German-American Catholics and the Social Order* (Notre Dame, Indiana: University of Notre Dame Press, 1968). The section on historical background in this chapter is heavily dependent upon Gleason. For two other books on the same topic but of much less value than Gleason's work, see Sister Mary Elizabeth Dye, *By Their Fruits: A Social Biography of Frederick Kenkel, Catholic Social Pioneer* (New York: Greenwich Book Publishers, 1960) ; Mary Liguori Brophy, *The Social Thought of the German Roman Catholic Central-Verein* (Washington, D.C.: Catholic University of America Press, 1941).
2. Emmet H. Rothan, *The German Catholic Immigrant in the United States (1830–1860)* (Washington, D.C.: Catholic University of America Press, 1946).
3. Gleason, *The Conservative Reformers*, pp. 7, 8; 19–21; 153–159.
4. Colman J. Barry, *The Catholic Church and the German Americans* (Washington, D.C.: Catholic University of America Press, 1953), pp. 183–236.
5. Ibid., pp. 131–182.
6. Cross, *The Emergence of Liberal Catholicism in America*, pp. 130–145.
7. Brophy, *Social Thought*, pp. 46–48 and throughout chapter 4, "The Central Verein and Education."
8. Gleason, *The Conservative Reformers*, pp. 36, 37.

9. The very title of the standard work on the Catholic abstinence movement indicates the problem for German-American Catholics: Joan Bland, *Hibernian Crusade: The Story of the Catholic Total Abstinence Union of America* (Washington, D.C.: Catholic University of America Press, 1951).

10. Brophy, *Social Thought*, p. 7.

11. For a brief historical sketch, see Brophy, *Social Thought*, pp. 1–14.

12. Gleason, *The Conservative Reformers*, pp. 69–115.

13. For a summary in English of Pesch's thought, see Richard E. Mulcahy, *The Economics of Heinrich Pesch* (New York: Henry Holt, 1952).

14. Gleason, *The Conservative Reformers*, pp. 116–121.

15. Ibid., pp. 73–83.

16. William Edward Hogan, *The Development of Bishop Wilhelm Emmanuel von Ketteler's Interpretation of the Social Problem* (Washington, D.C.: Catholic University of America Press, 1947).

17. Gleason, *The Conservative Reformers*, pp. 69–83.

18. Ibid., pp. 172–203.

19. For a brief description of Engelen's life, see the eulogy "Fr. William J. Engelen, S. J., Promoter of Christian Solidarism Has Died," *Central-Blatt and Social Justice* 30 (May 1937) : 57.

20. Gleason, *The Conservative Reformers*, pp. 131–138.

21. William J. Engelen, "Henry Pesch, S.J., the Economist," *CBSJ* 9 (April 1916): 7, 8; (May 1916): 41, 42; William J. Engelen, "Social Reconstruction XIII: Rev. Henry Pesch, S.J.," *CBSJ* 19 (June 1926): 77–79; (July 1926): 111, 112; (August 1926): 147, 148; (September 1926): 183, 184; (October 1926): 219, 220. In the future, references to Engelen's articles will not cite his name as author. *Central-Blatt and Social Justice* will be referred to as *CBSJ*.

22. Heinrich Pesch, *Lehrbuch der nationalokonomie*, 5 vols. (Freiburg im Breisgau, 1905–1923).

23. "Is It Socialistic to Call Society an Organism?" *CBSJ* 5 (November 1912) : 169.

24. "Social Reflections VI: Reconstruction and the Natural Law," *CBSJ* 13 (May 1920) : 41–43.

25. "Social Observations XIX: Back to the Old Spirit (2)," *CBSJ* 17 (August 1924) : 147–149.

26. "Social Reconstruction I: The Fundamentals of Solidarism," *CBSJ* 17 (September 1924) : 183.

27. "Capital and Labor under Solidarism: Postscript," *CBSJ* 8 (May 1915) : 37.

28. "Social Reconstruction XIII: Rev. Henry Pesch, S.J.," *CBSJ* 19 (June 1926) : 77.

29. "Rome Has Spoken: A Papal Encyclical on Labor Unions I," *CBSJ* 5 (January 1913) : 218.

30. "Social Reflections VI: Reconstruction and the Natural Law," *CBSJ* 13 (May 1920) : 41–43.

31. "Social Observations XIX: Back to the Old Spirit (2)," *CBSJ* 17 (August 1924) : 148.

32. "Social Observations VI: Deuteronomy versus Liberalism," *CBSJ* 15 (March 1923) : 407–409; "Social Observations VII: The Saviour's Social Principles and Liberalism," *CBSJ* 16 (April 1923) : 3–5; (May 1923) : 39–41.

33. "Social Reflections XX: Teaching the Social Gospel," *CBSJ* 14 (September 1923) : 178–180.

34. "The Blind Begin to See," *CBSJ* 6 (October 1913) : 185.

35. "Social Reflections VIII: Reconstruction of Duty," *CBSJ* 13 (July–August 1920) : 109–111.

36. "Social Observations VII: The Saviour's Social Principles and Liberalism (1)," *CBSJ* 16 (April 1923) : 4; "Social Reconstruction IV: A Solidaric Federation of Nations," *CBSJ* 17 (February 1925) : 363, 364.

37. "A Social Christmas to You," *CBSJ* 6(December 1913) : 251–254.

38. "Capital and Labor under Solidarism: A Program II," *CBSJ* (December 1914) : 266; "Social Reflections II: Reconstruction Congresses," *CBSJ* 12 (November 1919) : 246, 247; "Social Reflections IV: The Cornerstone of Reconstruction," *CBSJ* 12 (March 1920) : 381–383; "Social Reflections V: Reconstruction of Moral Standards," *CBSJ* 13 (April 1920) : 7–9.

39. "Social Observations VIII: Christianity's Influence on Roman Social Life," *CBSJ* 16 (June 1923) : 75–77.

40. "Social Observations IX: Medieval Social Ideal," *CBSJ* 16 (July 1923) : 111–113.

41. "Social Observations X: The Origin of Capitalism," *CBSJ* 16 (August 1923) : 147.

42. "The Blind Begin to See," *CBSJ* 6 (October 1913) : 184.

43. "Social Observations IV: A Lesson in Social History," *CBSJ* 14 (January 1922) : 322.

44. "Social Reflections V: Reconstruction of Moral Standards," *CBSJ* 13 (April 1920) : 8.

45. "Social Observations IV: A Lesson in Social History," *CBSJ* 14 (January 1922) : 321–323.

46. "Social Reflections XVI: The Stewardship of Authority," *CBSJ* 14 (May 1921) : 41–43.

47. "Social Observations IV: A Lesson in Social History," *CBSJ* 14 (January 1922) : 322, 323.

48. "Social Observations X: The Origin of Capitalism," *CBSJ* 16 (August 1923) : 147–149.

49. "Rome Has Spoken: What Must Be the Answer of American Catholics?" *CBSJ* 5 (February 1913) : 243–245; (March 1913) : 269–272.

50. "Social Reflections XII: Interest and Reconstruction," *CBSJ* 13 (December 1920): 266; "Social Observations XI: The Good and Evil in Capitalism," *CBSJ* 16 (September 1923): 183.

51. "Capital and Labor under Solidarism I: A Program," *CBSJ* 7 (November 1914): 233.

52. "Social Observations IX: Medieval Social Ideals," *CBSJ* 16 (July 1923): 111–113; "Social Reconstruction VII: Solidaric Spirit in Economic Life," *CBSJ* 18 (August 1925): 147, 148.

53. "Capitalism I," *CBSJ* 7 (August 1914): 135–137.

54. "Social Observations XI: The Good and Evil in Capitalism," *CBSJ* 16 (September 1923): 183, 184.

55. "Capital and Labor under Solidarism II: A Program," *CBSJ* 7 (December 1914): 264.

56. "Capitalism II: Abolition of Capitalism and Reform," *CBSJ* 7 (September 1914): 165, 166.

57. "Capital and Labor under Solidarism: A Program III," *CBSJ* 7 (January 1915): 319–321.

58. "Social Observations XVIII: Socialism As a Reformer," Part One, *CBSJ* 17 (May 1924): 39, 40; Part Two, *CBSJ* 17 (June 1924): 75, 76.

59. This central point is constantly stressed by Engelen; see, for example, "Social Observations XIX: Back to the Old Social Spirit," *CBSJ* 17 (July 1924): 111–113; (August 1924): 147–149.

60. "Is It Socialistic to Call Society an Organism?" *CBSJ* 5 (November 1912): 169–172.

61. "Social Reconstruction I: The Fundamentals of Solidarism," *CBSJ* 17 (September 1924): 183–185.

62. "Social Reconstruction" began in *CBSJ* 19 (October 1926): 219, 220. There were thirteen installments, but some of them included two or more parts in each installment.

63. "Social Reflections I: Reconstruction Programs," *CBSJ* 12 (October 1919): 203–205.

64. "Capital and Labor under Solidarism: A Program I," *CBSJ* 7 (November 1914): 233; IV, *CBSJ* 7 (February 1915): 320; "Capital and Labor under Solidarism: Postscript," *CBSJ* 8 (May 1915): 37.

65. "Capitalism II: Abolition of Capitalism and Reform," *CBSJ* 7 (September 1914): 165–167.

66. "Capital and Labor under Solidarism, Postscript," *CBSJ* 8 (May 1915): 37.

67. "Social Reconstruction X: Labor in the Light of Solidarism," *CBSJ* 18 (February 1926): 363, 364; (March 1926): 399–400.

68. "Social Reflections IX: The Bonds of Reconstruction," *CBSJ* 13 (September 1920): 151–153.

69. "The Need of Charity in Modern Society," *CBSJ* 24 (April 1931): 5, 6; "The Value of True Charity," *CBSJ* 24 (May 1931): 42–44; "The Moral Obligation of Charity," *CBSJ* 24 (June 1931): 79, 80.

70. "Social Reconstruction IX: Social Valuation of a Middle Class Policy (2)," *CBSJ* 18 (January 1926): 327–329; "Social Reconstruction XIII: Rev. Henry Pesch, S.J., (3)," *CBSJ* 19 (August 1926): 147, 148.

71. "Social Reconstruction VIII: A Modern Middle Class Society," *CBSJ* 18 (October 1925): 219–221; (November 1925): 255, 256; "Social Reconstruction IX: Social Valuation of a Middle Class Policy," *CBSJ* 19 (December 1925): 291–293; (January 1926): 327–329.

72. "Capital and Labor under Solidarism: A Program IV," *CBSJ* 7 (February 1915): 319–321; VI, *CBSJ* 8 (April 1915): 9–11.

73. Frederick P. Kenkel, "Some Arguments against the Proposed Child Labor Amendment," *CBSJ* 18 (July 1925): 114–116; (August 1925): 150–152.

74. John A. Ryan, "Two Important Points in the Social Programs of the Central-Verein," *Catholic Fortnightly Review* 16 (March 1909): 130–132.

75. John A. Ryan, "Minimum Wage Boards," *CBSJ* 3 (December 1910): 187, 188; "The Case against the Minimum Wage," *CBSJ* 5 (October 1912): 139–141. It should be noted that McGill does not mention these articles in her bio-bibliography of Ryan. For Ryan's participation in the summer school, see "Der Sociale Studienkursus des C-V," *CBSJ* 3 (August 1910): 107, 108.

76. Gleason, *The Conservative Reformers*, pp. 192, 193.

77. "Social Reconstruction XI: Solidaric Capital and the Middle Class," *CBSJ* 19 (April 1926): 3–5.

78. "Capital and Labor under Solidarism: A Program III," *CBSJ* 7 (January 1915): 289–291; IV, *CBSJ* 7 (February 1915): 319–321.

79. "Social Reflections X: Private Property and Its Social Regulation," *CBSJ* 13 (October 1920): 189–191; "Social Reflections XI: St. Thomas and Private Property," *CBSJ* 13 (November 1920): 223–225.

80. "Capital and Labor under Solidarism: A Program IV," *CBSJ* 7 (February 1915): 319.

81. "Social Reflections XIII: Interest and Reconstruction," *CBSJ* 13 (December 1920): 265–268.

82. "Social Reconstruction XIII: Rev. Henry Pesch, S.J., (3)," *CBSJ* 19 (August 1926): 148.

83. "Social Reconstruction X: Labor in the Light of Solidarism," *CBSJ* 18 (February 1926): 363, 364.

84. "Social Reflections XIX: The Right and Purpose of Organization," *CBSJ* 14 (August 1921): 144–146; "Social Observations XIV: Labor's Revolt against Capitalism," *CBSJ* 16 (December 1923): 291–293; "Social Observations XV: A Cornerstone in the New Structure," *CBSJ* 16 (January 1924): 327–329.

85. "Rome Has Spoken: A Papal Encyclical on Labor Unions I," *CBSJ* 5 (January 1913): 217–219.

86. "Rome Has Spoken: What Must Be the Answer of the

American Catholics? II," *CBSJ* 5 (February 1913): 243–245; III, *CBSJ* 5 (March 1913): 269–272.

87. "Social Reconstruction VIII: Solidaric Spirit in Economic Life (1)," *CBSJ* 18 (August 1925): 147, 148.

88. Raymond Philip Witte, *Twenty-Five Years of Crusading: A History of the National Catholic Rural Life Conference* (Des Moines: The National Catholic Rural Life Conference, 1948), pp. 45ff.

89. "The Farmers' Educational and Co-operative Union of America," *CBSJ* 6 (January 1914): 277, 278; (February 1914): 277, 278; (March 1914): 333–335.

90. "Social Observations XVI: A Sketch of the Modern Cooperative Movement," *CBSJ* 16 (February 1924): 363–365; "Social Observations XVII: Reconstructive Value of Cooperative Enterprises," *CBSJ* 16 (March 1924): 399–401; 17 (April 1924): 3–5; "Social Reconstruction XIII: Rev. Henry Pesch, S.J., (4)," *CBSJ* 19 (September 1926): 183, 184.

91. "Social Reconstruction IV: A Solidaric Federation of Nations," *CBSJ* 17 (February 1925): 363, 364; (March 1925): 399, 400.

92. "Social Reflections XV: Old Families and States for New," *CBSJ* 14 (April 1921): 7–9.

93. "Social Reflections XVIII: Social Representation," *CBSJ* 14 (July 1921): 109–111.

94. "Social Reflections XVI: The Stewardship of Authority," *CBSJ* 14 (May 1921): 41–43.

95. "Social Reconstruction V: A Truly Social Nation, (2)," *CBSJ* 18 (May 1925): 39, 40; "Social Observations VI: A Morally Sound Society," *CBSJ* 18 (June 1925): 75, 76; (July 1925): 111, 112.

96. "Social Reflections XIII: A Happy and Healthy Home," *CBSJ* 13 (January 1921): 299–301; "Social Reflections XIV: The Home As a Social Factor," *CBSJ* 13 (February 1921): 333, 334; (March 1921): 367, 368.

97. "The Negro Problem," *CBSJ* 2 (August 1909): 10, 11.

98. "A Social Christmas to You," *CBSJ* 6 (December 1913): 251.

99. "Rome Has Spoken: What Must Be the Answer of the American Catholics? II," *CBSJ* 5 (February 1913): 244.

100. "What Is the Social Unit?" *CBSJ* 2 (February 1910): 11. A good number of articles appeared in opposition to women's suffrage; e.g., *CBSJ* 5 (August 1912): 102, 103; (September 1912): 120, 122.

4. The Catholic Worker and Paul Hanly Furfey

1. For a history of the Catholic Worker movement, see William D. Miller, *A Harsh and Dreadful Love: Dorothy Day and the Catholic*

Worker Movement (New York: Liveright, 1973), paperback ed. (Garden City, New York: Doubleday Image Books, 1974). References will be to the more readily available paperback edition. There have been a number of books, articles, and theses written on the Worker. A mimeographed bibliography with supplements has been compiled by Alex Avitable, S.J., and is available from the author at Fordham University—"A Bibliography on Peter Maurin, Dorothy Day and the Catholic Worker." The thesis most directly pertinent to our study is John Stuart Sandberg, "The Eschatological Ethic of the Catholic Worker" (S.T.D. diss., Catholic University of America, 1979).

2. Miller, *A Harsh and Dreadful Love*, pp. 32–46. For the latest published biography of Maurin, see Marc H. Ellis, *Peter Maurin: Prophet in the Twentieth Century* (New York: Paulist Press, 1981); also Arthur Sheehan, *Peter Maurin: Gay Believer* (Garden City, New York: Hanover House, 1959).

3. Miller, *A Harsh and Dreadful Love*, pp. 47–74. Autobiographical materials can be found in her own works, which are listed in note 6.

4. For Maurin's description of the movement in one of his Easy Essays, see Peter Maurin, *The Green Revolution* (Fresno, California: Academy Guild Press, 1961). In recent years there has been some discussion about identifying the sources of the Worker's ideas. For an understanding of the Worker as grounded in the ideas of the French Catholic Right of the early part of this century, see Anthony Novitsky, "Peter Maurin's Green Revolution: The Radical Implications of Reactionary Social Catholicism," *Review of Politics* 37 (1975): 83–103. For an interpretation which sees affinities between the Worker and left-wing American equalitarianism as found in Thoreau and Emerson, see Wayne Lobue, "Public Theology and the Catholic Worker," *Cross Currents* 26 (1976): 270–285.

5. There have been four editions of Maurin's Easy Essays: Peter Maurin, *Easy Essays* (New York: Sheed and Ward, 1936); Maurin, *Catholic Radicalism: Phrased Essays for the Green Revolution* (New York: Catholic Worker Books, 1949); Maurin, *The Green Revolution* (Fresno, Cal.: Academy Guild Press, 1961); *Radical Christian Thought: Easy Essays by Peter Maurin*, ed. Chuck Smith (West Hamlin, West Virginia: The Green Revolution Press, 1971).

6. Dorothy Day's books in chronological order are: *From Union Square to Rome* (Silver Spring, Md.: Preservation of the Faith Press, 1938); *House of Hospitality* (New York: Sheed and Ward, 1939); *On Pilgrimage* (New York: Catholic Worker Books, 1948), paperback ed. (New York: Curtis Books, 1972); *The Long Loneliness* (New York: Harper and Brothers, 1952), paperback ed. (New York: Curtis Books, 1972); *Therese* (Notre Dame, Indiana: Fides Publishers, 1960); *Loaves and Fishes* (New York: Harper and Row, 1963), paperback ed. (New York: Curtis Books, 1972); *On Pilgrimage: The Sixties* (New York: Curtis Books, 1972).

7. *Long Loneliness*, pp. 266–270.

8. Ammon Hennacy, *The Book of Ammon* (Salt Lake City, Utah: Ammon Hennacy Publications, 1970) ; Hennacy, *The One Man Revolution in America* (Salt Lake City, Utah: Ammon Hennacy Publications, 1970).

9. Tom Cornell, "Tributes and Recollections," *America* 127 (November 11, 1972) : 390, 391.

10. Paul Hanly Furfey, *Fire on the Earth* (New York: Macmillan, 1936), pp. vii, viii. A reprint edition was published in 1978 by the Arno Press of New York as a part of their collection The American Catholic Tradition.

11. The principal books written by Furfey which are of interest for our study are the following (in chronological order) : Paul Hanly Furfey, *Fire on the Earth* (New York: Macmillan, 1936); *Three Theories of Society* (New York: Macmillan, 1937); *This Way to Heaven* (Silver Spring, Md.: Preservation of the Faith Press, 1939); *A History of Social Thought* (New York: Macmillan, 1942); *The Mystery of Iniquity* (Milwaukee: Bruce Publishing Co., 1944); *The Scope and Method of Sociology* (New York: Harper, 1953); *The Respectable Murderers* (New York: Herder and Herder, 1968); *The Morality Gap* (New York: Macmillan, 1969); *Love and the Urban Ghetto* (Maryknoll, New York: Orbis Books, 1978).

12. Paul Hanly Furfey, "From Catholic Liberalism to Catholic Radicalism," *American Ecclesiastical Review* 166 (1972): 678–686; *The Morality Gap*, pp. 99–113; *Love and the Urban Ghetto*, pp. vii-xii. These are the best published sources for information about Furfey's life and development. In addition, Furfey has circulated privately a duplicated autobiographical essay, "The Light at the End of the Tunnel."

13. His doctoral dissertation, illustrating the case-study approach, was commercially published—Paul Hanly Furfey, *The Gang Age: A Study of the Preadolescent Boy and His Recreational Needs* (New York: Macmillan, 1925).

14. *Three Theories of Society*, pp. 3–67.

15. Ibid., pp. 71–155.

16. Ibid., pp. 159–176. See also Furfey, "The Challenge of Modern Social Thought to Neo-Scholasticism," *Proceedings of the American Philosophical Association* 12 (1936) : 45–58.

17. *History of Social Thought*, p. 138.

18. *Fire on the Earth*, p. 67.

19. *This Way to Heaven*, p. 122.

20. *Morality Gap*, pp. ix, x.

21. *Three Theories of Society*, p. 181. Note that even the manuals of theology distinguish between the assent of faith and the religious assent of intellect and will, but Furfey recognizes no such distinction. For him all involves faith.

22. *Mystery of Iniquity*, p. 174.

23. *Fire on the Earth*, chapter 3, "The Mystical Body," pp. 39–59.

24. Paul Hanly Furfey, "Liturgy and the Social Problem," in *National Liturgical Week 1941* (Newark, New Jersey: Benedictine Liturgical Conference, 1942), pp. 181–186. Virgil Michel, the founder of the liturgical movement in the United States, was a strong advocate of the connection between the liturgy and the social apostolate. See Paul Marx, *The Life and Work of Virgil Michel* (Washington: Catholic University of America Press, 1957).

25. *Fire on the Earth*, p. 6 and throughout.

26. As a succinct example of this approach which is present throughout Furfey's writings, see Paul Hanly Furfey, "Five Hard Sayings Repugnant to Natural Man," *America* 56 (April 3, 1937): 604, 605.

27. *History of Social Thought*, p. 152.

28. Paul Hanly Furfey, "Plousios and Cognates in the New Testament," *Catholic Biblical Quarterly* 5 (1943): 243–263.

29. Paul Hanly Furfey, "Christ as Tekton," *Catholic Biblical Quarterly* 17 (1955): 204–215.

30. Paul Hanly Furfey, "The Mystery of Lawlessness," *Catholic Biblical Quarterly* 8 (1946): 179–191.

31. Paul Hanly Furfey, "The Semantic and Grammatical Principles in Linguistic Analysis," *Studies in Linguistics* 2 (Summer 1944): 56–66; Furfey, "The Verbal Interpretation of Social Documents," *American Catholic Sociological Review* 9 (1948): 272–282.

32. *American Ecclesiastical Review* 166 (1972): 680–682.

33. *Mystery of Iniquity*, pp. 68–83.

34. Paul Hanly Furfey, "Value Judgements in Sociology," *The American Catholic Sociological Review* 7 (1946): 83–95; *Fire on the Earth*, pp. 10–11.

35. Paul Hanly Furfey, "Why a Supernatural Sociology?" *The American Catholic Sociological Review* 1 (1940): 167–171.

36. *Scope and Method of Sociology*; Paul Hanly Furfey, "The Need for the Clarification of Basic Concepts: A Memorandum from Furfey to Lundberg," *Sociological Inquiry* 31 (1961): 107–116. For an appeal to Furfey's later approach—which tries to integrate faith, philosophy, and sociology without denying the legitimate methodological autonomy of sociology—as a way to avoid the extremes of a value-free sociology and of the approach proposed by Alvin Gouldner, see Joseph P. Fitzpatrick, "Catholic Sociology Revisited: The Challenge of Alvin Gouldner," *Thought* 53 (1978): 123–132.

37. *Fire on the Earth*, pp. 1–38; *Three Theories of Society*, pp. 159–176.

38. *This Way to Heaven*, pp. 185, 186.

39. *Morality Gap*, pp. 1-32.

40. *Respectable Murderers*, pp. 17–28.

41. Paul Hanly Furfey, "Catholic Extremism," *Catholic Digest* 1,

no. 3 (January 1937) : 38–43.

42. *Fire on the Earth,* p. 136.

43. *History of Social Thought,* pp. 133–135; *Mystery of Iniquity,* pp. 55–67.

44. *Fire on the Earth,* pp. 60–78; *Mystery of Iniquity,* pp. 13–29.

45. *Three Theories of Society,* p. 213.

46. *Fire on the Earth,* pp. 82–86; *Three Theories of Society,* pp. 213–217.

47. *Fire on the Earth,* pp. 1–28.

48. *Respectable Murderers,* p. 21.

49. *Morality Gap,* p. 114.

50. *Fire on the Earth,* pp. 39–59.

51. *Three Theories of Society,* pp. 228–248.

52. *Fire on the Earth,* p. 137.

53. Ibid., pp. 137–156.

54. *Three Theories of Society,* pp. 221–227; *This Way to Heaven,* pp. 24–35; "Liturgy and the Social Problem," *National Liturgical Week 1941,* pp. 181–186.

55. *This Way to Heaven,* pp. 36–89.

56. Mary Elizabeth Walsh, *The Saints and Social Work* (Silver Spring, Md.: Preservation of the Faith Press, 1937).

57. *Fire on the Earth,* p. 116; *Mystery of Iniquity,* p. 70; *This Way to Heaven,* pp. 90–100; *Morality Gap,* pp. 36–42.

58. *Fire on the Earth,* pp. 22–38; *Three Theories of Society,* pp. 192–200.

59. *Fire on the Earth,* pp. 134, 135.

60. Furfey sees the modern application of this in the approach of the Catholic Worker movement or of the Jocist movement founded by Father Cardijn in Belgium. *Morality Gap,* pp. 105, 106.

61. Paul Hanly Furfey, "Social Action in the Early Church, 30–180 A.D.," *Theological Studies* 2 (1941): 171–197; 3 (1942): 89–108; Furfey, "Catholic Social Thought in the First and Second Centuries," *American Catholic Sociological Review* 1 (1940): 3–20.

62. *Fire on the Earth,* pp. 89–97.

63. Paul Hanly Furfey, "Personalistic Social Action in the 'Rerum Novarum' and 'Quadragesimo Anno'," *American Catholic Sociological Review* 2 (1941): 204–216.

64. *Mystery of Iniquity,* pp. 13; 168–179.

65. *Morality Gap,* p. 121.

66. *Three Theories of Society,* pp. 218, 219.

67. *Fire on the Earth,* pp. 123–136.

68. This debate will be discussed at greater length in the next chapter.

69. *Morality Gap,* pp. 122–124.

70. *Fire on the Earth,* pp. 98–116.

71. *Morality Gap,* pp. 133–135.

72. Ibid., pp. 143–145.
73. *Three Theories of Society*, p. 219.
74. *Respectable Murderers*, p. 139.
75. *Three Theories of Society*, pp. 218, 219.
76. *Respectable Murderers*, pp. 17–111.
77. "Plousios and Cognates in the New Testament."
78. *Three Theories of Society*, p. 43.
79. *Respectable Murderers*, p. 89.
80. *Three Theories of Society*, p. 51.
81. *Mystery of Iniquity*, chapter 6, "The Mammon of Wickedness," pp. 84–101; *Morality Gap*, pp. 100–104.
82. *Fire on the Earth*, pp. 119; 145–147.
83. *Respectable Murderers*, pp. 29–49.
84. *Mystery of Iniquity*, pp. 138–141.
85. Ibid., pp. 141–151; *Fire on the Earth*, pp. 12, 13; 51, 52.
86. *Mystery of Iniquity*, p. 150.
87. *Fire on the Earth*, pp. 49–51.
88. *Mystery of Iniquity*, pp. 152–167.
89. *Respectable Murderers*, pp. 50–85.
90. *Mystery of Iniquity*, p. 161.
91. Ibid., pp. 165, 166; Paul Hanly Furfey, "Bombing of Noncombatants Is Murder," *The Catholic C.O.* 2 (July–December 1945): 3, 4. John Ford, a Jesuit moral theologian, also courageously condemned such bombing—John C. Ford, "The Morality of Obliteration Bombing," *Theological Studies* 5 (1944): 261–309.
92. *Respectable Murderers*, pp. 69–85.
93. *Mystery of Iniquity*, pp. 162–165.
94. *Respectable Murderers*, p. 83.
95. *Mystery of Iniquity*, p. 161.
96. *Fire on the Earth*, pp. 137–156.
97. *Morality Gap*, pp. 89–98.
98. Miller, *A Harsh and Dreadful Love*, pp. 157–185.
99. Paul Hanly Furfey, "There Are Two Kinds of Agrarianism," *The Catholic Worker* 7 (December 1939): 7, 8; Furfey, "Unemployment on the Land," *The Catholic Worker* 7 (October 1939): 8; O'Brien, *American Catholics and Social Reform: The New Deal Years*, p. 200.
100. Novitsky, "Peter Maurin's Green Revolution."
101. *Fire on the Earth*, pp. 144, 145; Paul Hanly Furfey, "Art and the Machine," *The Catholic Art Quarterly* 1, no. 3 (Pentecost 1944): 1–6.
102. *Mystery of Iniquity*, p. 114.
103. Sandberg, "The Eschatological Ethic of the Catholic Worker," pp. 80–96.
104. *Long Loneliness*, pp. 267–269.
105. For a good discussion and evaluation of the Worker's anarchism, see Mary C. Segers, "Equality and Christian Anarchism: The Political and Social Ideas of the Catholic Worker Movement," *Review*

of Politics 40 (1978): 196–230; also Sandberg, "The Eschatological Ethic of the Catholic Worker," pp. 96–113.
106. Sandberg, "The Eschatological Ethic of the Catholic Worker," pp. 80–96.
107. For the Worker's approach to freedom, see ibid., pp. 38–55.
108. *Mystery of Iniquity*, pp. 115–122; *Morality Gap*, pp. 105, 106.
109. *Fire on the Earth* (New York: Arno Press, 1978), introduction.
110. *Love and the Urban Ghetto*, pp. 33–91.
111. Ibid., pp. 1–32.
112. Ibid., pp. 92–110.
113. Ibid., pp. 111–130.
114. Ibid., pp. 131–151.
115. *American Ecclesiastical Review* 166 (1972): 683.

5. John Courtney Murray

1. See Neil G. McCluskey, ed., *The Catholic University: A Modern Appraisal* (Notre Dame, Indiana: University of Notre Dame Press, 1970); Philip Gleason, "The Crisis of Americanization," in *Contemporary Catholicism in the United States*, ed. Philip Gleason (Notre Dame, Indiana: University of Notre Dame Press, 1969), pp. 3–31.
2. Donald F. Crosby, *God, Church and Flag: Senator Joseph R. McCarthy and the Catholic Church, 1950–1957* (Chapel Hill, North Carolina: University of North Carolina Press, 1978).
3. John F. Cronin, *Social Principles and Economic Life* (Milwaukee: Bruce Publishing Co., 1959), revised edition, 1964.
4. John F. Cronin, *Communism: Threat to Freedom* (New York: Paulist Press, 1962).
5. *Social Principles and Economic Life*, revised ed., pp. 130–140.
6. Ibid., pp. 17–25.
7. Ibid., p. 62.
8. Gary Wills, *Nixon Agonistes* (New York: Signet Books, 1971), pp. 34–39.
9. For a recent biography of Murray which concentrates especially on the major controversy over church-state and religious freedom, see Donald E. Pelotte, *John Courtney Murray: Theologian in Conflict* (New York: Paulist Press, 1976). This book contains a complete bibliography of Murray's writings.
10. The only book published by Murray on the subjects under consideration here was a collection of his essays on the American proposition: John Courtney Murray, *We Hold These Truths: Catholic Reflections on the American Proposition* (New York: Sheed and Ward, 1960). Murray's significant article "The Problem of Religious Freedom," *Theological Studies* 25 (1964): 503–575, was published in book

form: *The Problem of Religious Freedom* (Westminster, Md.: Newman Press, 1965).

11. John Courtney Murray, *The Problem of God, Yesterday and Today* (New Haven: Yale University Press, 1964). This book also originally appeared as a long article: "On the Structure of the Problem of God," *Theological Studies* 23 (1962) : 1–26.

12. For the most complete view of Murray's work at the council, see Richard J. Regan, *Conflict and Consensus: Religious Freedom and the Second Vatican Council* (New York: Macmillan, 1967).

13. John Courtney Murray, "The Declaration on Religious Freedom," *Concilium* 15 (May 1966) : 6–16.

14. John Courtney Murray, "Intercredal Co-operation: Its Theory and Its Organization," *Theological Studies* 4 (1943) : 274; Murray, "Letter to the Editor," *Theological Studies* 4 (1943) : 472–474.

15. *Problem of Religious Freedom*, p. 28.

16. John Courtney Murray, "Reversing the Secularist Drift," *Thought* 24 (1949) : 36–46.

17. John Courtney Murray, "How Liberal Is Liberalism?" *America* 75 (April 6, 1946) : 6, 7.

18. John Courtney Murray, "Towards a Theology for the Layman: The Problem of Its Finality," *Theological Studies* 5 (1944) : 43–75.

19. John Courtney Murray, "The Roman Catholic Church," *The Catholic Mind* 46 (1948) : 580–588.

20. *We Hold These Truths*, pp. 189–193.

21. Ibid., p. 225.

22. Regan, *Conflict and Consensus*, pp. 117–129; *The Problem of Religious Freedom*, pp. 20–22.

23. John Courtney Murray, "Co-operation: Some Further Views," *Theological Studies* 4 (1943) : 109–111.

24. John Courtney Murray, "The Papal Allocution: Christmas," *America* 74 (January 5, 1946) : 370–371.

25. *We Hold These Truths*, pp. 327, 328.

26. Ibid., pp. 329–332; 111–113.

27. Ibid., pp. 109–123.

28. Ibid., pp. 295–298.

29. Ibid., p. 327.

30. Ibid., pp. 302–330.

31. Ibid., pp. 275–289.

32. John Courtney Murray, "Vers une intelligence du développement de la doctrine de l'Église sur la liberté religieuse," in *Vatican II: La liberté religieuse, declaration 'Dignitatis humanae personae'*, ed. J. Hamer and Y. Congar (Paris: Editions du Cerf, 1967), pp. 111–147.

33. John Courtney Murray, "Osservazione sulla dichiarazione della libertà religiosa," *Civilta Cattolica* 116 (1965): 536–554; Edward Gaffney, "Religious Liberty and Development of Doctrine: An Inter-

view with John C. Murray," *The Catholic World* 204 (September 1967):
277–283.

34. John Courtney Murray, "The Declaration on Religious Freedom: Its Deeper Significance," *America* 114 (April 23, 1966): 592, 593; "The Declaration on Religious Freedom," *Concilium* 15 (May 1966): 11–16.

35. "Co-operation: Some Further Views," p. 100.

36. "Intercredal Co-operation: Its Theory and Its Organization," pp. 281–286; John Courtney Murray, "On the Problem of Cooperation: Some Clarifications," *American Ecclesiastical Review* 112 (1945): 212–214.

37. "Intercredal Co-operation," pp. 257–281.

38. "Co-operation," pp. 100–111; "Intercredal Co-operation," pp. 257–261; 272, 273.

39. Francis J. Connell, "Catholics and 'Interfaith Groups'," *American Ecclesiastical Review* 105 (1941): 336–353.

40. John Courtney Murray, "Christian Co-operation," *Theological Studies* 3 (1942): 413–432; "Co-operation," pp. 100–111.

41. "Co-operation," pp. 107–111.

42. The bibliography of this debate between Furfey and Murray includes the following items in chronological order: Paul Hanly Furfey, "Letter to the Editor," *Theological Studies* 4 (1943): 467–472; John Courtney Murray, "Letter to the Editor," *Theological Studies* 4 (1943): 472–474; Furfey, "Intercredal Cooperation: Its Limitations," *American Ecclesiastical Review* 111 (1944): 161–175; Murray, "On the Problem of Cooperation: Some Clarifications," *American Ecclesiastical Review* 112 (1945): 194–214; Furfey, "Why Does Rome Discourage Socio-Religious Intercredalism?" *American Ecclesiastical Review* 112 (1945): 364–374.

43. Furfey, "Intercredal Cooperation," pp. 161–175.

44. "On the Problem of Cooperation," pp. 198–201.

45. Furfey, "Intercredal Cooperation," pp. 168–170.

46. "On the Problem of Cooperation," pp. 201–209.

47. Furfey, "Why Does Rome Discourage Socio-Religious Intercredalism," pp. 366–367.

48. "Co-operation," pp. 109–111.

49. The first and perhaps still the best account of Murray's position on church and state was written by a Protestant—Thomas T. Love, *John Courtney Murray: Contemporary Church-State Theory* (Garden City, New York: Doubleday, 1965). Pelotte is also a good source for Murray's teaching and his controversy with proponents of the older position. Two other dissertations written on this subject are most helpful: Faith E. Burgess, *The Relationship between Church and State according to John Courtney Murray, S.J.* Düsseldorf: Rudolf Stehle, 1971); Edward A. Goerner, "John Courtney Murray and the Problem of Church and State" (Ph.D. dissertation, University of Chi-

cago, 1959). Our discussion will not explore in depth the position of those who disagreed with Murray.

50. For Murray's own formulation of the older position, see *Problem of Religious Freedom,* pp. 7–17.

51. John Courtney Murray, "The Declaration on Religious Freedom," in *Vatican II: An Interfaith Appraisal,* ed. John H. Miller (Notre Dame, Indiana: University of Notre Dame Press, 1966), pp. 565–576.

52. John Courtney Murray, "Freedom, Authority, Community," *America* 115 (December 3, 1966) : 734–741.

53. *Problem of Religious Freedom,* pp. 25, 26.

54. John Courtney Murray, "Current Theology: Freedom of Religion," *Theological Studies* 6 (1945) : 85–113.

55. *Problem of Religious Freedom,* pp. 20–22.

56. Ibid., pp. 28–31.

57. Note that from his earliest writings Murray recognized the great difference between Continental liberalism and American democracy. This gave him a basis for the later development of his defense of religious liberty in the light of constitutional government. See, John Courtney Murray, "Separation of Church and State," *America* 76 (December 7, 1946) : 261–263.

58. John Courtney Murray, "Freedom of Religion, I: The Ethical Problem," *Theological Studies* 6 (1945) : 266ff.

59. John Courtney Murray, "Governmental Repression of Heresy," *Proceedings of the Catholic Theological Society of America* 3 (1948) : 26–98.

60. "Governmental Repression of Heresy," pp. 70–83.

61. George W. Shea, "Catholic Doctrine and 'The Religion of the State'," *American Ecclesiastical Review* 123 (1950) : 161–174.

62. John Courtney Murray, "The Problem of 'The Religion of the State'," *American Ecclesiastical Review* 124 (1951) : 327–352. This was also published as "The Problem of State Religion," *Theological Studies* 12 (1951) : 155–178.

63. "The Problem of State Religion," pp. 158, 159, n. 6.

64. Love, *John Courtney Murray,* pp. 149–154.

65. *Problem of Religious Freedom,* pp. 29, 30; John Courtney Murray, "The Declaration on Religious Freedom: A Moment in Its Legislative History," in *Religious Liberty: An End and a Beginning,* ed. John Courtney Murray (New York: Macmillan, 1966), pp. 34ff.

66. "The Declaration on Religious Freedom," *Vatican II: An Interfaith Appraisal,* pp. 565–576.

67. "Declaration on Religious Freedom," in *The Documents of Vatican II,* ed. Walter M. Abbott (New York: Guild Press, 1966), p. 687, n. 21. The footnotes, which are not in italics, are not official notes but are added by Murray himself.

68. "The Problem of State Religion," p. 162.

69. "The Declaration on Religious Freedom," *Concilium* 15 (May 1966) : 13–16.

70. *Problem of Religious Freedom*, pp. 26, 27.

71. "Governmental Repression of Heresy," pp. 26–98; John Courtney Murray, "St. Robert Bellarmine on the Indirect Power," *Theological Studies* 9 (1948) : 491–535; Murray, "Contemporary Orientation of Catholic Thought on Church and State in the Light of History," *Theological Studies* 10 (1949) : 177–234.

72. "Governmental Repression of Heresy," pp. 39–42.

73. "St. Robert Bellarmine on the Indirect Power," pp. 491–535; "Governmental Repression of Heresy," pp. 42–52.

74. "Contemporary Orientation of Catholic Thought," pp. 204–211.

75. Ibid., p. 205, n. 78.

76. Ibid., pp. 211–227.

77. "The Problem of 'The Religion of the State'," pp. 327–352; reprinted as "The Problem of State Religion," pp. 155–178.

78. "The Problem of State Religion," pp. 156–159.

79. "St. Robert Bellarmine on the Indirect Power," p. 424.

80. "Governmental Repression of Heresy," pp. 66–69; 75–85; "Contemporary Orientation of Catholic Thought," p. 231; "The Problem of State Religion," p. 164; see Love, *John Courtney Murray*, pp. 97–106.

81. "The Problem of State Religion," pp. 160, 161.

82. Pelotte, *John Courtney Murray*, p. 91; "Governmental Repression of Heresy," p. 37; "The Problem of State Religion," p. 162, n. 97.

83. *Problem of Religious Freedom*, pp. 98, 99.

84. John Courtney Murray, "The Church and Totalitarian Democracy," *Theological Studies* 13 (1952) : 552, n. 58.

85. John Courtney Murray, "Leo XIII: Separation of Church and State," *Theological Studies* 14 (1953) : 150.

86. *Problem of Religious Freedom*, pp. 47, 48.

87. "Governmental Repression of Heresy," p. 41; "St. Robert Bellarmine on the Indirect Power," pp. 522–532; "Leo XIII: Separation of Church and State," p. 190.

88. "Contemporary Orientation of Catholic Thought," pp. 227–234; "The Problem of State Religion," pp. 170–178.

89. "The Problem of State Religion," p. 165.

90. *Problem of Religious Freedom*, pp. 85–110.

91. The five articles published by Murray are: "The Church and Totalitarian Democracy," *Theological Studies* 13 (1952) : 525–563; "Leo XIII on Church and State: The General Structure of the Controversy," *Theological Studies* 14 (1953) : 1–30; "Leo XIII: Separation of Church and State," *Theological Studies* 14 (1953) : 145–214; "Leo XIII: Two Concepts of Government," *Theological Studies* 14 (1953) : 551–567; 'Leo XIII: Two Concepts of Government, II: Government and the Order of Culture," *Theological Studies* 15 (1954) : 1–33. The sixth article, which existed in galley proofs but was not allowed to be

published, was entitled "Leo XIII and Pius XII: Government and the Order of Religion."

92. "The Church and Totalitarian Democracy," pp. 525ff.

93. For Murray's summary judgments of Leo XIII, see *Problem of Religious Freedom*, pp. 52–64; "Vers une intelligence du développement," pp. 117–139.

94. "Leo XIII: Separation of Church and State," pp. 192–200; "Vers une intelligence du développement," p. 119.

95. "The Church and Totalitarian Democracy," p. 559.

96. *Problem of Religious Freedom*, pp. 61–63.

97. "Leo XIII: Separation of Church and State," pp. 206, 207.

98. Ibid., pp. 208, 209; "Leo XIII: Two Concepts of Government," pp. 558, 559.

99. "Vers une intelligence du développement," p. 118.

100. Ibid., p. 127.

101. Ibid., pp. 127, 128.

102. *Problem of Religious Freedom*, pp. 53–58.

103. "Vers une intelligence du développement," p. 134.

104. *Problem of Religious Freedom*, p. 70.

105. For the history of this period, see Pelotte, *John Courtney Murray*, pp. 27–73.

106. The most detailed account of Murray's contribution to the Declaration on Religious Freedom is found in Regan, *Conflict and Consensus*; see also Pelotte, *John Courtney Murray*, 74–114.

107. "The Declaration on Religious Freedom," in *Religious Liberty: An End and a Beginning*, pp. 15–42.

108. Declaration on Religious Freedom, par. 2, 3; Regan, *Conflict and Consensus*, pp. 174, 175; John A. Rohr, "John Courtney Murray's Theology of Our Founding Fathers' 'Faith': Freedom," in *Christian Spirituality in the United States: Independence and Interdependence*, ed. Francis A. Eigo (Villanova, Pa.: Villanova University Press, 1978), pp. 1–30.

109. "The Declaration on Religious Freedom," in *Religious Liberty: An End and a Beginning*, p. 16.

110. Francis J. Canavan, "The Catholic Concept of Religious Freedom As a Human Right," in *Religious Liberty: An End and a Beginning*, especially pp. 78, 79. See also the authors mentioned in note 108.

111. E.g., Enda McDonagh, *The Declaration on Religious Freedom of Vatican Council II* (London: Darton, Longman and Todd, 1967), pp. 37–50.

112. Abbott, *Documents of Vatican II*, pp. 676, 677, nn. 3 and 4. For other examples of Murray's defensiveness vis-à-vis the final declaration, see Burgess, *The Relationship between Church and State*, pp. 233, 234.

113. *We Hold These Truths*, pp. ix, x.

114. Ibid., pp. 22–24.

115. Ibid., p. vii.
116. "How Liberal Is Liberalism," pp. 6, 7; *We Hold These Truths,* pp. 28, 29.
117. *We Hold These Truths,* pp. 28–39.
118. Ibid., p. 35.
119. Ibid., pp. 48–56.
120. "Separation of Church and State," p. 261.
121. John Courtney Murray, "Paul Blanshard and the New Nativism," *The Month,* new series 5 (1951) : 214.
122. "Separation of Church and State," pp. 261–263.
123. "Paul Blanshard and the New Nativism," pp. 214–225.
124. *We Hold These Truths,* pp. 62–78.
125. Ibid., p. 41.
126. Ibid., pp. 39–43.
127. Ibid., p. 109.
128. Ibid., pp. 334, 335.
129. Ibid., pp. 117–121.
130. Ibid., pp. 221–247.
131. Ibid., pp. 249–273.
132. John Courtney Murray, "War and Conscience," in *A Conflict of Loyalties: The Case for Selective Conscientious Objection,* ed. James Finn (New York: Pegasus, 1969), pp. 19–30.
133. Among Murray's essays dealing with federal aid to Catholic schools are the following: "Separation of Church and State: True and False Concepts," *America* 76 (February 15, 1947): 541–545; "The Court Upholds Religious Freedom," *America* 76 (March 8, 1947): 628–630; "Dr. Morrison and the First Amendment II," *America* 78 (March 20, 1948): 683–686; *We Hold These Truths,* pp. 143–154.
134. "Dr. Morrison and the First Amendment," p. 686.
135. *We Hold These Truths,* pp. 153–169. The crux of the problem concerns the exact meaning of public morality.
136. *Problem of Religious Freedom,* p. 55.
137. See, for example, Gustavo Gutierrez, *A Theology of Liberation* (Maryknoll, New York: Orbis Books, 1973), pp. 56–77. Gutierrez criticizes what he calls the distinction of planes approach which leads to the perception of two missions in the church and to a sharp differentiation between the roles of priest and laity. For Gutierrez there are not two histories, spiritual and secular, but only one salvation history embracing all reality.
138. In correspondence with his Roman superiors at the time of his silencing, Murray describes himself as "natively of a pessimistic turn of mind." Pelotte, *John Courtney Murray,* p. 53.
139. John Courtney Murray, "The Roman Catholic Church," *Catholic Mind* 46 (1948) : 580–588.
140. For a discussion of this question in the light of Murray's work, see David Hollenbach, ed., "Theology and Philosophy in Public: A Symposium on John Courtney Murray's Unfinished Agenda"

Theological Studies 40 (1979) : 700–715.

141. "The Church and Totalitarian Democracy," 552, n. 58. This criticism has been made by Edward A. Goerner, *Peter and Caesar: The Catholic Church and Political Authority* (New York: Herder and Herder, 1965), pp. 186–191.

142. *Problem of Religious Freedom*, p. 19.

143. Ibid., p. 41.

144. Ibid., pp. 102, 103. Murray's relativism during this stage of his writings has been criticized by A. F. Carillo de Albornoz, "Religious Freedom: Intrinsic or Fortuitous? A Critique of a Treatise by John Courtney Murray," *The Christian Century* 82 (September 15, 1965): 1122–1126.

145. Goerner, *Peter and Caesar*, pp. 186–191.

146. Rohr, "John Courtney Murray's Theology," pp. 21, 22.

147. John Courtney Murray, "The Vatican Declaration on Religious Freedom," in *The University in the American Experience* (New York: Fordham University Press, 1966), p. 8.

148. Goerner, *Peter and Caesar*, p. 190.

149. For a somewhat similar but further-developed explanation of Murray's position, see Rohr, "John Courtney Murray's Theology," pp. 22–26.

150. John Courtney Murray, "The Status of the Nicene Creed As Dogma of the Church," in *The Status of the Nicene Creed As Dogma in the Church: Theological Consultation between Representatives of the U.S.A. National Committee of the Luthern World Federation and the Bishops' Commission for Ecumenical Affairs Held July 6–7, 1965, in Baltimore, Maryland* (Washington: United States Catholic Conference, 1965), pp. 16–30.

151. Francis J. Connell, "Reply to Fr. Murray," *American Ecclesiastical Review* 126 (1952) : 56, 57; Joseph Clifford Fenton, "Principles Underlying Traditional Church–State Doctrine," *American Ecclesiastical Review* 126 (1952) : 453.

152. "The Church and Totalitarian Democracy," pp. 551, 552, n. 58.

153. John Courtney Murray, "Leo XIII and Pius XII: Government and the Order of Religion." Unpublished manuscript, galley p. R–79.

154. Rohr, "John Courtney Murray's Theology," pp. 4, 5.

155. *We Hold These Truths*, p. 179.

156. Regan, *Conflict and Consensus*, pp. 124, 125.

6. The Catholic Peace Movement and James W. Douglass

1. It is too soon to have a definitive history of this movement. For a good beginning, with a heavy emphasis on oral history, see Charles A. Meconis, *With Clumsy Grace: The American Catholic Left, 1961–*

1975 (New York: Seabury Press, 1979).

2. Dogmatic Constitution on Divine Revelation, par. 24. For documents of the Second Vatican Council, see Walter M. Abbott, ed., *The Documents of Vatican II* (New York: Guild Press, 1966).

3. The Decree on Priestly Formation, par. 16; Abbott, *The Documents of Vatican II*, p. 452.

4. Charles Moeller, "History of the Constitution," in *Commentary on the Documents of Vatican II, V: Pastoral Constitution on the Church in the Modern World*, ed. Herbert Vorgrimler (New York: Herder and Herder, 1969), pp. 1–76.

5. Pastoral Constitution on the Church in the Modern World, par. 43; Abbott, *The Documents of Vatican II*, p. 243.

6. Pastoral Constitution on the Church in the Modern World, par. 4; Abbott, *The Documents of Vatican II*, pp. 201, 202.

7. Pastoral Constitution on the Church in the Modern World, par. 46; Abbott, *The Documents of Vatican II*, p. 248.

8. For commentaries on this section of the Pastoral Constitution on the Church in the Modern World, see Rene Costé, "Commentary on Chapter V," in *Commentary on the Documents of Vatican II, V*, pp. 347–369; Dominique Dubarle, "Schema XIII and War," in *The Church Today: Commentaries on the Pastoral Constitution on the Church in the Modern World*, ed. Group 2000 (New York: Newman Press, 1967), pp. 229–282.

9. Pastoral Constitution on the Church in the Modern World, par. 77–80; Abbott, *The Documents of Vatican II*, pp. 289–294.

10. Pastoral Constitution on the Church in the Modern World, par. 81, 82; Abbott, *The Documents of Vatican II*, pp. 294–297.

11. Patricia F. McNeal, *The American Catholic Peace Movement, 1928–1972* (New York: Arno Press, 1978), pp. 204, 205.

12. For a similar judgment, see J. Bryan Hehir, "The Just War Ethic and Catholic Theology: Dynamics of Change and Continuity," in *War or Peace? The Search for New Answers*, ed. Thomas A. Shannon (Maryknoll, New York: Orbis Books, 1980), pp. 15–58. McNeal (*The American Catholic Peace Movement*, p. 306) maintains that the council did not completely shut the door on the just-war theory.

13. This short section is based on David J. O'Brien, "American Catholic Opposition to the Vietnam War," in *War or Peace?*, pp. 119–150.

14. McNeal, *The American Catholic Peace Movement*, pp. 15–32; 169–177; 196–203. McNeal's doctoral dissertation is the most important source for peace movements in the American Catholic Church.

15. Ibid., pp. 58–122.

16. Gordon C. Zahn, *A Descriptive Study of the Social Backgrounds of Conscientious Objectors in Civilian Public Service during World War II* (Washington, D.C.: Catholic University of America Press, 1953).

17. Gordon C. Zahn, *German Catholics and Hitler's Wars: A Study in Social Control* (New York: Sheed and Ward, 1962). The volume *War or Peace?* is dedicated to Zahn, who wrote the "Afterword."

18. McNeal, *The American Catholic Peace Movement*, pp. 192–206.

19. Meconis, *With Clumsy Grace*, p. 9; McNeal, *The American Catholic Peace Movement*, pp. 220–222.

20. McNeal, *The American Catholic Peace Movement*, pp. 222–225.

21. Ibid., pp. 223–236.

22. Meconis, *With Clumsy Grace*, pp. 17–24.

23. Ibid., pp. 24–81; 153–166.

24. For a very readable account of the Berrigans until the time of Catonsville, see Francine du Plessix Gray, *Divine Disobedience: Profiles in Catholic Radicalism* (New York: Alfred A. Knopf, 1970), pp. 45–228; also John Deedy, *Apologies, Good Friends . . . An Interim Biography of Daniel Berrigan, S.J.* (Chicago: Fides/Claretian, 1981). For a summary of their activities, see McNeal, *The American Catholic Peace Movement*, pp. 241–299.

25. Meconis, *With Clumsy Grace*, pp. 81–131; McNeal, *The American Catholic Peace Movement*, pp. 282–290.

26. McNeal, *The American Catholic Peace Movement*, pp. 290–293; Meconis, *With Clumsy Grace*, pp. 131–141.

27. Gordon C. Zahn, "The Berrigans: Radical Activism Personified," in *The Berrigans*, ed. William VanEtten Casey and Philip Nobile (New York: Avon, 1971), pp. 97–112.

28. Thomas Merton, "Peace and Revolution: A Footnote from Ulysses," in *Thomas Merton on Peace* (New York: McCall Publishing Co., no date), pp. 70–75; "Note for *Ave Maria*," in *Thomas Merton on Peace*, pp. 231–233.

29. For Merton's own approach, see *Thomas Merton on Peace*. See also Gordon C. Zahn, "Original Child Monk: An Appreciation," in *Thomas Merton on Peace*, pp. ix–xli; Zahn, "Thomas Merton: Reluctant Pacifist," in *Thomas Merton: Prophet in the Belly of a Paradox*, ed. Gerald Twomey (New York: Paulist Press, 1978), pp. 55–79; James H. Forest, "Thomas Merton's Struggle with Peacemaking," in *Thomas Merton: Prophet in the Belly of a Paradox*, pp. 15–54; also McNeal, *The American Catholic Peace Movement*, pp. 123–168.

30. Meconis, *With Clumsy Grace*, pp. 9; 37, 38.

31. James W. Douglass, *The Non-Violent Cross: A Theology of Revolution and Peace* (New York: Macmillan, 1968). This work is not really systematic in the fullest sense, for some of the chapters had previously been published as articles in different journals. Douglass, *Resistance and Contemplation: The Way of Liberation* (Garden City, New York: Doubleday, 1972); Douglass, *Lightning East to West* (Portland, Oregon: Sunburst Press, 1980).

330

32. The biographical information can be found scattered throughout *Lightning East to West.*
33. *Non-Violent Cross*, p. 5.
34. *Lightning East to West*, p. 17.
35. Ibid., pp. 5, 6.
36. Ibid., pp. 90, 91.
37. *Non-Violent Cross*, pp. 48–79.
38. *Resistance and Contemplation*, pp. 99–105; *Non-Violent Cross*, pp. 183–190.
39. *Non-Violent Cross*, pp. 284–292.
40. Ibid., pp. 70–77.
41. Ibid., p. 55.
42. Ibid., p. 95.
43. Ibid., pp. 69–72.
44. *Lightning East to West*, p. 1.
45. Ibid., pp. 1–24.
46. Ibid., pp. 19–33.
47. Ibid., pp. 33–36; *Resistance and Contemplation*, pp. 71–78.
48. Ibid., pp. 35–39.
49. *Non-Violent Cross*, pp. 217–239.
50. Ibid., p. 211.
51. *Lightning East to West*, p. 51.
52. *Non-Violent Cross*, pp. 21, 22.
53. *Resistance and Contemplation*, pp. 88, 89.
54. *Non-Violent Cross*, pp. 3–25; 48–78.
55. *Resistance and Contemplation*, pp. 42–45.
56. *Non-Violent Cross*, pp. 29ff.; *Resistance and Contemplation*, pp. 125; 177.
57. *Lightning East to West*, p. 8.
58. *Resistance and Contemplation*, pp. 178–181.
59. *Non-Violent Cross*, pp. 29–44.
60. James Douglass, "Birth of Christ, Death of the World," in *Catholic Northwest Progress*, December 29, 1978.
61. *Non-Violent Cross*, pp. 262–265.
62. Ibid., pp. 177, 178.
63. Ibid., pp. 239–254.
64. Ibid., pp. 81–94.
65. Ibid., pp. 94–98.
66. Ibid., p. 135, n. 56.
67. *Pacem in terris*, par. 137 in *Acta Apostolicae Sedis* 55 (1963): 291. *Quare aetate hac nostra quae vi atomica gloriatur, alienum est a ratione, bellum iam aptum esse ad violata iura sarcienda.*
68. Pope Paul VI, "Address to the General Assembly of the United Nations (October 4, 1965)," par. 19, 23, in *The Gospel of Peace and Justice*, ed. Gremillion, pp. 383, 384.
69. *Non-Violent Cross*, pp. 100–111.

70. Ibid., pp. 115–124.
71. Ibid., pp. 124–126.
72. Ibid., p. 126.
73. Ibid., pp. 155–181.
74. *Resistance and Contemplation*, pp. 18–25.
75. Ibid., pp. 52, 53; 67.
76. *Lightning East to West*, especially pp. 62–72.
77. *Resistance and Contemplation*, pp. 70, 71.
78. Ibid., 58–64; *Lightning East to West*, pp. 60–66.
79. *Resistance and Contemplation*, pp. 109–136.
80. *Lightning East to West*, pp. 63, 64.
81. *Resistance and Contemplation*, 186–190.
82. *Lightning East to West*, pp. 11–13.
83. *Resistance and Contemplation*, pp. 15–45.
84. *Lightning East to West*, p. 58.
85. Ibid., pp. 59, 60; *Resistance and Contemplation*, pp. 138, 139.
86. *Resistance and Contemplation*, pp. 137–149.
87. Ibid., 157–169.
88. Sentencing statement given by Jim Douglass on March 28, 1980.
89. *Resistance and Contemplation*, pp. 170–181; *Catholic Northwest Progress*, October 27, 1978.
90. *Resistance and Contemplation*, pp. 182–192.
91. James Douglass, "Pilgrimage to Ground Zero," *Sojourners 9* (March 1980) : 20–23.
92. *Resistance and Contemplation*, pp. 10, 11.
93. *Lightning East to West*, pp. 29, 30.
94. Ibid., pp. 9–11; 24–28.
95. Ibid., pp. 73–95.
96. Ibid., p. 93.
97. *Catholic Northwest Progress*, October 27, 1978.
98. *Non-Violent Cross*, pp. 182–214.
99. Ibid., pp. 257–280.
100. Ibid.
101. Ibid., pp. 182–214.
102. Ibid., pp. 257–283.
103. Ibid., p. 211.
104. *Lightning East to West*, pp. 90, 91.
105. For an overview of the present discussion about methodology in Christian ethics and for my own position, see Charles E. Curran and Richard A. McCormick, eds., *Readings in Moral Theology No. 1: Moral Norms and Catholic Tradition* (New York: Paulist Press, 1979).
106. *Lightning East to West*, pp. 79–88.
107. *Resistance and Contemplation*, p. 107.

Epilogue

1. Two of the most significant treatises on liberation theology are Gustavo Gutierrez, *A Theology of Liberation* (Maryknoll, New York: Orbis Books, 1973) and Juan Luis Segundo, *The Liberation of Theology* (Maryknoll, New York: Orbis Books, 1976).

2. For a discussion including different approaches to this question, see Charles E. Curran and Richard A. McCormick, eds., *Readings in Moral Theology No. 2: The Distinctiveness of Christian Ethics* (New York: Paulist Press, 1980).

3. For a discussion of this issue, see David Hollenbach, Robin W. Lovin, John A. Coleman, and J. Bryan Hehir, "Theology and Philosophy in Public: A Symposium on John Courtney Murray's Unfinished Agenda," *Theological Studies* 40 (1979) : 700–715.

4. For the understanding of the state in the Catholic tradition with its insistence on a positive function for the state, see Heinrich A. Rommen, *The State in Catholic Thought: A Treatise in Political Philosophy* (St. Louis: B. Herder Book Co., 1945).

5. This distinction was developed at great length in Ernst Troeltsch, *The Social Teaching of the Christian Churches*, 2 vols. (New York: Harper Torchbooks, 1960).

6. See note 3. The footnotes to this symposium in *Theological Studies* refer to other works by these authors.

7. Justice in the World, par. 6, in *The Gospel of Peace and Justice*, ed. Gremillion, p. 514.

8. *Octogesima adveniens*, par. 4, in *The Gospel of Peace and Justice*, ed. Gremillion, p. 487.

INDEX